The Military Advantage

The Military.com Guide to Military and Veterans Benefits

Foreword by
General Norman Schwarzkopf, USA (Ret.)

Christopher P. Michel
and Terry Howell

Naval Institute Press
Annapolis, Maryland

Naval Institute Press
291 Wood Road
Annapolis, MD 21402

Grateful acknowledgment is made to each branch of the U.S. Military, Defense Finance and Accounting Service, Department of Defense, Department of Homeland Security, Department of Veterans Affairs, Internal Revenue Service, TRICARE Military Health System and all the agencies, organizations and individuals, too numerous to mention, who contributed the programs, resources, and information that support the military community and form the basis of this book. For updates, questions and suggestions, visit www.military.com/book.

The ideas and opinions in this book are those of the author and do not represent the views of any government agency or other party. While every attempt has been made to ensure the accuracy of the information in this book, readers should always verify information.

Library of Congress Cataloging-in-Publication Data

Michel, Christopher P., 1967–
    The military advantage : a comprehensive guide to your military & veterans benefits / Christopher P. Michel ; foreword by Norman Schwarzkopf.
        p. cm.
    Includes bibliographical references and index.
    ISBN 978-1-59114-499-1 (acid-free paper) 1. United States—Armed Forces—Pay, allowances, etc. 2. Military pensions—United States. 3. Veterans—Services for—United States. I. Title.
    UC74.M52 2009
    362.86'0973—dc22

                                                                                2009000123

Manufactured in the United States of America

15 14 13 12 11 10 09   9 8 7 6 5 4 3 2

First Printing

To all who have answered the call to serve.

And in memory of Andy McKelvey, founder of Monster, and Adm. Phil Coady, USN (Ret.).

Contents

Foreword

For 35 years I had the privilege of serving in the United States Army. My career was defined by two conflicts—Vietnam and Desert Storm, wars that challenged and taught me as a leader of brave men and women. But over my decades of service, in times of war and peace, I also experienced firsthand the importance of benefits designed for those who have answered the call to serve. Whether you are in uniform today, a family member, a veteran, or a retiree, you have the thanks of a grateful nation. You also have a suite of valuable benefits at your disposal.

In the years since my retirement from active duty, I've developed an even greater appreciation for the array of military benefits. I've also discovered that many benefits go unused. Too often veterans are either unaware of their eligibility or unsure of how to access programs that could have tremendous impact on their lives and their families.

Enter this updated version of *The Military Advantage*. Chris Michel and his team have spent the last seven years building the nation's largest military membership organization—Military.com—dedicated to "cutting the red tape" between servicemembers, veterans, and military dependents and their earned benefits. This book is an extension of those tireless efforts, at once a comprehensive reference resource as well as a "how to" guide. Built for the community with the input of the community, this book makes it easier to understand and use your benefits.

I follow in the footsteps of the late congressman G. V. "Sonny" Montgomery, who authored the foreword to the 2006 edition. Sonny Montgomery spent three decades in Congress advocating for servicemembers and veterans. The cornerstone of his efforts was the Montgomery GI Bill, a benefit millions have used to continue their education. It is my honor to pick up his torch at the head of these pages.

America has been challenged during the twenty-first century in ways we never imagined at the time I left active duty. Now as much as any other period in our nation's history we need to ensure that the benefits of service to America are easily accessible. *The Military Advantage* is a vital step toward that end.

General Norman Schwarzkopf, USA (Ret.)

Introduction

By opening this book, you've already taken the first steps to getting the benefits you have earned in service to America. Over the next eight chapters, you'll learn how to quickly understand and use hundreds of extremely valuable programs. This book could even change your life.

No nation has done more to provide for its military and veteran community. On March 4, 1865, President Abraham Lincoln proclaimed our nation's duty "to care for him who shall have borne the battle, and for his widow, and his orphan." Since then, more than one trillion dollars have been spent to provide for servicemembers, veterans, and their families, creating the world's largest benefits system. Landmark programs like the GI Bill and VA Loan have transformed America. Despite the overwhelming success of military benefits, many of these important programs go unused because they are either hidden or too complicated. I believe that this book and its companion website, Military.com, can change all that.

In the late 1990s, I was in the Naval Reserve following seven years on active duty. While on a reserve drill weekend, I asked for advice from one of the more senior sailors about navigating a particularly tricky benefits program. His answer was succinct, useful, and insightful—yet wasn't available anywhere except from him. In that very moment, it struck me that there must be a better way to help people easily access their benefits—that the Internet was the perfect vehicle to connect, empower, and inform the military community. Four weeks later, I started Military.com with one mission in mind: to connect servicemembers, veterans, and their families to all the benefits earned in service to America.

Today, Military.com is the largest military and veteran membership organization in the country. The company helps its 10 million members cut through the benefits red tape. By negotiating discounts and keeping members connected to their service friends and mentors, we help make the most of the military experience. In addition, we help over 500,000 veterans with career services each month. As always, membership in Military.com is free.

This book is the culmination of years of experience in helping millions of servicemembers make full use of their benefits. Many of our members have provided feedback, helping us supply even more of what you really need.

Additionally, we have worked closely with the Department of Defense, Veterans Administration, and other agencies while writing this book. Their dedicated teams are the source of much of this valuable information.

So, *The Military Advantage* was written partly by you—the military community. Many of the lessons that you have learned—and communicated to us—are available for others in these pages. Like the advice my squadronmate passed on, this hard-to-find information can now help the 30 million members of the military and veteran community. I hope you'll carry on in that tradition of shipmates helping one another by providing us your feedback, insider tips, and stories for future editions.

Finally, it is a great honor to have General Norman Schwarzkopf write the foreword for this edition of the book. General Schwarzkopf is a worthy successor to the late congressman G. V. "Sonny" Montgomery, who was the lead sponsor of the Montgomery GI Bill legislation and who wrote the foreword for the first edition of this book. Like Congressman Montgomery, General Schwarzkopf has been a champion for our nation's veterans, and I am deeply honored to have him involved in a book that advocates for our men and women in uniform, veterans, and their families.

It is my sincere wish that this book helps you take full advantage of all the benefits you've earned. Thank you for your service to America.

Note: Eligibility for many of the benefits covered in this guide are determined by your duty status. In many cases, recalled reserve and guard members, who have been activated under Federal law (Title 10), enjoy the same benefits as their active duty counterparts. Servicemembers should contact their personnel, VA or other appropriate office for assistance in determining benefits eligibility. Contact information appears in relevant sections of the book.

Also, many of the benefits covered in this book are subject to change. For the latest benefits updates and news, changes, and reader suggestions and feedback, please visit www.military.com/book.

Part One

The
Money
Advantage

A s a member of the military community, you earn discounts and valuable benefits (besides pay) that have a direct impact on your personal finances. Tax breaks, VA home loans, and a retirement savings plan (Thrift Savings Plan) are just a few of the programs designed to stretch your dollars.

Knowing your financial benefits helps you make informed choices for yourself and your family on banking, life insurance, home-buying, and money management. The insider tips in this chapter can save you money and provide the peace of mind that you deserve, especially as you deploy, transition, or retire.

You'll also find information on the safety net that protects our military community in times of emergencies or unexpected expenses. Knowing of these resources could help you, your friends, and your troops.

Military and Veteran Discounts

As more businesses and retailers seek ways to support the troops, more special deals and discounts are available for military personnel today than ever before. Food, car rentals, long-distance telephone service, gifts, airline tickets—you name it, and more likely than not there is a military discount for it somewhere. These special discounts on items and services extend to veterans, retirees, and

The Money Advantage at a Glance

military family members. In addition, the military has its own shopping facilities that offer built-in savings for servicemembers, retirees, and their families.

Discounts are always changing, but here are some choice websites for keeping up with the latest and best retail discounts for servicemembers, retirees, veterans, and their families:

• www.military.com/discounts.

• www.militarynow.com.

• www.4militaryfamilies.com/militarydiscounts.htm.

In fact, if you know of a discount that's not listed, visit Military .com/discounts and post it online—so that others can take advantage, too. If your favorite retailer doesn't offer a military discount, you might want to ask for one anyway. You will be surprised how often they say yes.

To take advantage of certain discounts, such as shopping at military commissaries and exchanges (page 5), you need a military identification card. This card also helps servicemembers, retirees, and military families access many benefits, including health care.

Take Advantage
Use the form letter at www.military.com/discounts to write retailers and request a military discount.

Military Identification Cards

The military identification card is essential for unlocking benefits and discounts for you and your family members. Active-duty, reserve, and guard members receive an ID upon entering service; retirees get a retiree ID card upon leaving service. To get military identification, military dependents need to register with the Defense Enrollment Eligibility Reporting System (DEERS), the same system used to register servicemembers and families for TRICARE health benefits. (A full overview of DEERS and TRICARE is in chapter 3).

Getting ID Cards

Along with servicemembers, those who are eligible for military ID cards include the servicemember's:

• Spouse (and certain former spouses)

• Unremarried widow or widower

• Children at age 10 and unmarried children under age 21 (including adopted children or step-children)

Take Advantage
Find your ID Card Office at www.dmdc.osd.mil/rsl /owa/home.

Contact

To update your DEERS information in person, find the nearest uniformed services personnel office at www.dmdc.osd.mil/rsl/owa/home. Call in address changes to the Defense Manpower Data Center Support Office at 800-538-9552, or fax changes to 831-655-8317.

Update information directly to the TRICARE website at www.tricare.osd.mil/deers. Mail address changes to the Defense Manpower Data Center Support Office, Attn. COA, 400 Gigling Road, Seaside, CA 93955-6771.

- Children under age 10 may be eligible if they do not presently live with an eligible family member or under special circumstances, such as if they live with a single parent.

- Unmarried children between ages 21 and 23 who are attending college full-time.

- Unmarried children older than 21, who cannot support themselves due to a physical or mental incapacity that existed either prior to their 21st birthday or between the 21st and 23rd birthdays while a legal dependent as a full-time student. This must be established in DEERS, and the child must be dependent upon the servicemember for more than one-half of his or her financial support.

Under certain circumstances, other family members can be certified as legal dependents and be eligible for ID cards. Such cases may include unmarried children, parents or parents-in-law, and an unmarried person in the servicemember's legal custody for at least 12 months. Ask your personnel or legal assistance officer on your installation for advice if you have a special case.

If you need to apply for an ID card or update ID card information, you should go to a certified ID Card/DEERS verifying office. You will need to prove eligibility to get your family's ID cards verified, so be prepared to show the following documents, as applicable:

- Marriage certificate (clear photocopy is acceptable).

- Children's birth certificates (clear photocopy is acceptable).

- Social Security card (not just the number; a clear photocopy is acceptable).

- Certified copy of court order for adoption (if applicable).

- Certified copy of court order establishing paternity (for illegitimate children if applicable).

- Certified copy of death certificate(s) (if applicable).

- Certified copy of divorce decrees (if applicable).

- Statement from licensed physician or medical officer indicating physical handicaps and period of incapacity for dependent children older than 21 years of age.

- Certificate of full-time enrollment from school registrar for dependent children older than 21 and younger than 23 (if applicable).

Commissaries and Exchanges

Active-duty, reserve, and guard servicemembers, their families, and military retirees have a major shopping benefit through access to on-base commissaries and exchanges. Everyday household items, as well as a wide range of services and products, are offered at these venues at a discount compared to civilian retail prices. You also pay no sales tax. Profits from these stores also fund Morale, Welfare, and Recreation (MWR) activities in the military community.

Commissaries

Commissaries, the equivalent of civilian supermarkets, are usually located on military installations. They sell food, sundries, and cleaning products at below-market prices, and are available to servicemembers, their families, and retirees. Guard and reserve members previously were restricted to 24 visits a year to the commissary, but they now have unlimited access. A military ID is required for all servicemembers, retirees, and family members who use the commissary.

Overseen by the Defense Commissary Agency, there are 274 commissaries around the world that net a combined $5 billion a year. Check the commissaries website for updates on sales, contests, savings opportunities, and gift certificates. The website also has a nationwide commissary directory with information on opening and closing hours, contact phone numbers, and even sales-floor layouts.

Many installations have shopping malls on base as part of the exchange system. Services can include uniform shops, barbershops, beauty parlors, dry cleaners, bookstores, optical shops, florists and watch-repair shops. Some bases even contain food courts.

Take Advantage

If you are eligible, you can shop at *any* commissary or exchange, regardless of your service affiliation.

Take Advantage

An independent study conducted by the Defense Commissary Agency found that average consumers save 30 percent on their grocery bills when using the commissary.

Take Advantage

The latest DeCA feature allows you to shop for pre-packaged commissary assortments and other gifts online. You can have gifts shipped anywhere including to your deployed loved ones and friends. Visit www.commissaries .com to learn more.

Get Involved: Commissary Focus Groups

Commissaries are required by law to add a five percent surcharge to all purchases. This helps reduce the cost of operating and building commissaries, saving the taxpayers money. Commissary shoppers save an average of 30 percent on their grocery bills.

Contact

Defense Commissary Agency: www. commissaries.com.

Take Advantage

Commissaries feature many unadvertised specials ("manager's specials") that offer extra savings—keep an eagle eye out when you shop. Be sure to ask if a discount is available before you make a purchase, especially for case-lot sales, which provide even more savings than usual.

Exchanges

The exchange is the military equivalent of a combined department and drug store. Post exchanges (PXs), Base exchanges, the Army and Air Force Exchange Service (AAFES), Navy exchanges, Marine Corps exchanges, and shopettes—military convenience stores—are all examples of military exchange stores. You can also shop online at the major exchange websites.

The Army and Air Force Exchange Service, which serves both Army and Air Force bases, is by far the largest exchange and its sales exceed $7 billion a year. It operates 224 retail stores.

A Collection of Canteens

Since 1895, when the War Department asked commanders at 48 posts to try to establish exchanges, Army and Air Force Exchange Service offerings have grown amazingly. What started more than 100 years ago as a collection of canteens and general stores has expanded to thousands of retail facilities in 25 countries.

Contact

Army and Air Force Exchange Service: www.aafes.com.

Navy Exchange Service: www.navy-nex.com.

Marine Corps Exchange: www.usmc-mccs.org.

Coast Guard Exchange: www.cg-exchange.com.

The Navy's exchange system is under the control of the Navy Exchange Command (NEXCOM). NEXCOM's website has information on Navy exchange locations and services, Navy lodging locations and amenities (for more details, see page 148), ship stores, and Navy uniforms. Customers can order Navy uniforms online; they can also make, change, or cancel a Navy lodging reservation online. Shipping and handling charges are included in the listed prices. Its sales from exchange complexes at bases and ship stores top $2 billion annually.

The Marine Corps' system has 16 main stores and annual sales of about $600 million. Coast Guard stores are run by the U.S. Coast Guard Exchange and Morale Division in Chesapeake, Virginia.

Exchange service facilities include gas stations, laundries, and auto service centers. Some may offer bookstores, one-hour photo development shops, video-rental stores, and more. All the military services operate their package, or liquor stores, as exchange operations.

Credit. Stateside and overseas exchanges accept MasterCard, Visa, American Express, and Discover credit cards. Exchanges also offer their own credit plan through the joint-exchange Military Star Card. Exchanges cash personal checks at no charge when you present a valid military ID.

Military Matters

In addition to their land-based stores, the Navy and Coast Guard operate floating exchanges known as ship stores. There are 180 Navy ship stores, stocked largely with toiletries and snack foods, uniforms, CD's, and personal electronics such as mp3 players and hand-held games.

Eligible shoppers. Eligible shoppers at exchanges include active-duty servicemembers, retirees, guard and reserve members and their families, some disabled veterans and their families, surviving spouses, and former spouses. Limits or restrictions may apply—check with your local exchange for eligibility requirements. If you are eligible, you can shop at any exchange, in person or online, regardless of service affiliation. As with commissaries, your military ID is required for access to exchanges (see page 3).

Mail order. The Exchange Catalog is available for $5 to all eligible shoppers. Individual exchanges offer specialty catalogs for uniform pieces, furniture, and other items. You can also check exchange websites for products—it's fast and free.

Contact

Military Star Card: www.aafes.com.

Contact

You can order exchange catalogs by calling toll-free 800-527-2345 in the United States, 24 hours a day, seven days a week. Or write: Exchange Catalog Address P.O. Box 660202 Dallas, TX. 75266-0202

Exchange Extras

Today's military exchanges may offer many services, including:

- Rental carpet-cleaning equipment
- On-site film processing service
- Optical and optometry shops
- Contact lens replacement
- Digital-imaging services
- Flowers by wire
- Fruit gift baskets
- Professional hair care shops and products
- Money order service

- Money transfer services
- Video / DVD rental shops
- Watch and jewelry repair service
- Stationery store
- Car and truck rental
- Overseas car sales
- Shop Online
- Mail Order
- Dental Clinics

Take Advantage

For tips on household budgeting, saving, banking, and more, see www.military.com/money.

Dealing with Credit and Debt

Success in personal financial management requires planning and perseverance. If you are currently serving on active duty or in the Reserve or Guard, it is especially critical for you to stay out of serious debt—any serious problems have the potential to negatively affect your career. For instance, failing to pay your bills could mean losing your security clearance or receiving poor marks on your evaluation. Fortunately, if you find yourself in debt, there are resources available to help you deal with the situation.

Debt-relief organizations and societies can evaluate your finances and help you budget your way out of debt. Some also provide interest-free loans for essentials or emergencies so that you can get back on your feet. (For more on these organizations, see page 9.)

Avoid "predatory" and "payday" lenders that take advantage of borrowers (often with poor credit) by engaging in questionable sales practices and charging excessive interest rates, fees, and more. You can find tips on how to avoid these kinds of lenders at the Federal Trade Commission website.

Even if you're not protected under the Servicemembers Civil Relief Act (see page 13), you may still be able to negotiate lower rates or loan extensions. Creditors don't want you to fall into bankruptcy because they could end up

Take Advantage

To find a reputable credit counseling service check out the National Foundation for Credit Counseling: www.nfcc.org.

Your Credit Report

It's important to check your credit report, a critical barometer of your financial health.

Credit reports also warn you if something is amiss (e.g. if someone has stolen your identity). Your credit report is accessed by lenders when you apply for major loans such as auto financing, and has an impact on the rate they offer you, or whether they can even extend you a loan. Some civilian employers also check credit reports before they hire. You can get your credit scores from www.equifax.com, www.transunion.com, or www.experian.com. By law, you can also request a free credit report once every 12 months. (See www.annualcreditreport.com for details.)

How long does information stay on your credit report? Here are examples:

Accounts in good standing: 10 years	Bankruptcies: 10 years
Late or missed payments: 7 years	Credit inquiries: 2 years
Collections: 7 years	Tax liens: indefinite
Judgments: 7 years	

with nothing. You can negotiate on your own or consider a credit counseling service. Credit counselors evaluate your budget, negotiate lower payments on your behalf, bring overdue accounts up to date, and consolidate your debts.

Remember your financial situation is unique. Follow the advice of professionals from aid organizations, legal assistance and financial counselors on your base, nonprofit credit counseling services, or civilian law firms if you can.

Contact

Federal Trade Commission: www.ftc.gov.

Banking Options

Many banks have financial services specially designed to serve the military. From military credit unions on bases, to organizations such as USAA to national banks such as Bank of America and Wells Fargo, you'll find savings and investment plans, financial planning services, credit and check cards, loans, mortgages—just about every kind of financial offering you can think of. The financial plan (or plans) you choose will depend on some important decisions on your part. When you're deciding on a bank or service to use, consider these factors:

Take Advantage

For additional tips on maintaining good credit and avoiding debt, see www.military.com/credit and *Military Money Magazine*.

• What range of services does the bank provide? Do they fit your needs?

• Will you be able to use your bank's services even if you move to a different location, or are deployed? Is the bank accessible?

• Do the bank's interest rates compare favorably with those of other banks?

• What fees or premiums will you be charged? How do they compare with those of other banks? Can you reasonably afford them?

Consider your own particular needs along with the above factors in determining which banking plan is best for you.

Take Advantage

For more information on bank services for the military, see www.military.com/banking.

Emergency Relief Organizations

If you are a servicemember, retiree, or family member experiencing financial difficulties, you can turn to charitable organizations that stand ready to assist you.

Air Force Aid Society

The Air Force Aid Society (AFAS) is the official charity of the United States Air Force. Founded in 1942, AFAS is a private nonprofit organization whose

Contact

Air Force Aid Society: www.afas.org.

mission is to help relieve the financial distress of Air Force members and their families. Active-duty and retired Air Force members and their dependents are eligible for AFAS assistance, as are the dependents of Air Force personnel who died on active duty or in retired status. Reservists and National Guard members serving on extended active duty for more than 30 days are eligible as well, but limited to emergencies resulting from the applicant's active-duty tour.

AFAS Loans and Grants. Most AFAS interest-free loans and grants are for short-term or one-time emergencies such as food, rent and utilities, car repairs, and emergency travel requirements. Each case, regardless of the request, is treated individually. If the local commander recommends help, and if the assistance falls within the general thrust of the AFAS charter, in most cases the request will be granted.

For more information, visit the AFAS office at your home base. Branches are located on all Air Force bases worldwide, usually in the Family Support Center. If you are away from your home base, and not near another Air Force base, the Air Force Aid Society has reciprocal agreements that allow you to receive assistance from Army Emergency Relief, the Navy-Marine Corps Relief Society, or American Red Cross chapters.

Army Emergency Relief

Army Emergency Relief (AER) is a private nonprofit organization founded in 1942 to help soldiers and their dependents deal with financial crises. Soldiers and their dependents, as well as retirees and their dependents, are eligible for help.

Army Emergency Relief helps with food, rent or utilities, transportation and vehicle repair, funeral expenses, medical/dental expenses, and personal needs when pay is delayed or stolen. Army Emergency Relief generally does not cover the following:

• Payment for nonessential items.

• Financing ordinary leave or vacation.

• Payment of fines or legal expenses.

• Liquidation or consolidation of debt.

• Assistance for home purchasing or home improvements.

• Help for purchasing, renting, or leasing a vehicle.

• Coverage for bad checks or payment of credit card bills.

Contact

Army Emergency Relief Services
703-428-0000
Fax:
703-325-7183
www.aerhq.org.

Navy-Marine Corps Relief Society

The Navy-Marine Corps Relief Society (NMCRS) gives emergency financial assistance to active-duty and reserve servicemembers, as well as retired Navy and Marine Corps personnel and their families. Basic living expenses such as food, rent, utilities, transportation, funerals, medical and dental bills, essential car repair, pay problems, and other emergency needs are covered. Assistance is provided in the form of loans or grants, depending on financial need.

The following personnel are eligible for help:

- Active-duty and retired members of the regular Navy and Marine Corps.

- Reservists on extended active duty, and certain retired Reservists.

- Dependents and dependent survivors of the above members.

- Mothers (65 years or older) of deceased servicemembers who have limited resources and no family to provide for their welfare.

- Ex-spouses (unremarried) whose marriage to a servicemember lasted for at least 20 years while the service member was on active duty.

- Uniformed members of the National Oceanic and Atmospheric Administration.

Take Advantage
Some Navy-Marine Corps Relief Society locations have thrift stores that offer secondhand merchandise, including military and civilian clothing, small appliances, household items, and baby furniture. If you wish to donate items to the shop, check with your local office for details.

Contact
Navy-Marine Corps Relief Society
703-696-4904
Fax:
703-696-0144
www.nmcrs.org.

Coast Guard Mutual Assistance

A non-profit organization that supports servicemembers, veterans, and their families in times of financial need, its services include interest-free loans, personal grants, education assistance, and confidential financial counseling and referral services.

Contact
Coast Guard Mutual Assistance
800-881-2462
www.cgmahq.org.

Military Matters

The Red Cross collaborates with the military aid societies in providing financial assistance when an urgent personal crisis arises. It helps cover emergency travel, burial assistance, or health and welfare needs such as food and shelter. Red Cross workers also assist veterans in obtaining evidence to support financial-benefits claims through the Board of Veterans Appeals. (See also 162 for more information.)

Contact
Red Cross
202-303-4498
www.redcross.org.

Deployment and Your Money

Take Advantage

If you buy a great keepsake in Japan and your spouse can't pay the bills in North Carolina, there's bound to be trouble. Consider opening a second bank account for discretionary deployment funds to avoid misunderstandings with regular household money.

Deployments are covered in more detail in the Career Advantage chapter, but the effects of deployment on your personal finances cannot be underestimated. While you cannot avoid some stresses of deployment, you can minimize others or avoid them altogether with a little careful preparation. One of the more important aspects of predeployment planning is deciding how to handle finances while you're away. (For more deployment issues and deployment checklists, see page 239.)

During deployment, life-as-usual will change dramatically for you. But responsibility for financial obligations, unfortunately, will not. Advance financial preparation is vital to preventing overdue bills, overdrawn accounts, and unwanted "special attention" from your command.

If you are married, you should work together with your spouse to establish a budget, determining how money will be spent. Make sure that both you and your spouse are listed on your bank account or possess a valid power of attorney. If you are single, you may wish to authorize a trusted individual with a limited power of attorney to act on your financial behalf, if needed. (For more on power of attorney, see www.military.com/attorney).

One important benefit related to financial assistance during deployment is the Servicemembers Civil Relief Act (SCRA). Be sure to read more about SCRA on page 148.

Take Advantage

When you're deployed, you may find temporary refuge from your debt in the Servicemembers Civil Relief Act (SCRA), which requires creditors to lower interest rates on debts incurred before entering military service. Reservists and guard members are also eligible for this protection while on active duty.

You can get a good estimate of your deployment expenses by reviewing past expenditures. If this is the first time you'll be shipping out, consider meeting with a financial counselor from a relief organization (i.e. Air Force Relief Society, Navy-Marine Corps Relief Society) for assistance. Be aware that changes may occur in your standard pay. Married servicemembers who receive subsistence allowance for meals should plan for its deduction while they are deployed. Reserve and guard families may need to adjust for changes in pay from civilian employment to that of active-duty service.

With the right planning you and your family can avoid worrying about finances during the stress of deployment. Then you can concentrate on the important things—like a job well done and the countdown until the day you return.

Taxes

When you're in the military (and especially when you're deployed), there are many tax rules to keep in mind. Fortunately, your tax situation is different from—and often more advantageous than—what your civilian counterparts face. Armed with the right knowledge, you can get important breaks on your taxes.

While this book covers military tax highlights, you should go to the IRS for the most comprehensive resource on tax regulations for military personnel. The IRS publishes the Armed Forces Tax Guide, available online along with annual updates on military tax laws.

New Law Provides Military Tax Relief

The Heroes Earning Assistance and Relief Tax (HEART) Act, passed in June of 2008, allows active-duty reservists to make penalty-free withdrawals from retirement plans, and makes the Earned Income Tax Credit a permanent inclusion into Soldiers' combat pay. Additionally, the new law ensures that reservists called to active duty do not suffer pay cuts; and provides a small tax credit to small businesses that continue to pay reservists and guardsmen who are deployed.

Other provisions are designed to ease the financial burden on military families by doing the following:

- Permitting an employer to make contributions to a qualified retirement plan on behalf of an employee killed or disabled during combat.

- Counting extra pay for active-duty military personnel from their previous civilian employer for retirement purposes.

- Making thousands of veterans eligible for low-interest loans by changing the qualified mortgage bond programs used to help veterans achieve homeownership.

- Permitting recipients of military death benefit gratuities to roll over the amounts received tax free, to a Roth IRA or Education Saving Account.

- Revising tax rules relating to U.S. citizens and permanent residents (expatriates) who relinquish citizenship or residency to avoid U.S. taxation.

Contact

Find the Armed Forces Tax Guide and updated tax information: www.military.com/taxes.

Take Advantage

Many private tax-preparation agencies offer discounts to military personnel. It may be worth using these services instead of spending both the time and energy to do your taxes yourself, especially if you're deployed or you are a spouse taking care of the family finances. Visit www.military.com/discounts for a list of these services.

Servicemembers Civil Relief Act

The Servicemembers Civil Relief Act (SCRA) ensures favorable tax benefits for reserve and guard members called to active duty. For example, you may be able to delay payment of income tax that becomes due before or during your military service for up to 180 days after your release from service. If you have been called to active service, or may be called up soon, see the Tax section of Part Four for further SCRA and tax benefit details.

Combat Zone Tax Exclusion

If you are an enlisted member, warrant officer, or commissioned warrant officer and you serve in a combat zone during any part of a month, all of your military pay for that month is excluded from your taxable income. You can also exclude military pay earned while you are hospitalized as a result of wounds, disease, or injury incurred in the combat zone. The exclusion of your military pay while you are hospitalized no longer applies to any month that begins more than two years after the end of combat activities in that combat zone. You do not need to be hospitalized in a combat zone to exclude pay earned during that period.

If you are a commissioned officer (other than a warrant officer), you can claim a tax exclusion according to the rules just discussed. However, the amount of your exclusion is limited to the highest rate of *enlisted* pay available (e.g. an E-9 with maximum time in service), plus imminent danger or hostile fire pay you received for each month in which you served in a combat zone, or were hospitalized as a result of your service there.

Combat zone tax exclusions include:

- Active-duty pay earned in any month you served in a combat zone.

- Imminent danger or hostile fire pay.

- A reenlistment bonus if the voluntary extension or reenlistment occurs in a month you served in a combat zone.

- Pay for accrued leave earned in any month you served in a combat zone.

Tax Exclusions

You can exclude the following items from gross income, whether or not each item is furnished in kind or is a reimbursement or allowance.

Housing allowances:
- Basic Allowance for Housing (BAH)
  You can deduct mortgage interest and real estate taxes on your home even if you pay these expenses with your BAH.
- Basic Allowance for Subsistence (BAS)
- Housing and cost-of-living allowances abroad, whether paid by the U.S. government or by a foreign government
- Overseas Housing Allowance (OHA)

Moving allowances:
- Dislocation
- Move-in housing
- Moving of household and personal items
- Moving of trailers or mobile homes
- Storage
- Temporary lodging and temporary lodging expenses

Family allowances:
- Emergencies
- Evacuation to a place of safety
- Separation

Health expenses and in-kind benefits:
- Medical/dental care
- Defense counseling
- Disability, including payments received for injuries incurred as a direct result of a terrorist or military action
- Group-term life insurance

Education allowances and benefits:
- Certain educational expenses for dependents

- Professional education
- ROTC educational and subsistence allowances

Death allowances:
- Burial services
- Death gratuity payments (up to $100,000) to eligible survivors
- Travel of dependents to burial site

Travel allowances:
- Annual round trip for dependent students
- Leave between consecutive overseas tours
- Reassignment in a dependent-restricted status
- Transportation for you or your dependents during ship overhaul or inactivation
- Per diem

Other exclusions:
- Survivor and retirement benefit plan premiums
- Uniform allowances
- Uniforms furnished to enlisted personnel

Excludable special pay:
- Compensation for active service while in a combat zone or a qualified hazardous duty area

Excludable in-kind military benefits:
- Legal assistance
- Space-available travel on government aircraft
- Commissary and exchange discounts

Source: Internal Revenue Service

Contact

IRS combat zone relief: combatzone@irs. gov.

The Department of Defense (DoD) must determine that the unused leave was earned during that period.

- Pay received for duties as a member of the Armed Forces in clubs, messes, post and station theaters, and other nonappropriated fund activities. The pay must be earned in a month you served in a combat zone.

- Awards for suggestions, inventions, or scientific achievements you are entitled to because of a submission you made in a month you served in a combat zone.

- Student loan repayments that are attributable to your period of service in a combat zone (provided a full year's service is performed to earn the repayment).

- Career Status Bonus (retirement bonus), during your time in a combat zone.

New Tax Break

The new "Heroes Earned Retirement Opportunities Act" allows servicemembers to include combat zone compensation in determining their allowable income tax deduction for contributions to IRAs.

If you are in a combat zone while on leave from a duty station located outside the combat zone, or traveling over or through a combat zone between two points that are outside a combat zone, your pay does not qualify as a combat zone exclusion.

Form W-2. The wages shown in box 1 of your annual Form W-2 should not include military pay set aside according to the combat zone exclusion provisions. If you do include these wages, you will need to get a corrected Form W-2 from your finance office. You cannot exclude as combat pay any wages mistakenly shown in box 1 of Form W-2.

Notifying the IRS by email about Combat Zone Service. Working with the DoD, the IRS identifies taxpayers who are serving in a combat zone in order to suspend compliance actions, such as audits or enforced collections, until 180 days after the taxpayer has left the zone.

If you qualify for such combat zone relief, you may also notify the IRS directly of your status by writing to a special email address. Include your name, stateside address, date of birth, and the date of your deployment to the combat zone: combatzone@irs.gov.

Military Matters

The President of the United States designates a combat zone as an area in which the U.S. Armed Forces are engaging or have engaged in combat. An area usually becomes a combat zone and ceases to be a combat zone based on the dates of the president's executive order. For a list of current combat zones, see www.military.com/combatzones.

Do not include any Social Security numbers in nonsecure email messages.
This notification can be made by the taxpayer, the taxpayer's spouse, or an authorized agent or representative. The IRS cannot provide tax account information by email, but it will respond to any questions about a taxpayer's account by regular mail within two business days using the address it has on file. The IRS may provide general answers to questions regarding the status of individual combat zone updates via this email address.

Other Tax Benefits

Death gratuity. The $100,000 death gratuity paid to survivors of deceased Armed Forces members is not taxable. Taxpayers amending a return to use this provision should write "Military Family Tax Relief Act" in red in the top margin of Form 1040X, the amended U.S. Individual Tax Return form. For more on the death gratuity, see the Surviving Family Benefits section of Part Four.

National Guard and Reserve deduction for overnight travel expenses. If you are in the Reserve or Guard and stay overnight more than 100 miles away from home while in service (e.g. for a drill or meeting), you can deduct unreimbursed travel expenses (transportation, meals, and lodging). This deduction follows rates used for federal-government employees, including per diem in lieu of subsistence. Use Form 2106 or 2106-EZ to calculate the deduction amount, and carry it as a "write-in" to Form 1040, line 33, putting the letters "RC" along with the amount on the dotted line.

DoD Homeowners Assistance Program. As a fringe benefit, payments made under this program to offset the adverse effects due to military base realignments or closures on property value will be excludable.

Dependent-care assistance programs. Dependent-care assistance programs for military personnel are also tax-free benefits.

Doing Taxes Overseas

If you're abroad, you are expected to file a tax return by the April 15 deadline. However, all U.S. citizens overseas, including military members and their families, are eligible for a two-month filing extension until June 15. You can qualify for an extension if either of the following situations applies to you: (1) you live outside the United States and Puerto Rico and your main place of business or post of duty is outside the United States and Puerto Rico; or (2)

Contact

Tax forms for National Guard and Reserve deductions are at www.irs.gov/pub/irs-pdf/f2106.pdf or at www.irs.gov/pub/irs-pdf/f2106ez.pdf.

Earned Income Tax Credit

Many junior servicemembers with families may qualify for the Earned Income Tax Credit. The amount of this tax credit is determined by your income and number of dependents. The EITC for the 2008 tax year will range from $428 to $4,716.

Take Advantage

If you are unable to pay the tax you owe or estimate, file Form 9465 (www.irs.gov/pub /irs-pdf/f9465.pdf) to arrange an install-ment payment agreement with the IRS that reflects your ability to pay the tax owed.

you are in military or Naval service on an assigned tour of duty outside the United States and Puerto Rico for a period that includes the due date of the return.

This extension is automatic, but if you use it, you must attach a statement to the return showing that you have met the requirement. You can request a sec-ond two-month extension, until August 15, by filing Form 4868 by June 15. Write "Taxpayer Abroad" across the top of Form 4868.

You can request an additional two-month extension beyond August 15 by filing Form 2688 or by writing a letter to the IRS. Except in undue-hardship cases, this additional extension will be granted only if Form 4868 has been filed previously.

A filing extension does not mean you have an extension to pay any tax due. If you owe taxes and pay your taxes after the regular due date, you will be charged interest based on the period from the regular due date to the time of payment. You must estimate your tax due, and pay it by the April 15 deadline.

Contact

Tax Forms 4868 and 2688 are available at www.military.com/ taxes.

Military Matters

Generally, U.S. citizens working abroad can get an exemption on their tax returns—specifically, they don't have to pay taxes on the first $80,000 they earn from a foreign employer. U.S. servicemembers are not exempt from paying taxes on salary they earn while stationed abroad. If you incor-rectly claim this exemption on your tax return, you will have to pay addi-tional taxes, and possibly be penalized.

Filing Joint Returns

If one spouse is overseas on military duty, there are two options when filing a joint return. The first option is for one spouse to prepare the return, sign it, and send it to the other spouse to sign in time to file. The second option is for the spouse who expects to be overseas to file Form 2848, specifically designating that the spouse who remains in the United States can sign the return for the absent spouse.

However, when a spouse is unreachable, in a combat zone or qualified hazardous duty area, in a missing status, or incapacitated, a power of attorney may be needed to file a joint return.

Contact

Form 2848 is available at www.irs.gov/pub/ irs-pdf/f2848.pdf.

You can gain power of attorney by filing Form 2848, available at your near-est legal assistance office. While other power of attorney forms may be used, they must contain the information required by Form 2848. For assistance on this and related legal issues, see page 150.

If one spouse is unable to sign the return and the other does not have a power of attorney or other required statement, the present spouse should still sign for the absent spouse. Along with the return the present spouse should include a statement that explains the absent spouse is serving in a combat zone.

To qualify for a filing extension, only one spouse needs to meet the extension requirements if you file jointly. If you are married but filing separate returns, only the spouse who meets the requirements qualifies for the automatic extension to June 15.

IRS International Offices

If you are a taxpayer who lives outside the United States, the IRS has full-time permanent staff in U.S. embassies and consulates located in Berlin, London, Paris, and Puerto Rico. These offices have tax forms and publications, and employees who help you with account problems and answer your questions about notices and bills. You can reach these offices at the following telephone numbers, which include country or city codes if you are outside the local dialing area. If you have technical or tax account questions that can't be answered overseas, call, fax, or write the IRS in Washington, D.C.

Contact

If you're overseas, call the IRS in Washington at 215-516-2000. If you are in Guam, the Bahamas, the U.S. Virgin Islands, or Puerto Rico, call 800-829-1040. You can also access www.irs.gov.

The IRS Overseas

Assistant Commissioner (International), IRS
950 L'Enfant Plaza SW
Attn: CP:IN:D:CS
Washington, D.C. 20024
    Tel: 202-874-1460
    Fax: 202-874-5440

Germany
IRS
U. S. Consulate Frankfurt
Geissener Str. 30
60435 Frankfurt am Main
Tel: [49] (69) 7535-3834
FAX: [49] (69) 7535-3803
M-F 8 a.m. - 4 p.m. (Closed U.S. and German Holidays)

London
United States Embassy/IRS
24/31 Grosvenor Square
London W1A 1AE UK
Walk-in assistance 9 a.m. to 4 p.m.
    (Tuesday through Thursday)

Tel: [44] (207) 408-8077
(9 a.m. to noon, Monday through Friday)
Fax: +44-207-495-4224

Paris
United States
Internal Revenue Service (International)
P.O. Box 920
Bensalem, PA 19020
Tel: 215-516-2000 (not toll-free)
Fax: 215-516-2555

Puerto Rico
7 Tabonuco Street
Guaynobo, Puerto Rico 00918
    Tel: 787-622-8929
    (8:30 a.m. to 4 p.m., Monday through Friday)

VA Home Loans

One of the most significant benefits of military service is the VA home loan, which can help you purchase a home with no down payment or refinance an existing loan. This gives you the opportunity to get a mortgage with a competitive interest rate as well as a lower cost at closing without prepayment penalty. With all these benefits, you have the potential to purchase a more expensive home than you might otherwise have been able to afford.

VA does not give you the actual loan for your home; rather, they simply guarantee a loan made to you by private lenders (such as banks, savings and loans, or mortgage companies). If a home loan is approved by your lender, VA will guarantee a portion of the loan to the lender.

A VA loan can be used for the following expenses (only for your principal primary residence, not a second home or home you rent out):

Home purchase or repair

- Buying a home, townhouse, or condo.

- Building a home.

- Buying a manufactured home with or without a lot.

- Repairing, altering, or improving a home.

- Simultaneously purchasing and improving a home with energy-efficient improvements.

- Installing a solar heating or cooling system or other weatherization improvements.

Loan refinancing

- Refinancing an existing home loan.

- Refinancing an existing VA home loan to lower the interest rate.

- Refinancing a manufactured home with or without a lot.

Source: Dept. of Veterans Affairs

There is technically no maximum VA loan, but lenders will generally limit the total amount of a VA-guaranteed loan to $417,000. VA actually guarantees up to 25 percent of the $417,000 loan limit. While not a down payment, the guarantee often satisfies the lenders' requirement that a portion of the home price be paid for up front (e.g. the down payment). This can save the home buyer the burden of making a down pay-

Take Advantage

VA home loans are not always your best option. You may be better off getting a conventional home loan with a lower interest rate. You should investigate to see which option is best for you.

Take Advantage

Recent legislation has temporarily increased the VA Home Loan limit to more than $1 million, depending on location.

Take Advantage

Veterans with permanent and total service-connected disabilities may be eligible to receive a VA Specially Adapted Housing (SAH) grant for up to $50,000 to adapt a house to meet their disability needs. Or they may be eligible for a grant to cover the appraised market value of necessary adapted features already in a house when they purchased it. For details, see www.homeloans.va.gov/sah.htm.

ment. The loan maximum itself may be up to 100 percent of the VA-established reasonable value of the property, though generally it may not exceed $417,000 (this figure increases every year—see www.military.com/valoans for updates). In addition, certain funding fees and closing costs apply, and you must be able to pay a portion of these fees up front. Generally, these fees range from 1.25 percent to 3 percent of the total loan.

Eligibility for a VA Home Loan

The major eligibility categories for a VA home loan include:

- Veterans and servicemembers who have served 181 active-duty days during peacetime, unless discharged or separated from a previous qualifying period of active-duty service.

- Veterans who served during World War II, Korea, or Vietnam, if they served for 90 days and were honorably discharged.

- If you have served for any period since August 2, 1990, you can also qualify if you have served 24 months of continuous active duty, or the full period (at least 90 days) that you were called to active duty.

- Those who have completed a total of six years in the Selected Reserves or National Guard.

- An unremarried spouse of a veteran who died while in service or from a service-connected disability, or a spouse of a serviceperson missing in action or a prisoner of war. (Note: A surviving spouse who remarries on or after attaining age 57, and on or after December 16, 2003, may also be eligible for the home loan benefit.)

See Appendix, page 350, for military service requirements for VA loan eligibility.

Applying for a VA Loan In Four Steps

There are four basic steps in the VA home loan application process. The first step is to find a lender or lending institution that provides home loans. At this stage, you should also gather the documents you'll need when applying for the loan. The second step involves getting a purchase agreement for your new home and asking VA for a property inspection or appraisal. For the third step, you'll need to submit a VA home loan application. In the fourth and final step, your loan is approved, the funding is confirmed, and you can close on your new home.

Take Advantage
Veterans with a VA-rated disability of 10% or higher are eligible to have their VA Loan fees waived. This could save them thousands in loan origination fees.

Take Advantage
Find out if you are eligible for a VA loan with an easy eligibility calculator at www.military.com/Finance/VA-eligibility.

Contact
For a current table of VA funding fees, go to www.homeloans.va.gov/docs/funding_fee_tables.doc.

Contact

To find a VA-approved lender in your area, visit www.military.com/valoan.

Military Matters

A VA guaranteed home loan allows eligible borrowers to obtain a home loan with favorable terms (e.g. a no downpayment loan). The guaranteed home loan must be repaid, and failure to make payments could result in the loss of your home through foreclosure. If your loan is foreclosed and VA is forced to pay the guaranty to the lender, you will not be able to reuse your eligibility until such time as you repay VA for the loss.

Contact

National Personnel Records Center Military Personnel Records 9700 Page Ave. St. Louis, MO 63132-5100 Toll-free: 866-272-6272 www.archives.gov/regional/mpr.html.

Step 1: Selecting a Lender

A lender can help you review your financial situation and credit history and determine the loan amount you qualify for. Choose a lending institution that both is VA-approved and can handle home loans. Different lenders have different closing costs and other fees, so it pays to shop around.

The loan application and approval process depends on accurate and complete documentation. To ensure a smooth transaction, make sure to gather all necessary documents you need prior to your initial loan application.

You will need to give your lender a VA Certificate of Eligibility. This form is required to process your loan. You can request your Certificate of Eligibility for VA home loan benefits by sending a completed VA Form 26-1880 along with your proof of service documents to the Winston-Salem VA Eligibility Center. A list of required documents can be found on page 2, section D of the request form.

Automated Certificate of Eligibility. You can also get your Certificate of Eligibility from your lender through the ACE system. This Internet-based application can establish your eligibility and issue an online Certificate of Eligibility in a matter of seconds. However, not all requests can be processed through ACE—only those veterans for whom the VA has sufficient data are eligible for this streamlined process.

Contact

Winston-Salem VA Eligibility Center P.O. Box 20729 Winston-Salem, NC 27120 888-244-6711.

Step 2: Home Purchase Agreement and Appraisal

Now comes the big decision: choosing the home you wish to buy. Once you sign a purchase agreement, you need to get a property appraisal from VA.

Advantages of a VA Loan

A VA home loan offers you many advantages that you don't receive with a conventional home loan and mortgage:

- No down payment required in most cases.
- Loan maximum up to 100 percent of the VA-established reasonable value of the property.
- Negotiable interest rate.
- No monthly mortgage insurance premium to pay.
- Buyer informed of reasonable value by a license appraiser.
- Limitation on buyer's closing costs; may result in lower closing costs.
- Thirty-year loans with a choice of repayment plans.
- An assumable mortgage, subject to VA approval of the assumer's credit.
- Right to prepay loan without penalty
- Personal loan servicing performed by VA as well as financial counseling to help veteran borrowers in default due to temporary financial difficulty.
- Without penalty the borrower can prepay the entire loan or any part not less than the amount of one installment or $100 (whichever is less).
- In case a borrower becomes temporarily unable to meet the terms of the loan, VA encourages holders to extend forbearance.
- For most loans on a new or recently built house, construction is inspected at appropriate stages to ensure compliance with the approved plans, and a one-year warranty is required from the builder to ensure that the house is built to conform to VA-approved plans and specifications. (In cases where the builder provides an acceptable 10-year warranty plan, only a final inspection may be required.)
- In cases of new construction completed under VA or HUD inspection, VA may pay or otherwise compensate the veteran borrower for correction of structural defects seriously affecting livability if assistance is requested within four years of a home loan guaranty.

Source: Dept. of Veterans Affairs

(Usually this is done by the lender.) This property appraisal, known as the Certificate of Reasonable Value (CRV), is an appraiser's estimate of the value of the property to be purchased. Because the loan amount may not exceed the CRV, it is important to request an appraisal early in the home loan process.

Once completed, the CRV form can be mailed to the Loan Guaranty Division at the nearest VA office for processing.

Contact your VA Regional Loan Center for information concerning its assignment procedures. Meanwhile, the appraiser will send a bill for his or her services to the requester according to a fee schedule approved by VA. To

Contact

VA Loan Office:
800-827-1000.

simplify the process, VA and the Department of Housing and Urban Development/Federal Housing Administration (HUD/FHA) use the same appraisal forms. Also, under certain limited circumstances, if the property was recently appraised by HUD, the HUD conditional commitment can be converted to a VA CRV. Employees at your VA Regional Loan Center can explain how this is done.

Military Matters

Although the VA-approved appraiser must view the property from both the exterior and interior to determine its overall condition, the appraisal process is not intended to be a formal inspection of the property. This means the appraiser is not responsible for recommending cosmetic repairs, ensuring that mechanical, electrical, and plumbing systems work properly, checking the roof, and so forth.

Step 3: Submit the Application

For instructions on how to receive and submit your home loan application, contact your lender directly. Most lenders will allow you to submit the application online, by fax, over the phone, by mail, or in person.

After your application and paperwork are submitted, the lender reviews all your information to ensure there are no discrepancies in presentation. Any possible problems are addressed at this stage. If you did not provide all the original documents needed, you will be requested to provide them again. In the processing stage, all the following documents are gathered: certificate of eligibility, verifications of employment, verifications of deposit credit report, escrow instructions, preliminary title reports, appraisal, and additional supporting documents.

Step 4: Loan Approval, Funding, and Closing

If all your paperwork checks out and the lender approves your loan, you may still need to provide updated or additional information before the closing of your loan. Such items or conditions will eventually go to the lender, so that your loan can move to the next stage: ordering your loan documents. To finalize your transaction you need these legal binding documents:

• Promissory note indicating amount borrowed, interest rate charged, and terms of repayment.

• Deed of Trust placing the property as security against the loan and note.

• HUD-1 Form (pages 1 and 2) itemizing all fees incurred for obtaining the loan

Contact

VA Regional Loan Center website: www.homeloans. va.gov/rlcweb.htm.

Once your loan documents have been prepared, signed, and returned, the funding process begins. After a final check of all signed documents is completed, the lender funds the loan. Usually through an electronic wire transfer, the money you borrowed is given to the escrow or closing attorney for disbursement. The last step is the issuance of your HUD-1, which often takes place on the same day as the recording of your loan. The recording is considered the true closing of the loan.

By law, a VA loan user must pay a funding fee (usually around 2 percent of the loan), but VA can lower this fee if the borrower makes a down payment of at least 5 percent. You may also be exempt from this fee if you fall under one of these categories:

• You receive VA compensation for service-connected disabilities.

• You are a veteran who would be entitled to receive compensation for service-connected disabilities if you did not receive retirement pay.

• You are a surviving spouse of a veteran who died in service or from service-connected disabilities.

VA Loan Repayment

If you are having trouble repaying your loan, it's best to talk with the lender as soon as possible. Explain why the payments may be late and when and how those late payments will be made. If you've lost a job, been divorced, or had another serious problem, and you can't make regular monthly payments, VA may be able help you in arranging a repayment plan. VA offers home loan counseling through its regional offices. For the nearest loan service representative, call VA's toll-free number. Should all else fail, there are alternatives to foreclosure, such as selling your home.

If you do sell your home, but the expected proceeds from the sale are not enough to pay off your existing loan, the VA guaranty will pay the lender for the difference between your loan amount and the amount your home sold for. As with any claim payment by VA, you usually remain liable to VA for the amount of the claim payment.

Take Advantage

If you pay off a VA loan, save the paperwork—this can help if you ever apply for a second VA loan and want to ask for the maximum amount you're allowed. For more on getting a second VA loan, see page 27.

VA Loan Documents Checklist

VA Eligibility Information
- Certificate of Eligibility. Obtain VA Form 26-1880, Request for a Certificate of Eligibility for VA Home Loan Benefits (www.military.com/forms).
- Certificate of Release or Discharge from Active Duty (DD Form 214) if you are a veteran. If you do not have this form, apply for one using Standard Form 180 (www.military. com/forms).

Employment Information
- Complete tax returns from the past two years, with all schedules
- W-2s and 1099s from the past two years
- Most recent pay stubs covering a one-month period
- If applicable: tax returns and Year-to-Date Profit and Loss Statement from the last three years for self-employed veterans
- If applicable: copies of spouse's employer addresses and phone numbers

Savings Information
- Complete bank statements from the most recent three months for all accounts
- Most statements from retirement, 401k, mutual funds, money market, stocks, bonds, and inheritances
- If applicable: Copies of spouse's financial accounts and phone numbers

Credit Information
- Latest credit card statements, indicating minimum payments and account numbers

- Name, address, and phone number of your landlord, or 12 months of cancelled rent checks
- If applicable: if you have no credit cards, copies of your most recent utility bills
- If applicable: copy of complete bankruptcy and discharge papers
- If applicable: if you co-signed for a mortgage, car, credit card, etc., copies of 12 months' cancelled checks, front and back, indicating you are not making payments
- If applicable: copies of spouse's credit card accounts

Personal Information
- Copy of driver's license
- Copy of Social Security card
- If applicable: copies of complete divorce, palimony, or alimony papers
- If applicable: copy of green card or work permit

If You Are Refinancing or Own Rental Property
- Copy of note and deed from current loan
- Copy of property tax bill
- Copy of hazard (homeowners) insurance policy
- Copy of payment coupon for current mortgage
- If applicable: If property is multi-unit, you need copies of rental agreements. Upon review of your file on a case-by-case basis, additional documents may be requested.

These documents will only be used in the verification process.

Source: Dept. of Veterans Affairs

Refinancing Your VA Home Loan

You can use your VA home loan benefit to refinance your existing VA home loan to a lower interest rate, with little or no out-of-pocket cost. This is called an Interest Rate Reduction Refinancing Loan (IRRRL), also known as a "rapid refinance" or a "streamline refinance."

Generally, no appraisal, credit information, or underwriting is required for this refinancing option, although some lenders may require an appraisal and credit report. The fees and charges associated with the refinancing loan may be incorporated into the new VA loan. Remember: The interest rate on the new loan must be lower than the rate on the old loan (unless you refinance an adjustable-rate mortgage to a fixed-rate mortgage).

To receive an IRRRL, work with your lender to process your application. It's generally a good idea to compare several lenders' rates first, as there may be large differences in the terms they offer. Also, some lenders may contact you suggesting that they are the only lenders with the authority to make IRRLs, but according to VA, any lender can make you an IRRRL.

An IRRRL can be done only if you have already used your eligibility for a VA loan on the property you intend to refinance. If you have your Certificate of Eligibility, take it to the lender to show your prior use of the entitlement.

The occupancy requirement for an IRRRL is different from that for other VA loans. When you originally got your VA loan, you certified that you occupied or intended to occupy the home. For an IRRRL, you need only certify that you previously occupied it.

The loan may not exceed the sum of the outstanding balance on the existing VA loan, plus allowable fees and closing costs, including the funding fee.

Take Advantage

An online calculator that compares VA loans to conventional home loans is available at www.military.com/mortgages.

Reusing Your VA Home Loan Benefit

The VA home loan benefit can be reused if you have paid off your prior VA loan and sold the property. In addition you may, on a one-time only basis, be able to reuse or restore your benefit eligibility if your prior VA loan has been paid in full and you still own the property.

In either case, to restore your eligibility, you must send a completed VA Form 26-1880 to your VA Eligibility Center. (See VA Loan Documents on page 26 for information.)

To prevent delays in processing, you should also include evidence that the prior loan has been paid in full and, if applicable, the property disposed of. This evidence can be presented in the form of a paid-in-full statement from the former lender, or a copy of the HUD-1 settlement statement completed in connection with a sale of the property or refinance of the prior loan.

Depending on the circumstances, if you have already used a portion of your VA-guaranteed amount (up to $89,912), and the used portion cannot be restored, any remaining portion of your VA guarantee is available for use on another loan. You will have to ask your lender if your remaining VA-guaranteed portion will be enough, or if you will need to make a down payment to qualify for the loan. If you have a question about your specific case, contact VA.

Life Insurance

A life insurance policy is critical for financial reasons, and because of the nature of military service. Fortunately, there are good life insurance options for servicemembers, veterans, retirees, and family members. When you join the military, the government automatically provides coverage and deducts premiums from your pay. You can elect to decline this coverage and get coverage through private life insurance companies, including nonprofit organizations created to serve the military community.

Selecting the right life insurance policy for you and your family is also important when you retire or separate from the military. In deciding on the best plan for you, consider the following questions:

• Will the plan adequately cover you and your family?

• How do the premiums and overall coverage compare with other plans? Which plan gives you the most "bang for the buck"?

• Are you interested in term life insurance (which covers you and your family only for a specified period; i.e. the next 20 years) or whole life insurance (which covers you for your entire life, but also generally costs more)?

Servicemembers Group Life Insurance

Servicemembers Group Life Insurance (SGLI) is for servicemembers on active duty, Ready Reservists, National Guard members, members of the Commissioned Corps of the National Oceanic and Atmospheric Administration and the Public Health Service, cadets and midshipmen of the four service academies, and members of the Reserve Officer Training Corps (ROTC).

Currently, you may elect to take up to $400,000 of coverage, in increments

Military Matters

The four main types of life insurance are:
- Term: lasts for a specific period; has no savings component.
- Whole Life: combines term insurance with an investment component (i.e. stocks, bonds).
- Permanent: requires you pay premiums until your death, but you also build savings.
- Variable: has a flexible structure designed to allow greater return on the savings portion of the policy.

Take Advantage

To reduce or cancel your SGLI, complete and file form 3286, "Servicemembers Group Life Insurance Election and Certificate," with your uniformed service.

of $50,000 regardless of age. Your monthly cost for coverage is 6.5 cents per every $1,000 of coverage (for example, $27 for $400,000 of coverage). This premium includes an additional $1.00 per month for Traumatic Injury Protection coverage, which is mandatory and added automatically.

Special note: Servicemembers serving in OEF/OIF receive an allowance to defray the premium costs for the first $150,000 of SGLI coverage; if you elect to be insured for less than $150,000 of SGLI, then the amount of the allowance will equal the amount of your premium deduction for SGLI coverage.

SGLI is term insurance; it does not pay dividends. In addition, there are no loan, cash, or extended insurance values, or any provision for waiver of premiums or benefit because of total disability, accidents, etc., though there are exceptions.

Members on active duty, active duty for training, or inactive duty for training, and members of the Ready Reserve are automatically covered for $400,000, with premiums deducted from your pay. If you elect to be insured for less than the maximum amount, or to decline coverage entirely, you must also complete the Servicemembers Group Life Insurance Election and Certificate.

Upon your separation from service, you can convert your full-time SGLI coverage to term insurance under the Veterans Group Life Insurance (VGLI) program or to a permanent insurance plan with a participating commercial insurance company. Coverage under the group life insurance policy does not affect your right to retain any other government or private insurance, or your entitlement to other veterans' benefits. For example, you can be insured for up to $30,000 in Service-Disabled Veterans Insurance (S-DVI) coverage (see page 34) and have $400,000 of SGLI coverage at the same time.

Complete a copy of the Servicemembers Group Life Insurance Election and Certificate to designate one or more beneficiaries to receive payment of the insurance proceeds. A copy of this form also serves as a certificate of coverage.

Take Advantage

For more on the life insurance options mentioned here, plus additional tips, see www.military.com/insurance.

Military Matters

If you and your spouse are both in the military and participate in SGLI, each of you can be insured under basic SGLI as well as SGLI family coverage for the maximum coverage amount of $400,000 for each spouse. To ensure that both of you have spousal coverage, you must list each other as spouses on your DEERS record.

SGLI Costs

If you're on active duty or in the Ready Reserve or are a reserve or guard member called to active duty for over 31 days, you pay $3.50 a month per every $50,000 of coverage. The premium for part-time coverage for Ready Reservists is $28 per year for $400,000 insurance. Members of the Individual Ready Reserve (IRR) will be charged a premium of $1.25 for $400,000 insurance for one-day call-ups.

Traumatic Injury Protection

Under SGLI, you can be issued a traumatic injury benefit (TSGLI) of between $25,000 and $100,000 if you sustain one of the following types of injury:

- Total and permanent loss of sight.

- Loss of a hand or foot.

- Total and permanent loss of speech.

- Total and permanent loss of hearing in both ears.

- Loss of thumb and index finger on the same hand by severance at or above the metacarpophalangeal joints.

- Quadriplegia, paraplegia, or hemiplegia.

- Burns greater than second degree, covering 30 percent of the body or 30 percent of the face.

- Coma or the inability to carry out the activities of daily living resulting from traumatic injury to the brain.

Payment under this section may be made only if you are insured under Servicemembers Group Life Insurance when the traumatic injury is sustained, and when the loss results directly from that traumatic injury and from no other cause. Payments will be made by a schedule decided upon by the secretary of your service in collaboration with the Secretary of Defense.

Contact

Office of Servicemembers Group Life Insurance
290 W. Mt. Pleasant Ave.
Livingston, NJ 07039
800-419-1473
Fax:
800-236-6142
Death and accelerated benefits claims only:
877-832-4943.

Are You Eligible for SGLI?

If you are or have been on full-time active duty or active duty for training (for more than 31 days), and belong to one of the groups below, you can receive full-time SGLI coverage:

• Commissioned, warrant, and enlisted members of the Air Force, Army, Marine Corps, Coast Guard, and Navy, and commissioned members of the National Oceanic and Atmospheric Administration and Public Health Service/

• Members of the Reserve or Guard who are assigned to a unit or position in which they may be required to perform active duty or active duty for training and who each year will be scheduled to perform at least 12 periods of inactive-duty training/

• Members of the Individual Ready Reserve and the National Guard who volunteer for assignment to a mobilization category/

• Cadets or midshipmen of the United States Air Force Academy, United States Coast Guard Academy, United States Military Academy, or United States Naval Academy/

Part-time coverage is provided to the following reservists who do not qualify for full-time coverage while performing active duty or active duty for training under calls or orders specifying periods of less than 31 days:

• Commissioned, warrant, and enlisted members of the Air Force, Army, Navy, Marine Corps, and Coast Guard Reserves (except temporary members of the Coast Guard Reserves)/

• Members of the Individual Ready Reserve who volunteer for assignment to a "mobilization" category/

• Reserve Corps of the Public Health Service/

• The Army National Guard and Air National Guard/

• Members, cadets, and midshipmen of the ROTC while attending field training or practice cruises.

Source: Dept. of Veterans Affairs

Long-Term Care Insurance

Active duty and retired servicemembers are eligible to purchase long-term care insurance for themselves and their families. This insurance covers a wide range of expenses associated with assisted living that are not covered by TRACARE. Visit www.opm.gov/insure/ltc to learn more.

Family Servicemembers Group Life Insurance

Contact

For details on Family Servicemembers Group Life Insurance, see www.insurance.va.gov/sgliSite/FSGLI/sglifam.htm.

Family Servicemembers Group Life Insurance (FSGLI) is an insurance program for the spouses and dependent children of servicemembers insured under the SGLI program. Spouse and family members of active-duty servicemembers and members of the Ready Reserve and National Guard are eligible. FSGLI provides up to a maximum of $100,000 of insurance coverage for spouses and $10,000 for dependent children. However, you cannot purchase more coverage for your spouse than you have for yourself: i.e., if you have purchased $50,000 of coverage for yourself, your spouse cannot have more than $50,000 of coverage. Spousal coverage is issued in increments of $10,000, at a cost ranging from $.55 to $5.20 per increment.

FSGLI coverage for family members begins automatically if servicemembers:

- Were married when the program began on November 1, 200.1

- Enter active-duty or Ready Reserve service, and are married or have dependent children.

- Get married or gain a dependent child during service, and have full-time SGLI coverage.

Veterans Group Life Insurance (VGLI)

Veterans Group Life Insurance (VGLI) is a program that allows you to convert your SGLI coverage to renewable term insurance once you separate from the military. VGLI is administered by the Office of Servicemembers Group Life Insurance but supervised by the Department of Veterans Affairs. You can buy coverage in increments of $10,000 up to a maximum of $250,000, but not more than the amount of your SGLI when you separated from military service.

Full-time coverage is available if you have full-time SGLI insurance and are separated from active duty or the Reserves. Ready Reservists who have part-time SGLI coverage and who, while performing active duty or inactive duty for training for a period of less than 31 days, incur a disability or aggravate a preexisting disability that makes them uninsurable at standard premium rates, also qualify. Members of the Individual Ready Reserve and Inactive National Guard can purchase VGLI as well.

To convert your plan to VGLI you must submit an application to the Office of Servicemembers Group Life Insurance within 120 days of separating from active duty. The insurance becomes effective on the 121st day, or the day the premium is received in the SGLI office. (After 121 days, you may still be granted

VGLI, provided initial premium and evidence of insurability are submitted within one year after your SGLI coverage is terminated.) Members with full-time SGLI coverage who are totally disabled at the time of separation and who are eligible for VGLI may purchase the insurance while remaining totally disabled for up to one year following separation. The effective date of VGLI will be either at the end of the one-year period following separation or the date the disability ends, whichever is earlier. If you are insured under part-time SGLI coverage and incurred a disability or aggravated a preexisting disability during a reserve active or inactive period, you can apply for VGLI within 120 days following the period during which the disability was incurred or aggravated.

Totally disabled servicemembers must submit proof of disability with an application and the first premium. If you separate from active duty, reenlist, or your duty status changes in another way, you may be eligible for both SGLI and VGLI. If you're insured under VGLI and become eligible again, you are automatically returned to coverage under SGLI. You can participate in both plans if that is somehow advantageous, as long as the combined amount of SGLI and VGLI does not exceed $200,000.

Military Matters

Your private life insurance policy is protected against lapse, termination, and forfeiture for nonpayment of premiums or indebtedness during military service. Professional liability insurance of persons called to active duty will be suspended upon written request to the insurance carrier. The insured person or beneficiary must apply to VA for protection by calling 800-419-1473.

Contact

For a list of participating insurance companies, see www.insurance.va.gov/SgliSite/forms/ParticList.htm.

As a VGLI policyholder, you can convert to an individual commercial policy at standard premium rates, regardless of your health, with any participating insurance company licensed to do business in your state. The individual policy will be effective the date after your VGLI terminates, which will occur at the end of any five-year period. The SGLI office will let you know of the impending date of termination and explain how to convert VGLI to an individual policy.

If you remain in the Individual Ready Reserve or Inactive National Guard throughout your period of VGLI coverage, you can renew your VGLI for additional five-year periods instead of converting to an individual policy. At the end of these subsequent periods of coverage, you are still free to convert to an individual policy. For further information, contact your nearest VA office or the Office of Servicemembers Group Life Insurance.

Contact

New VGLI Applications and VGLI Reinstatements Office of Servicemember Group Life Insurance P.O. Box 5000 Millville, NJ 08332-9928 800-419-1473.

VGLI Premium Rates

Your age and amount of insurance determine VGLI premium rates. To cut into the high cost of term insurance as you get older, you can opt for a Decreasing Term Option, starting at age 60. While you pay the same premium for life, the insurance coverage declines by 25 percent for three subsequent five-year renewals. At that point, coverage will be reduced to 25 percent of the original amount.

Service-Disabled Veterans Insurance

If you are a veteran who has been granted a service-connected disability but are otherwise in good health, you may apply to VA for up to $10,000 life insurance coverage at standard insurance rates. This insurance is limited to veterans who left service after April 24, 1951; veterans who are totally disabled may apply for a waiver of premiums. If you are eligible for this waiver, an additional policy of up to $20,000 is available. Premiums, however, cannot be waived on the additional insurance.

You can apply for Service-Disabled Veterans Insurance (S-DVI) if:

• You have received a rating of any percentage for a service-connected disability.

• You apply for the insurance within two years after the date the service connection is established.

• You are in good health with the exception of your service-connected disability.

You can apply for supplemental S-DVI if:

• You are eligible for a waiver of premiums.

• You apply for the coverage within one year after notice of the waiver has been granted.

• You are under age 65.

Premiums For Service-Disabled Veterans Insurance Insurance

The annual premium for S-DVI cannot exceed $69.73 per $1,000 of coverage. Premiums are based on the rates a healthy individual would have been charged when the program began in 1951. The program insures so many veterans with severe disabilities that premiums alone cannot cover all the claims: 29 percent of S-DVI policyholders are totally disabled, and their premiums are waived.

Therefore, S-DVI is supplemented on an annual basis by additional Congressional appropriations to ensure adequate funds are available.

S-DVI provides the following disability benefits:

- A waiver of premiums at no extra cost based on the insured person's total disability, starting before age 65, and lasting six months or longer

- A total disability premium waiver in cases where the total disability began prior to the effective date of the policy, providing the total disability is service-connected

You can apply for S-DVI online by going to the VA Autoform system and following the instructions.

Contact

The VA Autoform system for insurance applications is located at https://insurance.va.gov/Autoform/index.asp.

Military Matters

Service-Disabled Veterans Insurance insurance protects veterans who become incompetent from a service-connected disability while eligible to apply for S-DVI, but who die before an application is filed. Issued posthumously, gratuitous S-DVI is payable to the veteran's relatives in a lump sum only.

Veterans Mortgage Life Insurance

Veterans Mortgage Life Insurance (VMLI) is restricted to those veterans who receive Specially Adapted Housing (SAH) purchase grants, which are available to veterans who are entitled to compensation for service-connected, permanent, and total disabilities. VMLI provides financial protection to cover your home mortgage in the event that you die.

The maximum amount of mortgage life insurance available is $90,000. Protection is automatic unless you decline in writing or fail to respond to a final request for information on which your premium can be based. Premiums are either automatically deducted from VA benefit payments or paid directly, as long as you don't draw compensation. This continues until the mortgage has been liquidated, or the home is sold, or until the coverage terminates when you reach age 70 or you die. If a mortgage is disposed of through liquidation or sale of the property, you can still retain VMLI on a second or subsequent home.

Contact

To apply for Veterans Mortgage Life Insurance, fill out VA Form 29-8636, located at www.military.com/forms.

Help with VMLI Insurance

Specialists are available to discuss premium payments, insurance dividends, changes of address, policy loans, naming of beneficiaries, and reporting the death of the insured person or a beneficiary. If you are calling after business hours, leave a recorded message, which will be responded to on the next work-day. If the policy number is unknown, send the veteran's VA file number, Social Security number, military serial number or military service branch, and dates of service with date of birth to one of the two VA insurance centers.

For states east of the Mississippi River, or for any policy that is being paid through a deduction from VA benefits, military retired pay, or a checking account, contact the VA Insurance Center in Philadelphia. For states west of the Mississippi River, and the states of Minnesota, Wisconsin, Illinois, Indiana, and Mississippi, contact the VA Insurance Center in St. Paul, Minnesota.

Accelerated Benefits for the Terminally Ill

Servicemembers Group Life Insurance and Veterans Group Life Insurance offer accelerated benefits to the terminally ill, or those whose condition warrants a written medical prognosis of nine months or less to live. For SGLI and VGLI, up to 50 percent of the policy coverage may be paid out in a lump sum to the insured member. This payment is not taxable. To apply for these benefits, submit Benefit Option Form 8284, available at www.military.com/forms. Spouses covered under Family SGLI can apply for benefits using form 8284A, available at www.military.com/forms.

Thrift Savings Plan

The Thrift Savings Plan (TSP) is a government savings and investment plan that provides retirement income. The program is completely voluntary and offers the same type of savings and tax benefits that many private corporations offer their employees under 401(k) plans. The savings you contribute under TSP are yours to keep, even if you transition out of the service before you are eligible for military retirement pay. As with a 401(k) plan, you decide on a certain amount of money that you want to be taken from your pay each month and placed in an investment fund or funds. The major advantage of this program is that your TSP contributions are taken out of your pay before taxes are with-held, so you pay less tax altogether. TSP earnings are tax-deferred. You don't pay federal or, in most cases, state income tax on your contributions or earnings until you withdraw the money—at retirement, when you will likely be in a lower tax bracket. Over the years, the money in your account will accrue earnings. These earnings are also tax-deferred.

Unlike the Federal Employee TSP and most 401(k) plans, the uniformed services TSP does not allow for matching contributions from the employer—in this case, the Armed Forces.

The retirement income that you receive from your TSP account will depend on how much you have contributed to your account during your working years and on the earnings on those contributions. Like any investment, it is a risk, and you must monitor how well your contributions are doing and make adjustments accordingly. But like 401(k), TSP can bring great benefits.

You have the flexibility to contribute as little as 1 percent, or as much as 10 percent, of your basic pay—plus any amount of incentive pay or special pay, including bonus pay. The limit of total annual contributions has been set at $16,500 for 2009.

You can elect to contribute basic pay, incentive pay, or special pay (including bonus pay) to the TSP—but you must contribute basic pay to be eligible to contribute incentive pay or special pay.

Thrift Savings Plan Eligibility

Uniformed members of the Air Force, Army, Coast Guard, Marine Corps, National Oceanic and Atmospheric Administration, Navy, and Public Health Service serving on active duty, and members of the Ready Reserve or National Guard of those services in any pay status, can contribute to the TSP.

How to Enroll in the Thrift Savings Plan

In the past, the TSP would only allow enrollments and changes during "open seasons," but you can now enroll or change your contribution amount at any time. To enroll or change your contribution amount, submit a completed TSP Election Form (see page 40) unless your service branch requires you to use the myPay system. (See page 64 for more on myPay.) Your contributions to the TSP will generally begin not later than the first full pay period after the filing date.

You can stop contributing to the TSP at any time by completing the appropriate sections of Form TSP-U-1 and submitting it to your service. Your contributions will usually be stopped no later than the end of the pay period in which your service accepts the form. Because of cutoff dates for processing elections, your service will advise you of the date your election will be made effective.

Contact

Department of Veterans Affairs Regional Office and Insurance Center
P.O. Box 8079
Philadelphia, PA 19101
800-669-8477
8:30 a.m. to 6 p.m., Eastern Time

Department of Veterans Affairs Regional Office and Insurance Center
Bishop Henry Whipple Bldg.
Fort Snelling
St. Paul, MN 55111
800-827-1000.

Your Thrift Savings Plan Contribution Options

You can distribute your TSP contributions however you want among six different investment funds:

• Government Securities Investment (G) Fund.

• Fixed Income Index Investment (F) Fund.

• Common Stock Index Investment (C) Fund.

• Small Capitalization Stock Index Investment (S) Fund.

• International Stock Index Investment (I) Fund.

• Life Cycle (L) Funds—Targeted investment portfolio based on your forecasted retirement date.

You can transfer any amount of money into the TSP from qualified retirement savings plans in which you are already invested. For example, if you have money in a 401(k) plan from previous employment, you can transfer all or part of that money into the TSP. Similarly, you can transfer your TSP account balance to an eligible retirement plan if you leave federal service. (See page 41.)

To keep track of how these funds are doing, you have several options. You can obtain the daily share prices for each of the funds from the TSP website. Or you can obtain the rates of return for the most recent month or the most recent 12-month period, as well as historical rates of return for the funds and their related indexes. Returns for each fund are updated monthly. Rates of return are also available by calling the ThriftLine.

If you are a federal civilian employee and a member of the Reserve or Guard, you should know this important information about your TSP account—especially if you are called to active duty.

• When you return from active duty, you may make up TSP contributions missed as a result of your military service.

• If you have a loan from your civilian TSP account (see page 41 for more on TSP loans), your payments will be suspended when you begin your non pay status to perform military service. Your agency will resume your loan payments when you return to pay status.

• If you separated from civilian service and your Agency Automatic (1 percent) Contributions were forfeited because you were not vested, you are entitled to have these funds and their earnings restored to your account when you return to civilian service.

- If you separated from civilian service and your TSP account was paid to you as an automatic cash-out, you may return the funds to reestablish your account when you return to civilian service. If applicable, you may re-establish a TSP loan.

- You may contribute to a uniformed services TSP account from your Reserve pay or your active-duty pay.

Submit Electronic Form. The best way to sign up for the TSP is through the Defense Finance and Accounting Service employee/member self-service website. This secure site will provide the enrollment form and automatically submit it for you. A confirmation screen (only shown at the time of enrollment) alerts you that your enrollment has been accepted. If you make errors or you later change your mind about percentages and so forth, simply complete a new TSP enrollment on-screen—the system will override your old submission and accept the most recent one.

Download enrollment form on the web. You can download and print the official enrollment form TSP-U-1 from the TSP website. Deliver the completed form to your installation Financial Servicing Office (FSO) for input into the pay system.

Get enrollment form on base. Hard copies of enrollment forms and other TSP materials may also be picked up at your installation's Family Support Center.

Taking Out a Loan from TSP

As with a 401(k) plan, you are discouraged from taking out a loan from TSP while you are enrolled in the plan, since you would lose the tax benefit of this program. But if you must, your loan will have the following conditions attached:

- A $50 fee is deducted from the amount of each new loan. For example, if you take out a loan of $2,000, you will receive $1,950 after the $50 fee.

- The minimum loan that you can take out is $1,000.

- You can take out one general-purpose loan and one residential loan, but you cannot have more than one general-purpose loan at a time.

- Your loan repayment schedule will be determined by the TSP office, which will send you a Loan Agreement.

- When you pay off a TSP loan, you are not eligible to apply for another loan of the same type for 60 days.

Take Advantage

The Army is now offering a TSP Matching Funds Program to qualified non-prior service recruits. Visit or call your local Army recruiter to learn more.

Take Advantage

You can contribute to the TSP within 60 days of joining the uniformed services. At any time while serving in the military, you can change the amount of your TSP contributions (or start contributing, if you had previously passed up the opportunity).

Contact

DFAS employee/member self-service website: www.dod.dfas.mil/emss.

Military Matters

If you are in the Reserve or Guard and are already contributing to a TSP account as a civilian employee of the federal government, the sum of your contributions to the two TSP accounts during the same calendar year cannot exceed the applicable Internal Revenue Code contribution limit (the limit is $16,500 for 2009). In addition, civilian employees enrolled in the Federal Employee Retirement System (FERS) who also contribute from Reserve or Guard pay should take care not to reach their contribution limit before the end of the calendar year. Otherwise, they will miss out on their civilian agency matching contributions.

Take Advantage

You can download from the TSP website a copy of the booklet, "Summary of the Thrift Savings Plan for Uniformed Services," which contains an extensive explanation of the TSP.

Your Thrift Savings Plan Options Upon Separation

When you separate from the uniformed services, you can do the following with your Thrift Savings Plan (TSP) account:

Leave your money in the TSP. Your money remains in the TSP, where it will continue to accrue earnings. Although you will not be able to continue to make contributions, you will be able to make transfers to other retirement funds. You must begin withdrawing funds from your account no later than April 1 of the year following the year you turn age 70 and are separated from service.

Receive a single payment to rollover into another retirement plan. All or a portion of your account can be transferred to a traditional individual retirement account (IRA), or a 401(k) plan.

Request a series of monthly payments based on a dollar amount or on your life expectancy. All or a portion of certain monthly payments can be transferred to a traditional IRA or eligible employer plan.

Request a TSP annuity. You must have at least $3,500 in your account in order to purchase an annuity.

While you are in service, any tax-deferred money you withdraw before age 59 is subject to the IRS's 10 percent early withdrawal penalty, as well as to regular income tax. If you separate from service during or after the year when you turn 60, your withdrawal will not be subject to the early withdrawal penalty tax. If you separate from the military at any point (whether you are a veteran or retiree), you can transfer, or "roll over," your TSP account to a traditional IRA, or an eligible employer plan (i.e. a 401(k) plan) without penalty.

Individual Retirement Accounts

Individual Retirement Accounts (IRAs) are a good way to supplement your savings for retirement after you maximize the amount you can invest in your TSP.

IRAs let you augment your pension and Social Security income, while potentially giving you a break on your taxes. You can reduce your current tax bill by deferring income tax on the dividends the account earns until you begin withdrawals—which usually happens after you retire, when your tax rate is lower. Part or all of the money you deposit may be tax-deferred, depending on your overall income and pension plan participation status.

Take Advantage

To transfer your TSP funds into another account, use a "Request for Full Withdrawal" (Form TSP-70), or "Request for Partial Withdrawal When Separated" (Form TSP-77), both available at the TSP website.

Military Service and Social Security

Social Security is intended to provide income in the event of retirement, injury or disability, or death. Middle-income workers can expect a retirement benefit of about 40 percent of their average lifetime earnings. Low-income workers get a higher percentage, while those with upper incomes get a lower percentage. This design is not meant to punish any one group, but rather to even out the benefits each person receives. Servicemembers need to be just as knowledgeable as civilian workers regarding Social Security—the same regulations and benefits apply to all.

Special Social Security Wage Credits for Military Personnel. If you are a veteran applying for Social Security benefits, you can be credited with up to $1,200 more income per year for each year you served on active duty. Check on your eligibility when you contact your Social Security office.

Social Security benefits are available to:

• Retired, insured workers 62 years of age or older.

• The survivors and dependents of a retired or disabled worker.

• Insured workers under 65 who are disabled.

• The survivors and dependents, upon the death of an insured worker, as a one-time lump sum payment of up to $255. To receive the benefit, survivors must apply for it through their local Social Security office.

Many financial advisors say that when you retire, you'll need about 70 percent of your pre-retirement earnings to comfortably maintain your pre-retirement standard of living. Social Security benefits, along with pensions, savings, and investments, make up the major elements of most retirement portfolios.

Contact

Call the Social Security Administration at the toll-free number, 800-772-1213, TTY/TDD 800-325-0778. The website is www.ssa.gov if you live within the United States, and www.ssa.gov/ foreign if you live abroad.

Receiving Social Security

You are eligible for full retirement Social Security benefits as soon as you reach full retirement age. The full retirement age has increased; the full retirement age for 2008 through 2020 is 66. . You can retire as early as age 62, but if you do, your Social Security benefits will be reduced permanently.

To get the ball rolling on receiving benefits, the Social Security Administration recommends you apply three months in advance of your retirement date. You may apply online, or use the online locator to find your local Social Security office. You can call your local office to get a free estimate of the retirement, disability, and survivors benefits you may be entitled to. Be sure to have your Social Security number at hand when you call.

Take Advantage

If you are a veteran applying for Social Security benefits, you can be credited with up to $1,200 more income per year for each year served on active duty. Check on your eligibility when you contact your Social Security office.

Special Savings Program for Combat Zones

The Savings Deposit Program allows members who are deployed to combat zones, qualified hazardous duty areas, or certain contingency operations to make deposits from their pay into a DoD managed savings account. The maximum deposit amount per deployment is $10,000. The Savings Deposit Program offers an annual rate of 10 percent that compounds quarterly.

Take Advantage

To help you decide the best time to retire, check the government publication *Retirement Benefits* at www.ssa.gov/pubs/ 10035.html.

Part Two

The Pay Advantage

W ith basic pay and 70 types of special pays and allowances, understanding military pay can be challenging. Changes in pay grade, duty status, your military occupation, duty station, or deployment status can have a material impact on your pay.

In this chapter, we'll help you navigate your pay, including how to use online tools for adjusting your allotments, obtaining tax information, viewing your leave and earnings information, and asking questions.

You'll also find tips on making the most of unused leave when you are ready to transition, and you'll learn how to calculate retirement pay, disability compensation, veterans pension, and survivor benefits.

Your Standard Pay

Servicemembers usually qualify for three types of basic pay: basic pay, basic allowance for subsistence, and basic allowance for housing. In addition, you receive special pays (i.e., for special career fields or for serving in a combat zone). Of course, as you advance or are promoted, or when Congress increases pay rates, you receive pay raises.

The Pay Advantage at a Glance

Basic Pay

You can think of basic pay as the standard paycheck for your job. Listed in terms of dollars per month, basic pay rates are the same across all branches of service. Your individual basic pay depends on two factors: your pay grade (E-1 through E-9 for enlisted servicemembers, OE-1 through OE-3 for prior enlisted officers, and W-1 through W-5 and O-1 through O-9 for officers), and the number of years you have been in service.

See Appendix, page 348, for 2009 pay charts.

Basic Allowance for Subsistence

The Basic Allowance for Subsistence (BAS) is meant to offset costs for your meals. Adjusted annually, the amount granted is linked to the price of food. For 2008, officers received $202.76 per month in BAS, while enlisted members received $294.43 per month.

Military Matters

Every year, the Office of the Secretary of Defense (OSD) comptroller announces a government meal rate to be effective January 1. The rate is reviewed and revised, if necessary. For more information on government meal rates, visit www.military.com/pay.

Basic Allowance for Housing

When you're in the military, the maxim "There's no place like home" takes on a new meaning. Depending on where you are stationed, the cost of your housing will vary. For example, renting a home in the San Diego area could cost twice as much as renting a home in a small Midwestern town. The Basic Allowance for Housing (BAH) addresses this imbalance, providing you with what is judged to be equitable housing compensation based on housing costs in local civilian housing markets. Also based on pay grade and number of dependents, this benefit is paid out automatically when you apply for off-base housing. (If you live in government quarters by yourself and have no dependents, you are entitled to partial BAH.)

Here's an example of how much BAH can vary: If you are an E-5 with depend-

Take Advantage

For updates on military pay and current pay tables, visit www.military.com/pay.

Basic Pay

Military pay was increased by 2.2 percent and the pay charts were extended to cover 40 years of service on January 1, 2007. On April 1, 2007, selected midgrade enlisted and warrant officer pay grades will receive a targeted pay raise of up to 8.3 percent. Go to www.military.com/pay to view the latest pay charts.

Take Advantage

To calculate your BAH rate based on your location, pay grade, and dependency status, go to www.military.com/BAH.

ents, and you lived in San Diego in 2008, you would have received $1,857 a month in BAH. The same E-5 living near Fort Rucker, Alabama, would get $766 per month.

BAH-II. BAH-II is the housing allowance for Reservists on active duty for less than 30 days. The same amount for all locations, the BAH-II is based on the old basic allowance for quarters (BAQ), which drew its figures from the national average costs for housing. BAH-II is published annually and is determined by increasing the previous year's table by the percentage growth of housing costs.

BAH Differential. Servicemembers who live in government housing and pay child support are eligible for the BAH differential. Servicemembers who pay child support and live on the local economy receive the "with dependent" BAH rate for their locality.

Special Circumstances. In the case where a servicemember is married to another servicemember, they reside together, and they have dependents, one servicemember can claim dependents for BAH at the "with dependents" rate, while the other servicemember must claim the "single" rate.

Additional Allowances

Several variables can add to your pay, including increases in the annual cost of living, increases in allowances for housing and subsistence, separation from family, overseas housing, and more. Depending on your situation, you may qualify for allowances as described in the following pages.

Cost of Living Allowance

As a servicemember, you may be assigned to places where the cost of living will vary widely. Although private-sector pay scales tend to reflect local living costs in U.S. locations, military pay does not. To make up for this imbalance, you are eligible to receive a cost-of-living allowance (COLA) if you meet any of these conditions:

- You are assigned to a high-cost area in the continental United States. As of this writing, there are over 52 such locations across the country.

- You are assigned to an unaccompanied tour of duty outside the continental United States, and your primary dependent resides in a high-cost area in the continental United States.

- Your primary dependent must reside in a high-cost area in the continental United States due to your duty location or other circumstances.

The cost-of-living allowance in the continental U.S. is based on the zip code of your duty station, not your home address. COLA is computed differently for members with and without dependents.

Take Advantage

You receive COLA payments regardless of whether you live on or off base.

Clothing Allowances

To help pay for your uniform and other clothing costs if appropriate clothing has not been furnished, you may be given a clothing allowance. The basic allowance is for necessary replacement and maintenance of unique military items; eligibility for this allowance varies by service.

Initial Clothing Allowance. This is provided to you upon initial enlistment or upon a special qualification for a prescribed uniform or uniforms.

Cash Clothing Replacement Allowance. This is paid annually on the anniversary of your initial clothing allowance. Cash clothing replacement allowances cover replacement of required uniform items.

Extra Clothing Allowance. This is separate from initial and replacement allowances. It covers unusual circumstances when you may require additional uniform items, or when an officer (with a permanent duty station outside the United States) or enlisted member may require civilian clothing to perform his or her assigned duties.

Clothing Maintenance Allowance. This monthly allowance is paid automatically to all eligible enlisted servicemembers.

See Appendix, page 353, for clothing allowance amounts for all services.

Overseas COLA

Overseas Cost of Living Allowance equalizes the income level between those serving overseas and their CONUS-based counterparts. The average supplement is $300 per month. Overseas COLA is provided at approximately 600 locations overseas, including Alaska and Hawaii. Visit www.military.com/oconus-cola.

Per Diem

If you are traveling on official military business, your lodging and meal expenses are paid for with a per diem. To receive per diem, you must submit a travel claim through the Department of Finance and Accounting Services (DFAS) for Department of Defense (DoD) servicemembers, or the Coast Guard Personnel Support Center (PSC) for the Coast Guard. Check with your personnel office for more information on the travel claim process.

Contact

For full listings of per diem rates, both in and out of the United States, go to www.military.com/perdiem.

Dislocation Allowance

Contact

For current Dislocation Allowance rates, see www.military.com/DLA.

A Dislocation Allowance (DLA) reimburses you partially for your expenses when you relocate your household during a permanent change of station, for any housing moves ordered for the government's convenience, or because of an evacuation. This allowance may be paid in advance and ranges from $748 to $3,592. It does not apply if you are reporting to your first duty station after initial training.

Family Separation Allowance

Take Advantage

Although normally a reservist or guard member is not eligible for Dislocation Allowance, there is an exception: when you come on active duty for more than 20 weeks at one location, are authorized permanent change of station allowances, and move your dependents from your home to your new permanent duty station or another designated place.

If you have dependents, you may be entitled to a Family Separation Allowance (FSA) of $250 per month, in addition to any per diem or other entitlements. The allowance requires that:

- Movement of dependents to the permanent duty station at government expense is not authorized; the dependents do not already live at or near that station.

- You are on duty on board a ship away from the ship's home port for a period of more than 30 continuous days.

- You are on temporary duty away from the permanent duty station for a continuous period of more than 30 days, and your dependents do not live at or near the temporary duty station.

If you choose to serve an unaccompanied tour of duty at a permanent duty station where the movement of dependents at government expense is authorized, you are not entitled to the Family Separation Allowance. If you are married to another servicemember, the allowance is authorized for one spouse if you resided together immediately before the separation.

Overseas Housing Allowance

Contact

Joint Federal Travel Regulations website: www.dtic.mil/perdiem/trvlregs.html.

A monthly Overseas Housing Allowance (OHA) is paid to servicemembers assigned to a permanent duty station outside the continental United States, and authorized to live in private housing. An OHA defrays your housing costs and includes the following three components: rent, utility and recurring maintenance expenses, and a move-in housing allowance.

According to the DoD, the average annual OHA payment is $11,800. Take a look at the Joint Federal Travel Regulations website for details on the OHA.

Overseas Temporary Lodging Allowance

A Temporary Lodging Allowance (TLA) reimburses you partially for higher-than-normal housing expenses if you are living overseas for a limited amount of time. It is available in the following situations:

- When you first report to a permanent duty station (PDS) outside the continental United States (OCONUS) and are waiting for a government-quarters assignment, or while completing arrangements for other permanent living accommodations when government quarters are not available.

- When you must vacate permanent quarters either permanently or temporarily and use temporary lodgings in the permanent duty station (PDS) vicinity while looking for other permanent quarters or waiting to reoccupy the vacated permanent quarters.

- While seeking permanent housing following a temporary duty period.

- Immediately preceding your departure from an OCONUS PDS, after you have vacated government quarters in connection with a permanent change of station order.

- When you have been hospitalized and are en route between permanent duty stations, and your dependents are required to use OCONUS temporary lodgings.

If you retire, stay in the PDS area, and then move at a later date, you are not eligible for a Temporary Lodging Allowance. For more information on Temporary Housing Allowances check the Joint Federal Travel Regulations website.

Move-In Housing Allowance

When you are eligible for Overseas Housing Allowance, you also qualify to receive a Move-In Housing Allowance (MHA), paid in lump-sum supplements. It includes three components:

Move-In Housing Allowance/Miscellaneous. Payments cover the purchase of household necessities, such as sinks, toilets, light fixtures, kitchen cabinets, and a refrigerator and stove (not always provided in overseas dwellings). No receipts are needed.

Move-In Housing Allowance/Rent. Onetime, nonrefundable, rent-related expenses are covered here—receipts are required. Examples are real estate agent fees, redecoration fees, and onetime lease taxes.

Move-In Housing Allowance/Security. These expenses apply to members assigned to areas where dwellings must be modified to minimize exposure to a terrorist or criminal threat. Receipts are required. Expenditures unrelated to the physical dwelling, such as personal security guards or dogs, are not reimbursed. All security payments must be approved by the senior officer in the country.

Move-In Housing Allowance rates change with currency fluctuations and location—check with your base relocation manager for rates in your area. For more detailed information on move-in housing allowances, see the Joint Federal Travel Regulations site.

Leave

Take Advantage

Even if you do not qualify for special leave accrual, you may still qualify for leave carryover if you have been deployed for 60 or more days. Your unit commander can put in a request for you.

If you are on active duty in any of the five branches of the Armed Forces or the National Oceanic and Atmospheric Administration (NOAA), you earn 30 days of paid vacation, or leave, every year.

You earn two and a half days of leave for each month of service. You can accrue up to 60 days of leave over a two-year period, but your leave balance is checked on the first day of the fiscal year (October 1), and any leave in excess of 60 days is forfeited. This formula is the same for the Reserve and Guard when members are activated.

If you serve in a combat zone and have more than 75 days on the books the new policy will grant you up to four years to reduce your accrued leave to the new 75-day cap.

Unused Leave

Take Advantage

Leave cannot be taken without permission from your command, so coordinate any leave with your unit commander. If you plan to take leave during the course of your orders, let your command know you have accrued leave and wish to take it.

If you have accrued leave at the time of your discharge, reenlistment, or retirement, you may be entitled to receive payment in lieu of leave. The monetary value of your leave is based on basic pay, not including special pay or allowances. In other words, each day of leave is worth a single day's basic pay. However, you can't sell back more than 60 days of accrued leave. You also can't sell back leave if you have been discharged to accept a commission or a warrant in any uniformed service, or if you elect to have leave carried over to a new enlistment in any uniformed service on the day after the date of your discharge. On the other hand, you can sell back any leave you elect not to carry over to a new enlistment. For example, if you have 72 days of leave left on the books when you reenlist, you may choose to sell back 12 and carry over 60.

The leave sell-back rate is based on base pay only and is normally subject to taxation and withholding tax, except when you are serving in a combat zone or hazardous duty area. (For more information on taxes, see page 12.)

Note: A new leave policy allows enlisted members to sell back up to 30 days of special accrued leave—leave earned in a combat zone or designated contingency operation—that would be lost due to the new 75-day cap. Leave accrued in a combat zone is more valuable than regular leave because it is not taxed.

If you are a reserve or guard member, you can sell back accrued leave beyond the authorized 60-day career limitation if you are on orders for active duty for more than 30 days (but not more than 365 days).

Reserve and National Guard Pay

If you are serving as a member of the Reserve or National Guard, you are eligible for regular drill pay and might qualify for some special pays. Many of the pays mentioned in the Special Pays section on page 52 are also open to reserve and guard members, and are noted as such when applicable.

All reserve and guard members receive pay for participating in weekend drills and exercises as part of their service commitment. Your drill pay is calculated by number of drill periods (one drill period is four hours, and one drill weekend is usually four drill periods), your current pay grade, and your minimum time in service (i.e., less than two years, three years, four years, etc.).

For more on reserve and guard retired pay, see page 77. See page 349 for 2009 monthly drill pay charts.

Reserve and National Guard Incentive Program

The Ready Reserve Incentive Program offers bonuses for enlistment, reenlistment, prior-service enlistment, affiliation in the Selected Reserve, and enlistment in the Individual Ready Reserve. Reenlistment bonuses can change frequently, depending on service needs.

Prior Service Enlistment Bonus

If you were formerly enlisted in any branch of the military and choose to affiliate or enlist in the Reserve or Guard, in a critical military skill, for a period of three or six years, you may be eligible for a prior enlistment bonus, if you meet each of the following requirements:

• You completed a military service obligation, but have less than 14 years of total military service, and you received an honorable discharge at the conclusion of your service obligation.

Take Advantage
Calculate your individual drill pay at www.military.com/drillcalculator.

• You were not released, or are not being released, from active service for the purpose of enlistment in a reserve or guard component.

• You are projected to occupy, or are occupying, a position as a member of the Selected Reserve in a specialty, or you have otherwise completed training or retraining in the specialty skill.

A prior enlistment bonus will vary depending on service and position, but at this time is:

• $20,000 for enlisting for a period of six years.

• $10,000 for enlisting for a period of three years.

Reenlistment Bonus for Individual Ready Reserve

Combat Injury Pay

CIP is $430 per month (minus Hostile Fire/Imminent Danger Pay (HF/IDP)) paid to members hospitalized during rehabilitation from wounds, injuries, and/or illness incurred in a combat operation or combat zone. Visit http://www.military.com/CIP to learn more.

If you served in the Armed Forces, and enlist, reenlist, or voluntarily extend an enlistment in a combat or combat-support skill of the non-drilling Individual Ready Reserve for a period of three to six years beyond your obligation, you may be paid a bonus. A bonus may not be paid if you have failed to complete satisfactorily any original term of enlistment in the Armed Forces.

Special Pays

In addition to the basic pay benefits and allowances already mentioned, you may receive special pays and incentive pays depending on your career field or location—even when you first join the military. We've included the major types of special pay as follows.

Overseas Extension Pay

The military may offer servicemembers an added incentive for extending their overseas tour. This special incentive can come in the form of an $80 monthly special pay, $2,000 annual bonus or up to 15 days of special rest and recuperation. Be sure to speak to your personnel office to learn more.

Reenlistment Bonuses

Prior Service Enlistment Bonuses are available if you have been separated from the military, possess a critical military skill, and decide to rejoin active duty.

Reenlistment bonus amounts are generally computed using bonus multipliers based on your rating, career specialty, or Military Occupational Specialty (MOS) and how many years you served. The military has placed a cap on the maximum amounts authorized, and the current cap is $90,000 for the most critical specialty (there are exceptions, like Enlisted Supervisor Retention Pay).

The bonus you receive is typically based on this formula: *bonus multiplier x your monthly base pay x number of months you are reenlisting for.*

Each branch of service also provides reenlistment bonuses, which change based on current service needs. The amount may further depend on your permanent duty station. You may be eligible for a bonus, provided:

- You have completed at least 17 months of continuous active duty (other than for training) but not more than 14 years of active duty.

- You are qualified in a military skill designated as critical by the Secretary of Defense or the Secretary of Homeland Security.

- You are willing to accept less desirable assignments (AIP – Assignment Incentive Pay).

- You are not receiving special nuclear training pay.

- You have reenlisted or voluntarily extended your enlistment for a period of at least three years.

- You have enlisted in a regular component of the service concerned, or you continue in a reserve component of the service concerned.

Contact

For more on reenlistment bonuses, see www.military.com/bonuses.

Military Matters

If you do not complete the term of enlistment for which a bonus was paid, you must refund a prorated amount of the bonus. A refund-of-bonus applies if you leave voluntarily or because of misconduct, but does not apply if you did not finish your service due to injury, illness, or other impairment.

Contact

For detailed regulations on Hostile Fire and Imminent Danger Pay, see www.dtic.mil/comptroller.

Hostile Fire/Imminent Danger Pay

Active-duty, reserve, and guard members are eligible for Hostile Fire and Imminent Danger Pay. You may earn a special pay of $225 for any month in which you:

- Are subject to hostile fire or explosion of hostile mines.

- Are in imminent danger of being exposed to hostile fire or explosion of hostile mines.

- Are injured or wounded by hostile fire, explosion of a hostile mine, or any other hostile action.

- Are on duty in a foreign area and subject to the threat of physical harm or imminent danger on the basis of civil insurrection, civil war, terrorism, or wartime conditions.

SDAP

Another special pay based on assignment is Special Duty Assignment Pay (SDAP)–for extremely difficult duties, or those not part of the servicemember's normal occupation.

Hardship Duty Pay

Hardship Duty Pay for Location (HDP-L), formerly called Foreign Duty Pay, is granted in recognition of the extraordinarily difficult living conditions, excessive physical hardship, or unhealthful conditions that exist in certain areas.

All members stationed in designated HDP-L locations qualify for a monthly pay of $50, $100, or $150 depending on their location. You must be in the location for at least 30 days to qualify for the pay. Your residence for HDP-L pay purposes must be the same as your designated legal residence for tax purposes. If you are a resident of a designated Hardship Duty Pay area while serving on permanent duty within that state, possession, or foreign country, you will also receive HDP-L at the current rates.

Members who change their state of legal residence to Alaska or Hawaii, and are stationed in that state, lose entitlement to HDP-L pay.

Hardship Duty Pay for Mission Assignment (HDP-M) is payable to servicemembers for performing designated hardship or specialized missions. The monthly payment for HDP-M is $150.

Hazardous Duty Incentive Pay (For Noncrewmembers)

As the name suggests, Hazardous Duty Incentive Pay is a monthly pay of $150 for servicemembers who perform the following duties:

- Parachute or Flight Deck Duty.

- Demolition Duty.

- Experimental Stress Duty.

- Toxic Fuels (or Propellants) Duty, Toxic Pesticides Duty, or Dangerous Viruses (or Bacteria) Lab Duty.

- Chemical Munitions Duty.

If you are engaged in high-altitude, low-opening parachute technique (HALO) jumps, you can earn Hazardous Duty Pay at $225 a month.

You may be entitled to receive up two types of hazardous duty pay if you are assigned to a unit whose mission involves more than one kind of hazardous duty.

Aviation Career Incentive Pay for Officers

Aviation Career Incentive Pay (ACIP) is for regular and reserve officers who hold, or who are training to hold, an aeronautical rating or designation. To be eligible, you must remain in aviation service on a career basis. ACIP ranges from $125 to $840 per month depending on the number of years you have served as an aviation officer in an operation aviation billet.

Warrant officers with more than 22 years of aviation service are paid the same rate as commissioned officers with more than 14 years of aviation service.

Take Advantage

To apply for Aviation Continuation Pay, fill out and submit DA Form 4127, available at www.military.com/forms.

Aviation Continuation Pay

Officer aviators who remain on active duty after the end of their active-duty service commitment are eligible for this type of pay. To receive the ACP, you must submit an application. Annual amounts vary depending on each service's needs and the length of time the aviator agrees to serve. For 2008, the maximum bonuses by service are:

- Air Force: up to $25,000 per year.

- Navy: up to $25,000 per year.

- Marine Corps: up to $18,000 per year.

- Army (for AH-64 and MH-47 warrant officer pilots only): up to $25,000 per year.

Hazardous Duty Incentive Pay for Flying

This is also known as "aircrew pay." Officers and enlisted members qualify for this pay as nonpilots or navigators aboard military aircraft if they are not already drawing career-incentive or flight pay.

Air weapons controllers aboard AWACS planes qualify for $150 to $350 per month, depending on rank and years of service. Non-AWACS officers receive $150 to $250 per month, depending on rank. Enlisted aircraft aircrew members earn $150 to $240 a month, depending on rank.

Career Sea Pay

If you are a servicemember on sea duty, you are entitled to Career Sea Pay at a monthly rate of up to $730. Your pay rate depends on your rank and number of years served and ranges from $50 to $730. If you have served 36 consecutive months of sea duty, you are also entitled to a Career Sea Pay Premium for the 37th consecutive month and for each subsequent consecutive month of sea duty served. The monthly premium amount is determined by the secretary of the service concerned, but it does not exceed $350.

Diving Duty Pay

You are entitled to special pay for periods in which you are assigned by orders to diving duty. To qualify for this pay, you must be certified by the specific military branch concerned, maintain proficiency as a diver by frequent and regular dives, and either actually perform diving duty while serving in an assignment for which diving is a primary duty or meet requirements to maintain proficiency while serving in an assignment that includes diving duty as something other than a primary duty.

Enlisted personnel are entitled to Diving Duty Pay of up to $240 per month, while officers can earn up to $340.

Foreign Language Proficiency Pay

If you have been certified as proficient in a foreign language, you may earn Foreign Language Proficiency Pay. To do so, you must meet one of the following conditions:

• You are qualified in a career military linguist specialty.

• You have received training under prescribed regulations to develop such a proficiency.

- You are assigned to military duties requiring such a proficiency.

- You are proficient in a foreign language for which the military has identified a critical need.

Contact

For more on Foreign Language Proficiency Pay, see www.military.com/flpp.

Written *and* spoken ability must be certified—don't expect that a few years of a language in high school will get you past the language tests. Members in a noncareer linguist military occupational specialty may receive Foreign Language Proficiency Pay, but at reduced rates.

Reserve and guard members called to active duty, active duty for training, and inactive duty training who are entitled to basic pay and meet the qualifications above may receive a prorated amount of proficiency pay for each day of duty or for each period of instruction performed.

Active-duty servicemembers can receive up to $1,000 per month for Foreign Language Proficiency Pay, while reservists may be entitled to up to $6,000 per year. Pay can be awarded for proficiency in multiple foreign languages, but the monthly rate may not exceed the limits noted above.

Judge Advocate Continuation Pay

The Judge Advocate Continuation Pay (JACP) program applies to all officers who have completed 10 years of service as a judge advocate on, or after, October 1, 1999. Its aim is to help the Judge Advocate General (JAG) Corps officers to relieve the large student-loan debts many of them incur. JACP is taxable income, and taxes will be deducted from the payments prior to electronic transfer to the officer's account.

An eligible judge advocate who signs a written agreement to remain on active duty for a period of service specified in the agreement may be paid continuation pay. The term "eligible judge advocate" refers to an officer in the Armed Forces on full-time active duty who is qualified and serving as a judge advocate and has completed his active-duty service requirements. The total amount paid to an officer under one or more agreements has a limit of $60,000.

Take Advantage

Naval personnel who serve under orders on a submarine, operate or crew an operational submersible or undersea exploration or research vehicle can earn up to $835 a month. This includes those who are undergoing training for assignment to, or are rehabilitating from, an assignment to a nuclear-powered submarine

Nuclear Career Bonuses

Nuclear Career Accession Bonus. If you are selected for officer nuclear power training for duty in connection with the supervision, operation, and maintenance of naval nuclear propulsion plants, you may be paid a bonus of up to $20,000.

Nuclear Career Annual Incentive Bonus. Qualified Naval officers may be paid an annual incentive bonus of up to $22,000 a year, which is payable in either a lump sum or annual installments, for each service year during which they meet the following conditions:

- Entitlement to basic pay.

- Pay grade not above O-6.

- Completion of initial obligated active service as an officer.

- Completion of training for duty in connection with the supervision, operation, and maintenance of naval nuclear propulsion plants.

- Possession of current technical qualifications for duty in connection with the supervision, operation, and maintenance of naval nuclear propulsion plants.

Nuclear Qualified Officers Extending Period of Active Service. Navy nuclear officers who have the technical qualifications for duty in connection with naval nuclear propulsion plants, and who agree to remain on active duty in connection with supervision, operation, and maintenance of naval nuclear propulsion plants for a period of three, four, or five years, may receive a bonus of up to $25,000 for each year of the active-service agreement.

Special Pay for Dental Officers

Air Force dental officers or Army or Navy Dental Corps Officers on active duty for not less than one year are eligible for both contractual special pay bonuses and monthly special pays.

An Accession Bonus of up to $75,000 is paid to all qualified dentists who contract to serve on active duty for four years. The contractual agreement must be signed within 60 days of your call to active duty. Officers are not eligible to receive the bonus if the following situation applies: they are entering the Commissioned Corps as an interservice transfer, with prior extended active duty in any uniformed service within 24 months of their call to duty in the Commissioned Corps, or in order to fulfill scholarship or training obligations.

Variable Special Pay is available to all dentists based on years of creditable service. The Creditable Service Entry Date (CSED) reflects your years of active duty as a dental officer in any of the uniformed services or else the years spent participating in an accredited dental internship or residency training while not on active duty in a uniformed service. Variable Special Pay rates range from $3,000 to $12,000 per year, depending on your CSED.

Board Certified Pay is based on board certification in a specialty recognized by the American Dental Association, Federal Services Board, or American Board of Oral Medicine, Oral Diagnosis, or Oral Radiology. Rates range from $2,500 to $6,000 annually based on years of CSED. In order to receive Board Certified Pay, you must provide documentation of the certification. Note that the National Dental Examiners Board is not a specialty exam board and does not entitle you to Board Certified Pay.

Additional Special Pay is available to all dental officers who execute a contract to remain on active duty for at least one year and meet the eligibility requirements. Amounts range from $4,000 to $15,000 annually, depending on CSED.

A Multiyear Retention Bonus is payable to dental officers trained in recognized dental specialties who execute a contract to remain on active duty for a period of two to four years. The rate of a Multiyear Retention Bonus depends on the dental officer's specialty training and length of contract, and ranges from $13,000 to $50,000 annually.

> **Contact**
>
> For the latest special pay rates for medical and health professionals, see www.military.com/medicalpay.

Special Pay for Medical Officers and Health Professional Officers

If you are an Army or Navy Medical Corps officer or the Public Health Service, or an Air Force officer designated as a medical officer and on active duty under a call or order to active duty for a period of not less than one year, you are entitled to special pay. A medical officer may not be paid any additional special pay unless he or she first agrees to remain on active duty for a period of not less than one year beginning on the date of acceptance of the award of special pay.

If you agree to remain on active duty for two, three, or four years after completion of any other active-duty service commitment, you may be paid a retention bonus of up to $14,000 for each year of the agreement. In addition, you may qualify for a loan repayment program for more than $114,000 through the Active Duty Health Professions Loan Repayment Program (ADHPLRP).

Special Warfare Officer Continuation Pay

If you are an officer serving in a military occupational specialty designated as "special warfare," and you remain on active duty in special warfare service for at least one year, you may be paid a retention (continuation) bonus of up to $25,000 for each year of continuation.

You can apply for continuation pay if you are in pay grade O-3 or O-4 and are not on a list of officers recommended for promotion at the time you apply. You also must have completed at least six, but not more than 14, years of active commissioned service; and you must have completed any service commitments to be commissioned as an officer.

Take Advantage

DD Form 2558 is available at www.military.com/ forms.

Special Pay for Veterinary Officers

Commissioned officers on active duty who are designated as veterinary officers or hold a degree in veterinary medicine are eligible for $100 a month in special pay. In addition, military veterinarians receive annual awards ranging from $2,000 to $5,000, depending on their years of service.

Allotments

An allotment is a designated amount of money that is automatically distributed from your pay each month. The many reasons to have an allotment include setting aside funds for family, paying off loans, and paying for your life insurance premiums. There are two types of allotments: discretionary and nondiscretionary. You can have up to six discretionary allotments per month and any number of nondiscretionary allotments, as long as the total allotments per month is 15 or fewer.

Your allotment is evenly divided between your paychecks. For example, if you decide on a monthly allotment of $100, your take-home pay will be reduced on the first and 15th by $50.

All servicemembers paid through the active-duty pay system are eligible to set aside allotments from their pay. In addition, retirees are eligible to continue all existing authorized allotments, easing the transition for servicemembers to retirement.

If you have an allotment question or problem, you should first address the matter to your assigned pay office. If your pay office can't resolve the problem, it should officially refer your question to DFAS (see page 64).

Discretionary Allotments

Discretionary allotments are useful in that they allow you to make payments directly—you don't have to remember to do it each month. This is especially useful if you are deployed or in the field when your bills are due. To institute or change an allotment, you should fill out and submit DD Form 2558. All discretionary allotments are under your control, meaning you can start, stop, or adjust a discretionary allotment. Below are examples of discretionary allotments:

• Payment of premiums for commercial life insurance for you, your spouse, or your children.

• Voluntary payment to a dependent or other relative.

• Deposits to a financial institution, mutual fund company, or investment firm.

• Payment of car loans.

• Payment of mortgage or rent.

• Repayment of a personal loan.

• Deposits into the Thrift Savings Plan (page 39).

• For Air Force members only: payments to the Air Force Enlisted Members Widows Home.

• Allotments to VA for deposit to the Post-Vietnam Era Veterans Educational Assistance Program.

If you have the Veterans Educational Assistance Program allotment, it is not counted against your limit of six discretionary allotments, unless you make a change to it, at which point it will be treated as a new allotment and require you to have six or fewer before it can be restarted.

Nondiscretionary Allotments

Nondiscretionary allotments may be voluntary or involuntary, and they cannot be started or stopped at will. Nondiscretionary allotments are limited to the following:

Voluntary Nondiscretionary Allotments:

• Purchase of U.S. savings bonds.

• Repayment of loans to the Air Force Aid Society, American Red Cross, Army Emergency Relief, and Navy and Marine Corps Relief Society.

• Voluntary liquidation of indebtedness to the United States that includes the following:

—Any debt due to defaulted notes insured by the Federal Housing Administration (FHA) or guaranteed by the VA.

—Any other indebtedness to any department or agency of the United States government (except to the military department paying the member).

—Payment for pledges for charitable contributions to the following: Combined Federal Campaign (CFC), Army Emergency Relief, Navy and Marine Corps Relief Society, affiliates of the Air Force Assistance Fund and Coast Guard Mutual Assistance.

Involuntary Nondiscretionary Allotments:

• Court-ordered payments, such as child support, which is considered a garnishment.

- Any repayment of debts owed to an organization for funds administered on behalf of the U.S. government and any such debts assigned to a collection agency.

—Payment of delinquent federal, state, or local income or employment taxes.

Managing Your Pay: The myPay System

Now that you know the major pay benefits you have access to during military service, let's look at how you receive, monitor, and seek corrections to your pay. The Defense Finance and Accounting Service (DFAS) is the agency responsible for all military fiscal tasks, including payment of servicemembers. Since its inception in 1991, DFAS has worked to minimize the paperwork that threatens to slow its vast system. One recent innovation is an online system called myPay, which manages servicemember, civilian, military retiree, and annuitant pay accounts and other related information. myPay puts you in control of processing certain discretionary pay data items without the hassle of paper forms. You can also get your pay and tax statements and advice for travel payments using the myPay website.

If you need to speak to a representative for assistance, contact the DFAS Centralized Customer Support Unit at 1-800-390-2348. You can also find helpful information available under the Contact Us button on the myPay home page.

(Any changes you make using myPay can be corrected using myPay at any time. Submit your change only once, and it will be posted according to your pay system's update schedule.)

Leave and Earnings Statement: Display and Delivery

Contact

A complete breakdown of the items on a standard Leave and Earnings Statement is available at www.dod.mil/dfas/money/civpay/les.htm.

Your Leave and Earnings Statement (LES) is the monthly record of your earnings, deductions, and leave information. All active-duty, Reserve, and Guard members, along with civilians, annuitants, retired military and Army non-appropriated employees can view and print their Leave and Earnings (or pay) Statement online at myPay. Active-duty servicemembers can view their 12 most recent statements online. If you prefer to view and print your LES electronically, you can use myPay to stop the delivery of your hard copy LES. For instructions on how to print your LES from myPay, go to the myPay site and click on "LES Display and Delivery" under "Popular FAQs."

Military Matters

Federal law requires that the pay of active, reserve, guard, and retired members be garnished (or attached) to the payment of child and/or spousal support. In order to implement a garnishment or wage attachment against a military member, a spouse must serve an income-withholding order, or similar document, to the Defense Finance and Accounting Service (DFAS).

Contact

For a full directory of Defense Finance Accounting offices, along with their responsibilities and contact information, visit www.dod.mil/dfas/about/locations.

Online Tax Statements

Active-duty, Reserve, and Guard members may view, print, and save their W-2 Wage (your annual wage statement provided by your employer) and Tax Statement online. Access your W-2 from the "Main Menu" by clicking on the "Tax Statement (W-2)" option.

Retirees and civilians on the military payroll can view, print, and save their end-of-year tax statements through myPay. If the tax statement displayed is incorrect, contact your customer service representative. You can also access myPay and view your tax statement for one year after you are separated from duty.

(If you are active duty, Reserve, or Guard, you will not be permitted to add or change a state tax authority. To change your state tax authority, you must see your customer service representative or local finance office.)

Contact

myPay:
877-363-3677; outside of the continental U.S.: 478-757-3119; www.mypay.dfas.mil

DFAS Centralized Customer Support Unit:
800-390-2348 or 216-522-5122; or DSN: 580-5122 Monday through Friday, from 7 a.m. until 7:30 p.m. Eastern Time.

Crunching Numbers

In one year, the Defense Finance and Accounting Service:
- paid 5.9 million military members, civilian personnel, retirees, and annuitants (retirees who receive regular payments).
- processed 12.3 million contractor invoices.
- made 6.8 million travel payments.
- disbursed $416.1 billion.
- recorded 121 million accounting transactions.
- accounted for 279 active Defense Department appropriations.
- managed $197.4 billion in military-retirement trust funds.

Take Advantage

If you are a service-member, a military retiree, or a civilian on the military payroll, you can change direct deposit allotments using myPay.

The Military Pay Information Line

The Military Pay Information Line provides servicemembers access to their pay information. You will be able to use the Interactive Voice Response System (IVRS) to access your pay information 24 hours a day at 1-888-332-7411 or DSN 580-5096.

Servicemembers can use the IVRS to access the following information:

All Callers—General Information
- Non-receipt of allotments
- Information on bonds in safekeeping
- Reporting procedures for lost of stolen bonds
- Inquiries regarding estimated earnings for purposes of civilian retirement
- Direct access to a bond technician

Reserve and National Guard
- Net Pay
- Direct Deposit Information
- SGLI Election Information
- Tax Information

Active Duty
- Net Pay
- Direct Deposit Information
- Allotment Information
- Bond Information
- Tax Information
- Leave Balance Information

Recently Separated Servicemembers
- Final Account Audit Status
- W2 Information
- W2 Information

DFAS Toll Free Customer Service Lines:

Army (active duty)	1-888-332-7411
Army (reserve)	1-877-462-7782
Army (National Guard)	1-877-276-4729
Navy (active duty/reserve)	1-888-332-7411
Air Force (active duty/reserve/Natl Guard)	1-888-332-7411
Marine Corps (active duty & reserve)	1-888-332-7411
Out-of-Service Debts (all services)	1-800-962-0648
Garnishments (all services)	1-888-332-7411

Savings Bonds

The myPay service also allows you to manage savings bonds. To obtain bonds held in safekeeping, requests must contain your name, Social Security number, a valid mailing address, and the bonds you wish to be mailed. Allow thirty days before claiming nonreceipt of a bond.

Retired Pay

This section focuses on your retired pay options, retired pay procedures, special retired pay such as disability compensation, and how you can make updates to your retired pay account.

Military Retirement System

Unlike most organizations, the Armed Forces offers a pension, with benefits, when you retire from the military, no matter how old you are. That means you could start collecting a regular retirement pension as young as age 37. What's more, that pension check will grow with a cost-of-living adjustment each year.

Many factors determine exactly how much your pension will be. In addition, over the past 25 years, the government has made some significant changes to the military retirement system.

The Three Basic Plans

Each of the three military retirement systems has a common thread: If you stay in the Armed Forces for 20 years or more, you are eligible to receive a pension based on a percentage of your basic pay, and if you stay for a maximum of 30 years, you are eligible for 75 percent of your basic pay. But that's where the similarities end and the differences begin, because each of these systems determines your amount of pension differently. The three plans are as follows:

If you entered service:	Your retirement plan options are:
Prior to September 1980	Final Pay system
Between September 8, 1980, and August 1986	High 36 system
After August 1986	High 36 system or Career Status Bonus/REDUX (CSB) system

If you entered the service after August 1986 you are eligible to choose either the High 36 retirement system or the Career Status Bonus/REDUX (CSB) retirement system. You need to understand the differences because you will have to choose the plan you want at the 15-year mark in your military career. If you decline to make a choice, you will automatically receive the High 36 retirement plan.

Contact

Air Force, Army, Marine Corps, and Navy:
Defense Finance and Accounting Service—
Cleveland Center/ ROCAD
P.O. Box 99191
Cleveland, OH 44199-2058
800-321-1080 (general)
www.dod.mil/ dfas/about/ locations/cl_index.htm.

Coast Guard/ National Oceanic and Atmospheric Administration:
Commanding Officer U.S. Coast Guard Personnel Support Center (PSC/RAS)
444 S.E. Quincy St. Topeka, KS 66683-3591
800-772-8724 local
785-357-3415
www.uscg.mil/hq/psc.

Public Health Service:
U.S. Public Health Service, Division of Commissioned Personnel
5600 Fishers Lane Rockville, MD 20857
800-638-8744
301-594-3389 (local)
www.dcp.psc.gov/ default.asp.

Contact

If you do not have a myPay Personal Identification Number, visit the myPay site at www.mypay.dfas.mil.

The three retirement systems contain major differences in four areas:

- Determining your highest retirement earnings.

- The multiplier (percentage of base pay you receive).

- The cost-of-living adjustment.

- The career status bonus.

Determining your Retirement Earnings

The Final Pay retirement system (for those who entered the service prior to September 1980) bases the amount of pension on your last month of pay. If you retire at 20 years of service on the Final Pay retirement system, you receive 50 percent of your final month's pay as your pension.

Under the High 36 and CSB/REDUX systems, your pension is based on the average of your highest 36 months of basic pay. So if you retire at 20 years under these systems, you would get a percentage of the average of 36 months of your highest basic pay.

The Multiplier

The multiplier is the percentage of your base pay you receive for each year of service. For the Final Pay and High 36 systems you earn 2.5 percent per year of service. That means you get 50 percent for 20 years of service up to a maximum of 75 percent or 30 years.

The multiplier for the CSB/REDUX system is 2 percent per year for the first 20 years, but you get an increase to 3.5 percent for each additional year past 20. That means you get 40 percent for 20 years, but up to a maximum of 75 percent for 30 years—a significant difference.

The Cost-of-Living Adjustment

All three retirement systems have an annual cost-of-living adjustment (COLA). This may seem relatively unimportant, but over the course of your retirement, the COLA could more than double your retirement check.

The COLA for the Final Pay and High 36 systems is determined each year by the national Consumer Price Index, but for the CSB/REDUX retirement system the COLA is the Consumer Price Index minus 1 percent. Therefore, retirees under the High 36 system may see a COLA increase in their retirement check of

5.8 percent in 2009, while a retiree under the CSB/REDUX plan would get a 4.8 percent COLA increase. COLA is usually updated every December, and reflected in January retirement payments. A prorated COLA is applied to those who retired before completing a full retirement year by January.

There is one more twist to the COLA for CSB/REDUX retirees. At age 62, their COLA and multiplier are readjusted so that they get the same monthly pay as High 36 retirees.

The Career Status Bonus

The CSB/REDUX system is a bit more complicated: When you reach your 15th year of service, you *must* choose between taking the CSB/REDUX with a $30,000 cash bonus (approximately $21,000 after taxes) and a 40 percent pension check, and the High 36 retirement system with no bonus and a 50 percent pension check. This is a huge decision and cannot be made without serious consideration and a clear understanding of the details. (See Appendix, page 352, for the Retirement Systems Summary chart.)

Waiver of Retired Pay

If you receive a VA disability compensation you may be required to waive a portion of your retirement pay—equal to the amount of compensation you receive from VA. There are two exceptions to this rule: see the Combat Related Special Compensation (CRSC) and Concurrent Retirement and Disability Pay (CRDP) sections on page 73 for more information.

Retired Pay Centers: Answers to Your Questions

The Defense Finance and Accounting Service operates the Defense Retiree and Annuitant Pay System (DRAS). Military-retiree accounts are administered at the DFAS center in Cleveland. Annuitant accounts (accounts for those who receive payments from the Survivor Benefit Plan) are administered at the DFAS center in Denver. Keep in mind the following tips when you contact these centers:

- Include your complete name and Social Security number, as well as your signature, on any correspondence, including faxes.

- Keep your address current to ensure timely receipt of all mailings from the center, including your annual tax statement. Filing an address change will also update your official personnel file.

Take Advantage
The sooner you start saving, the more time your money has to grow. Put time on your side. Make saving for retirement a high priority. Devise a plan, stick to it, and set goals for yourself. Whatever your age, start saving now.

Take Advantage
If you have a choice of retirement plans, which should you choose? The Defense Department has retirement calculators that can help you pick the best plan for your situation at www.dod.mil/militarypay/retirement/calc.

Contact

Retired Pay Customer Service Line:

Toll Free: 800-321-1080
Commercial: (216) 522-5955
FAX: 800-469-6559

Defense Finance and Accounting Service
US Military Retirement Pay
P.O. Box 7130
London, KY 40742-7130

Annuitant Pay Customer Service Line

Toll Free: 800-321-1080
Commercial: (216) 522-5955
FAX: 800-982-8459

Defense Finance and Accounting Service
US Military Annuitant Pay
P.O. Box 7130
London, KY 40742-7131

You can make changes to your account, and print copies of your Retiree Account Statement (RAS)/Annuity Pay Account Statement and your IRS Form 1099, by accessing myPay. In particular, you can:

—Change your Federal and State withholding.

—Change your payment address.

—Change your correspondence address.

—Manage certain allotments.

—Manage deductions for a U.S. savings bond.

Military Retirement Payment Procedures

Unless you waive all your pay in favor of VA compensation or civil service annuity, your retired pay is electronically transferred to your financial institution on the first business day of each month. Retired pay is administered by Retired Pay Operations, at the DFAS Center in Cleveland. See Waiver of Retired Pay page 69 for further explanation.

Retired servicemembers who waive all retired pay in favor of VA compensation will be paid by VA. Retired servicemembers who waive a part of their retired pay to receive VA compensation will receive monthly payments from both VA and Retired Pay Operations.

Receiving Your Retirement Pay

If you retired on or after October 1, 1990, you must have your retired pay sent by electronic-funds transfer to a financial institution. If retired pay is sent to the same financial institution as for your active-duty pay, a new form isn't necessary. However, the routing number and the account number of the financial institution must be provided to DFAS. To initiate direct deposit of retired pay by electronic transfer, you should contact your financial institution for an SF 1199A, the Direct Deposit Sign-up Form. This form must be completed by the financial institution and submitted by you to the military finance office during out-processing.

Paychecks for retired servicemembers residing in certain overseas areas are mailed directly to the individual. If you do not use direct deposit, and believe a check has been lost, stolen, or destroyed, or if it has not been received within 10 days after the normal delivery date, you should contact Retired Pay Operations at the DFAS Cleveland Center and request a "stop payment" for the missing check. A substitute check will then be sent you, though you should anticipate some delay in receiving the new check.

Retiree paychecks are mailed at the end of each month. If you are an annuitant or retiree living overseas (see below), you need to send a Report of Existence (ROE) to Retired Pay Operations certifying your current status. For further information concerning Certificates of Eligibility (COEs) and other requirements, contact Retired Pay Operations at the DFAS Cleveland Center.

Changes of address. You must sign any notification of changes of address.

Special Situation Retirees

For the protection of the government, certain safeguards are required for retiree paychecks mailed through the international postal system, or payable to legal representatives of mentally incompetent members.

Overseas retirees. U.S. military retirees and annuitants who live overseas may have their monthly payments sent directly to their local banks through the DFAS International Direct Deposit Program (IDD). IDD is not available at all overseas locations.

Through IDD DFAS electronically deposits funds into an individual's bank account, normally on the first business day of the month. Those retirees and annuitants currently receiving their pay by check can avoid postal delays, misrouted, lost or stolen checks. Contact the DFAS Military Retirement Center at London KY for enrollment forms.

Mentally incompetent retirees. Forwarding checks directly to retirees who are found mentally incompetent to manage their own affairs is prohibited. In such cases, checks may be drawn payable to a legal guardian, trustee, or other legal representative after receipt by Retired Pay Operations of proper documentation of the authority of the guardian, trustee, or other legal representative to receive such payments.

Military Retirement Allotments

With the exception of Combined Federal Campaign pledges, TRICARE Retiree Dental Plan (TRDP), Veterans' Group Life Insurance (VGLI), and deposits in the Veterans' Educational Assistance Program (VEAP), retired servicemembers are permitted to continue allotments that had been in effect while they were on active duty. (For more on SGLI, see page 28. For more on VEAP, see page 193.)

As noted earlier, military retirees are authorized a maximum of six discretionary allotments. Examples of discretionary allotments include insurance premiums for health, auto, or life; voluntary payments to a family member;

Coast Guard/ National Oceanic and Atmospheric Administration (NOAA)
Commanding Officer (RAS)
U.S. Coast Guard Pay and Personnel Center
444 S.E. Quincy St.
Topeka, KS 66683-3591
800-772-8724 (toll-free) or
785-339-3415

Public Health Services (USPHS)
Compensation Branch
Parklawn Bldg.
5600 Fishers Lane, Room 4-50
Rockville, MD 20857
800-638-8744 (toll-free) or
301-594-2963.

Take Advantage
You should inform Retired Pay Operations before the 10th day of the month if you want to make changes in retired pay. Changes received after the 10th may not be made until the following month. All change requests must contain your signature and Social Security number.

Setting Up and Changing Your Retirement Account

The following steps establish your retirement account, and should be completed as part of your preretirement preparation.

Separation from Active Duty. When you separate, your command must close your active-duty account in order to establish your retirement account.

Data for Payment of Retired Personnel (DD Form 2656). This form must be completed and submitted in accordance with the policy of your branch of service and prior to your retirement or transfer date. It requires you to provide DFAS with dependency information, your Survivor Benefit Plan (SBP) election, information regarding the beneficiary of your retired pay when you die, and withholding information for federal and state tax purposes. All these materials are used to build your retired pay account. This form is available at www.military.com/forms.

Survivor Benefit Plan (SBP) Election Statement for Former Spouse Coverage (DD Form 2656-1). In addition to the DD Form 2656, if you elect for some type of Former Spouse SBP coverage, you must also complete a DD Form 2656-1. This form is available at www.military.com/forms.

Payment method/schedule. Your retired pay should be sent to your financial institution by direct deposit unless you reside in a foreign country in which direct deposit is not available. Your retired pay will be deposited in your account on the first business day of the month following the end of the month.

Allotment authorization. You can start, stop, or change current allotments by requesting action by the office that takes care of your active duty pay account. Changes should be processed 30 days before retirement. When reviewing your information for retirement, ensure that your allotment total will not exceed your retirement pay. (See page 73 for more information.)

Retired Pay Operations will mail a Retiree Account Statement (RAS) to you when an account is established. Revised RASs are sent only when a change occurs in net retired pay or beneficiary information.

Source: DFAS

Contact

If you do not receive your paper check on time, contact the DFAS Treasury Operations Center at 800-390-2347 or 216-522-5470 outside the U.S.

deposits into a financial institution, mutual fund, or investment firm; and payment of an auto or personal loan, mortgage, rent, or consumer debts.

Retirees are authorized an unlimited number of nondiscretionary allotments. Examples of nondiscretionary allotments are U.S. government savings bonds; payment of delinquent federal, state, or local taxes; repayment of Army Emergency Relief (AER) and Red Cross loans; any court-ordered garnishment; and charitable contributions to Armed Forces Retirement Homes and AER.

Garnishment of Retirement Pay

Retired pay may be garnished, or withheld, for enforcement of a retired servicemember's legal obligations to provide child support or make alimony payments under the USFPA. Upon receipt of a court order, DFAS may use retired pay, including any allotments, to satisfy the amount owed, which can include all retroactive amounts for which a retired servicemember may be delinquent in child support or alimony payments. DFAS will attempt to notify a retired servicemember of any garnishment against retired pay, with only the retiree's disposable retirement income subject to garnishment.

Disposable retirement income is gross retired pay minus amounts owed to the United States; federal income taxes required or authorized by law (additional amounts for tax withholding are considered only when the servicemember submits evidence of the tax obligation); state taxes under certain conditions; compensation deductions under Title 5 or 38 (dual compensation/forfeiture or VA compensation); and Survivor Benefit Plan (SBP) cost deductions regardless of the beneficiary.

The garnishment amount is limited to 50 percent of disposable income if the retiree is supporting a second family and 60 percent if the retiree is not supporting a second family. When a retiree is more than 12 weeks in arrears for support, the limitation is 55 percent if the retiree is supporting a second family and 65 percent if the retiree is not supporting a second family.

Compensation paid by VA is garnishable if the retiree waived all or part of his or her retired pay in order to receive such compensation from VA. All other VA compensation (e.g., pension, payments for service-connected disability or death) may not be garnished.

Combat-Related Special Compensation

Combat-Related Special Compensation (CRSC) provides military retirees a monthly compensation of between $123 and over $3,100, which replaces their VA disability offset. This means that qualified military retirees that have a 10 percent "combat related" VA-rated disability no longer have their military retirement pay reduced by the amount of their VA disability compensation. Instead they will receive both their full military retirement pay and their full VA disability compensation.

To qualify for CRSC you must meet the following criteria:

- Eligible for military retired pay as a result of:
    —20 years of creditable military service.
- or -

—Medical Chapter 61, Temporary Early Retirement Act (TERA) and Temporary Disabled Retirement List (TDRL) retirees – regardless of the number of years of service.

- Have 10% or greater VA rated injury.

- Have your military retired pay reduced by VA disability payments (VA Waiver).

- Be able to provide documentary evidence that your injury was a result of one of the following:

—Training that simulates war (e.g., exercises, field training) .

—Hazardous duty (e.g., flight, diving, parachute duty) .

—An instrumentality of war (e.g., combat vehicles, weapons, Agent Orange).

—Armed conflict (e.g., gun shot wounds [Purple Heart]).

To receive Combat Related Special Compensation you must submit your application (DD form 2860), through your parent military service branch. Each service branch has the authority to determine your eligibility. Veterans who retired from a branch of service can submit their claim to that branch. See the contact information on the following page.

Concurrent Retirement Disability Pay

Concurrent Retirement Disability Pay (CRDP), formerly known as Concurrent Receipt, means that qualified military retirees will receive both their full military retirement pay and their VA disability compensation. This recently passed law phases out the VA disability offset, which means that military retirees with 20 or more years of service and a 50 percent (or higher) VA-rated disability will no longer have their military retirement pay reduced by the amount of their VA disability compensation. However, CRDP is both taxable and divisible (i.e., in the case of divorce).

Unlike CRSC, full concurrent receipt CRDP will be phased in over 10 years, unless you are a veteran rated at 100 percent disabled, in which case you will receive full CRDP immediately. If you are less than 100 percent disabled, you will see your retirement pay increase by approximately 10 percent each year until the phase-in is complete in 2014.

CRDP is automatic. If you qualify, you will see an increase in your monthly retirement check.

Concurrent Retirement and Disability Pay Qualifications

To qualify for CRDP, you must:

- Be a military retiree with 20 or more years of service, including:

    —Chapter 61 Medical Retirees with 20 or more years

    —Reserve or National Guard with 20 or more qualifying years

    —Includes certain Temporary Early Retirement Act (TERA) retirees with less than 20 years of service.

- Have a service-related VA disability rating of 50 percent or higher

2008 Update: Those members who have been rated less than 100 percent, but rated 100 percent disabled by the VA under the unemployability code (UI), will now receive CRDP. It has not been made clear when the first payments will be sent. Contact the VA for details on your personal payment situation. 1-800-827-1000.

Comparing CRSC and CRDP

Many retirees qualify for both CRSC and CRDP, However, it is important to note that you cannot receive both CRSC and CRDP and must elect one each year through an annual "program election." Many retirees are confused about which is better for them. When making this decision, please note the following characteristics of CRSC and CRDP:

	CRSC	CRDP
Full Concurrent Receipt	Yes	No - 10 Year Phase In *(Except for 100% rated Disabled Retirees)*
Sample Payment for 50% Disability Rating	$728 (2008)	$633 (2008)
Required VA Disability Rating:	10%	50%
Taxable	No	Yes
VA Individual Unemployment (IU) Eligible	Yes	Yes
Survivor Benefit	No	No
Application Requirement	Yes - DD 2860	No - Automatic
Type of Disability	Combat Related	Service-Connected

Source: Army CRSC Division

200 Stovall Street
Alexandria, VA 22332
1-866-281-3254
Email: crsc.info@us.army.mil
Website: www.CRSC.army.mil

COAST GUARD
Commander (adm-1-CRSC)
U.S. Coast Guard Personnel Command
4200 Wilson Boulevard
Arlington, VA 22203-1804
1-800-772-8274
Website: www.uscg.mil/hq/cgpc/adm/adm.htm

NAVY and MARINE CORPS

Secretary of the Navy Council of Review Boards
Attn: Combat-Related Special Compensation Branch
720 Kennon Street SE, Suite 309
Washington Navy Yard, DC 20374
Fax: 202-685-6882
Website: www.donhq.navy.mil/corb/crscmainpage.htm

Suspension of Retirement Pay

Your retirement pay may be placed in a suspended (nonpayment) status to comply with statutory or regulatory requirements or military department procedures. Such suspensions don't necessarily affect continued or future entitlement once the requirements or procedures that prompted the suspension no longer apply.

Military departments may suspend your pay if you fail to take necessary administrative actions on time or if you decline to receive further payments. For example, retired pay is suspended if you don't furnish a required Report of Existence (ROE); fail to notify your military department of an address change and your current address is unknown; or have been overpaid because there is some doubt concerning a specific entitlement. When a retired member is missing and there is no information concerning his or her whereabouts, the member's retired pay must be suspended from the date that he or she was last known to be alive.

Upon the death of a retiree, notification should be made by calling DFAS Cleveland (see numbers on page 76). The caller needs to provide the following information:

(see numbers on page 76)

- Date of the member's death.

- Spouse's name, Social Security number, date of birth, if the spouse is alive, address, and telephone number.

- Identity and relationship of the caller, along with address and telephone number.

- Next of kin addresses and telephone numbers.

The call should be followed up by faxing or mailing a copy of the member's death certificate. Some Air Force Retiree Affairs Offices have access to the Retired Pay System and can take information on the death of a retiree as well. Any paper retired paychecks received subsequent to the member's death should be returned to the DFAS. Any payments direct-deposited subsequent to the member's death should remain in the account. DFAS Cleveland will automatically reclaim those funds.

CRDP and CRSC Updates

Both of these compensation programs are often revised and updated. Visit military.com/cr to keep up with the latest changes in these programs.

Guard and Reserve Retired Pay: The Points System

Reservists and National Guard members earn credit toward retirement based on points. You earn one point for each day of active-duty, one point for four hours of inactive-duty training, and one point for every three hours of Extension Course Institute (ECI) courses. Your pension is calculated based on these points when you reach age 60.

You must have 20 qualifying years of service to be eligible for retired pay at age 60. A qualifying year is one in which you earn a minimum of 50 retirement points.

Computing Reserve and Guard Retired Pay

To determine how much retired pay you may be eligible to receive, the first step is to calculate the number of equivalent years of service (comparable to full-time service) by dividing your total creditable retirement points by 360. For example, 3,600 points equals 10 years.

If you separate before age 60, you will be credited for basic pay purposes only with the years up until your discharge. If you transfer to the Retired Reserve before age 60, you will receive credit (for basic pay purposes only) for the years spent in the Retired Reserve until you reach age 60.

In other words, a retirement-eligible reserve or guard member can increase his or her retirement base by remaining affiliated with the Retired Reserve instead of being discharged or resigning his or her commission.

Depending on the Date of Initial Entry into Military Service (DIEMS), your monthly reserve retired pay will be calculated under the Final Basic Pay or High-3 formula as follows:

Final Basic Pay. DIEMS date before September 8, 1980: Multiply your years of satisfactory service by 2.5 percent, with a result no higher than 75 percent. Multiply the result by the basic pay in effect on the date your retired pay starts.

High-3. DIEMS date on or after September 8, 1980: Multiply your years of satisfactory service by 2.5 percent, with a result no higher than 75 percent. Then multiply the result by the average of your highest 36 months of basic pay. Normally the highest 36 months for a member who transfers to the Retired Reserve until age 60 will be the 36 months before he or she turns 60. Members who request a discharge from the Retired Reserve before age 60 can only use the basic pay for the 36 months prior to their discharge.

Your retired pay will increase annually through a cost-of-living allowance, which typically occurs every year on January 1.

Calculation example: A retiring E-7 reservist has 7,200 points (20 years), and the average monthly pay for his highest 36 months is $3,400.

Multiply years of service by 2.5 percent to determine percentage rate:

$$20 \times 2.5\% = 50\%$$

Multiply percentage rate by the average of the highest 36 months of pay:

$$50\% \times \$3,400 = \$1,700$$

So $1,700 is the monthly retirement rate.

As noted, however, a cost-of-living adjustment (averaging 3 percent) will in-

Contact

Defense Manpower Data Center
www.dmdc.mil/CRSC.

Air Force
United States Air Force Personnel Center—Disability Division (CRSC)
550 C St. West, Suite 6
Randolph AFB, TX 78150-4708
866-229-7074

Army
U.S. Total Army Personnel Command
U.S. Army Physical Disability Agency (CRSC)
c/o The Adjutant General Directorate
2461 Eisenhower Ave.
Alexandria, VA 22331-0470
866-281-3254

Marine Corps and Navy
Department of Navy—Naval Council of Personnel Boards
Combat-Related Special Compensation Branch
720 Kennon St. SE, Suite 309
Washington Navy Yard, D.C. 20374-5023
877-366-2772.

Contact

To notify DFAS of a retiree's death, call 800-321-1080, or 216-522-5955 if you are outside the continental United States. The death certificate should be copied and faxed to DFAS at 800-469-6559 or mailed to the Defense Finance and Accounting Service, U.S. Military Retirement Pay P.O. Box 7130 London, KY 40742-7130.

crease the retirement rate to approximately $2,900 per month by the time the retiree reservist hits 60 years old. (For more on COLA, see page 48.)

Veteran Disability Pay

Veterans receive many benefits from the government—many are covered in the Benefits chapter. Below are more details about veteran and death pensions.

Veterans Disability Pension

You may be eligible for a pension if you have limited income and had 90 days or more of active military service, at least one day of which was during a period of war. If you qualify, payments are made to you to bring your total income, including other retirement or Social Security income, to a level set by Congress.

Reasons for Suspension of Pay

A retiree's pay is suspended if the retiree:
• Is recalled to active duty.
• Requests a waiver of retired pay because of:
    —award of VA disability compensation or pension payments.
    —military service being used for U.S. civil service retirement annuity purposes .
• Completes five years on the Temporary Disability Retired List (TDRL.)
• Fails to report for a required physical examination while on the TDRL or while a member of the Fleet Reserve/Fleet Marine Corps Reserve.
• Is employed by a foreign government (including local government units within a foreign country as well as the national government itself) without applicable congressional or secretarial approval.
• Is a retired regular officer doing business with the DoD or other specified agencies during the three years immediately after retirement.
• Is reported to be, or is found to be, mentally incapable of managing his or her own affairs, and no guardian, trustee, or other legal representative has been appointed.
• Is repaying readjustment pay information.

Source: DFAS

Retired Pay Eligibility for Reserve and Guard Members

To be eligible for retirement as a reserve or guard member, you must meet all the following criteria:

- Be at least 60 years old.
- Have performed at least 20 years of qualifying service.
- Be entitled, under any other provision of law, to retired pay from a branch of the Armed Forces or retainer pay as a member of any reserve component.
- Apply for retired pay by submitting DD Form 108 to the branch of service you were assigned to at the time of your discharge or transfer to the Retired Reserve.

Unreimbursed medical expenses may reduce your countable income level. A pension is not payable to those who have sufficient assets to provide for adequate living. Currently, normal pensions range from $18,181 to over $22,000. To apply, submit VA Form 21-526, available at www.military.com/forms.

Veterans' Pension

To be eligible for veterans pension, you must meet the following criteria:

- Your discharge from active duty must have been honorable.

- You are permanently and totally disabled for reasons not traceable to willful misconduct.

- You are not incarcerated. However, if you are incarcerated, your dependents may receive a portion of benefits. (Failure to notify VA of your incarceration will cause the loss of all financial benefits until any overpayment is recovered.)

Income Limits for Veterans Pension

To qualify for veterans pension, your annual income must be less than the amounts listed below. Your income subtracted from the maximum amount equals your pension.

- Veteran without dependents: $11,583.

- Veteran with one dependent: $15,493.

Military Matters

Service Secretaries are required to notify members of the reserve components when members have completed enough service to qualify for retired pay. You will receive a letter titled "Notification of Eligibility for Retired Pay at Age 60," also known as the 20-year letter. You should get this letter within one year of completing 20 qualifying years of service.

Take Advantage

The Department of Veterans Affairs offers three payment options. Most veterans choose the convenience of receiving their benefit payments by direct deposit. However, veterans who do not have a bank account may choose to establish an Electronic Transfer Account, which allows a cash withdrawal through certain ATMs. The third option is to receive the benefits by monthly check. To learn more call 1-877-2778 Weekdays 7:3o a.m. to 4:50 p.m. CST.

- Housebound veteran without dependents: $14,493.

- Housebound veteran with one dependent: $18,120.

- Veteran married to another veteran: $15,493.

- Added amount per additional child in any category above: $2,020.

The pension program stipulates a maximum annual rate of pension. The payment is reduced by the veteran's countable income and the income of the spouse or dependent children. When a veteran without a spouse or a child is being furnished nursing home or domiciliary care by VA, the pension is reduced to an amount not to exceed $90 per month after three calendar months of care. The reduction may be delayed if nursing home care is being continued for the primary purpose of providing the veteran with rehabilitation services.

Pensioners entitled to benefits as of December 31, 1978, who do not elect to receive a pension under the Improved Pension program, continue to receive pension benefits at the rate they were entitled to receive on December 31, 1978, as long as they remain permanently and totally disabled, do not lose a dependent, and their incomes do not exceed the income limitation, adjusted annually.

VA Disability Compensation

VA Disability Compensation is a benefit paid to veterans due to injuries that happened while on active duty, or were made worse by active military service. The benefits are tax-free, and range from $123 to $3,000 per month, depending on how disabled you are and how many dependents you have. You are eligible if you have a service-related disability and you were discharged under other than dishonorable conditions.

The Application Process

You can apply for disability compensation by filling out and submitting VA Form 21-526 (available at www.military.com/forms), Veterans Application for Compensation or Pension. If you have any of the following material, attach it to your application:

• Marriage and children's birth certificates.

• Medical evidence (doctor and hospital reports).

Once you have submitted your application, you will be given an appointment at your local VA clinic or hospital to have a medical examination. This is the first step in your claim evaluation process. Next your application, support documents, and examination report will be evaluated to determine if you have a claim for VA disability compensation.

The board may take up to a year to make their determination. You will be notified whether you have any applicable service-connected disabilities and the overall percentage of disability of VA Disability Rating. This rating ranges from 0 to 100 percent and determines the amount of your compensation pay.

You have the right to appeal the VA evaluation board's determination (see page 163).

Take Advantage

Holders of the Medal of Honor are eligible to receive a monthly pension, plus an annual clothing allowance and a one-time $11,000 automobile allowance.

Death Pension

Surviving spouses and unmarried children of deceased veterans with wartime service may be eligible for a non-service-connected pension based on need. Your family qualifies for death pension if the family's annual income is below the following levels set by law:

• Surviving spouse with no dependents: $7,933.

• Surviving spouse with one dependent: $10,395 (add $2,020 for each additional child).

• Housebound surviving spouse with no dependents: $9,696.

• Housebound surviving spouse with one dependent: $12,144 (add $2,020 for each additional child).

• Surviving spouse who needs aid and attendance with no dependents: $13,195.

• Surviving spouse who needs aid and attendance with one dependent: $15,527 (add $2,020 for each additional child).

• Surviving child with no eligible parent: $2,020.

Contact

VA Disability Compensation rates are available at www.vba.va.gov /bln/21/Rates/ comp01.htm.

The death pension paid annually will be the amount that brings the family income up to the levels mentioned above. For example, if a surviving spouse with no children has an annual income of $4,000, the annual death pension the spouse receives will be $3,094, to bring the spouse's total income up to $7,094.

Spouses must not have remarried and children must be under age 18, or under age 23 if attending a VA-approved school. Pension is not payable to those who leave estates large enough to maintain the family's lifestyle. In addition, the veteran must have been discharged under conditions other than dishonorable and must have had 90 days or more of active military service, at least one day of which was during a period of war, or a service-connected disability justifying discharge for disability. If the veteran died in service but not in the line of duty, benefits may be payable if the veteran had completed at least two years of honorable service.

Children who became incapable of self-support because of a disability before age 18 may be eligible for a pension as long as the condition exists, unless the child marries or the child's income exceeds the applicable limit.

A surviving spouse who is a patient in a nursing home, is in need of the regular aid and attendance of another person, or is permanently housebound may be entitled to higher income limitations or additional benefits.

Contact

For more details on the death pension and how to apply, see www.military.com/ benefits.

The Improved Pension program provides a monthly payment to bring an eligible person's income to a support level established by law. The payment is reduced by the annual income from other sources such as Social Security paid to either the surviving spouse or dependent children. Medical expenses may be deducted from countable income. Pension is not payable to those who have assets that can be used to provide adequate maintenance.

Special Monthly Compensation (SMC)

SMC is a monetary compensation (paid in addition to the regular VA Disability Compensation) to a veteran who, as a result of military service, incurred the loss or loss of use of specific organs or extremities. Loss or loss of use is described as either an amputation or having no effective remaining function of an extremity or organ. The VA will pay higher rates for combinations of disabilities such as loss or loss of use of the feet, legs, hands, and arms, in specific monetary increments, based on the particular combination of the disabilities. There are also higher payments for various combinations of severe deafness with bilateral blindness. Additional SMC is available if a veteran is service connected for paraplegia with complete loss of bowel and bladder control.

More details about SMC can be found at www.military.com/benefits/veteran -benefits/smc-explained.

Part Three

The
Health Care
Advantage

A s a member of the military community, one of your most important benefits is health care coverage. Both the Department of Defense (DoD) and the Department of Veterans Affairs offer health care benefits. The more you know about your coverage, the better equipped you'll be to access your benefits. In this chapter, we demystify the system, clarify your options, and help you find nearby health care providers.

The Health Care Advantage at a Glance

If You Are on Active Duty
• TRICARE Prime 92
• TRICARE Pharmacy Program 106
• TRICARE Vision Benefits 94
• TRICARE Reserve Select 109
• TRICARE Plus 99
• TRICARE Prime Travel 91
• TRICARE Costs for Active Duty Families 99

If You Are a Military Retiree and Under 65
• TRICARE Prime 92
• TRICARE Standard 99
• TRICARE Extra 102
• TRICARE Retiree Dental Plan 119
• TRICARE Pharmacy Program 106
• TRICARE Supplement Programs 109

If You Are a Military Retiree and Over 65
• Continued Health Care Benefit Program 117
• TRICARE for Life 111
• TRICARE Retiree Dental Program 117
• Veteran Health Program 127

If You Are a Reservist or Guard Member
• TRICARE Prime 92
• TRICARE Standard 99
• TRICARE Extra 102

• TRICARE Pharmacy Program 106
• TRICARE Dental Program 104

If You Are a Reservist or Guard Member Activated for 30 Days or More
• TRICARE for Activated Guard and Reserve 85
• TRICARE Pharmacy Program 106
• TRICARE Prime 92
• TRICARE Vision Benefits 94

Health Programs Related to the War on Terror
• Health Care for Combat Veterans 111
• Transitional Health Care 112
• TRICARE Select for Reserve and Guard 113

If You Are a Family Member
• TRICARE Prime 92
• TRICARE Standard 99
• TRICARE Extra 102
• TRICARE Dental Program 104
• TRICARE Vision Benefits 94
• TRICARE Pharmacy Program 106
• Extra Care Health Option (ECHO) 109

If You Are A Veteran
• Veteran Health Program 127

TRICARE

Contact

Call TRICARE Active Duty Claims (Military Medical Support Office) at 800-876-1131. Weekdays 8 a.m.–11 p.m., Saturday 9 a.m.–8 p.m., Sunday 10 a.m.–5:30 p.m. Closed holidays.

TRICARE is the health care program for servicemembers and retirees, along with their families and survivors. When called to active duty for more than 30 days, reservists, National Guard members, and their families also receive TRICARE health benefits. TRICARE offers additional health care programs for active and retired servicemembers, including TRICARE Pharmacy, TRICARE Dental (United Concordia), and TRICARE for Life.

Although TRICARE appears complicated, it's really not that hard to understand if you break it down and are aware of the best ways to access your benefits.

TRICARE has three main coverage plans. You may not be enrolled in more than one of these TRICARE plans, but you and your family may be enrolled under different categories.

- TRICARE Prime is for active-duty personnel, activated Guard, and Reserve. Family members have the option to enroll, as well. Consisting of military hospitals and outpatient clinics, Military Treatment Facilities (MTFs) are the principal health care providers for users of TRICARE Prime. For people who live more than 50 miles from a MTF, TRICARE Prime Remote and the U.S. Family Health Plan are TRICARE Prime options.

- TRICARE Standard is a fee for service option that gives you more flexibility in choosing health providers. Military families are enrolled automatically in this option.

- TRICARE Extra offers a preferred provider network for military families that may save you money as there is no enrollment or annual fee.

For most family members the savings in deductible and cost-shares generally make TRICARE Prime the best choice. However, if money is not a concern, and you prefer to see civilian providers, then TRICARE Standard may be the right choice. If you want to see civilian doctors, would like to avoid filing claims, and don't mind using preferred providers, then TRICARE Extra may be the best selection.

A "provider" refers to the person, business, or institution that gives you health care. For example, doctors, hospitals, labs, and ambulance companies all count as providers.

Providers must be authorized under TRICARE and must have their authorized status verified (certified) by their regional TRICARE contractor. Being authorized usually means that the providers are licensed by their state, are accredited by a national organization, and meet other standards of the medical

Take Advantage

For a self-help tutorial on TRICARE, visit www.tricareu.tricare.osd.mil. Additional TRICARE information is available at www.military.com/TRICARE.

TRICARE Reference

TRICARE My Benefits Website
www.tricare.mil/mybenefits

DEERS Registration
https://www.dmdc.osd.mil/deers/

Military Treatment Center Locator
http://www.tricare.mil/mtf/

TRICARE Customer Service Locator
http://www.military.com/benefits/tricare
/tricare-service-centers

community. If a provider is not authorized, TRICARE Standard cannot help pay for care from that provider. Most hospitals and doctors are authorized by TRI-CARE. (Check with them, just to be certain.) But for other types of providers, such as labs and ambulance companies, it's a good idea to check with your Beneficiary Counseling and Assistance Coordinator or TRICARE Service Center before getting care to make sure they're authorized.

If you aren't a servicemember, you may still qualify for inpatient and outpatient care through TRICARE, provided you fall into one of these general groups:

- Family members of active-duty uniformed servicemembers and activated Guard and Reserve.

- Family members of uniformed service retirees, and family members of uniformed servicemembers who died while on active duty or during retirement.

- Individuals who were either voluntarily or involuntarily separated from a uniformed servicemember (e.g., by divorce).

The Military Family

When it comes to designating a benefits-eligible family member, the Department of Defense is very specific. In the Armed Forces, a family member is defined as a spouse, a widow or widower (if not remarried), an unmarried child younger than 21, or a dependent parent or parent-in-law. Adopted children and stepchildren qualify as family members, but illegitimate children do not except under certain circumstances. A child who is older than 21, but younger than 23 and a full-time student, is considered an eligible family member. A former spouse who is not remarried, and who does not have private medical insurance, is also entitled to family member benefits.

TRICARE for Transitioning Servicemembers

Congress has granted up to 180 days of eligibility for TRICARE benefits to certain former active-duty, reserve, and guard members, as follows:

Each service branch determines this limited, transitional eligibility. For details about eligibility, contact your nearest service personnel representative or transition office. The military does offer the Continued Health Care Benefit Program—consider taking advantage of it to avoid gaps in your medical coverage. The details of this program are covered on page 121. The main categories of transitioning servicemembers who are eligible for TRICARE include:

- A member involuntarily separated from active duty.

- A reserve or guard member separated from active duty who was called up for an active-duty period of more than 30 days, and his or her family.

- A member separated from active duty after being involuntarily retained in support of a contingency operation.

- A member separated from active duty following a voluntary agreement to stay on active duty for a period of less than one year in support of a contingency mission.

Take Advantage
Early TRICARE Benefit
Members of the Guard and Reserve issued delayed-effective-date active-duty orders for more than 30 days in support of a contingency operation are eligible for "early" TRICARE medical and dental benefits, which means they can enroll for benefits as much as 90 days prior to reporting for active duty.

Special Provisions for Reserve and Guard Members Called to Active Duty

As a reserve or guard member called to active duty for more than 30 days, your family becomes eligible for TRICARE Standard and TRICARE Prime on the day you report for active duty. With TRICARE Standard, family members can receive care at the Military Treatment Facility on a space-available basis. If they use civilian doctors, they will pay only their TRICARE Standard cost-shares. By using TRICARE network doctors, they'll pay even less out of pocket.

There are a few things you must do to make this process easier. Make sure all information on your Defense Enrollment Eligibility Reporting System (DEERS) record is correct. (See page 90 for more on DEERS.) Get current military identification cards for all family members 10 years of age or older. Though you will have a chance to update your DEERS record during mobilization, it is best to keep this information current at all times.

If you want your spouse to be able to inquire about your claims, you should complete and sign an Authorization to Disclose Information form and send it to the claims processor for your region. Give your spouse a copy of your orders for documentation.

If you're activated for contingency operations, you and your family can keep your TRICARE benefits for up to 180 days after your release from active duty, unless your civilian insurance takes effect before that time. For more on this and other health benefits related to deployment, see page 108.

Enrolling in TRICARE: DEERS

Many people don't realize there is a difference between *qualifying* for and *registering* with TRICARE. You need to be registered with the Defense Enrollment Eligibility Reporting System (DEERS) in order to receive coverage and many other military benefits. DEERS is the computerized database of military personnel, families, and others worldwide who are entitled under law to TRICARE and other benefits, such as access to commissaries. If you're an active-duty or retired servicemember, you're automatically registered in DEERS, but you must register your family members and ensure they're correctly entered into the database. Reserve and guard members who are activated are automatically enrolled in TRICARE. Any time you change your address, or need to

Health Care for Active-Duty Servicemembers and Family Members

	TRICARE Prime	TRICARE Extra	TRICARE Standard
Annual Deductible	None	$150/individual or $300/family for E-5 and above; $50/$100 for E-4 and below	$150/individual or $300/family for E-5 and above; $50/$100 for E-4 and below
Annual Enrollment Fee	None	None	None
Civilian Outpatient Visit	No cost	15% of negotiated fee	20% of negotiated fee
Civilian Inpatient Admission	No cost	Greater of $25 or $11.90/day	Greater of $25 or $11.90/day
Civilian Inpatient Mental Health	No cost	Greater of $20/day or $25/admission	Greater of $20/day or $25/admission

change the enrollment status of family members, you are also responsible for alerting DEERS. Mistakes in the DEERS database can cause problems with TRICARE claims, so it is critical to keep your DEERS information current.

You can verify your DEERS information by contacting your local TRICARE service center, regional TRICARE managed care representative, or the nearest uniformed services personnel office, which is the same place you get your identification card. Any registered family members may make address changes, but only the primary insured person can add or take away a family member from DEERS. You'll need the appropriate document (marriage certificate, divorce decree, or birth certificate) to do so. If an eligible servicemember or retiree is not accompanied by family members to the personnel office for DEERS enrollment and dependent identification cards, they need you to provide the necessary documentation and complete and sign an "Application for Uniformed Services Identification Cards and DEERS Enrollment" (DD Form 1172), available at www.military.com/forms. In addition, each family member's eligibility record must be updated separately.

Life changes (marriage, birth, divorce, death) also need to be reported to DEERS so that the Department of Defense can keep track of your eligibility. If you are on active duty and reenlist, separate, retire, or move, make sure your information gets updated in DEERS as soon as possible. If you don't, you and your family might experience a break in health care coverage.

As soon as you reenlist, take your reenlistment paperwork to your personnel support center or ID card facility so that your information can be updated prior to the expiration of your previous service obligation. When you retire, make sure DEERS reflects your change to retiree status.

Keep in Mind

A few more points to remember when dealing with DEERS:

- Pharmacies check TRICARE eligibility through DEERS. Your prescriptions will be filled only if you are in the system.

- If you have a child who is older than age 21 and a full time student, be sure to get his or her student status entered into DEERS so that TRICARE eligibility is not interrupted and access to health care is not lost. Your child loses eligibility at age 21 if not a full-time student.

- If you or members of your family are Medicare eligible, you must update DEERS to reflect Medicare parts A and B status to retain TRICARE coverage. When you turn 65, the medical section of your military ID card may also need to be updated.

Contact

For general TRICARE information, call 877-363-6337; for hearing- or speech-impaired information, TTY/TDD 877-535-6778. Weekdays 8 a.m.–8 p.m. Eastern time. Closed holidays.

Contact

To update your DEERS information in person, find the nearest uniformed services personnel office at www.dmdc. osd.mil/rsl. Call in address changes to the Defense Manpower Data Center Support Office at 800-538-9552, or fax changes to 831-655-8317.

Update information directly to the TRICARE website at www.tricare.osd. mil/deers. Mail address changes to the Defense Manpower Data Center Support Office, Attn. COA, 400 Gigling Road, Seaside, CA 93955-6771.

Make sure you use a TRICARE provider or receive (verified) authorization before you visit a specialist or provider other than your Primary Care Manager (PCM). Otherwise, you must pay a deductible of $300 per person ($600 per family member) and a cost-share of 50 percent of the TRICARE maximum allowable charge, after you meet the deductible.

TRICARE must authorize certain medical treatments before you can receive them. The doctor who is going to provide treatment must seek authorization from TRICARE. You can ask your provider if authorization is needed.

Now that you know how to register for TRICARE, you are ready to weigh the pros and cons of each option—Prime, Standard, and Extra—with their different combinations of cost, service, and delivery methods.

All About TRICARE Prime

TRICARE Prime is the lowest-cost health care option and is used by most active-duty servicemembers and their families. TRICARE Prime is a managed care option similar to a civilian health maintenance organization (HMO), and it offers fewer out-of-pocket costs than any other TRICARE option. TRICARE Prime enrollees receive most of their care from a Military Treatment Facility, augmented by the TRICARE contractor's Preferred Provider Network. Moreover, if you are on active duty, you do not pay for enrollment or regular office visits. However, retirees and their family members must pay an annual enrollment fee of $230 for an individual, or $460 for a family.

Enrollment in TRICARE Prime is not automatic, eligible family members must be enrolled individually using the TRICARE Prime enrollment form.

TRICARE Prime at a Glance

Advantages:

- No enrollment fee for active-duty members and families.

- No fee for visits to military treatment facilities.

- No fee for active-duty members to see civilian providers.

Contact

A directory of TRICARE providers is available online at www.tricare.osd .mil/Provider Directory.

- Primary Care Manager supervises and coordinates care.

- Point of Service option (receive services without a referral or authorization).

- Affordable enrollment fee for retirees and their families.

Limitations:

- Limited provider choice.

- Specialty care is available by referral only.

- Not available in all geographic regions.

- Minimum one-year enrollment period.

Take Advantage

Saving your receipts can save you both money and headaches. Keep every receipt, Explanation of Benefits (EOB), copayment record, etc. for at least one year. Many health care expenses can be deducted from your taxes, and you never know when you may be incorrectly double billed.

Are You Eligible for TRICARE Prime?

In addition to all active-duty personnel, the following people may choose TRICARE Prime:

- Family members and survivors of active-duty personnel.

- Retirees, their family members, and survivors under age 65.

- Reserve and guard members called to active duty for more than 30 days, and their families.

Active Duty

Your maximum out-of-pocket expense is $1,000 per fiscal year. If your family is not enrolled in TRICARE Prime, the annual deductible depends on your pay grade. Up to E-4, the annual deductible is $50 per family member or $100 per family. For E-5 and above, it's $150 per family member or $300 per family. There is no annual deductible for TRICARE Prime, unless you choose the Point of Service option.

In most cases with TRICARE Prime, you and your family will see military doctors, physician's assistants, and nurses at a Military Treatment Facility (MTF). If the Primary Care Manager (PCM) or principal health care provider in your PRIME area (outside a 50 mile radius of your home *and* work) is not an MTF, TRICARE Prime allows you to enroll in TRICARE Prime Remote and choose a local civilian TRICARE-authorized PCM. See page 95 for more information on TRICARE Prime Remote.

Your first medical contact is always your PCM, the person who provides

Take Advantage

TRICARE Prime members should *always* seek the advice of their Primary Care Manager (your local MTF) before seeking medical attention from any specialists or other medical facilities.

Take Advantage

The Point of Service annual deductible and cost-share amounts do not count toward your enrollment-year maximum out-of-pocket expense, but instead are credited to your fiscal year maximum. There is no limit to the amount of a patient's responsibility under the POS option.

and oversees your main care and is in charge of your health records. For example, if you need to see a specialist of any kind, either in or out of the TRICARE network, your PCM will make the referral and arrange the visit. A TRICARE nurse called a "health care finder" can also be asked to help locate specialists and make appointments.

You can opt to use a Point of Service (POS) feature of your TRICARE Prime coverage. Point of Service gives you the freedom to use any TRICARE-authorized civilian provider, in or out of the network, without a referral from your Primary Care Manager. However, POS claims can be very costly. You pay outpatient deductibles ($300 per individual, $600 per family annually), 50 percent of outpatient and inpatient costs, and excess charges up to 15 percent over the allowed amount.

TRICARE Vision Benefits

TRICARE Prime enrollees ages three and older are entitled to a comprehensive eye examination once every two years. You can make an appointment with any TRICARE network provider without a referral or authorization from your Primary Care Manager or Health Care Finder. If an eye examination is not available from a network provider, you can go to a non-network provider if you have a referral from your Primary Care Manager and authorization from the Health

Cost-shares and deductibles

The following chart shows the costs TRICARE Prime enrollees pay if they use the Point of Service option.

Charges	Individual	Family
Deductible per fiscal year (10/1-9/30) for outpatient care only	$300	$600
Cost-share for outpatient care	50% of TRICARE allowable charge, after annual deductible is met	
Cost-share for inpatient care	50% of TRICARE allowable charge	

Source: TRICARE

Care Finder. However, if you see a non-network provider without the proper referral and authorization, the TRICARE Prime Point of Service option will kick in and you will have to pay some of the cost.

Two exceptions to the general vision benefit: Pediatric vision screening is available at birth and approximately six months of age, and diabetic patients, at any age, are allowed annual comprehensive eye examinations.

For most participants, vision exams are excluded from the TRICARE Extra and TRICARE Standard plans, unless the exam is related to a covered medical condition. Retirees and their family members who use TRICARE Standard, TRICARE Extra, and TRICARE for Life are not eligible for routine eye examinations.

TRICARE Prime Travel Reimbursement

TRICARE Prime and TRICARE Prime Remote beneficiaries may qualify to have "reasonable travel expenses" reimbursed by TRICARE when they are referred by their primary care manager (PCM) for medically-necessary, non-emergent specialty care at a location more than 100 miles (one way) from their PCM's office. Reasonable travel expenses are the actual costs incurred while traveling, including meals, gas, tolls, parking and tickets for public transportation (i.e., airplane, *bus, or ferry*).

Active duty and members of the Guard and Reserve on active duty do not qualify for reimbursement under this program.

Contact your local MTF or TRO travel representative if you think you may qualify for this travel reimbursement.

Beyond TRICARE Prime

For people who cannot use normal TRICARE Prime due to geographic distance, there is TRICARE Prime Remote, and in specific parts of the country, there is also the U.S. Family Health Plan.

TRICARE Prime Remote

TRICARE Prime Remote provides health care coverage for servicemembers and their families who are on assignment at least 50 miles, or approximately one hour's drive or more, from a military hospital or clinic. This program allows you to see civilian network TRICARE-authorized providers for your medical needs.

Contact
Call TRICARE Prime Remote 800-363-2273. Weekdays 8 a.m.–11 p.m., Saturday 9 a.m.–8 p.m., Sunday 10 a.m.–5:30 p.m. Closed holidays.

Military Matters

TRICARE Prime Remote requires family members to enroll; however, if your family is enrolled in TRICARE Prime, do not disenroll them until you have checked into your new unit. This will ensure your whole family is covered by Prime while you are in transit from your old unit. By remaining enrolled with TRICARE Prime, you can avoid TRICARE Standard copayment and cost-shares if your family requires urgent care. Retirees and their family members must also enroll in the TRICARE Prime Remote option when geographic circumstances necessitate a change from regular TRICARE Prime.

Reserve and guard members and their families who meet the same location requirements also are eligible for TRICARE Prime Remote, if called to active duty for more than 30 consecutive days. Reserve and guard family members' eligibility requires that they and the servicemember must be living together on the effective date of the orders to active-duty service. The eligible servicemember does not need to enroll in TRICARE Prime Remote in order for his or her family members to be enrolled. Remember enrollment for family members in TRICARE Prime is not automatic.

- You must be eligible for TRICARE health benefits in order to enroll in TRICARE Prime or Prime Remote.

- TRICARE Prime is not available everywhere.

U.S. Family Health Plan

Depending on your location, you may be eligible to enroll in the U.S. Family Health Plan (USFHP). USFHP is available to eligible persons—including those who are age 65 and older—living near selected civilian medical facilities around the country. These facilities are called designated providers (DPs). At these DP facilities, the USFHP provides TRICARE Prime benefits and cost-shares for eligible persons who enroll, including those who are Medicare-eligible, plus lower costs compared to TRICARE for Life (see page 115).

While USFHP is not widely available, nor is it the least expensive option, you may want to consider it if you prefer the convenience offered under a POS arrangement, or if you wish to be seen at one of the six DP facilities listed on page

Contact

Find more information about U.S. Family Health Plan at www.usfhp.com.

98. USFHP is also the only TRICARE option that remains the same even after you turn 65, provided you are Medicare Part A eligible and enrolled in Medicare Part B.

USFHP's TRICARE-like benefits do not include the Point of Service option, under which TRICARE Prime enrollees can get nonemergency care outside their TRICARE Prime network without their PCM's authorization but must pay higher cost-shares and deductibles for the privilege. All care for a USFHP enrollee that will be cost-shared by the government must be received from the DP, unless the enrollee is traveling.

USFHP enrollees must live within specific ZIP codes around one of the designated hospitals. They may not seek care at military hospitals, or under TRICARE at other civilian medical facilities, during the period of enrollment. Medicare-eligible enrollees must also agree not to use their Medicare benefits for services covered under TRICARE Prime.

Enrollment is on a space-available basis, and again, you must reside in an appropriate service area. Unless you move out of the area or your eligibility status changes, you must make a one year commitment to the plan.

There is no enrollment fee for active-duty family members. Enrollment forms are available at participating hospitals and clinics. Like for TRICARE Prime, US Family Health Plan military retirees pay an annual enrollment fee of $230 for one person or $460 for a family. The enrollment fee is waived for persons who are Medicare Part A eligible and who are enrolled in TRICARE for Life and Medicare Part B.

TRICARE Overseas Prime

If you and your family are stationed overseas, you can enroll in TRICARE Prime as you would stateside. Like TRICARE Prime, TRICARE Prime Overseas enrollment is not automatic for family members, so you must make sure to enroll them. Active-duty families pay no enrollment fees, fees for office visits, or deductibles while overseas.

Note that servicemembers signed up for TRICARE Prime are automatically signed up for TRICARE Prime Overseas coverage. However, family members are not automatically enrolled. Also, military retirees and their families who live overseas are not *eligible to enroll in TRICARE Prime, but they can use TRICARE Standard.*

TRICARE Prime Overseas enrollees have access both to military medical facilities and to networks of local civilian providers. Wherever possible or available, your assigned Primary Care Manager provides most of your care and refers you to specialists.

If a care network for this program is not available in a given location, active duty families can have their cost-shares and deductibles waived by getting a Primary

Contact

For help with TRICARE Prime Overseas, call toll-free 888-777-8343.

Uniformed Services Family Health Plan Providers

The six Uniformed Services Family Health Plan hospitals and clinics are:

Brighton Marine Health Center
(with St. Elizabeth's Medical Center)
77 Warren St.
Brighton, MA 02139
800-818-8589
www.usfamilyhealthplan.org (click on link for
Massachusetts and Rhode Island)

CHRISTUS Health (covering southeast Texas
and southwest Louisiana)
(CHRISTUS St. Joseph Hospital, in downtown
Houston; CHRISTUS St. Catherine's Hospital,
Houston; CHRISTUS St. John Hospital, in
Nassau Bay; and CHRISTUS St. Mary
Hospital, in Port Arthur—all located in Texas)
P.O. Box 924708
Houston, TX 77292-4708
800-678-7347
www.usfamilyhealthplan.org/texas.htm

Johns Hopkins Medical Services Corporation
6704 Curtis Court
Glen Burnie, MD 21060
800-808-7347
www.hopkinsmedicine.org/usfhp

Martin's Point Health Care
P.O. Box 9746
Portland, ME 04104-5040
888-241-4556
www.martinspoint.org

Pacific Medical Clinics
1200 12th Ave. South
Seattle, WA 98144
888-958-7347
www.pacmed.org

Saint Vincent Catholic Medical Centers
of New York
450 West 33rd St.
New York, NY 10001
800-241-4848
www.svcmc.org

Care Manager's referral to non-network health care authorized by the regional military service center. *Be warned:* Without preauthorization from the regional military service center, hefty Point of Service cost-shares and deductibles will apply.

TRICARE Global Remote Overseas

TRICARE Global Remote Overseas (TGRO) is an option offered in designated remote overseas locations for active duty service members and their families. TGRO health care providers are carefully selected to ensure quality care no matter where you're stationed.

To learn more about TGRO, visit http://www.military.com/benefits/tricare.

All About TRICARE Standard

TRICARE Standard gives you the greatest flexibility in terms of doctor selection. You can see any doctor you choose, civilian or military, as long as the doctor is an authorized care provider under TRICARE Standard. You do pay a price for this considerable freedom—TRICARE Standard is the most costly of the three TRICARE programs. For example, you are responsible for charges beyond the 80 percent of the bill covered under TRICARE Standard. For retirees and retiree family members (under age 65), TRICARE Standard pays only 75 percent of the authorized cost of care. Also, keep in mind that if the medical provider charges more than what TRICARE has established as the authorized cost for the care you receive, you have to pay the additional difference.

An annual deductible of up to $300, depending on your military status, adds to your out-of-pocket expenses, although no enrollment fee is charged.

Active-duty family members, retirees, and their families who are enrolled in DEERS and eligible for TRICARE are enrolled automatically in TRICARE Standard. You do not, however, have to enroll to use TRICARE Standard, and you do not have to commit to use TRICARE Standard for any set period of time. Before TRICARE will begin covering its portion of the cost for your care, you must pay a deductible. When covered under TRICARE Standard, you do not have a Primary Care Manager, and you may need to file your own claims.

Since TRICARE Standard offers the greatest freedom in choosing health care providers, it is the most convenient option when you are traveling or away from home. If you choose TRICARE Standard, you may still be eligible for treatment at a military treatment facility on a space-available basis, after TRICARE Prime patients have been served.

Some military associations offer Supplemental Health Insurance as a companion to TRICARE Standard to help defray out-of-pocket expenses. See page 104 for additional details.

Take Advantage

Submit all claims separately; do not bundle multiple claims. Because processors manage claims separately, if you send multiple claims in together, a problem with one claim will delay payment on all claims.

Take Advantage

TRICARE suggests conducting business online whenever possible, calling during nonpeak hours, and visiting TRICARE service centers for face-to-face assistance as ways to beat phone congestion.

TRICARE Standard at a Glance

Advantages:

- Broadest choice of providers.

- Wide availability.

- No enrollment fee.

- Option also to use TRICARE Extra (see page 102).

Limitations:

- No Primary Care Manager.

- You pay deductible and copayment.

- You pay the balance if the bill exceeds the allowable charge and the provider is nonparticipating (up to 15 percent extra).

- You may need a statement from a military hospital stating that it cannot provide care to you if you receive civilian inpatient care in areas surrounding military treatment facilities.

- You have to do most, if not all, of your own paperwork and file your own claims.

Ins and Outs of TRICARE Standard

Even though TRICARE Standard has no enrollment fees, it is not free. You pay a portion of your medical costs, called copayments, as well as deductibles. There are special rules or limits on certain care, and some care is not covered at all. TRICARE Standard only pays for necessary medical services at what is defined as an "appropriate level of care."

Military Matters:

If your health care provider has agreed to accept TRICARE, then you are *not* responsible for paying any portion above or beyond your co-payment. This means that if your doctor, anesthesiologist, or other specialist is not paid by TRICARE for any reason, he or she cannot come after you for the balance—it's the law!

Remember that you must be enrolled in the DEERS computerized eligibility database before TRICARE claims can be paid.

Your Provider Charges

The individual providers you see may or may not participate in TRICARE Standard. Participation, in this case, simply means that a provider has agreed to charge only the established amount allowable or authorized for services pro-

10 Steps to a Healthy TRICARE Standard Claim

1. Always ask your provider, "Who is filing the claim?" If you are using a non-network provider, the provider may not be filing for you.
2. Use DD Form 2642, available at www.military.com/forms, and be sure to fill it out properly. If you do not know how to fill out this form, call your regional TRICARE Service Center (TSC) and ask them to assist you.
3. Be sure to send DD Form 2642 to the correct address. You can get the correct address from your regional TSC. (See www.tricare.osd.mil/tricareservicecenters for the complete list.)
4. Submit your claim as soon as service is rendered. Submitting a complete and accurate claim as soon as possible will assure you payment in a timely manner. Claims must be received within one year of the date of service, unless you have a waiver.
5. Submit all claims separately; do not bundle them. If there is a problem with one claim, all the claims may be held pending correction, and payment will be delayed.
6. File with your other health insurance (OHI) first. (OHI includes civilian health insurance you may have, as well as insurance through a spouse's.) After your OHI has paid its share, a claim may be filed with TRICARE. Not telling either your TRICARE provider or the claims processor about OHI may result in a denied or delayed payment.
7. Make sure your DEERS information is current. To do so, contact your nearest military personnel office or DEERS (address corrections only) at 800-538-9552.
8. Accident claims must include DD Form 2527, available at www.military.com/forms. If you are hurt in an accident for which someone else may be legally responsible, that person or that person's insurance may have to pay some or all of the medical bills. While you or the provider can file claims with TRICARE right away, be sure to point out that another person may be responsible by attaching a DD Form 2527 to all claims submitted.
9. Keep copies of everything you send to claims processors, including paperwork from your other health insurance (OHI).
10. Try to resolve problems at the lowest level first. With only one phone call on your part, a TSC staff member may be able to fix your problem.

Source: myTRICARE.com

vided under TRICARE Standard. You are free to see a nonparticipating provider, but you can be, and most likely will be, billed up to 15 percent more than the TRICARE Standard allowable charge.

It's your responsibility to arrange with your doctor how you will pay the bill. When you file the TRICARE Standard claim, TRICARE pays you its share of the allowable charge.

All About TRICARE Extra

Anyone who is TRICARE eligible may use TRICARE Extra, with the exception of active-duty servicemembers. TRICARE Extra may be a good option if you don't already have a relationship with a doctor. Under this program, you choose a doctor from a list of certified network providers. Paperwork is limited because you don't need to file any claims. You may use TRICARE Extra on a case-by-case basis simply by seeing one of the network providers. There's no need to commit to using TRICARE Extra for any set period of time. Under TRICARE Extra, you do not have a designated Primary Care Manager, and the list of providers is limited. Note that TRICARE Extra is not available in all areas.

As far as costs are concerned, TRICARE Extra requires no annual enrollment fee, though you must be enrolled in this option. Deductibles and cost-sharing work the same way for TRICARE Extra as for TRICARE Standard. In general, after the annual outpatient deductible has been met, the cost-share under TRICARE Extra for an active-duty family member is 15 percent of the TRICARE Extra network provider fee. All other TRICARE Extra participants pay a 20 percent cost-share of the contracted fee.

TRICARE Extra at a Glance

Advantages:

- Co-payment for active-duty family members is 5 percent less than TRICARE Standard co-payment.

- No balance billing.

- No enrollment fee.

- No forms to file.

- You may also use TRICARE Standard.

Limitations:

Contact

You can get a list of TRICARE Extra providers by contacting your local TRICARE Service Center at www.tricare.osd .mil/tricareservice centers.

TRICARE Costs for Active Duty Families

	TRICARE Prime	TRICARE Extra	TRICARE Standard
Annual Deductible	None	$150/individual or $300/family for E-5 & above; $50/$100 for E-4 & below	$150/individual or $300/family for E-5 & above; $50/100 E-4 below
Annual Enrollment Fee	None	None	None
Civilian Outpatient Visit	No cost	15% of negotiated fee	20% of allowable charges for covered service
Civilian Inpatient Admission	No cost	$ 15.15/day rate (multi-day stay) or $25 charge per admission, whichever is greater	$ 15.15/day rate (multi-day stay) or $25 charge per admission, whichever is greater
Civilian Inpatient Behavioral Health	No cost	$20/day rate (multi-day stay) or $25 charge per admission, which is greater	$20/day rate (multi-day stay) or $25 charge per admission, which is greater
Civilian Inpatient Skilled Nursing Facility Care	$0 per diem charge per admission No separate cost share for separately billed professional charges	$ 15.15/day rate (multi-day stay) or $25 charge per admission, whichever is greater	$ 15.15/day rate (multi-day stay) or $25 charge per admission, whichever is greater

- No Primary Care Manager.

- Limited provider choice.

- You pay a deductible.

- You have copayments.

- Not available overseas.

TRICARE Plus

TRICARE Plus is a primary care enrollment program offered at selected military treatment facilities. The program allows you to seek enrollment for primary care at military treatment facilities where enrollment capacity exists. If you are enrolled in TRICARE Prime or Medicare Advantage HMO, you are not

Take Advantage

For a list of TRICARE supplemental plans, see www.tricare.osd.mil /supplemental insuranceplans.cfm.

eligible for Plus. TRICARE Plus is not available at all military treatment facilities, and it does not guarantee access to specialty care at the military treatment facility where you are enrolled. In addition, TRICARE Plus is not a portable benefit; your enrollment at one facility does not guarantee access to care at another facility. For more information call your local MTF.

Supplemental Health Insurance

If you choose TRICARE Standard or Extra, the cost of copays and deductibles can be substantial. To defray these costs, insurance policies designed to supplement TRICARE are offered by some military associations and by some private firms. These policies reimburse you for your civilian medical care bills, copayments, and deductibles, after TRICARE pays the government's share of the cost.

Each TRICARE supplemental policy has its own rules on preexisting conditions, eligibility requirements for family members, deductibles, mental health limitations, long term illness, well baby care, disabilities, and allowable charges.

Take Advantage

TRICARE will now cover dental anesthesia and associated costs for beneficiaries with developmental, physical, or mental disabilities. This new coverage also includes children age 5 and below.

Contact

The directory of participating dentists is available online at www.ucci.com/ tdp/tdp.html.

TRICARE Dental Program

Active-duty members automatically receive dental care through military dentists, whom you can access at your Military Treatment Center. For family members, retirees, and members of the Reserve and Guard called to active duty, there is the TRICARE Dental Program. United Concordia administers this comprehensive dental program worldwide for TRICARE Prime, Standard, and Extra participants.

Family members, including spouses and unmarried children (natural, step, adopted, and wards) qualify for dental care. Eligibility may be extended at age 21 and older if:

- The dependent is enrolled full time at an accredited college or university and is more than 50 percent dependent on the military member for financial support (eligibility continues until the dependent turns 23 or until the month when his or her education terminates, whichever comes first).

- The dependent has a disabling illness or injury that occurred before his or her 21st birthday, or between the ages of 21 and 23 while enrolled as a full-time student.

Those ineligible for dental benefits include former spouses, parents, in-laws, disabled veterans, and foreign personnel.

Dental Benefits For Reserve, Guard, and Family Members

For activated reserve and guard members and their families, TRICARE Dental (United Concordia) offers an annual maximum payment of $1,200 per enrollee, per contract year, for nonorthodontic services. Payment for certain diagnostic and preventive services is not applied against the annual maximum. There is a lifetime maximum of $1,500 per person for orthodontic treatment, but orthodontic diagnostic services will be applied to the general $1,200 annual maximum.

If you are in the Reserve or Guard and are called up to active duty for more than 30 days, you automatically become eligible for free dental care at MTFs under TRICARE Prime.

Contact

You can contact United Concordia Dental Program at 800-866-8499; for enrollment applications, call 888-622-2256.

Enroll online at www.secure.ucci.com/TOE/process.jsp. To choose a dentist, go to www.ucci.com/tdp/tdp.html.

Your Dental Benefits at a Glance

Percent copayment for various dental services:

Type of Service	Pay Grades E-1—E-4 Continental U.S.	All Other Pay Grades Continental U.S	Outside Continental U.S.
Diagnostic	0%	0%	0%
Preventive (except sealants)	0%	0%	0%
Emergency Treatment	0%	0%	0%
Sealants	20%	20%	0%
Basic Restorative	20%	20%	0%
Endodontic	30%	40%	0%
Periodontic	30%	40%	0%
Oral Surgery	30%	40%	0%
Other Restorative	50%	50%	50%
Prosthodontic	50%	50%	50%
Orthodontic	50%	50%	50%
General Anesthesia	40%	40%	0%
Intravenous Sedation	50%	50%	0%
Consultation/Office Visit	20%	20%	0%
Implant Services	50%	50%	50%
Post-Surgical Services	20%	20%	0%
Miscellaneous Services (occlusal guard, athletic mouthguard, bleaching)	50%	50%	0%

Source: TRICARE

When you enroll, you will receive a complete directory of participating dentists. Although using a United Concordia network dentist saves you both time and money, you are always free to use any licensed dentist, although going outside the network will increase your out-of-pocket costs. If you live in a remote area, and do not have access to a United Concordia dental facility, you can visit a civilian dentist at no additional cost as long as you complete a non-availability and referral authorization to receive care.

Two TRICARE Dental plans

Single Plan: Under this plan, only one eligible member is covered. This can be one active-duty family member, a reserve or guard member, or one reserve or guard family member. The sponsor's enrollment is separate from his or her family member's enrollment.

Family Plan: Enrollment consists of two or more covered eligible active-duty family members, or two or more reserve and guard family members.

TRICARE Remote Dental Program

If you are an active-duty servicemember, you'll receive most care from military dental treatment facilities at no cost. But, if you are enrolled in TRICARE Prime Remote, you're automatically covered by the Tri-Service Remote Dental Program (RDP). The RDP augments military dental care by providing for routine, specialty, and emergency dental services. There are no out-of-pocket costs for using the RDP.

TRICARE Pharmacy Program

TRICARE provides a world-class pharmacy benefit to all eligible Uniformed Services members, including TRICARE for Life (TFL) beneficiaries entitled to Medicare Parts A and Parts B based on their age, disability and/or end-stage renal disease.

Any prescriptions you fill at your nearest Military Treatment Facility (MTF) are free under the TRICARE Pharmacy Program. If you cannot visit an MTF pharmacy, TRICARE network, non-network, and mail-order pharmacies can serve your needs.

In-Network Pharmacies

If you need a prescription filled right away and are unable to use an MTF pharmacy, your best bet is one of the TRICARE-approved civilian pharmacies—otherwise known as retail network pharmacies.

While the TRICARE Mail Order Pharmacy is more cost effective for long term medications, another option is to use a retail network pharmacy for new prescriptions your health care provider wants you to start taking immediately. Through the retail network pharmacies, you can order up to a 30 day supply of most prescription medications for a small copayment.

To be eligible for the TRICARE benefit at a retail network pharmacy, your family's information must be up to date in DEERS.

> **Contact**
>
> To register for mail-order prescriptions, call 866-363-8667. When outside the United States, call 866-275-4732. Online registration is at www.express-scripts.com.

Prescriptions by Mail

The most convenient way to fill your regular prescriptions, such as medication to reduce blood pressure, is through the TRICARE Mail Order Pharmacy. Other than the Military Treatment Facility option, the Mail Order Pharmacy is least expensive both for you and for the government. You simply mail your written prescription, along with your payment, to receive up to a 90 day supply of most medications. Register first with the TRICARE Mail Order Pharmacy by sending in a registration form.

Prescription drugs purchased through the TRICARE Mail Order Pharmacy are $3 for up to a 90-day supply of generic medications, and $9 for up to a 90-day supply of brand-name medications. Using a credit card is the easiest way to pay for mail-order prescriptions.

To use the TRICARE Mail Order Pharmacy (TMOP), register online at the Express Scripts website or call the TMOP. Make sure your address is current in the Defense Enrollment Eligibility Reporting System (DEERS).

After you are registered, you can simply mail your doctor's written prescription along with your payment to the TMOP, and you'll receive your medicine in the mail.

Using generic drugs, as prescribed by your physician, can save you additional money.

> **Contact**
>
> To appeal a denied prescription claim, call 866-363-8779 or write to Express Scripts, P.O. Box 60903, Phoenix, AZ 85082-0903.

Medicare Part D Prescription Drug Benefit

Medicare Part D prescription drug coverage recently became available to everyone with Medicare Part A and/or Part B. For nearly all TRICARE-Medicare beneficiaries, there is no added value in purchasing this Medicare prescription drug coverage if you have TRICARE. The exception to this general rule may be for

Your Prescription Costs

TRICARE Pharmacy Cost-Shares in the United States (Including Puerto Rico, Guam, Virgin Islands):

Place of Service	Generic	Formulary	Nonformulary
Military Treatment Facility (MTF) pharmacy (up to a 90-day supply)	$0	$0	Not Applicable
TRICARE Mail Order Pharmacy (TMOP) (up to a 90-day supply)	$3	$9	$22
TRICARE Retail Pharmacy Network pharmacy (TRRx) (up to a 30-day supply)	$3	$9	$22
Non-network retail pharmacy (up to a 30-day supply) *Note: Beneficiaries using non-network pharmacies may have to pay the total amount of their prescription first and then file a claim to receive partial reimbursement.*	For those who are *not* enrolled in TRICARE Prime: $9 or 20 percent of total cost, whichever is greater,after deductible is met (E-1-E-4: $50/person, $100/family. All others, including retirees: $150/person, $300/family) TRICARE Prime: 50 percent cost-share after Point of Service deductibles ($300 per person, $600 per family deductible)	For those who are *not* enrolled in TRICARE Prime: $22 or 20 percent of total cost, whichever is greater, after deductible is met (E-1-E-4: $50/person, $100/family. All others, including retirees: $150/person, $300/family) TRICARE Prime: 50 percent cost-share after Point of Service deductibles ($300 per person, $600 per family deductible)

Beneficiary Cost-Share at All Other Overseas Locations

	Active-duty servicemembers	Active-duty family members enrolled in Prime	Active-duty family members not enrolled in Prime	Retirees and family members
Cost-Share	No cost-share	No cost-share	25% cost-share	25% cost-share

those with limited incomes and assets who qualify for Medicare's extra help with prescription drug plan costs.

When deciding whether to enroll in Medicare Part D, you should consider monthly premiums, deductibles, copays, and drug coverage under other prescription drug plans, including the TRICARE Pharmacy Program. The Medicare Part D drug plan options will also vary by location.

TRICARE Extended Care Health Option (ECHO) Program

Take Advantage
General Exceptional Family Member Program information is available at www.efmconnections .org.

ECHO is a supplemental TRICARE program that provides financial assistance to eligible active-duty family members who have a qualifying mental or physical disability. The program offers services and supplies beyond the basic TRICARE benefits covered in Prime, Extra, and Standard. The ECHO benefit also provides a monthly government cost share of up to $2,500 per eligible family member. Additionally, some beneficiaries may qualify for ECHO Home Health Care (EHHC). EHHC provides medically necessary skilled services to eligible homebound beneficiaries.

Eligibility. ECHO benefits are available with a qualifying condition to an active-duty TRICARE-eligible child or spouse of the following individuals:

1. A member of one of the Uniformed Services of the United States, including members of the Reserve Component activated for a period of more than 30 days.

2. Family members eligible for continued TRICARE medical benefits through the Transitional Assistance Management Program (TAMP).

3. A former member of a Uniformed Service of the United States when the child or spouse is the victim of physical or emotional abuse.

The following are qualifying conditions under ECHO:

• Moderate or severe mental retardation.

• A serious physical disability.

The law added an additional qualifying condition to cover an extraordinary

Monthly ECHO Copayments

If your pay grade is	You pay
E-1 to E-5	$ 25
E-6	$ 30
E-7, O-1	$ 35
E-8, O-2	$ 40
E-9, W-1, W-2, O-3	$ 45
W-3, W-4, O-4	$ 50
W-5, O-5	$ 65
O-6	$ 75
O-7	$100
O-8	$150
O-9	$200
O-10	$250

physical or psychological condition of such complexity that the beneficiary is homebound.

Recipients may retain their eligibility for ECHO services as long as the sponsor remains on active duty. Even children of sponsors who reach the usual TRICARE eligibility age limit (21 or age 23 if enrolled in college full-time) retain their eligibility for ECHO services, as long as the sponsor remains on active duty, the child is incapable of self-support because of a mental or physical incapacity that occurs prior to the loss of his or her eligibility, and the sponsor is responsible for more than one-half the child's support.

Benefits. The following benefits may be offered through ECHO:

- Medical and rehabilitative services.

- Training to use assistive technology devices.

- Special education.

- Institutional care when a residential environment is required.

- Transportation under certain circumstances.

- Assistive services, such as those from a qualified interpreter or translator.

- Durable equipment, including adaptation and maintenance.

- Expanded in-home medical services through TRICARE ECHO Home Health Care.

- In-home respite care services.

- TRICARE ECHO Respite care: 16 hours per month when receiving other authorized ECHO benefits.

- TRICARE ECHO Home Health Respite care: up to 40 hours per week (eight hours per day, five days per week) for those who qualify.

Costs. After the monthly cost share is paid, TRICARE will pay up to $2,500 per month for authorized ECHO benefits, except for the EHHC benefit.

If two or more persons with the same sponsor receive benefits under ECHO, the sponsor will only have to pay one monthly cost share and TRICARE will pay up to $2,500 for each ECHO-eligible beneficiary, except for the EHHC benefit.

If the costs exceed $2,500 for any individual in any month, the sponsor is responsible for additional costs.

TRICARE Beneficiary Web Enrollment

The Beneficiary Web Enrollment website allows beneficiaries living in the United States to manage their TRICARE Prime or TRICARE Prime Remote enrollments online, update personal information in the Defense Enrollment Eligibility Reporting System (DEERS) or add/update information regarding other health insurance.

For technical assistance when using the Beneficiary Web Enrollment tool, call the Defense Manpower Data Center at 1-800-477-8227. For questions about enrollment processing, contact your regional TRICARE contractor.

Health Programs Related to the War on Terror

In support of the Global War on Terror, several new health care programs and services have been introduced. These programs especially affect reserve and guard members who have been called up to active duty. Read on to see what you qualify for.

Post-Deployment Health Assessment

If you are returning from deployment, you will be required to complete a Post-Deployment Health Assessment, DD Form 2796, and receive a health assessment by a health care provider. This assessment will evaluate your current physical and mental health and focus on any deployment-related health concerns.

VA Health Care for Combat Veterans

Further details on extended health care coverage for combat veterans can be found in the Veterans Health Care section.

Contact

For more information on special VA health care, check with your local VA office (see Appendix) or call 800-827-1000.

Eligibility

You are eligible if you served on active duty in a theater of combat operations after the Gulf War, or in combat against a hostile force after November 11, 1998, and have been discharged under other than dishonorable conditions. National Guard and Reserve members are also eligible for VA health care if they were ordered to active duty by a federal declaration, served the full period for which they were called or ordered to active duty, and have separated from active military service under other than dishonorable conditions. Active-duty, guard, and reserve members who were activated to a combat mission and then separated from active duty receive a Certificate of Release or Discharge from Active Duty, DD Form 214, which should show an award of the Armed Forces Expeditionary Medal. Individuals seeking services under this authority should bring their DD Form 214 when reporting to a VA health care facility.

For the paperwork required to qualify you for VA medical benefits, see page 136.

Take Advantage

The National Defense Act of 2006 authorized payment of travel and lodging for families of hospitalized servicemembers wounded in combat zones or other designated areas.

Traumatic Injury Protection

You can be issued a traumatic injury payment ranging from $25,000 to $100,000 if you sustain a serious injury resulting from active duty. You can only receive this payment if you were insured under Servicemembers Group Life Insurance (SGLI) when you received the traumatic injury. For more details on this benefit and SGLI, see page 28 in the Money chapter.

Hospitalization Benefits

If you are entitled to basic allowance for subsistence, you will not be charged for meals received in a military medical facility while undergoing medical recuperation or therapy for an injury, illness, or disease incurred or aggravated while on active duty in Operations Iraqi Freedom or Enduring Freedom. You will also have access to telephone service at such a facility, worth up to $40 of calling minutes per month.

Transitional Health Care Coverage

If you are an active-duty servicemember, your current TRICARE health coverage for you and your family will continue through your deployment and after it. If you are transitioning out of the military following deployment, read up on your veteran or retiree health benefits later in this chapter.

If you are in the Reserve or Guard, you may be eligible for continued TRICARE benefits for up to 180 days after you return from active duty, under the Department of Defense Transitional Assistance Management Program (TAMP). You must fulfill one of the following requirements:

- You are involuntarily separating from active duty under honorable conditions.

- You are a reserve member (certain members of the National Guard also qualify) separating from active-duty service of more than 30 days in support of a contingency operation.

- You are separating from active-duty service following involuntary retention (Stop-Loss) in support of a contingency operation.

- You are separating from active-duty service following a voluntary agreement to stay on active duty for less than one year in support of a contingency operation.

For answers to specific questions regarding this program, contact your TRICARE regional contractor.

TRICARE Reserve Select

TRICARE Reserve Select (TRS) is now available to ALL members of the Selected Reserve (National Guard and Reserve) regardless of active duty service, with the exception of those who are eligible for or are currently covered under the Federal Employees Health Benefits program.

TRS now has only one premium amount for each type of coverage. The

Contact

For more details on the TRICARE Reserve Select program, see www.tricare.osd.mil/reserve/reserveselect and dmdc.osd.mil/guard-reserve-portal.

Member-Only coverage premium $47.51 a month, while the Member-and-Family premium was $180.17 (2009 rates). TRS premiums are adjusted annually effective January 1.

Eligible members may now purchase the insurance at anytime throughout the year. Enrolling in TRS is a 2-step process:

Step 1: Qualify:

1. Log on to the Guard and Reserve Web Portal at https://www.dmdc .osd.mil/appj/trs/.
2. Click on the "TRICARE Reserve Select" box.
   - Select the type of coverage that you want to purchase: TRS Member-Only or TRS Member-and-Family.
   - Certify that you are not eligible for or enrolled in the FEHB program.
   - Select when you want your coverage to begin.
3. Print and sign the TRS Request Form (DD Form 2896-1).

Step 2: Purchase

Mail or fax your completed TRS Request Form along with the first month's premium payment to your regional contractor.

Visit www.military.com/benefits/tricare, to learn more about the changes to the TRICARE Reserve Select health care plan and how they affect you and your family.

Take Advantage

It's a good idea to sit down and discuss retirement issues with your local Transition Assistance Program (TAP) manager as soon as you know you are retiring. For more on TAP, see page 273.

TRICARE After Retirement

As a military retiree, you are entitled to all the same health care that is provided to active-duty members at Military Treatment Facilities. This provision is, of course, subject to the availability of facility space and the capabilities of the medical and dental staff.

The overlap of benefits for retirees and veterans can be tricky to sort through. To start, former active-duty members of the U.S. Armed Forces (regardless of rank) who receive retired pay may also be eligible for Department of Veterans Affairs (VA) medical benefits. Military retirees are eligible for VA medical care only after they agree to pay a copayment. If you do not agree to make this copayment, you will not be eligible. You may, however, be offered VA medical care as a beneficiary of the Department of Defense at its expense, but only on a space- and resource-available basis. Beneficiaries of the Department of Defense, with the exception of those in need of emergency medical services, need authorization prior to receiving VA medical care.

TRICARE for Retirees: Options

When you retire from active duty, the Reserve, or Guard, you and eligible family members will experience changes in your TRICARE benefits, depending on your age and options. If you are under 65, you will need to decide which TRICARE program is best for you and eligible family members. Use the chart on page 118 in helping you choose. Remember that as you transition, you also need to update your information in DEERS.

If you are a military retiree age 65 or older, your health care coverage will change from TRICARE to Medicare and TRICARE for Life (TFL). The following section will give you all the information you need on your new benefits.

When a retiree reaches age 65 and becomes eligible for TRICARE for Life, a spouse maintains regular TRICARE eligibility until he or she reaches 65 years of age.

TRICARE for Life

Put simply, TRICARE for Life (TFL) is Medicare-wraparound coverage for military retirees. It gives you expanded medical coverage if you are 65 or older, Medicare Part A eligible, and have purchased Medicare Part B. There is no special enrollment or enrollment fees for TRICARE for Life.

Who Is Eligible?

TRICARE for Life is available for all uniformed services retirees, including retired members of the Reserve or Guard who receive retired pay, along with Medicare-eligible family members, Medicare-eligible widows and widowers, certain former spouses, and anyone under age 65 who is entitled to Medicare Part A because of a disability or chronic renal disease. Dependent parents and parents-in-law are not eligible for TRICARE for Life benefits, although they may continue to receive services within a Military Treatment Facility on a space-available basis.

Take Advantage
If you retire with at least 15 but less than 20 years of service—so-called "15-year retirees"—you are eligible for the same TRICARE benefits as those who retire at the traditional 20 years or more of service.

Contact
You can call the TRICARE for Life program at 866-773-0404 weekdays 8 a.m.–11 p.m., Saturday 9 a.m.–8 p.m., Sunday 10 a.m.–5:30 p.m. Closed holidays.

A General Retires

General Douglas MacArthur probably would never have retired from the military if left to his own devices. After his 1951 dismissal as Commander in Chief of the United Nations forces in Korea, he addressed Congress as follows: "I am closing my 52 years of military service. When I joined the Army, even before the turn of the century, it was the fulfillment of all my boyish hopes and dreams. The world has turned over many times since I took the oath on the plain at West Point, and the hopes and dreams have long since vanished, but I still remember the refrain of one of the most popular barracks ballads of that day, which proclaimed most proudly that old soldiers never die; they just fade away. And like the old soldier of that ballad, I now close my military career and just fade away, an old soldier who tried to do his duty as God gave him the light to see that duty. Good-bye."

Contact

To locate the nearest military ID card facility, visit www.dmdc.osd.mil/rsl.

How to Use TRICARE For Life

Using your TRICARE for Life benefits is easy. You simply show your military ID card, and the service provider will not collect a copayment from you at the time of your visit. Rather, the service provider will send the claim to Medicare, and Medicare will send the claim to TFL. While TFL users don't need authorization to see a medical or surgical specialist, you do, however, need prior authorization for a mental-health-related admission to a hospital. TFL users do not need to see a TRICARE-authorized provider; TRICARE will use the service provider's Medicare number to file the claim. If TFL users cannot travel to a military ID card center, they can contact their nearest uniformed services personnel office for specific instructions on how to get an ID card.

TFL users should note that they will not be issued a TRICARE for Life identification card. Instead, only your Medicare card, reflecting Part B enrollment, and your Uniformed Services ID card will be required.

Your TRICARE for Life

For more information about TRICARE for Life, visit the TRICARE website at www.tricare.osd.mil/tfl or www.tricare4u.com.

Fact sheets on eligibility and DEERS are available at www.tricare.osd.mil/Factsheets/index.cfm.

If you have trouble finding copies of the TRICARE for Life beneficiary letter, brochure, information card, or cost-matrix files, you can download them from www.military.com/tfl.

About Medicare Part B

Within 90 days before your 65th birthday, the DEERS system will notify you that your medical benefits are about to change. You'll be asked to contact the nearest Social Security or Medicare office regarding your Medicare eligibility. In order to be eligible for TRICARE for Life, you must enroll in Medicare Part B. Once you're enrolled in Medicare Part B, TRICARE for Life pays health care costs that exceed Medicare coverage, beginning on the first day of the month you turn 65.

If you already are age 65 or older and don't have Part B, you may sign up during the general enrollment period, which runs every year from January 1 to March 31. Medicare Part B coverage begins on July 1 of the year in which you enroll. If you're entitled to Medicare Part A because of a disability or chronic renal disease, you still must enroll in Medicare Part B to be eligible for TRICARE for Life (unless you are an active duty family member).

TRICARE now recognizes all health care providers who accept Medicare as TRICARE-authorized providers who can participate on a claim-by-claim basis, but note that these providers may or may not accept TRICARE's payment as payment-in-full for covered benefits. Remember that TRICARE will not process claims for a nonauthorized provider.

TRICARE for Life Overseas

If you live overseas, you may use TRICARE for Life as long as you are enrolled in Medicare Part B. Since Medicare does not typically provide health care coverage overseas, TRICARE provides the same TRICARE Standard benefits available to retirees under age 65. You are responsible for the TRICARE Standard copayments and deductibles.

TRICARE Retiree Dental Program

Administered by Delta Dental Plan of California, the TRICARE Retiree Dental Program is another bonus for your retirement. Enrollment is open to retired uniformed services members and their families. At first, you commit to a minimum of 24 months in the program, after which enrollment is renewable for 12-month periods.

Newly retired members of the uniformed services who enroll in the enhanced TRICARE Retiree Dental Program within 120 days after their retirement from active duty have a special opportunity—normally subject to a 12 month waiting period—to begin immediate coverage with additional benefits. Highlights of this coverage include 50 percent cost coverage of major dental work such as crowns, bridges, dentures, and orthodontics.

The TRICARE Retiree Dental Program offers dental coverage throughout the

Contact

To learn more about TRICARE for Life benefits, call 888-363-5433. To file claims, call TRICARE for Life at 866-773-0404, or TDD 866-773-0405.

Contact

For more information about enrolling in Medicare Part B, and its monthly premiums, check with the Social Security Administration online at www.ssa.gov, call toll free at 800-772-1213, or visit www.medicare.gov.

TRICARE Costs for Retirees and Their Families

	TRICARE Prime	TRICARE Extra	TRICARE Standard
Annual Deductible	None	$150/individual or $300/family	$150/individual or $300/family
Annual Enrollment Fee	$230/individual $460/family	None	None
Civilian Outpatient Visits	$12	20% of negotiated fee	25% of allowable charges for covered service
Emergency Care	$30	20% of negotiated fee	25% of allowable charges for covered service
Outpatient Behavioral Health Visit	$25 (individual) $17 (group visit)	20% of negotiated fee	25% of allowable charges for covered service
Civilian Inpatient Cost Share	$11/day (minimum $25 charge per admission); no separate co-payment for separately billed professional charges.	Lesser of $250/day or 25% of negotiated charges plus 20% of negotiated professional fees	Lesser of $535/day or 25% of billed charges plus 25% of allowable professional fees
Civilian Inpatient Skilled Nursing Facility Care	$11/day (minimum $25 charge per admission)	$250 per diem cost share or 20% cost share of total charges, whichever is less, institutional services, plus 20% cost share of separately billed professional charges	25% cost share of allowable charges for institutional services, plus 25% cost share of allowable for separately billed professional charges.
Civilian Inpatient Behavioral Health	$40 per day; no charge for separately billed professional charges	20% of total charge. Plus, 20% of the allowable charge for separately billed professional services	High Volume Hospitals - 25% hospital specific per diem, plus 25% of the allowable charge for separately billed professional services; Low Volume Hospitals - $187 per day or 25% of the billed charges, whichever is lower, plus 25% of the allowable charge for separately billed services

TRICARE Retiree Dental Program Coverage

Covered Services	* Delta Pays:	Applied to Annual Deductible	Applied to Annual Maximum
Available during the first 12 months of enrollment:			
Diagnostic (exams)	100%	No	No
Preventive (cleanings)	100%	No	No
Basic Restorative (fillings)	80%	Yes	Yes
Endodontics (root canals)	60%	Yes	Yes
Periodontics (gum treatment)	60%	Yes	Yes
Oral Surgery (extractions)	60%	Yes	Yes
Emergency (treatment for minor pain)	80%	Yes	Yes
Dental Accidents	100%	No	No
Additional services available after 12 months of continuous enrollment:			
Cast Crowns, Onlays, and Bridges	50%	Yes	Yes
Partial/Full Dentures	50%	Yes	Yes
Orthodontics	50%	No	No

Deductibles and Maximums	
Annual Deductible	$50 per person, limit $150 per family, per benefit year
Annual Maximum	$1,200 per person/benefit year
Orthodontics Maximum	$1,200 per person/lifetime
Dental Accident Maximum	$1,000 per person/benefit year
Benefit Year	May 1-April 30

Source: TRICARE

* Percentage paid by Delta is based on the allowed amount for each procedure. This chart depicts coverage for those seeking treatment from a network dentist. Your total out-of-pocket costs may be higher if care is received from a nonparticipating provider.

50 United States, the District of Columbia, Puerto Rico, Guam, the U.S. Virgin Islands, American Samoa, the Commonwealth of the Northern Mariana Islands, and Canada. You pay all premiums, which vary depending on where you live.

Your bottom-line cost does not differ whether you visit one of the 67,000 participating providers from the TRICARE Retiree Dental Program (called DeltaSelect USA) or any licensed dentist of your choice. The only difference is that you must pay a non-network dentist directly and then submit a claim to Delta for reimbursement. If you visit a DeltaSelect USA dentist, TRICARE will submit all claims for you, and you'll only be responsible for your percentage of the allowable TRICARE costs (see chart, page 119).

The annual deductible is $50 per person, with an annual maximum coverage of $1,200 per person. The deductible and maximum do not apply to the diagnostic and preventive services, which are covered at 100 percent, or to dental-accident procedures and orthodontia. Orthodontic services have a separate $1,200 lifetime maximum, and dental-accident coverage has a separate $1,000 annual maximum benefit.

Retiree Dental Program Eligibility

You are eligible to enroll in the TRICARE Retiree Dental Plan if you are:

- A member of the uniformed services who is entitled to retired pay, including those age 65 and over.

- A member of the Retired Reserve/Guard, including "gray area" reservists (retired guard or reserve members entitled to retired pay but who will not begin receiving it until age 60).

- A current spouse of an enrolled member.

- A child of an enrolled member, up to age 21 (or to age 23 if a full time student, or older if disabled before losing eligibility) .

- An unremarried surviving spouse or eligible child of a deceased member who died while in retired status or on active duty.

- A Medal of Honor recipient and eligible immediate family member, or an unremarried surviving spouse or eligible immediate family member of a deceased recipient.

- A current spouse and/or eligible child of certain nonenrolled members, with documented proof that the nonenrolled member is:
  —eligible to receive ongoing, comprehensive dental care from the Department of Veterans Affairs .

—enrolled in a dental plan, through other employment, which is not available to family members, or

—unable to obtain benefits due to a current and enduring medical or dental condition.

Continued Health Care Benefits

Contact

Call the Continued Health Care Benefit Program at 800-444-5445, option 4, or write Humana Military Healthcare Services, Inc., P.O. Box 740072, Louisville, KY 40201. Or check online at www.humana-military.com.

Even if you lose your TRICARE eligibility (i.e., if you separate from the military), you have access to a military-administered safety net. People with no other military health system coverage are eligible for temporary enrollment in the Continued Health Care Benefit Program. Though not a part of TRICARE, the Continued Health Care Benefit Program provides similar benefits and operates under most of the same rules. You must enroll within 60 days after separation from active duty or you will lose eligibility for military health care. The premiums for this coverage are $933 per quarter for individuals and $1,996 per quarter for families.

Humana Military Healthcare Services, Inc., administers the Continued Health Care Benefit Program. For information, including eligibility details, to request a copy of the enrollment application, details on available benefits, and out-of-pocket costs once you are enrolled, you can contact them in writing or by phone.

Transitional Assistance Management Program

The Transitional Assistance Management Program (TAMP) provides 180 days of transitional health care benefits to certain uniformed services members and their families, if the sponsor is:

- Involuntarily separating from active duty under honorable conditions.
- A National Guard or Reserve member separating from active duty for a period of more than 30 consecutive days in support of a contingency operation.
- Separating from active duty following involuntary retention (stop-loss) in support of a contingency operation.
- Separating from active duty following a voluntary agreement to stay on active duty for less than one year in support of a contingency operation.

For those who qualify, the 180-day TAMP period begins upon the active duty sponsor's separation. During TAMP, sponsors and family members are eligible to enroll in TRICARE Prime, TRICARE Prime Overseas or use TRICARE Standard and Extra or TRICARE Standard Overseas.

TRICARE Benefits for Survivors

Eligible surviving family members, whose sponsor dies while on active duty or retirement from active-duty, are entitled to continue to receive TRICARE health care benefits. The only requirement is that the deceased was serving, or was ordered to active duty for more than 30 days, at the time of death. Claims are paid at the active-duty family member rate for the first three years, and thereafter at the retiree rate. Widows or widowers remain eligible until they re-marry, and children remain eligible until age 21. Full-time students retain eligibility until age 23.

Covered under TRICARE

In addition to general medical and diagnostic treatment, here are some examples of specific items covered under TRICARE programs. Check with your Health Benefits Advisor for restrictions and limitations before receiving care.

Durable Medical Equipment

Medical equipment, like wheelchairs, hospital beds, and respirators, can be cost-shared by TRICARE Standard. You can rent, sometimes "lease/purchase," or buy the equipment (whichever method is least expensive). With your claim, you send a doctor's prescription for the particular type of equipment you need, along with why and for how long you need it.

Eye Examinations

Family members of active-duty servicemembers are authorized to receive one eye examination per 12-month period. The exam may include a check of the inside and outside of the eye for disease and an evaluation of the patient's vision.

Family Planning

TRICARE covers infertility diagnosis and treatment, intrauterine devices (IUDs), diaphragms, birth control pills or prescribed injections, the Norplant System (long-term reversible contraceptive implants), in-office pregnancy tests, vasectomies, and tubal ligation.

Contact

For general information about the military Anthrax Vaccine Immunization Program, visit www.anthrax.osd.mil.

Genetic Testing

Some tests to find out if your unborn child has genetic defects are covered. But TRICARE Standard helps pay only if you are pregnant and age 35 or older; if you had rubella during your first three months of pregnancy; if you or your husband has had a child with a genetic (congenital) defect; or if you or your husband comes from a family with a history of genetic (congenital) defects. TRICARE Standard does not help pay for genetic tests to determine the father or gender of a child.

Home Health Care

TRICARE covers a maximum of 28 hours per week part time or 35 hours per week intermittent, skilled nursing care, home health aide services, any physical, speech and occupational therapy. All care must be provided by a participating home health agency.

Hospice

Hospice care is available in lieu of other TRICARE benefits for terminally ill patients who are expected to live less than six months. Hospice care must be provided by a Medicare-approved program and may include physician services, nursing care, counseling, inpatient respite care, medical supplies, medications, home health aide services, and short-term acute patient care related to terminal diagnosis. There are no deductibles, and TRICARE Standard pays the full cost of covered hospice care services, except for small cost-share amounts for such items as drugs and inpatient respite care.

Implants

Surgical implants are covered if approved by the Food and Drug Administration (FDA). Examples include intraocular lenses, which are implanted in the eye after cataract surgery; cochlear implants, which are electronic instruments surgically implanted in the ear to assist hearing; breast implants for reconstructive surgery; and penile implants, whether to correct a malformation that has existed since birth, to correct organic impotency, or to correct what the medical profession calls "ambiguous" reproductive organs. There are limitations to coverage for all of these procedures.

Mammograms and Pap Smears

Routine mammograms and Pap smears are covered as diagnostic or preventive health care measures.

Mental Health

TRICARE covers mental/behavioral health care that is medically or psychologically necessary. There are many different types of outpatient and inpatient mental/behavioral health care, and the coverage varies by the type of care.

TRICARE coverage includes inpatient and outpatient psychotherapy, treatment for substance abuse, and up to 150 days of care in authorized residential treatment centers for children and adolescents (some up to age 21) who have psychological disorders that require continued treatment in a therapeutic environment.

TRICARE also offers a voluntary, anonymous self-assessment to help you determine if your symptoms are consistent with a condition that would benefit from further treatment or evaluation.

Visit http://www.tricare.mil/mybenefit/ to learn more.

School Physical Exams

TRICARE-eligible dependents who are at least five years old, and younger than 12 years old, may get physical exams at school. This benefit does not include physical exams that the school may require for participation in sports activities.

Skilled Nursing Facility

TRICARE covers skilled nursing facility (SNF) care for an unlimited number of days. Skilled services are those directed by a doctor, and they can only be provided by professionals. Under the SNF benefit, TRICARE covers medically necessary skilled nursing care and rehabilitative (physical, occupational, and speech) therapies, room and board, prescribed drugs, laboratory work, supplies, appliances, and medical equipment.

Substance Abuse

TRICARE helps pay for up to seven days of detoxification in a TRICARE-certified substance-abuse-disorder rehabilitation facility. In addition, TRICARE Standard helps pay for up to 21 days of rehabilitation.

TRICARE Appeals

You have the right to appeal TRICARE decisions regarding payment of your claims or denial of service authorization. For information on filing an appeal with TRICARE, contact a representative at your TRICARE Service Center through www.tricare.osd.mil/servicecenters. Remember that you must:

Not Covered under TRICARE

The following list of services is not typically covered by any TRICARE option. This list does not include all items not covered, so before receiving any care, check with your Beneficiary Counseling and Assistance Coordinator, Health Benefits Advisor, or TRICARE Service Center through www.tricare.osd.mil/tricareservicecenters.

Abortions
Acupuncture
Anabolic Steroids
Artificial Insemination
Autopsy Services or Post-Mortem Examination
Bone Marrow Transplants for Treatment for Ovarian Cancer
Camps
Christian Science "Absent Treatment"
Chronic Fatigue Syndrome
Cosmetic Drugs
Cosmetic, Plastic, or Reconstructive Surgery
Counseling Services
Custodial Care
Dental Care and Dental X-rays
Education or Training
Electrolysis
Experimental Procedures (also referred to as "Unproven" procedures)
Eyeglasses and Contact Lenses
Family Furnished Care or Supplies
Food, Food Substitutes or Supplements, or Vitamins Outside of a Hospital
Foot Care
Hearing Aids

Hearing Examinations
Immune Globulin
Investigational Drugs
Learning Disabilities
Mind Expansion or Elective Psychotherapy
Naturopathic Treatment
Orthotics, Orthopedic Shoes, or Arch Supports
Orthomolecular Psychiatric Therapy
Over the Counter Drugs
Private Hospital Rooms
Rest Cure
Retirement Homes
Self Help Courses
Sex Changes
Smoking-Cessation Products
Speech Therapy
Sexual Dysfunction or Inadequacy Treatment
Surgical Sterilization Reversals
Telephone Services or Advice
Unproven Procedures or Care
Vitamins (except for formulations of folic acid and niacin, and vitamins D, K, and B12 injections)
Weight Control
Workers' Compensation Medical Review

Source: TRICARE

- Meet all the required appeal deadlines.

- Send appeals in writing with signatures.

- Include copies of all supporting documents in your appeal; if you do not have the paperwork available, send your letter within the deadline and note that more information will be sent.

- Keep copies of everything for yourself.

Frequently Asked Military Health Care Questions

Can I use the Beneficiary Web Enrollment (BWE) website if I live in Hawaii/Alaska/US Territory?
You can use the Beneficiary Web Enrollment Web site if you live in Hawaii or Alaska. However, the Beneficiary Web Enrollment isn't available in US territories or in overseas locations.

Where do I file my overseas claims?
Mail your claim form and bill to Wisconsin Physician Services, P.O. Box 7985, Madison, WI, 53707-7985.

Who can I contact if I am having problems with my claim and the claims processor is unable to resolve the problem?
If you have problems with your claim, you should contact your regional contractor or the Beneficiary Counseling and Assistance Coordinator (BCAC) at the local MTF. If you have received a notice from a collection agency or a negative credit report because of a TRICARE bill, you should contact the nearest Debt Collection Assistance Officer (DCAO) at the local MTF.

Who do I contact if my claim was not paid and I was sent to collections?
If you have received a notice from a collection agency or a negative credit report because of a TRICARE bill, you should contact the nearest Debt Collection Assistance Officer (DCAO) at the local MTF.

I've heard that combat veterans can receive 2 years of free health care. Is this true?
Yes. The Department of Veterans Affairs (VA) provides free health care for conditions possibly related to military service. The benefit is provided to veterans with combat service after November 11, 1998 and may last for a period of up to five years beginning on the date of the veteran's separation from active duty.

Does TRICARE pay for the shingles vaccine?
Yes. As of October 19, 2007, Zostavax™, the vaccine that helps reduce the risk of getting shingles (herpes zoster) is reimbursable under TRICARE.

May I go to a doctor who is not my PCM?
Yes. TRICARE will then pay Point of Service (POS) benefits. But if you do, you will have to meet an annual deductible of $300 (or $600 per family), and you will pay a 50 percent cost-share after meeting your annual deductible.

I am enrolled in TRICARE Prime but I have other health insurance. Is this the best option for me?
Generally speaking, you enjoy the greatest advantage from TRICARE Prime if TRICARE is your primary coverage. When you have other health insurance, TRICARE is always secondary. Talk with your Beneficiary Service Representative at your local TRICARE Service Center to discuss your options.

I did not get a referral before I went into the hospital. Will TRICARE pay benefits?
Yes, TRICARE will pay under the Point of Service option. But as noted before, you will have to meet an annual deductible of $300 (or $600 per family) and you will pay a 50 percent cost-share after meeting your annual deductible.

If I choose the Point of Service option for a doctor's visit, does that apply to the maximum out-of-pocket expense?
No. The POS annual deductible and cost-share amounts are not calculated in the enrollment-year maximum out-of-pocket expense, but they are credited to your fiscal year maximum. There is no limit to the amount of a patient's responsibility under the POS option.

Source: myTRICARE.com

Veteran Health Care

In October 1996, Congress passed the Veterans' Health Care Eligibility Reform Act, paving the way for the Medical Benefits Package plan. The Medical Benefits Package emphasizes preventive and primary care, offering a full range of outpatient and inpatient services. The care you are eligible for will depend on your disability rating, income, and other factors (see chart page 133).

If you served on active duty in the Army, Navy, Air Force, Marine Corps, or Coast Guard, and received honorable discharge or release under honorable conditions, you are eligible for VA health care. If you served after September

Take Advantage

Even if you fall into a priority group with a high number (i.e., 7 or 8), you should still enroll in the VA Health Care System. The simple enrollment process may prove vital in helping you meet unanticipated future medical needs. VA is already tightening up the enrollment process and is not accepting additional veterans in some categories within Priority Group 8. This trend is likely to continue, so don't delay!

1980, you must have served 24 months of active duty to be eligible. If you served in the National Guard or Reserve and were ordered to active duty, you are eligible for VA health care if you served the full period for which you were called or ordered to active duty and received an honorable discharge or release under honorable conditions.

VA Health Care Enrollment

When you apply for enrollment with the Veterans Health Administration, your health care eligibility will be verified. Then, based on your specific eligibility status, you will be assigned a priority group.

The priority groups currently range from 1 to 8. Number 1 is the highest priority for enrollment, but the same services are generally available to all enrolled veterans. You can apply for VA health care by completing VA Application for Health Benefits Form 10-10EZ. This form may be obtained by visiting, calling, or writing any VA health care facility or Veterans' benefits office. Additional VA health care information and forms are available at www.military.com /vahealth. An important aspect of enrollment is choosing your preferred VA health care facility, where you receive your primary care. If for any reason a selected facility cannot provide the health care needed, then that facility's staff will make arrangements for referral.

What does "service-connected" mean?

In this context, the term service-connected means that VA has determined a condition or disability was incurred during or aggravated by military service.

Any medical condition or injury that occurs while you are on active duty is service-connected, unless you demonstrated a blatant disregard for safety, or you were injured while committing a crime.

Extended Eligibility for Combat Veterans

On January 28, 2008, the "National Defense Authorization Act of 2008" was signed into law. This law extends the period of health care eligibility from two years to up to five years for many veterans who served in a theater of combat operations after November 11, 1998. Under this authority, the Department of Veterans Affairs (VA) now provides cost-free health care services and nursing home care for conditions possibly related to military service and enrollment in Priority Group 6 or higher. This applies to the following:

- Currently enrolled veterans and new enrollees who were discharged from active duty on or after January 28, 2003, are eligible for the enhanced benefits, for five years after discharge.

- Veterans discharged from active duty before January 28, 2003, who apply for enrollment on or after January 28, 2008, are eligible for the enhanced benefit until January 27, 2011.

For those veterans who do not enroll with VA during their enhanced eligibility period, eligibility for enrollment and subsequent care is based on other factors such as a compensable service connection rating, VA pension status, catastrophic disability determination, or the veteran's financial circumstances. For this reason, combat veterans are strongly encouraged to apply for enrollment within their enhanced eligibility period, even if no medical care is currently needed.

Contact

Veterans Health Administration Facilities locations and contact information are available at www1.va.gov/directory.

VA Medical Benefits Package

The basic health care services for which enrolled veterans are eligible include the following:

- Outpatient medical, surgical, and mental health care, including care for substance abuse.

- Inpatient hospital, medical, surgical, and mental health care, including care for substance abuse .

- Prescription drugs, including over the counter drugs and medical and surgical supplies available under the VA national formulary system.

- Emergency care in VA facilities.

- Emergency care in non-VA facilities under certain conditions: This benefit is a safety net for veterans requiring emergency care for a service-connected disability or enrolled veterans who have no other means of paying a private-facility emergency bill. If another health insurance provider pays all or part of a bill, VA cannot provide any reimbursement. To qualify for payment or reimbursement for non-VA emergency care service for a service connected disability, all the following criteria must be met:

    —The service must be for a medical emergency.

    —VA or other federal facilities are not feasibly available at the time of the emergency event.

Take Advantage

When completing the VA enrollment form, do not try to fill out sections you do not understand. Service Officers with the Veterans of Foreign Wars (VFW) and Disabled American Veterans (DAV) offer free assistance in completing forms and explaining your VA benefits.

Contact

If you have any questions concerning completion of the veterans health benefits application form 10-10EZ, call VA at 877-222-VETS (8383) or 800-827-1000. Service Officers with the Veterans of Foreign Wars (VFW) and Disabled American Veterans (DAV), who offer free assistance in completing forms and understanding VA benefits, can be located at www.vfwdc.org /NVS/sor.htm or www.dav.org/help /service_offices .html.

—The emergency was related to a service-connected disability.

To qualify for payment or reimbursement for non-VA emergency care services for a non-service-connected condition, you must meet all the following criteria:

• You are enrolled in the VA Health Care System.

• You have been provided care by a VA clinician or provider within the last 24 months.

• You were provided care in a hospital emergency department or similar facility that provides emergency care.

• You have no other form of health insurance.

• You do not have coverage under Medicare, Medicaid, or a state program.

• You do not have coverage under any other VA programs.

• A reasonable layperson would judge that any delay in medical attention would endanger your health or life.

• You are financially liable to the provider of the emergency treatment for that treatment.

• You have no other contractual or legal recourse against a third party that will pay all or part of the bill.

The services you may qualify for under VA health care include the following:

• Bereavement counseling.

• Comprehensive rehabilitative services other than vocational services.

• Consultation, professional counseling, training, and mental health services for the members of the immediate family or legal guardian of the veteran.

• Durable medical equipment and prosthetic and orthotic devices, including eyeglasses and hearing aids.

• Home health services.

• Reconstructive (plastic) surgery required as a result of a disease or trauma but not including cosmetic surgery that is not medically necessary.

• Respite, hospice, and palliative care.

• Payment of allowable travel and travel expenses for eligible veterans.

• Pregnancy and delivery service, to the extent authorized by law.

- Completion of forms.

- Periodic medical exams.

- Health education, including nutrition education.

- Maintenance of drug use profiles, drug monitoring, and drug-use education.

- Mental health and substance-abuse preventive services.

Limited Coverage

The Medical Benefits Package covers a few special situations, including the following:

- You may receive certain types of VA hospital and outpatient care not included in the Medical Benefits Package, such as humanitarian emergency care for which you will be billed, compensation and pension examinations, dental care, readjustment counseling, care as part of a VA-approved research project, seeing eye or guide dogs, sexual trauma counseling and treatment, or special registry examinations.

- You may receive an examination to determine whether you are catastrophically disabled and therefore eligible for inclusion in a priority category.

- Commonwealth Army Veterans and new Philippine Scouts may receive hospital and outpatient care provided for in the Medical Benefits Package.

- For details on conditions concerning nonenrolled veterans, contact your local VA office. (See Appendix, page 357.)

Even if you have a service-connected disability, different regulations and payment requirements may apply to your non-service-connected medical conditions.

Veteran Benefits Not Covered

The following health care is not covered under veteran benefits:

- Abortions and abortion counseling.

- In vitro fertilization.

- Drugs, biologicals, and medical devices not approved by the Food and Drug Administration (FDA) unless the treating medical facility is conducting formal clinical trials under an Investigational Device Exemption (IDE) or an Investigational New Drug (IND) application, or the drugs, biologicals, or

Take Advantage

My HealtheVet is the gateway to veteran health benefits and services. It provides access to trusted health information, links to Federal and VA resources, the Personal Health Journal, and online VA prescription refills. Visit www .myhealth.va.gov/ for more information.

Frequently Asked VA Health Care Questions

How do I apply?

An application form is available at any VA facility or by calling for an appointment. Applications are also available online at www.va.gov/1010ez.htm.

What services can I receive through the VA health system?

You will receive all necessary inpatient and outpatient services, including preventive and primary care, and diagnostic and treatment services, as well as rehabilitation, mental health treatment, substance-abuse treatment, home health, respite and hospice care, women's clinic services, and prescribed drugs.

What does VA care cost me?

While you pay no monthly premium for VA care, copayments may be required, depending on your eligibility and income level. (If you have insurance, it may cover the cost of the copayments.)

Are there restrictions on getting care in private facilities at VA expense?

Yes. Care in private facilities at VA expense is provided only under certain circumstances. For additional information, contact your local VA health care facility.

What about emergency services?

VA provides urgent and emergency care in VA facilities. VA's ability to pay for emergency care in non-VA facilities is very limited.

What if I get sick while traveling?

You may receive health care at any VA facility in the country. For a list of VA facilities nationwide, visit the VA Facilities Directory at www.va.gov/facilities.

Can I get free prescriptions from VA?

Medications are provided to veterans who are enrolled with the VA and receive health care provided by a VA Primary Care Provider. Medications are prescribed for treatment of a condition for which a veteran is receiving health care from the VA provider. A copayment may be required.

Can I get dental care?

Dental benefits are limited to service-connected dental conditions or to veterans who are permanently and totally disabled from service-connected causes.

Does VA provide hearing aids and eyeglasses?

Yes, if you have a service-connected disability rating of 10 percent or more. Otherwise, hearing aids and eyeglasses will only be provided in special circumstances and not for common hearing or vision loss.

Does VA provide maternity services?

VA does provide maternity care, but not care to a newborn child, even immediately after birth.

I've heard that VA will now pay for treatment in the emergency rooms of private hospitals. How do I get VA to pick up the bill?

This new coverage for non-VA emergency care has a narrow scope: It is designed as a safety net for veterans who do not have any way to pay for emergency health care services. If you are treated at a civilian facility for a nonemergency, you will not be covered under this benefit.

Source: Dept. of Veterans Affairs

VA Enrollment Priority Groups

Enrollment Priority 1

- Veterans with service-connected disabilities rated 50 percent or more disabling.
- Veterans determined by VA to be unemployable due to service-connected conditions.

Enrollment Priority 2

- Veterans with service-connected disabilities rated 30 percent or 40 percent disabling.

Enrollment Priority 3

- Veterans who are former POWs.
- Veterans awarded the Purple Heart.
- Veterans whose discharge was for a disability that was incurred or aggravated in the line of duty.
- Veterans with service-connected disabilities rated 10 percent or 20 percent disabling.
- Veterans awarded special eligibility classification under Title 38, U.S.C., Section 1151, "benefits for individuals disabled by treatment or vocational rehabilitation."

Enrollment Priority 4

- Veterans who are receiving aid and attendance or housebound benefits.

- Veterans who have been determined by VA to be catastrophically disabled.

Enrollment Priority 5

- Non-service-connected veterans and non-compensable service-connected veterans rated 0 percent disabled whose annual income and net worth are below the established VA Means Test thresholds.
- Veterans receiving VA pension benefits.
- Veterans eligible for Medicaid benefits.

Enrollment Priority 6

- World War I veterans.
- Mexican Border War veterans.
- Compensable 0 percent service-connected veterans.
- Veterans exposed to ionizing radiation during atmospheric testing or during the occupation of Hiroshima and Nagasaki .
- Project 112/SHAD participants.
- Veterans who served in a theater of combat operations after November 11, 1998 as follows:
- —Veterans discharged from active duty on or after January 28, 2003, who were enrolled as of January 28, 2008 and

veterans who apply for enrollment after January 28, 2008, for 5 years post discharge.

—Veterans discharged from active duty before January 28, 2003, who apply for enrollment after January 28, 2008, until January 27, 2011.

Enrollment Priority 7

• Veterans with income and/or net worth above the VA national income threshold and income below the geographic income threshold who agree to pay copays.

Enrollment Priority 8

Veterans who agree to pay specified copayments with income and/or net worth above the VA Means Test threshold and the HUD geographic index

• Subpriority a: Non-compensable 0 percent service-connected veterans enrolled as of January 16, 2003, and who have remained enrolled since that date.

• Subpriority c: Non-service-connected veterans enrolled as of January 16, 2003, and who have remained enrolled since that date.

Source: Dept. of Veterans Affairs

medical devices are prescribed under a compassionate-use exemption.

• Hospital and outpatient care for a veteran who is either a patient or inmate in an institution of another government agency, if that agency has a duty to give the care or services.

• Membership in spas and health clubs.

VA Health Care Costs

Most non-service-connected veterans and non-compensable 0 percent service-connected veterans (veterans who incurred an injury or disease during service not severe enough to qualify for VA compensation) are required to complete an annual means test, based on family income and net worth. If your annual income is above a certain cutoff, you will have to make copayments for your care and medications. However, you can apply for an exemption from those copayments to avoid a hardship if projections of your income for the current year are substantially below the applicable income threshold.

Whether or not you have other health insurance does not affect your eligibility for VA health care benefits. You will be asked to provide that information, however, because VA is required to submit claims to insurance carriers for treatment of all non-service-connected conditions. Reimbursement received

The Four Copayments for VA Health Care

Veterans in certain priority groups may have copayments.

- Medication: $8 for each supply of medications for 30 days or less provided on an outpatient basis for non-service-connected conditions. These co-pays apply to Priority Groups 2, 3, 5, 7, and 8.
- Outpatient: Based on preventive care visits (no charge), primary care visits ($15), and specialty care visits ($50). These co-pays apply to veterans in Priority Groups 7 and 8 only.
- Inpatient: The inpatient co-pay for first 90 days of care during a 365-day period is $1024 and drops to $512 for each additional 90 days of care. The Per Diem Charge is $10/day. These co-pays apply to veterans in Priority Groups 7 and 8 only.
  Note: Lower income veterans who live in high-cost areas may qualify for a reduction of 80% of inpatient co-pay charges.
- Long Term Care: Co-pays for Long-Term Care services range start on the 22nd day of care during any 12-month period—there is no co-pay requirement for the first 21 days. Actual co-pay charges will vary from veteran to veteran depending upon financial status. These co-pays apply to veterans in Priority Groups5, 7 and 8 only.

from insurance carriers is retained at the VA health care facility where treatment was received. These funds are used to provide additional health care services to all veterans.

VA Prescriptions

If you are receiving medical treatment, necessary prescriptions will be provided. Service-connected veterans rated 50 percent disabled or more, service-connected veterans receiving medications for a service-connected condition, or non-service-connected veterans who meet the criteria for low income are exempt from the prescription copayment. This income threshold changes annually.

VA Polytrauma Care Program

Polytrauma care is for veterans and returning service members with injuries to more than one physical region or organ system, one of which may be life threatening, and which results in physical, cognitive, psychological, or psychosocial impairments and functional disability.

Take Advantage

For updates on veterans' health services and charges, which change frequently, stay in touch with your local VA office or check www.va.gov /healtheligibility/costs or the Military Report website (www.militaryreport .com) to keep up with the latest revisions to your benefits.

Contact

Information on programs for women veterans is available at the VA Center for Women Veterans at www1.va.gov /womenvet.

Some examples of Polytrauma include:

- Traumatic Brain Injury (TBI)
- Hearing Loss
- Amputations

- Fractures
- Burns
- Visual Impairment

The Department of Veterans Affairs Polytrauma teams provide comprehensive, high-quality, and inter-disciplinary care to patients. Teams of physicians from every relevant field plan and administer an individually tailored rehabilitation plan to help the patient recover as much as possible.

There are four Polytrauma Rehabilitation Centers located in Richmond, VA; Tampa, FL; Minneapolis, MN; and Palo Alto, CA.

Documents You Need to Apply for VA Benefits

Medical Benefits:
- A copy of your discharge certificate, or Certificate of Release, or Discharge from Active Duty, DD Form 214, if available
- Complete VA Form 10-10EZ, Application for Health Benefits, online at www.va.gov/1010ez.htm.

In order to document your service in a theater of combat operations, it will be helpful if you have any of the following:
- A copy of your Leave and Earnings Statement (LES) showing receipt of Hostile Fire or Imminent Danger Pay.
- Receipt of the Armed Forces Expeditionary Medal.
- Kosovo Campaign Medal.
- Global War on Terrorism Expeditionary Medal.
- Afghanistan Campaign Medal.

- Iraq Campaign Medal.
- Southwest Asia Campaign Medal.
- Proof of exemption of federal tax status for hostile fire or imminent danger pay.
- Orders to a theater of combat operations.

Non-Medical Benefits:
- A copy of your discharge certificate, or Certificate of Release, or Discharge from Active Duty, DD Form 214, if available.
- Your VA claim number or Social Security number, if receiving benefits under prior service.
- A copy of all marriage certificates and divorce decrees (if any), for both servicemember and family.
- A copy of any service medical records for disabilities you intend to claim.

In addition there are 17 additional Polytrauma Network Sites:

- Augusta, GA
- Boston, MA
- Bronx, NY
- Cleveland, OH
- Dallas, TX
- Denver, CO
- Hines, IL
- Houston, TX
- Indianapolis, IN
- Lexington, KY
- Philadelphia, PA
- St. Louis, MO
- Seattle, WA
- Syracuse, NY
- Tucson, AZ
- West Los Angeles, CA
- Washington, DC

Special VA Programs

The government has taken care to address special issues and illnesses by offering specific treatment to veterans. Unless otherwise noted, contact your nearest VA facility (see Appendix, page 359) to enroll in any of these programs.

Post Traumatic Stress Disorder (PTSD) Resources

The Department of Veterans Affairs has several initiatives to assist those veterans who are dealing with the affects of PTSD. Vet Centers are one of the best resources for finding these programs. Vet Centers provide readjustment counseling and outreach services to all veterans who served in any combat zone. Services are also available for their family members for military related issues. Veterans have earned these benefits through their service and all are provided at no cost to the veteran or family. In addition you can contact MilitaryOneSource at 1-800-342-9647 for assistance and counseling.

Alcohol and Drug Dependency Treatment

If you are eligible for VA medical care, you can apply for substance-abuse treatment. Veterans without service-connected disabilities whose incomes exceed the threshold for free medical care may be authorized to receive treatment for alcohol and drug dependence if they agree to make a copayment.

Contact

For online resources and services for blind veterans, visit the Blinded Veterans Association at www.bva.org.

Contact

For information about assistance for homeless veterans, call 800-827-1000 or visit www.va.gov /homeless.

Contact

For information on Persian Gulf War veterans' benefits, call 800-749-8387. Veterans who believe they may have been exposed to depleted uranium (DU) can find related information at www.vethealth .cio.med.va.gov /DUProgram.htm.

Contact

Call the Agent Orange Helpline at 800-749-8387, or visit www1.va.gov /agentorange.

Programs for Women Veterans

Gender- specific services and benefits—including breast and pelvic examinations —and preventive care such as contraceptive services, menopause management, Pap smears, reproductive counseling, and mammography are available. VA health care professionals are trained to provide counseling and treatment to women who suffered from personal and sexual assault or harassment during military service. Care is available for any injury, illness, or psychological illness resulting from such trauma. Women Veterans' Coordinators are available at all VA facilities to assist female veterans in seeking treatment and benefits.

Blind Veterans Services

Blind veterans may be eligible for services at a VA medical center or for admission to a VA blind rehabilitation center or clinic for the blind. Services are available at all VA medical facilities through the Visual Impairment Services Coordinator. In addition, blind veterans entitled to receive disability compensation may receive VA aids for the blind.

Programs for Homeless Veterans

VA has many benefits and services to assist eligible homeless veterans, including disability benefits, education, health care, rehabilitation services, residential care, and compensated work therapy.

Treatment for Gulf War Syndrome and Related Illnesses

Veterans who served in the Persian Gulf War are provided with free, comprehensive medical examinations, including laboratory and other diagnostic tests deemed necessary by an examining physician to determine health status. Results of the examinations, which include review of the veteran's military service and exposure history, are entered into special, computerized databases, called registries. These databases assist VA in analyzing the types of health conditions being reported by veterans. Registry participants are advised of the results of their examinations in personal consultations. If veterans wish to participate, they should contact the nearest VA health care facility for an examination. VA operates a toll-free hot line to inform Persian Gulf War Veterans about VA programs, their benefits, and the latest information on benefits specific to those who served in the Gulf War.

Treatment for Agent Orange Exposure

VA provides treatment to any veteran who, while serving in Vietnam, may have been exposed to dioxin or to a toxic substance in an herbicide or defoliant used for military purposes, and who suffered conditions related to such exposure. Documentation and additional information are available at the VA Agent Orange website.

Treatment for Radiation Exposure

Health care services are available for medical conditions related to a veteran's exposure to ionizing radiation from the detonation of a nuclear device in connection with nuclear tests, or specifically with the American occupation of Hiroshima and Nagasaki, Japan, during the period beginning September 11, 1945, and ending July 1, 1946. Veterans exposed to ionizing radiation while on active duty may be eligible for disability compensation if they have disabilities related to that exposure. To determine eligibility, VA considers factors including amount of radiation exposure, duration of exposure, and elapsed time between exposure and onset of the disease.

My HealtheVet Program

My HealtheVet (MHV) is the gateway to veteran health benefits and services. It provides access to trusted health information, links to Federal and VA benefits and resources, the Personal Health Journal, and online VA prescription refill. In addition, MHV registrants will soon be able to view appointments, copay balances, and key portions of their VA medical records online, and much more! My HealtheVet is a powerful tool to help you better understand and manage your health.

Military Matters

VA has launched a national campaign to locate veterans exposed to mustard gas or the chemical agent Lewisite during their military service. Any veterans who suspect they were exposed to either substance during their service are strongly encouraged to contact VA by calling 800-749-8387.

VA Provides Chiropractic Care

Good news to those veterans who are suffering from back pain caused by neuromusculoskeletal conditions. VA medical centers and clinics may offer chiropractic spinal manipulative therapy for problems of the spine. However, this service is not offered at all VA facilities. In areas distant from the locations that offer this service, eligible veterans may be able to receive chiropractic care through VA's outpatient fee-basis program after a referral by their primary care provider, and prior authorization by the department. See your primary care provider at your nearest VA medical facility for assistance.

CHAMPVA

The Civilian Health and Medical Program of the Department of Veterans Affairs (CHAMPVA) is a health benefits program in which the Department of Veterans Affairs (VA) shares the cost of certain health care services and supplies with eligible beneficiaries. CHAMPVA is available to the spouse or child of a veteran who has either been rated permanently and totally disabled for a service-connected disability, died from a VA-rated service connected disability, was at the time of death rated permanently and totally disabled, or who died in the line of duty.

More detailed information can be found on the VA CHAMPVA website at www.va.gov/hac/forbeneficiaries/champva.

Part Four

The
Benefits
Advantage

A s a servicemember, in addition to pay, education benefits, and health care coverage, you've earned a wide variety of additional benefits. For example, did you know that you can travel internationally for next to nothing on a Department of Defense (DoD) aircraft? Or that financial and legal protections are in place to help you if you are a reserve or guard member called to active service?

This chapter is dedicated to the less well-known benefits of military service. Each year, millions in benefits go unused because people don't take advantage of these valuable programs, including military travel and lodging benefits, legal protections and entitlements, and burial and survivor benefits.

Military Travel and Lodging Benefits

The military offers a wide range of accommodation for travelers no matter what service branch you're affiliated with, and you can fly at no cost to reach all those destinations by using a special travel benefit.

The Benefits Advantage at a Glance

New Benefits Related to the War on Terror

If you are an active-duty servicemember or a member of the Reserve or Guard called to serve in Operations Enduring Freedom or Iraqi Freedom, you should be aware of new and improved benefits that are in place to support you and your family. These benefits are available in addition to the other benefits covered in this chapter, and have been either created or updated since September 11, 2001.

Education
New GI Bill Benefits for Activated Guard and
    Reserve (Chapter 1607) 191

Health Care
TRICARE Select for Guard and Reserve 113
VA Health Care and Mental Health Care 127

Insurance
Increased Servicemembers Group Life
    Insurance (SGLI) 29
Disability Insurance for Wounded
    Servicemembers 35

Legal Protection
Enhanced protection under SCRA 151

Veteran Assistance
Veterans Employment Training Service (VETS)
    303
Military Severely Injured Career Center 299

Survivor Benefits
Increased Death Gratuity Payment 176

Space Available Flights

Space Available Flight, better known as Space A or military hops, is a unique privilege provided to servicemembers, retirees, and their families. Eligible passengers can fill unused seats on DoD-owned or -controlled aircraft once all the passengers on duty and cargo have been accommodated. In other words, you may travel to hundreds of locations around the country and the world, for a fraction of what a commercial airline would cost.

Space A flights can be a good value, but you need to do some research to decide on your flight. There is no single flight-booking engine that shows flight schedules for military flights; Space A travelers must do the research themselves. In the post-September 11 world, flight information is more restricted, which makes travel planning more challenging. In addition, Space A passengers are never guaranteed a seat—priority is always given to operational requirements, military personnel under orders, etc. Space A travelers often spend a great deal of time in terminals waiting to see if they can get on a flight. Finally, it

TIP:
Be prepared to purchase a commercial airline ticket in case you find yourself stranded due to cancelled flights or other emergencies that may arise while traveling Space A..

Take Advantage

Using the closest airport for Space A travel may not necessarily be the quickest route. Going through major terminals may get you to your destination faster than if you fly directly out of a smaller terminal. Some of the major Space A hubs are Dover Air Force Base, McChord, Travis Air Force Base, Norfolk Naval Station, Ramstein, Rhein Main, and Mildenhall.

Take Advantage

Once accepted for a flight, a Space A passenger cannot be bumped by another Space A passenger, regardless of category.

Take Advantage

Have a backup travel plan. Most military flights make several stops on the way to and from the final destination, and conditions may warrant unscheduled changes.

is very difficult to travel with family—traveling Space A often means hitching a ride on aircraft not designed for passengers (cold, noisy, and without an in-flight movie). For these reasons, Space A is often appropriate only for people with a bit of time on their hands and a penchant for adventure. That said, if you know how to use Space A and have time on your hands, you might be able to use this valuable benefit to stretch your vacation dollars and venture to interesting places.

Space A Eligibility

The first thing to understand is your eligibility and your Space A category. Space A is only available to personnel with a Department of Defense or Uniformed Services ID card. Unfortunately, most veterans (non-retirees) are not eligible to use Space A. Under a new program, family members, in the company of servicemembers, can fly between stateside locations.

Your Space A category is essentially your priority level on the flight. If there is room on a qualifying Space A flight, base operations will assign the seats in order of category—ranging from category 1 (emergency leave) down to the lowest priority, category 6 (Reserve/Guard, retirees, dependents, ROTC, etc). Many nuances are involved in assigning categories, and you should research your unique circumstance. If you are on active duty, to qualify you *must* be on leave or pass status at the time you register for Space A travel, *and* while you're waiting to be accepted.

New Space A Regulations – Spouses and children of military personnel deployed 120 days or longer may now use military transport in CONUS, to/from CONUS, and within/between theater, provided they have a verification letter from the military member's commander. Visit www.military.com/spacea for more details.

Category I: Emergency Leave This includes emergency round-trip travel in connection with serious illness, death, or impending death of a member of the immediate family of the following:

- Uniformed servicemembers with emergency status indicated in leave orders.

- United States citizen civilian employees of the DoD (and their families) when stationed overseas.

- Full-time, paid personnel of the American Red Cross serving with United States military services overseas; or within the continental United States when accompanied by their sponsor, if the emergency exists there.

- Uniformed services family members whose sponsors are stationed within the continental United States and the emergency exists overseas.

Category II: Environmental Morale Leave This includes servicemembers on environmental and morale leave and accompanying family members. Military personnel must also be on ordinary leave. This category includes DoD-dependent school teachers and their accompanying family members in Environmental Morale Leave (EML) status.

Category III: Ordinary Leave and Certain Unaccompanied Dependents

- Members of the uniformed services in an ordinary or reenlistment leave status and uniformed services patients on convalescent leave.

- Military personnel traveling on permissive temporary duty orders for house-hunting may travel within the continental United States and internationally, and may be accompanied by one family member (with a valid identification card). For more details on family member ID cards, see the Money chapter.

- Foreign-exchange servicemembers on permanent duty with the DoD, when on leave status.

- Unaccompanied dependents of sponsors deployed for greater than 365 days.

    This privilege does not apply to travel of dependents to or from a sponsor's restricted or unaccompanied tour location. It applies only to round-trip travel to an overseas area or the continental United States along with the sponsor.

Category IV: Unaccompanied Dependents on Environmental Morale Leave

- Unaccompanied family members (18 years or older) traveling on Environmental Morale Leave orders.

- DoD-dependent school teachers or family members (accompanied or unaccompanied) in an Environmental Morale Leave status year-round.

- Unaccompanied dependents of sponsors deployed for 120 days or more.

Category V: Permissive Temporary Duty and Students

- Students whose parents are stationed in Alaska or Hawaii.

- Military personnel traveling on permissive temporary duty orders for activities other than house-hunting.

- Command-sponsored dependents (18 years or older) of servicemembers who are stationed overseas. Such individuals may travel unaccompanied from the sponsor's duty location to the continental United States and return. Dependents must have command-sponsored documentation signed by the commander verifying command sponsorship.

Take Advantage

Space A schedules and locations are subject to change. Visit John D's Space A Travel Index to get the latest information on space A travel. www.spacea.net/. You can also sign-up for Space A flights at www.takeahop.org.

Contact

Sign up for Space A travel online at www.spacea.info/signup. For the full list of Space A gateways (bases that support Space A travel) and fax information, go to www.takeahop.org

Take Advantage

When you apply for Space A travel, select "all" as your choice for a "fifth destination" to discover unscheduled, unique travel opportunities.

- Non-command sponsored dependents of active duty, permissive orders, TDY (Excluding house Hunting).

Category VI: Retirees, Guard, and Reserve

- National Guard, Reserve components, members of the Ready Reserve, and members of the Standby Reserve who are on the Active-Duty Status List.

- Retired military members who are issued an ID card and are eligible to receive retired or retainer pay.

- Family members (with a valid identification card) of retired members when accompanied by a sponsor.

How to Sign Up for Space A Flights

There are several ways to sign up for Space A. One option is to complete Air Mobility Command Form 140 and fax it to the gateway you intend to embark from, or you can sign up at any of the gateways from which you could travel. Once registered, your name remains on the Space A flights register for 60 days, or for the duration of your travel orders/leave authorization, whichever occurs first. After you register, an email is sent both to the selected departure location and to your email address. The date and time of your registration determines your selection status for all flights to your chosen destination. When you get to your final destination, be sure to sign up immediately for your return trip. This will give you the best date and time, as you are competing for seats on those flights.

Remote Sign-Up. Once you have selected a gateway, you must register. You can register either in person, or by e-mail, fax or online at www.takeahop .org.

Guard and Reserve members. If you have DD Form 2 (Red) identification and DD Form 1853 (available at www.military.com/forms), you may fly to, from, and between Alaska, Hawaii, Puerto Rico, the Virgin Islands, Guam, American Samoa, and the continental United States. Additionally, when on active duty, members may fly anywhere overseas.

You should be prepared to provide copies of all travel documents. During registration, you will be asked to select up to five destination countries—and may opt for one of the five to be "all," giving you the chance to fly to unique, and potentially unexpected, destinations. Passengers remain on the registration list for up to 60 days or until selected for travel. You should be ready to go, and in the vicinity of the terminal, during "show time"—often two hours prior to departure. Note: Not all terminals honor the 60-day sign-up.

All Space A passengers need appropriate documentation prior to travel. The most commonly required documents include Armed Forces Identification

Take Advantage

You can learn from the travel experiences of others, visit Dirk's Space A Message board to get the inside scoop on making the most of Space A travel at www.pepperd.com.

Contact

Air Mobility Command Form 140: www.military.com /spacea.

Cards, leave documents (as necessary), passports (with visas, as appropriate), and immunization records. While travelers can generally depart the continental United States (CONUS) from both civilian and military terminals, re-entry into the United States for non–active-duty personnel (those traveling on passports) may require that the reentry terminal have appropriate immigration facilities, which generally means returning to a commercial gateway (civilian airport).

Military Matters

If you are a passenger and your leave authorization has expired, you will not be able to register for Space A unless a leave extension has been approved. A verbal confirmation is normally acceptable. Passengers already on the Space A register who request a leave extension are required to notify passenger service personnel prior to their leave expiration date. Your name will remain on the space-available register as long as you are pursuing a leave extension. Passengers will not be selected or moved until an extension has been approved.

Look Up Flight Schedules

Because of increased tension and terrorist activities throughout the world, most flight scheduling information is no longer posted on the Internet. The exception is the Joint Operational Support Airlift Center (OSA) site at https://josac.transcom.mil/newfltschedules.htm, which allows you to check the daily OSA Space Available Flight schedule and a searchable OSA flight schedule. These schedules, however, can only be accessed from a military computer and a Common Access Card (CAC).

More About Space A Flights

Uniforms. Currently, all the services permit appropriate civilian attire on DoD-owned or controlled aircraft; you don't have to travel in uniform.

Baggage. As a Space A traveler, you may check two pieces of luggage at 70 pounds each per person. Space A travelers cannot pay to take excess baggage, but family members traveling together may pool their baggage allowance as long as the total does not exceed the total allowance. You may hand-carry only what fits under your seat or in the overhead compartment, if available.

Travel light. Take only essentials. Do not place valuables, medicine, or important documents in your checked baggage. Be sure your name and current address are on and inside your bags. Air Mobility Command terminals have baggage ID tags available for your use.

Space A costs. Some terminals must collect a head tax or a federal inspection fee from Space A passengers on commercial contract missions. Passengers usually may purchase meals at a nominal fee while traveling on military aircraft. Meal service on Air Mobility Command Category B full planeload charters is complimentary.

Insider Advice for Space A Travel

You are likely aware of the uncomfortable conditions on most military flights. If you are traveling with family members, make sure they know what to expect. Be prepared for the flight to be extra hot or cold, sometimes both. Always bring a jacket, no matter the current weather outdoors. The flights are usually cold due to the altitude, and in any case you may be diverted to a place much colder than your eventual destination.

Bring snacks, plenty of reading material, a personal music player, laptop, or other portable entertainment for the waiting period in the terminal and the flight. To be a successful Space A traveler, it helps to relax and be patient. Think of Space A as an adventure, and be open to changes in your itinerary. Going in with the right attitude can make all the difference.

Military Lodging

Another great benefit of military service is that you have many convenient and inexpensive lodging options. Thousands of rooms are available at temporary housing facilities, hotels, resorts, and guesthouses around the world. The two major categories of military lodging are on-base lodging and Armed Forces Recreation Centers.

Each branch of the military offers its own special lodging styles and locations. You do not have to be affiliated with a particular service to use the service's lodging. Whenever you travel, use the following information to take advantage of cost-effective lodging opportunities along the way. Military lodging services are generally available to:

• Military and civilian travelers on official orders.

• Air Force, Army, Coast Guard, Marine Corps, Navy, federal government, and DoD personnel on temporary duty.

• Servicemembers and their families.

- Military retirees and their families.

- Widows, widowers, and dependents of retired military personnel.

- Reserve and National Guard members and their families.

- Foreign military (on orders).

- Medical in-patients and family of the seriously ill.

- Medical out-patients.

- Official guests and visitors of the command.

Air Force Lodging

Staying at Air Force lodging is a simple process. First, choose where you want to stay. Available online, the Air Force Lodging Directory provides lodging information for each Air Force facility around the world. The directory also lists extensive information on:

- Contact / reservation information

- Airport information.

- Dining and shopping facilities.

- Other available amenities.

After you have checked out the directory, make your reservations by calling the toll-free reservation number listed in the margin.

Army Lodging

You can make reservations for Army lodging facilities worldwide, including the Armed Forces Recreation Center—Europe at the Army Morale, Welfare and Recreation (MWR) website. Army lodging units, temporary housing, and guesthouses are located at 80 locations in the United States, Korea, Japan, Belgium, Germany, Italy, Alaska, and Hawaii. They can all be reached with one toll-free call.

Coast Guard Lodging

The Coast Guard Morale, Well-Being, and Recreation site offers a directory of lodging choices. Active-duty military members and their dependents have first priority at the facilities, but a full listing of eligible patrons authorized to use these facilities is provided in the Coast Guard MWR Manual located on the website.

The Coast Guard MWR Recreational Lodging Facilities guide provides information for military personnel and their families to choose a facility. If you have

Contact

The DoD now offers DoD Lodging Net, a new website dedicated Air Force and Navy lodging facilities. On the web at: http://dodlodging.net

Contact

For army lodging, call 800-GO-ARMY-1 (800-462-7691), or go to www.armymwr.com.

Contact

For a directory of Coast Guard lodging options, http://www.uscg.mil/mwr/lodging/Lodging.asp, or www.uscg.mil/mwr/Cottages/RecreationCottages.htm for the Coast Guard Recreational Lodging Facilities guide.

Contact

For more information, visit www.hqmc.usmc. mil/lffweb.nsf and click on the link for Marine Corps Transient Billeting Quarters. For Marine Corps Temporary Lodging facilities, go to http://www.usmc-mccs.org/lodging/index.cfm. You can find phone and reservation information for each location on the website.

Take Advantage

If government lodging is certified "not available," ask the Commercial Travel Office on your installation to book a Navy Elite hotel for you. The Navy Elite Lodging Plan offers three different types of hotel accommodations—economy, mid-priced, and deluxe.

questions about specific housing locations, we recommend that you ask by phone or over the Internet when you make reservations. Some Coast Guard facilities allow reservations as early as three months in advance, while others require as little as seven days' notice.

Marine Corps Lodging

Marine Corps Transient Billeting Quarters provides temporary housing for the following people:

- Personnel (military and civilian) traveling on official temporary assignment duty or temporary duty orders.

- Personnel (military and civilian) traveling with a Permanent Change of Station status and their dependents.

- Personnel in a nonduty status (includes retirees, official guests of the command, etc.).

Reservations are accepted on a first-come, first-served basis for all authorized patrons. Those who do not make reservations are housed on a space-available basis.

Another option is short-term Marine Corps housing accommodations. A full list of such accommodations is available at the Marine Corps Temporary Lodging Facilities site.

Those eligible for this type of housing include:

- Military personnel and their families who are without housing due to Permanent Change of Station orders.

- Military members, Ready Reservists, and Department of Defense civilian personnel on temporary duty.

- Military personnel, retirees, Ready Reservists, Retired Reserves, and Department of Defense civilian personnel, their families, and guests of military personnel in nonduty status, as well as other authorized patrons.

Navy Lodging

Navy Lodges provide accommodations for active-duty, Reserve, Guard, retirees and their families. The Navy Lodge website offers a complete listing of all Navy Lodge facilities in the United States and abroad. Reservations for Navy lodging are accepted for all eligible personnel on a first-come, first-served basis. Reservations and room assignments are made without regard to rank.

In the U.S. and overseas, Navy bachelor quarters provide yet another option. A complete directory of such quarters is available at the Navy Bachelor Housing website. Navy transient facilities are for authorized military and DoD civilians and military retirees on official travel orders. Nonduty military and retirees may stay at these facilities on a space-available basis.

Special Military Lodging

The military and non-profit groups feature clubs and recreation centers in addition to the facilities already described. Some of the more prominent ones are mentioned below.

Shades of Green

Located within the Walt Disney World Resort in Florida, Shades of Green is an Armed Forces Recreation Center (AFRC). The newly expanded Shades of Green is the only AFRC located in the continental U.S. Shades of Green is a true resort destination, offering accommodations and amenities available to other Disney guests.

Hale Koa

Hale Koa, or House of the Warrior, is a world-class 817-room resort hotel for military personnel in Honolulu, Waikiki Beach. It opened on October 25, 1975, and now has more than one million visitors annually. Prices are affordable for military members and their families.

The Marines Memorial Club and Hotel

Established in 1946 as a living memorial to Marines who lost their lives in the Pacific during World War II, the nonprofit Marines' Memorial Association offers membership to former and retired members of all branches of the U.S. Armed Forces. The Marines Memorial Club and Hotel, located in downtown San Francisco, provides a full range of amenities in a building that dates to 1926. The famous Aviator Bar offers spectacular downtown views.

New Sanno Hotel

The New Sanno Hotel, operated by the U.S. Navy, is located in downtown Tokyo, Japan. It offers a swimming pool, recreational facilities, a Navy Exchange, and other services for military travelers.

Contact

You can make reservations through the Navy Lodge Central Reservation Center via www.Navy-Lodge.com (48 hours in advance required) or the toll-free number, 800-NAVY-INN (800-628-9466).

Contact

The websites for special military lodging are:

www.shadesofgreen.org

www.halekoa.com

www.marineclub.com

www.thenewsanno.com

www.dragonhilllodge.com/main.html

www.edelweisslodgeandresort.com

Take Advantage

Many "civilian" hotels and resorts offer special discounts for service-members and their families. See www.military.com/discounts to check out the latest offers available. Also check when you are making reservations.

Dragon Hill Lodge

The Dragon Hill Lodge is located in Seoul, South Korea, and operated by the U.S. Army for personnel assigned to or employed by the U.S. forces in Korea, their family members, and guests. Its amenities include a fitness center, specialized shopping mall, and restaurants, lounges, and pubs. Reservations are accepted 24 hours a day.

Edelweiss Lodge and Resort

The Edelweiss Lodge and Resort offers a vacation retreat designed for active-duty servicemembers, DoD civilians, and retirees. Located in Garmisch-Partenkirchen, Germany, in the Bavarian Alps, the resort includes a conference center and fitness club, and also retiree vacation packages.

Legal Rights, Entitlements, and Benefits

As a servicemember or veteran, you have many legal rights, entitlements, and benefits. These include financial and legal protection when you are mobilized or deployed, and assistance with personal legal matters. Key legal protections include:

- The Servicemembers Civil Relief Act (SCRA) for active-duty and certain reserve and guard members.

- United Services Employment and Reemployment Rights Act (USERRA) for reserve and guard members.

- Legal Assistance Entitlement for active-duty, reserve and guard members and retirees.

The Servicemembers Civil Relief Act (SCRA)

Today, more than 300,000 men and women in uniform are deployed overseas, and mobilization levels are at their highest point since World War II. Beyond the considerable operational challenges faced by military personnel, periods of prolonged conflict often create serious personal and financial challenges. Fortunately, there are resources, support networks, and laws designed to support military members and their families. In fact, new legislation has strengthened protection for those serving.

In 2003 SCRA significantly strengthened the civil protections afforded to active-duty (and recalled) military personnel. An update to the older Soldiers and Sailors Civil Relief Act of 1940, SCRA was enacted to allow servicemembers to "devote their full energy to the defense needs of the nation" by providing significant civil, legal, and financial protections. In other words, it aims to allow military personnel freedom to serve without experiencing undue worry about leases, civil proceedings, and excessive interest, among other possible burdens.

SCRA covers all active-duty personnel including reservists and guard members who are called to active duty. The protection begins on the date you enter active duty, and generally terminates within 30 to 90 days after you are discharged from active duty. Below are the more important benefits of SCRA.

Take Advantage

SCRA is not just for servicemembers who are being activated, mobilized, or deployed—it applies to all servicemembers on active duty. Check with your military legal assistance office to see how SCRA applies to you.

6 Percent Maximum Rate of Interest

One of SCRA's most significant provisions is that it limits interest that may be collected on your debts to 6 percent APR (annual percentage rate) during the period of active duty. No interest above 6 percent can accrue for credit obligations incurred, nor can that excess interest become due once you leave active duty. Instead, any amount above 6 percent is permanently forgiven. Furthermore, your monthly payment must be reduced by the amount of interest saved during the period covered. *This protection applies only to financial obligations you incur* before *you go on active duty.*

Legal Proceedings, Trials, and Judgments

Default judgment. If you do not officially respond to a lawsuit in time, a court issues a default judgment. If a default judgment is entered against you during your active-duty service, or within 90 days thereafter, SCRA allows you to reopen that default judgment and set it aside, as long as you:

- Make an application to the court within 90 days after leaving active duty.

- Show that you were judged unfairly by not being able to appear in person.

- Have a good and legal defense for the claims against you.

Remember, you must apply to the court within 90 days after your release from active duty.

Take Advantage

Most SCRA protection begins the day you receive your orders to active duty or deployment. You should expect to present a copy of those orders to whomever you ask for any right or benefit provided for under the act.

Take Advantage

If you are suing or being sued in a civil—not a criminal—case, your commander can ask the judge to temporarily delay the proceedings until you can appear.

Stay of execution of judgments/attachments. The court may stay (postpone) the execution of judgments, court actions, attachments, and garnishments if action is brought against you while you are on active duty, or if you were in service within the last 90 days. If you request a stay, it must be granted unless the court finds your ability to comply with the order or judgment is not affected by your military status.

Stay of proceedings. If you are involved in civil litigation, you can request a delay in proceedings if you can show that your military responsibilities would interfere with proper representation in court. This provision is invoked most often by servicemembers who are on an extended deployment, or stationed overseas.

Statute of limitations. Your time in service cannot be used to compute time limits for bringing any action or proceeding by or against you, whether in court or elsewhere. This does not apply, however, to time limitations established under federal tax laws.

Health Insurance Reinstatement

If you are called up to active duty, your health care needs are covered by the military's medical facilities. In addition, your family members become eligible for coverage (see page 87).

During your active-duty service, you may want to suspend any civilian coverage you may have had prior to entering service. If you do this, SCRA will require your civilian insurance company to reinstate your coverage when you complete your active duty. Your provider will have to write you a policy, and it cannot refuse to cover most preexisting conditions.

Installment Contracts and Mortgage Foreclosures

Contact

For information on how to obtain Soldiers and Sailors Certificates, which are often required before a default judgment may be set aside in a lawsuit, go to www.military.com /SCRA.

If you signed an installment payment plan to buy real estate or personal property prior to your entering active duty, you are protected under SCRA against contract termination or foreclosure if your ability to make payments is affected by your military service. To qualify, you must have paid (prior to active duty) a deposit or an installment under the contract. The seller is then prohibited from exercising any right or option to rescind or terminate the contract, to resume possession of the property for nonpayment of any installment due, or to breach the terms of the contract, unless authorized by the court.

SCRA also protects you against foreclosures of mortgages, as long as the following facts are established:

- The relief is sought on an obligation secured by a mortgage, trust deed, or other security in the nature of a mortgage on either real or personal property.

- The obligation originated prior to active duty.

- You or a family member owned the property prior to your active duty.

- You or a family member still owns the property at the time relief is sought.

- The ability to meet the financial obligation is materially affected by the servicemember's active-duty obligation.

Contact

For more information on how to apply for deferment of your private life insurance premiums, call the VA life insurance service branch toll-free at 800-669-8477.

Life Insurance Protection

SCRA also permits you to request deferment of private life insurance premiums for the period of military service and two years thereafter. You must apply for deferment of premiums through the Department of Veterans Affairs.

If VA approves your request, the federal government will guarantee your payments, your policy will continue in force, and you will have up to two years after release from military service to repay all premiums and interest. SCRA increases the amount of insurance this program will cover to $250,000 or the maximum limit of Servicemembers Group Life Insurance, whichever is greater.

Eviction Protection

Although SCRA does not excuse you from paying rent, it does give you some relief and protection from eviction if your military service makes payment difficult. To evict you or your dependents, your landlord must obtain a court order. This means that the court must determine that you cannot pay rent because your service pay isn't enough to cover it.

If you are unable to pay rent due to military service, the court *may* delay an eviction three months (unless the court decides on a shorter or longer period in the interest of justice) when you or your dependents request it. The requirements are:

(1) The landlord is attempting eviction during a period in which you are in military service or after receipt of orders to report to duty.

(2) The rental is used for housing by your spouse, children, or other dependents.

(3) The agreed rent does not exceed $2,615 per month. (The rent ceiling is subject to increases in future years.)

Take Advantage

If you think being called to active military service has reduced your ability to meet your financial obligations, contact your nearest legal assistance office to see if SCRA protection applies. For more, see www.military.com/law.

If you are threatened with eviction for failure to pay rent, you should see a legal assistance attorney.

Termination of Lease

You can terminate a lease for property occupied for dwelling, professional, business, agricultural, or similar purposes, as long as you have served on active duty for at least 90 days and the following two conditions are met:

- You entered into the lease before you started active duty.

- You or your dependents have occupied the leased premises for the purposes mentioned above.

To terminate your lease, you must deliver written notice to the landlord after your call to active duty or receipt of orders for active duty. Verbal notice is not enough. The effective date of termination is determined as follows:

- For month-to-month rentals—following the date of notice of termination, 30 days after the next rental payment is due. For example, if the rent is due on the first day of each month, and notice is given on July 30, then the next rental payment is due and payable on September 1, making the effective date of termination 30 days later, on October 1.

- For all other leases—on the last day of the next month after proper notice is given. So if the lease requires a yearly rental and proper notice of termination is given on July 20, the effective date of termination would be August 31.

You must pay rent for only those months before the lease is terminated. If rent has been paid in advance, the landlord must prorate and refund the unearned portion. If a security deposit was required, it must be returned to you upon termination of the lease.

Taxation

Through SCRA you are protected from a form of double taxation that can occur if your spouse works and is taxed in a state other than the state in which he or she maintains permanent legal residence. SCRA also prevents states from using the income you earn in determining a spouse's tax rate when he or she does not maintain permanent legal residence in that state. Finally, under certain conditions SCRA will allow you to defer paying taxes for up to 180 days after your release from service, if your inability to pay taxes is caused by military service. (For more information on taxes, see page 12.)

To learn more about these or other provisions of the Servicemembers' Civil

Military Matters

SCRA lease protection extends to automobiles leased for personal or business use by you and your dependents provided the lease began before you went on active duty. You can cancel such a lease if you receive active-duty orders for a period of 180 days or more.

In addition, an automobile lease entered into while you are on active duty may be terminated if you receive permanent change of station orders to a location outside the continental United States or deployment orders for a period of 180 days or more.

Relief Act, contact your unit or installation legal assistance office. You can also read the full text of the law online at www.military.com/SCRA.

Take Advantage

If your home of record (not necessarily where you live today) taxes military pay, you will have to pay those taxes. If you get assigned to another state, you remain legally a resident of your home of record state. The state to which the military assigns you cannot tax your military pay.

Uniformed Services Employment and Reemployment Rights Act (USERRA)

Reserve and guard members are increasingly confronted with the same challenges as their active-duty counterparts, as well as additional complexities arising from mobilization, including employer, financial, and family support issues. Fortunately, you can benefit from the same laws and support networks as active-duty personnel (including SCRA). You are also eligible for special protections designed to ease the burden of life—most notably, the Uniformed Services Employment and Reemployment Rights Act (USERRA).

One provision under USERRA is a right of reemployment with your civilian employer. Updated in 1994 in response to issues encountered at the end of the first Gulf War, the law requires most employers to reemploy demobilized servicemembers in positions comparable to those they held before being called up. The law also provides for returning employees to benefit from accrued seniority and additional training, if necessary. USERRA applies to voluntary as well as involuntary service, in peacetime as well as wartime.

Eligibility for USERRA Coverage

You are eligible for USERRA if you have been absent from a position of employment because you performed voluntary or involuntary duty in a uniformed service, including:

Take Advantage

Under USERRA, you are not required to provide your employer with a copy of military orders when you give notice for an upcoming period of service, but it's a wise idea to provide such documentation.

- Active duty (including reserve and guard members who have been called up).

- Active duty for training.

- Initial active duty for training.

- Inactive-duty training.

- Full-time National Guard duty.

- Absence from work for an examination to determine a person's fitness for any of the above types of duty.

- Funeral honors duty performed by the National Guard or Reserve.

In order to have reemployment rights following a period of service in the uniformed services, you must meet all five of these eligibility criteria:

- You must have held a civilian job.

- You must have informed your employer that you were leaving the job for service in the uniformed services.

- The period of service must not have exceeded five years.

- You must have been released from service under honorable conditions.

- You must report back to your civilian employer in a timely manner or submit a timely application for reemployment. Remember, by law your employer cannot treat you as if you were applying for a new job.

Take Advantage

All your benefits under USERRA depend on your reporting back to your employer or reapplying for employment with your former employer *as soon as possible* after demobilization. If you delay too long, you may no longer qualify for USERRA protection. For a sample application for reemployment, see www.military.com/USERRA.

Reemployment Protection

When you are released from military service, USERRA stipulates that you must be promptly reemployed, in the following order of priority:

1. In the job you would have held had you remained continuously employed (also known as the "escalator" principle), or a position of equivalent seniority, status, and pay so long as you are qualified for the job, or could become qualified after reasonable efforts by the employer to qualify you.

2. If you cannot become qualified for the position in priority 1, then in your pre-service position so long as you are qualified for the job or could become qualified after reasonable efforts by the employer.

3. If you cannot become qualified for the position in either priority 1 or 2, then in any other position that is the nearest approximation of priority 1 for which you are qualified, with full seniority.

If you're on active duty less than 31 days, you must return to work immediately upon your return. If you're on active duty between 31 and 180 days, you must apply for reemployment within 14 days after release from service. If you're on active duty for more than 180 days, you have up to 90 days after release from service to apply for reemployment.

Your employer is not required to reemploy you if any of the following conditions apply:

- The employer's circumstances have changed so as to make such reemployment impossible or unreasonable.

- Reemployment of you would impose an undue hardship on the employer.

- You had left to serve in the uniformed services for a brief, nonrecurrent period, and there was no reasonable expectation that your employment would continue indefinitely or for a significant period.

If you submit an application for reemployment, you are required to provide documentation to the employer only if the employer requests it. However, in all cases, you may find it helpful to provide documentation to establish that:

- Your application for reemployment is timely.

- You have not exceeded the time limitations for reemployment.

- Your entitlement to USERRA benefits has not been terminated.

Employer Discrimination

If you are eligible for USERRA, you cannot be denied initial employment, reemployment, retention in employment, promotion, or any benefit of employment by an employer based on your military obligations. Your employer also cannot discriminate against or take any adverse employment action against you if you do any of the following:

- Take action to enforce your protection under USERRA.

- Testify or make a statement in or in connection with any proceeding under USERRA.

- Assist or participate in an investigation under USERRA.

- Exercise a right provided for in USERRA.

Take Advantage
Under USERRA, your employer is not permitted to make you spend vacation time for your military training or service.

Take Advantage
If you feel you have been discriminated against in your right to reemployment or veterans hiring preference, you can contact the Department of Labor at 866-4-USA-DOL (866-487-2365), or Employer Support of the Guard and Reserve Ombudsman at 800-336-4590.

Contact

You can read a complete overview of USERRA at www.military.com /USERRA.

In short, the employer itself must prove that any discriminatory action on its part is *not* due to your military obligations.

Health Care Protection

USERRA also provides that if you are on active duty for more than 30 days, you may elect to continue your health coverage if you (or your dependents) had a health plan through your employer, and you are absent from your job due to military service. As a maximum period of coverage, you and your dependents would get the shorter of these two options:

• The 18-month period beginning on the date on which your absence begins.

• The day after the date on which you fail to apply for or return to a position of employment.

At no time can you be required to pay more than 102 percent of the full premium for coverage. If your active-duty period in the service was for 30 days or fewer, you cannot be required to pay more than the normal employee share of any premium.

On your return from service, your health insurance coverage must be reinstated without any waiting period or exclusions for preexisting conditions, other than waiting periods or exclusions that would have applied had you not been absent for uniformed service.

This rule does not apply to the coverage of any illness or injury determined by VA to have been incurred or aggravated during performance of service in uniform.

Employer Support for Guard and Reserve

With the current national defense strategy, the Reserve and Guard will be spending more time away from the workplace defending the nation. This increases the chance that issues may develop between you and your civilian employer regarding job rights, reemployment, and any other military-service-related issues. The National Committee for Employer Support of the Guard and Reserve (ESGR) can help.

Take Advantage

If your employer is doing *more than the law requires* to support your National Guard or Reserve participation, you can nominate your employer for an award through the ESGR website at www.esgr.org.

ESGR has a network of volunteers and committees located in each state and the District of Columbia, Guam, Puerto Rico, the Virgin Islands and Europe. ESGR's programs are directed at U.S. employers, employees, and communities to ensure understanding and appreciation of the role of the National Guard and Reserve in the context of the DoD Total Force Policy. ESGR services include:

Employer Recognition and Awards Programs. All employer recognition and awards originate from nominations by individual Reserve component members. Employer awards include the Patriot Award, the Local ESGR Committee Chair's Award, the PRO PATRIA Award, and the Employer Support Freedom Awards.

Ombudsman Services. This program provides information, informal mediation, and referral services to resolve conflicts between servicemembers and employers. ESGR volunteers and the Ombudsmen of the national staff are available to respond promptly to inquiries and conflicts presented by employees or employers.

Resolving Employer Conflicts

If you are a reserve or guard member who is having a conflict with your employer, your first approach should be to go to your employer. Often, talking the situation through in a calm, respectful manner can lead to a reasonable solution.

If you can't come up with a workable solution by just talking with your employer on your own, go to your unit commander or senior enlisted advisor for advice and support. In some situations, your unit commander may be better able to explain the situation to your employer and to suggest compromises or alternatives that will satisfy everyone's needs.

You can also contact ESGR Ombudsmen Services through your local ESGR Committee or the National ESGR Headquarters. Though ESGR is not an enforcement agency and does not offer legal counsel or advice, most employer-employee conflicts can be resolved without referral to the Department of Labor for formal investigation through this informal process.

Your Legal Assistance Entitlement

There will probably come a time when you need legal advice, whether it involves drafting a will, ethics counseling, tax issues, just wanting to know your rights, or filing a veteran claim or appeal. Fortunately, the military provides free legal assistance to its members. Based on availability, most legal assistance offices on base can provide advice concerning personal, nonbusiness, civil legal problems, including preparation of legal documents and taxes, and assistance in drafting letters. Although each service has its own legal branch, and most military bases have legal assistance officers, you can request assistance from the legal assistance office of any military branch.

Eligibility for Armed Forces legal assistance is established through federal law, subject to available legal staff resources. Legal assistance in connection with personal civil legal affairs can be provided to the following persons:

Contact

National Committee for Employer Support of the Guard and Reserve
1555 Wilson Blvd. Suite 200
Arlington, VA 22209-2405
800-336-4590
www.esgr.org.

Mission One: 800-336-4590.

Take Advantage

If you have a question about your employment rights, government experts suggest you start by contacting ESGR. This is not only your best option for speedy resolution; it also protects all levels of appeal if they are needed.

Contact

Check out the ESGR website at www.esgr.org. It has fact sheets, more information on USERRA, and links to related sites. Ombudsman Services can be reached toll-free at 800-336-4590.

1. Members of the Armed Forces who are on active duty.

2. Members and former members entitled to retired or retainer pay or equivalent pay.

3. Officers of the commissioned corps of the Public Health Service who are on active duty or entitled to retired or equivalent pay.

4. Members of the Reserve and Guard who are called to active duty for more than 30 days are eligible for assistance for twice the time they served on active duty. If you are activated for 30 days, for example, you can request assistance for up to 60 days after being released.

5. Dependents of members and former members described in the above four examples.

Some military offices may restrict legal assistance to certain categories, depending on resources and expertise. Each office may also provide legal assistance in unique subject areas. In most cases, legal assistance attorneys can do the following:

- Serve as advocate and counsel for an eligible client.

- Prepare and sign correspondence on behalf of an eligible client.

- Negotiate with another party or that party's attorney.

- Prepare legal documents.

- Draft powers of attorney and wills.

- Provide estate planning advice.

- Review contracts and leases (ideally, before you sign).

- Notarize documents.

- Provide family and domestic relations advice (divorce, separation, family support, adoption, custody, paternity, and name changes).

- Assist with consumer affairs.

- Provide tax advice on real and personal property and income (and in certain locations tax preparation and electronic filing).

- Answer questions about landlord-tenant issues (including leases, security deposits and evictions, and SCRA issues).

Contact

Locate a DoD Legal Assistance Office on the American Bar Association website at www.abanet.org/ legalservices/ findlegal-help/freehelp.html . You can also find legal assistance offices for your service branch at www.military.com/ law.

- Provide advice on immigration and naturalization issues.

- Assist with SCRA- and USERRA-related issues.

Ask your legal assistance office to review and explain questionable legal documents before you sign them. If you are unable to resolve a problem yourself, it is best to get advice as soon as possible. Delay rarely makes things better, and the law may limit your remedy if you do not act quickly.

Generally, the military services offer limited legal assistance even to guard and reserve members during inactive–duty training periods for preparation of legal documents such as wills and powers of attorney, which you'd need if called to active duty. These offices can be your first stop for help with SCRA, USERRA, and related laws.

Legal Assistance Limitations

Military legal assistance offices cannot:

- Provide legal assistance via a third party—the attorney must deal directly with the client, not his or her friend or relative.

- Provide assistance or counsel regarding legal problems arising from the client's business or commercial interests.

- Provide in-court representation for an individual (except in limited cases).

- Give advice over the telephone (under normal circumstances).

- Represent or provide counsel to both parties in a dispute (divorce, for example)

If a legal assistance attorney cannot resolve a given case or a specialized attorney is needed, the legal assistance attorney will refer you to a civilian attorney, normally through a local lawyer-referral service, who can handle the case. (Generally there will be a service fee.)

If you are a servicemember or dependent, you are encouraged to contact your local legal assistance office concerning eligibility and legal assistance subject areas.

Veterans Benefits Claims and Appeals

Take Advantage
Keep your address and contact information current with your local VA office staff at all times—they will need that information to inform you of changes in your benefits.

The Veterans Benefits Administration (VBA) is the branch of the Department of Veterans Affairs that manages your benefits. If you are a veteran, the VBA, in partnership with the Veterans Health Administration and the National Cemetery Administration, provides benefits and services to you and your family in recognition of your service to the nation.

Veterans Benefits Administration Claims

Contact
You can enroll in the VA benefit system online at www.1010ez. med.va.gov/sec/ vha/1010ez.

As a veteran, you may need to file a claim with the VBA, most likely involving compensation related to a medical condition. The claims process will vary depending on the type of claim you're filing. However, you will first need to be enrolled in the VA benefit system. (For more information, see page 127.) You can enroll by contacting the VA facility closest to you (page 357), at any time. Your enrollment will be reviewed annually, depending upon your priority group (see page 133) and available resources. If VA cannot renew your enrollment for the coming year, you will be notified in writing 60 days before your enrollment expires.

To apply for veteran benefits, it is your responsibility to file a claim and maintain an updated address where you can be contacted. You should also have your service record (or Official Military Personnel File) handy, or at a minimum your "Discharge from Active Duty" (DD Form 214). (See "Records and Awards," in chapter 7.)

Take Advantage
Your DD Form 214 discharge papers are the key to unlocking your veteran benefits. For more information on how to get these papers, see page 312.

Filing the Claim

A claim can be filed at any VA office or medical center. (See Appendix for addresses.) Many cities also have vet centers where a claim may be filed. You can file your claim online, and can get additional information about the specific claim you are filing.

A number of federally chartered veterans service organizations (VSOs), including the Veterans of Foreign Wars (VFW) and the Disabled American Veterans (DAV), may prepare, present, and prosecute VA claims, often at no cost to you. Each VSO's service officer will help prepare and manage your claims for benefits.

Service officers function as advocates for you and your family in any appeals you make. They will also aid you and your family in filing claims for VA disability compensation, rehabilitation, and education programs, pension and death benefits, employment and training programs, Social Security disability benefits, and many other programs.

VSOs have representatives at most VA regional offices. You may also get information about VSOs from your VA medical center's Voluntary Service program manager.

Contact

To file your veteran benefits claim online, go to www.vba.va.gov.

New Online Claims Filing Process

Veterans, survivors, and other claimants may now use the Department of Veterans Affairs VONAPP (Veterans On Line Applications) website to file initial applications for disability compensation, pension, education, and vocational rehabilitation and employment benefits online without the additional requirement to submit a signed paper copy of the application.

VONAPP is a Web-based system that benefits both internal and external users. Veterans, survivors and other claimants seeking compensation, pension, education, or vocational rehabilitation benefits can apply electronically without the constraints of location, postage cost, and time delays in mail delivery.

The on-line application also provides a link to apply for VA health care benefits and much more. Over 3.7 million veterans and beneficiaries receive compensation and pension benefits from VA and approximately 523,000 students receive education benefits. Approximately 90,000 disabled veterans participate in VA's Vocational Rehabilitation and Employment program. VONAPP can be found at www.vabenefits.vba.va.gov/vonapp/main.asp

Take Advantage

Don't go it alone! When enrolling or filing a claim, you should contact the Veterans Service Organization (VSO) service officer at your nearest VA office or clinic. Service officers can ensure that your enrollment and claims forms are filled out correctly and that your claims are processed right the first time.

Appealing a VA Decision

Were you awarded a VA disability compensation benefit smaller than what you feel you deserved? Or maybe you've recently had problems with VA's approving benefits for education, pensions, medication copayments, or some other items. If you feel you have a legitimate case, how do you contest a VA decision?

Veterans and other claimants for VA benefits have the right to appeal decisions made by a VA regional office or medical center. From the date of the notification of a VA decision, a claimant has one year to file an appeal. After that, the determination is considered final and cannot be appealed unless you can show a clear and unmistakable error by VA.

Anyone who has filed a claim for benefits with VA (i.e., veterans *and* other claimants) and has received a determination from a local VA office is eligible to appeal. You may appeal a complete or partial denial of your claim, or you may appeal the degree or amount of benefit granted.

Take Advantage

Keep a copy of everything—your correspondence, your evidence, everything—that's related to your veteran compensation case. This will help if you need to make an appeal later on.

The Appeals Process

If you have received a response on a VA benefits claim that you do not agree with, send a letter to the VA office where you originally processed your claim. This does not require a special form; it is simply your written statement that you disagree with your local VA office's claim determination, and you want to appeal it. If you want to appeal your claim, make sure you do this within one year of the date your determination was mailed to you. After you send in your letter, you can request that a Decision Review Officer at the VA office review your file.

After receiving your letter, your local VA office will send you a summary of reasons behind its ruling in what is called a Statement of the Case. The office will also send a VA Form 9, the document you need to file to make your official appeal. Be sure to fill out and mail back the "Appeal to the Board of Veterans Appeals" (VA Form 9) no later than 60 days after your Statement of the Case was mailed out to you, or within one year after the date your original determination was mailed to you, whichever is later.

After receiving your VA Form 9, your local VA office will forward all claim materials to the Board of Veterans Appeals. It will notify you when it sends these materials out. You have 90 days after this notification is mailed to submit additional evidence, appoint or change legal representation for your claim, or ask for a hearing.

The Board will conduct hearings, if requested, review your appeal, and issue a decision. You have the right to schedule a personal hearing with the board, either in Washington, D.C., at your local VA office, or through video conferencing. Video conferencing is usually the easiest of these options to set up.

These hearings are informal and not your standard "Court TV" showdowns. Usually, a member of the Board will hear your side of the case, and may ask some questions. You can represent yourself, have an attorney represent you, or a veterans service officer can represent you. The transcript of the meeting will be added to your case file and reviewed by the Board. Eventually, the Board will either grant, seek more information before making a final ruling, or deny your appeal. If your appeal is denied, you have three options:

• You can accept the ruling.

• You can file a motion for the Board to reconsider your case.

• You can take your case to the U.S. Court of Appeals for Veterans Claims.

If you choose the third option, you must take your appeal to the Court within 120 days after the date the original Board of Veterans Appeals ruling was mailed to you.

Decisions concerning the need for medical care or the type of medical treatment needed, such as a physician's decision to prescribe (or not pre-scribe) a specific drug, are not within the Board's jurisdiction, and thus cannot be appealed.

The Two-Level Process

1. The Board of Veterans Appeals. Your appeal will be reviewed by the Board of Veterans Appeals, which makes final decisions on appeals on behalf of VA. If you make an appeal, you can be represented by a VSO, an agent, or an attorney.

The Board reviews fee agreements between you and your attorneys or agents, along with determining whether attorneys or agents are eligible for payment of fees from your past-due benefits. You have the right to present your case in person to a Board member at a hearing in Washington, D.C., at a VA regional office, or by videoconference.

Board decisions can be viewed at the Board of Veterans Appeals Decisions website.

2. U.S. Court of Appeals for Veterans Claims. If you receive an unsatisfactory ruling from the Board of Veterans Appeals on your claim, you can then appeal to the Court of Veterans Appeals, which is independent from VA. Only claimants may seek a review by the court; VA cannot appeal Board decisions. To appeal to the court, you must have filed a Notice of Disagreement on or after November 18, 1988.

The court does not hold trials or receive new evidence; it simply reviews the record that was considered by the Board of Veterans Appeals. Oral argument is held only at the direction of the court. Either party may appeal a decision of this court to the U.S. Court of Appeals for the Federal Circuit and then to the Supreme Court of the United States. Appellants may represent themselves before the court, or have lawyers or approved agents as representatives. Court decisions, case status information, rules and procedures, and other special announcements can be obtained from the U.S. Court of Appeals for Veterans Claims website.

Burial Benefits

In return for the sacrifices that you and your family make as part of the Armed Forces, the Department of Veterans Affairs (VA) provides burial services for eligible servicemembers, Reserve, Guard, retirees, and veterans. Burial benefits include:

Take Advantage

Present as much clear evidence as you can to support your VA benefits claim. Use full names, addresses, and dates. You don't want to lose your case because you didn't provide all the information you have.

Contact

View Board of Veterans Appeals decisions at www.index.va.gov/search/va/bva.html.

Take Advantage

To ensure your case is not lost in a paperwork quagmire, put your VA claim number on all correspondence and evidence you send to VA regarding your claim or appeal.

Contact

You can contact the clerk's office at:
United States Court of Appeals for Veterans Claims
625 Indiana Ave. NW, Suite 900
Washington, D.C. 20004
202-501-5970.

Benefit Claims Forms

VA Form 21-530 (Application for Burial Benefits)

VA Form 9 (Appeal to the Board of Veterans Appeals)

VA Form 21-22 (Appointment of Veterans Service Organization as Claimant's Representative)

VA Form 22a (Appointment of Attorney or Agent as Claimant's Representative)

All forms can be found at www.military.com/forms.

Contact

To review your eligibility for burial benefits or to locate your nearest VA regional office or national cemetery, call a Veterans Benefits Counselor at 800-827-1000.

- A grave site in any of the 120 national cemeteries that have space available.

- Burial with military honors (if available).

- Opening and closing of the grave, as well as perpetual care.

- A government headstone or marker, a burial flag, and a Presidential Memorial Certificate at no cost to the family.

- Reimbursement payments as well as a burial allowance for transport of remains (Cremated remains are buried or inurned in national cemeteries in the same manner and with the same honors as casketed remains.)

Reimbursement of Burial Expenses

VA will reimburse you for several costs associated with the burial of an eligible servicemember, including:

- A burial allowance of up to $2,000 if the veteran's death is service-connected.

- The cost of transporting the remains of a service-disabled veteran to the national cemetery nearest the home of the deceased that has available grave sites. In such cases, the person who bore the veteran's burial expenses may claim reimbursement from VA.

- A $300 burial and funeral expense allowance for veterans who, at the time of death, were entitled to receive pension or compensation or would have been entitled to compensation if not for receipt of military retirement pay.

- A $300 burial (plot) allowance when the veteran is not buried in a cemetery that is under U.S. government jurisdiction, if the veteran meets the eligibility requirements.

Eligibility for Burial Benefits

Generally, servicemembers who die while on duty and veterans discharged under conditions other than dishonorable are eligible for burial in a VA national cemetery. Reserve and Guard members are eligible if they were entitled to retired pay at the time of death, or would have been entitled had they not been younger than 60 (gray-area retirees).

VA national cemetery directors, upon request of a funeral director acting for the decedent's family, have the primary responsibility for verifying eligibility for burial in VA national cemeteries. VA regional offices may also assist in determining eligibility for such burials. Other persons who may be eligible for a military burial include:

- Commissioned Officers of the National Oceanic and Atmospheric Administration.

- Commissioned Officers of the Public Health Service.

- World War II Merchant Mariners.

- Spouses and dependents, provided:

  —The spouse or unremarried surviving spouse of a veteran is eligible.

  —The remarriage of a surviving spouse who remarries an ineligible individual is rendered void.

  —A minor child is unmarried and under the age of 21 years, or is under 23 years of age and a full-time student.

Burial in a VA National Cemetery

No special forms are required when requesting burial in a VA national cemetery other than the servicemember's DD Form 214. The person making burial arrangements should have the funeral home contact the national cemetery once burial becomes necessary. Scheduling can be done seven days a week for interments

Who Shall Have Borne the Battle

The national cemetery system was established in 1862 as part of a veterans-benefit package designed, as President Lincoln said in his second inaugural address, "to care for him who shall have borne the battle and for his widow and his orphan." The first veterans' graveyards were small and located near Civil War battlefields and hospitals.

Contact

For a full list of all national cemeteries, visit www.cem.va.gov/ nchp.htm.

taking place on Mondays through Fridays. If possible, the following information concerning the deceased should be provided when the cemetery is first contacted:

- Full name and military rank.

- Branch of service.

- Social Security number.

- Service number.

- VA claim number, if applicable.

- Date and place of birth.

- Date and place of death.

- Date of retirement or last separation from active duty.

- Copy of any military separation documents, such as the Department of Defense Form 214.

Contact

For information on Arlington burials, call 703-695-3250, or write to Superintendent, Arlington National Cemetery, Arlington, VA 22211.

The same procedures are followed if the servicemember's eligible spouse or dependent dies before the servicemember. In most cases, one grave site is provided for the burial of all eligible family members and a single headstone or marker is provided. When both spouses are veterans, two grave sites and two headstones or markers may be provided if requested.

As of 1962, grave sites in VA national cemeteries cannot be reserved in advance; however, reservations made prior to 1962 will be honored.

Arlington National Cemetery

Under the jurisdiction of the Army, this cemetery has eligibility more limited than that of other national cemeteries. Eligibility for inurnment of cremated remains in Arlington's columbarium, however, is the same as eligibility for burial in VA national cemeteries. More than 5,000 burials a year are conducted at Arlington.

Contact

To download an application for a veteran's burial in a private cemetery, go to www.military.com /forms.

Interior Department-run Cemeteries

Eligibility criteria similar to that for VA national cemeteries apply to the two active national cemeteries administered by the Department of the Interior: Andersonville National Cemetery in Georgia and Andrew Johnson National Cemetery in Tennessee.

Rest in Peace

Arlington National Cemetery's 612 acres contain the graves of more than 200,000 veterans. Many civilians are buried there, too, usually by virtue of being related to someone in the military. Presidents John F. Kennedy and William H. Taft, as well as Supreme Court Justices Oliver Wendell Holmes, Thurgood Marshall, and Earl Warren, are all buried at Arlington.

Contact

For a listing of state cemeteries, visit www.cem.va.gov /lsvc.htm.

Burial in a State Cemetery

Many states have established veterans cemeteries. Eligibility is similar to VA national cemeteries, but may include residency requirements. Though these cemeteries may have been established or improved with government funds through the VA's State Cemetery Grants Program, state veterans cemeteries are run solely by the states. Contact the specific cemetery for information.

Burial in a Private Cemetery

If a veteran's burial will be in a private cemetery, the military still will supply a standard headstone or marker free of charge. The family should complete VA Form 40-1330 in advance and file it with the veteran's military discharge papers.

Headstones and Markers

VA provides headstones and markers for the graves of veterans anywhere in the world and for eligible dependents of veterans buried in national, state veteran, or federal cemeteries. Eligibility for a VA headstone or marker is the same as for burial in a national cemetery.

Headstones and markers are inscribed with the name of the deceased, the years of birth and death, and branch of service. Optional items that also will be inscribed at VA expense are: military grade, rank, or rate; war service (such as "World War II"); months and days of birth and death; an emblem reflecting one's beliefs, such as a cross or Star of David; and military decorations. Items not listed here may be inscribed at private expense. Information regarding style, inscription, shipping, and placement can be obtained from the cemetery.

Contact

To apply for headstones, complete VA Form 40-1330 (at www.military.com/ forms) and mail to:

Memorial Programs Service (41A1) Department of Veterans Affairs 5109 Russell Rd. Quantico, VA 22134.

Burial Flags

Contact

For information regarding the status of an application for a headstone, call 800-697-6947.

As an added expression of gratitude, and to honor the memory of the deceased's military service to his or her country, a United States flag is provided, at no cost, to drape the casket or accompany the urn of a deceased servicemember who served honorably in the U.S. Armed Forces.

Generally, the flag is given to the next of kin or to a family friend as a keepsake after its use during the funeral service. Families of servicemembers buried in national cemeteries may donate the burial flags of their loved ones to be flown on patriotic holidays.

Take Advantage

Unfortunately VA cannot replace a lost, destroyed, or stolen flag. However, some veterans organizations or other community groups may be able to help you get another flag.

You can apply for the flag by completing VA Form 2008, Application for United States Flag for Burial Purposes available at www.military.com/forms. To get the flag itself, you can go to any VA regional office or U.S. Post Office. Generally, the funeral director will help you in this process.

Military Funeral Honors

Military funeral honor details have long been provided (at no cost) whenever possible. However, the law now *mandates* that the DoD provide military funeral honors for a servicemember if requested by the family. The honor detail will, at a minimum, perform a ceremony that includes the folding and presenting of the American flag to the next of kin and the playing of "Taps." "Taps" will be played by a bugler, if available, or by electronic recording.

Take Advantage

A new law mandates that in addition to the surviving spouse, each surviving child shall be presented with a burial flag

Families of eligible veterans can request funeral honors through their funeral director. The funeral director will contact the appropriate office to arrange for the funeral honors detail.

Gold Star Lapel Buttons

The Gold Star Lapel Button identifies widows, parents, and next of kin of members

Avenue of Flags

Most of the Department of Veterans Affairs national cemeteries display an "Avenue of Flags" on patriotic holidays and during special events. The Avenues consist of donated burial flags. Donors receive a Certificate of Appreciation.

of the United States Armed Forces who lost their lives in the following campaigns:

- World War I.

- World War II.

- During any subsequent period of armed hostilities in which the United States was engaged before July 1, 1958 (Korean War).

- After June 30, 1958:

  —while engaged in an action against an enemy of the United States.

  —while engaged in military operations involving conflict with an opposing foreign force.

  —while serving with friendly foreign forces engaged in an armed conflict in which the United States was not a primary belligerent party against an opposing armed force.

The law provides that one Gold Star Lapel Button will be furnished, without cost, to the widow or widower and to each of the parents and the next of kin. If a Gold Star Lapel Button is lost or destroyed it can be replaced upon application and payment of the manufacture and distribution costs.

Presidential Memorial Certificates

A Presidential Memorial Certificate (PMC) is an engraved paper certificate, signed by the current President, to honor the memory of honorably discharged veterans who have died.

Initiated in March 1962 by President John F. Kennedy, this program has been continued by all subsequent Presidents. The Department of Veterans Affairs administers the program by preparing the certificates.

Eligible recipients include the deceased veteran's next of kin and loved ones. More than one certificate may be provided.

Eligible recipients, or someone acting on their behalf, may apply for a PMC in person at any VA regional office, by fax, or by mail. Requests cannot be sent via email. There is no form to use when requesting a PMC, but be sure to enclose a copy of the veteran's discharge and death certificate.

Contact

For the Gold Star Lapel Button application, download form DD3 at www.military.com /forms.

Contact

For questions about a Presidential Memorial Certificate you have received, a request you have already sent in, or about the program in general, call 1-800-827-1000. To request a certificate, or to check on a request made more than eight weeks ago, send your request and all supporting documents (copy of discharge and death certificate) by fax to 202-565-8054, or mail to:

Presidential Memorial Certificates (41A1C) Department of Veterans Affairs 5109 Russell Rd. Quantico, VA 22134-3903.

Contact

Survivors should report deaths to the DFAS Cleveland Center's casualty office at 800-269-5170. You can also fax the office at 800-469-6559.

Surviving Family Benefits

Dealing with the death of a servicemember or veteran is never easy, but surviving family members are entitled to benefits that can help ease financial difficulties. Looking into these benefits can be difficult emotionally, but you should plan ahead. Otherwise you risk facing unexpected circumstances that may prevent you from receiving your benefits.

It's best to plan ahead for all contingencies, even when the servicemember or veteran is still alive. Make lists of both routine and special tasks that must be taken care of—for instance, renewal dates for a spouse's and children's military ID and insurance policies, wills, due dates for driver's licenses, automobile tags, and personal property taxes, etc. Assign each item to a major category such as personal data, military service history, estate planning, financial assets, insurance policies, veteran benefits, or emergency planning guidance. For each item, provide a brief explanation and list tasks that need to be accomplished. If an essential document is missing or outdated, make a note to get it as soon as possible.

For these preparations, there is no one-size-fits-all format, so include as much content and detail as you believe will be necessary to enable your family to tend to these affairs. Counselors lament that they hear too many horror stories from survivors who suddenly lost a spouse who had provided everything for them. Many military and veteran organizations provide informational guidance on "estate planning." Another option is to visit with a certified financial planner. Above all, it's important to anticipate all possibilities, even while hoping for the best.

When a servicemember, retiree, or veteran dies, family members are offered several forms of compensation. These include Dependency and Indemnity Compensation, proceeds from SGLI, various basic benefits, and the Survivor Benefits Plan. Each military service branch has a Casualty Assistance branch that is dedicated to assisting you with your paperwork and applications for all of your benefits and compensation.

Take Advantage

Be sure contact a Casualty Assistance Calls Officer. A CACO Support Program can help you and your family leave no stone unturned, and get all the important benefits you are entitled to.

Tragedy Assistance Program for Survivors

If your family has suffered the loss of a servicemember or veteran, the Tragedy Assistance Program for Survivors (TAPS) is foremost among organizations that can help. The services this nonprofit organization offers to bereaved families include:

- Peer support networks.

- Crisis intervention hotline (24 hours a day).

- Assistance with casework associated with death benefits and burial.

- Grief counseling referrals, in partnership with the Department of Veterans Affairs Readjustment Counseling Service and its 206 centers around the country.

- Annual National Military Survivor Seminar and Good Grief Camp for Young Survivors, held every year during Memorial Day weekend in Washington, D.C.

- TAPS Chat through online support groups.

Dependency and Indemnity Compensation

For surviving spouses and family members, the financial burden that follows a death can be a harsh reality. One major VA program that can assist you with financial need is Dependency and Indemnity Compensation (DIC), through which a monthly amount of $1,091 is paid to eligible survivors of a deceased servicemember or veteran.

If you are an eligible survivor, an unremarried spouse, or an unmarried minor child, you qualify for DIC if your loved one fits any of the following eligibility categories:

- Servicemembers who died while on active duty.

- Veteran whose death resulted from a service-related injury or disease.

- Veteran whose death resulted from a non-service-related injury or disease, and who was receiving, or was entitled to receive, VA compensation for a service-connected disability rated as permanent and totally disabling.

  —For at least 10 years immediately prior to death.

  —Since the veteran's release from active duty and for at least five years immediately preceding death, or

  —For at least one year before death if the veteran was a former prisoner of war who died after September 30, 1999.

To be considered a surviving spouse in terms of benefits eligibility, any of the following criteria must be met:

- Married the veteran before January 1, 1957.

- Was married to a servicemember who died on active duty.

- Married the veteran within 15 years after his or her discharge from the period

---

Take Advantage

Don't use any retired or compensation payments received after the date of a retiree's death. A beneficiary can be required to pay back any money that was used after the date of death.

Contact

Find more information on TAPS at:

Tragedy Assistance Program for Survivors
1621 Connecticut Ave. NW, Suite 300
Washington, D.C. 20009
www.taps.org
Office:
202-588-TAPS
(202-588-8277)
Crisis hotline, toll-free:
800-959-TAPS
(800-959-8277)
Fax:
202-588-0784.

Take Advantage

You can get a free analysis of your family's survivor benefits online. Go to www.navymutual.org, and look through the "24/7 Survivor Benefits Analysis" feature on the homepage.

Casualty Assistance Contact Information

Air Force Casualty Assistance: 800-433-0048
www.afpc.randolph.af.mil/Casualty

Army Casualty Family Assistance Hotline: 800-833-6622
www.perscomonline.army.mil/tagd/cmaoc/cmaoc.htm

Coast Guard Decedent Affairs: 202-267-2085
www.uscg.mil/HQ/G-W/G-WP/G-WPM/g-wpm-2/Decedent.htm

Marine Corps Casualty Assistance: 800-847-1597
www.marines.mil/marinelink/mcn2000.nsf/oifassist

Navy Casualty Assistance: 800-368-3202
www.npc.navy.mil/commandsupport/casualtyassistance

of military service in which the disease or injury that caused the veteran's death began or was aggravated.

- Was married to the veteran for at least one year, or

- Had a child with the veteran, *and*

   —Cohabited with the veteran continuously until the veteran's death or, if separated, was not at fault for the separation, *and*

   —Is not currently remarried.

In a recent change to DIC, spouses who remarry on or after reaching age 57, and on or after December 16, 2003, can continue to receive DIC. In addition, certain adult children who cannot live independently may be entitled to DIC.

DIC benefit payments are currently the following:

In addition to the basic monthly payment rate of $1,154, survivors may be eligible for the following additional allowances:

- Add $246 if at the time of the veteran's death he or she had been entitled to compensation for a service-connected disability - rated totally disabling - for a continuous period of at least 8 years AND the surviving spouse was married to the veteran for those same 8 years.

- Add $286 per child for each dependent child under age 18.

- If the surviving spouse is entitled to aid and attendance, add $286.

- If the surviving spouse is entitled to Housebound rates, add $135.

If you are a surviving spouse who is eligible for payments under the military's Survivor Benefit Program (SBP) and DIC, your DIC benefit will offset your SBP benefit, dollar for dollar. You cannot receive both benefits simultaneously.

First-time applicants for DIC must complete VA Form 21-534 and submit it to the VA regional office serving your area. Other documents you will require include copies of birth and marriage certificates, as well as divorce and death records. VA will need to obtain verifications of military service from the service departments if these documents are not available. On requests for restored DIC, the process is simpler. If you have questions about supporting materials that VA may need or special instructions on requests for restoration of DIC, contact a veterans benefits counselor.

Contact

If you think you may qualify for DIC, call toll-free 800-827-1000, or visit the VA website at www.va.gov. Fill out VA Form 21-535, available at www.military.com/forms, and submit it to the VA regional office that serves your area.

Parents' DIC

Parents' DIC is an income-based monthly benefit for the surviving parents, or parent, of a deceased servicemember or veteran. This benefit is available for biological, adoptive, and foster parents and eligibility is based on need. To apply, follow the same instructions as for applying for DIC. Parents must report all sources of income to VA; for example, gross wages, retirement annuity, insurance proceeds or annuity, interest, and dividends. The spouse's income must also be included if both parents live together. A spouse may be the other parent of the deceased veteran, or from remarriage.

Military Matters

In cases where VA determines that the servicemember's death occurred outside the line of duty and that the survivors are not, therefore, eligible for DIC payments, the survivors may still be eligible for benefits from a VA Death Pension. Contact VA to determine if your family meets the current eligibility requirements.

Death Gratuity

Next of kin receive this gratuity upon the death of a relative who was in the armed services. They may also receive free housing or a housing allowance, as well as TRICARE benefits. The death gratuity is $100,000 (100 percent tax free), and is paid to the next of kin for active-duty, guard, reserve and ROTC servicemembers who have been killed either while on active duty or traveling to or from official active or inactive duty training.

Other Benefits for Surviving Family Members

Surviving family members of deceased servicemembers will continue to receive benefits under the TRICARE health care and dental system.

Surviving spouses continue under the same coverage for three years after the death of the servicemember. After that period, the spouse may pay an annual membership fee equal to that paid by retirees to enroll (or reenroll) in TRICARE Prime. Those who choose the TRICARE Standard or Extra options must pay the cost-shares and deductibles applicable to retirees and their families. Such coverage continues for life, or until the surviving spouse remarries or reaches age 65. TRICARE is coordinated with Medicare under TRICARE for Life.

Surviving children continue under the same coverage until age 21 or until age 23 if enrolled full-time in school.

If family members are no longer eligible for the TRICARE Family Dental Plan, they may be eligible for dental care under the TRICARE Retiree Dental Plan.

Contact a health benefit advisor at your local TRICARE medical treatment facility for more information. For more on TRICARE benefits for survivors, see the Health chapter, page 121.

Survivors' Basic Allowance for Housing

The spouse and children (including children from a previous marriage) of a deceased servicemember living in government quarters are entitled either to remain in government housing for up to one year or to relocate to private quarters and receive an up-to-one-year Basic Allowance for Housing or Overseas Housing Allowance, as appropriate. To receive this allowance for private quarters, the servicemember must have been eligible to receive those allowances for his or her dependents at the time of death. Note that the entitlement is for up to one year, which may be any combination of use of government quarters and/or allowances for private quarters. Housing benefits will generally be finalized within 7 to 14 days after the notification of next of kin.

In addition to the extended on-base housing and/or housing allowances, the military will pay to transport and store household goods and personal effects. The items to be moved must be turned over to a transportation officer or carrier within three years after the member's death for shipment to the desired location.

The Casualty Assistance Calls Officer (CACO) at your military installation will assist you in arranging for shipment and will contact the personal property officer at the nearest military installation to answer any questions you may have.

You may temporarily store a shipment of household goods for up to one year. With the exception of certain extenuating circumstances any temporary storage beyond one year will be at your own expense. To gain extended storage, you must send a written request to the transportation officer handling your move to show extenuating circumstances beyond your control. The CACO will also be able to assist you in this matter.

Nontemporary storage in connection with a shipment of household goods may not exceed one year from the date of death. Storage under these conditions will be in an approved commercial or government facility, whichever is nearest the point where the household goods are located on the date of the servicemember's death.

Federal Employment Preference Points

Surviving spouses who have not remarried, and certain mothers of a deceased member who served during a war period, are entitled to an additional 10 points to the rating they earned on the civil service examination. Information concerning preference eligibility may be obtained from the Office of Personnel Management, State Employment Office, or your local post office.

Your Casualty Assistance Calls Officer (CACO) will provide you with the claim application form and will help you arrange for an appointment.

Unpaid Compensation

Any unpaid compensation due the servicemember on the date of death will go to the designated beneficiary. If no beneficiary was designated, then the recipient will be in the following order of priority:

- Spouse.

- Children or their descendants.

- Parents.

- Person appointed by estate.

Contact

For more information about Federal Employment Preference Points, call 800-772-1213.

Take Advantage

Many states provide additional survivors' benefits such as educational assistance, land settlement preference, civil service preference, tax and license fee exemptions, loans, relief and rehabilitation, employment assistance, and bonuses. State veterans commissions usually supervise these programs and may be contacted for additional information. For details, see www.military.com /statebenefits.

Contact

Claim for Unpaid Compensation of Deceased Members of the Uniformed Services, Standard Form 1174, is available at www.military.com /forms.

If no representative was appointed, state probate laws governing the servicemember's estate determine its disbursement.

The CACO will assist you in completing the Claim for Unpaid Compensation of Deceased Members of the Uniformed Services, which is an application to receive the remaining money in the servicemember's account. The CACO will send the paperwork to the Defense Finance and Accounting Service (DFAS) and the branch Personnel Office. These claims are usually settled within 60 to 90 days after the servicemember's death, and may include pay and allowances accumulated up to the date of death (minus any debts owed to the government), as well as any unused leave due on the date of death.

Uniformed Services Identification and Privilege Card

The Uniformed Services Identification and Privilege Card identifies the holder as an authorized patron for privileges indicated on the card. Servicemembers' dependents older than age 10 must have a card to gain access to facilities such as the commissary and exchange, to obtain medical care at a government facility or through a civilian care facility, for base theater privileges, and so forth. As the surviving dependent of a deceased member, your present card expires on the date of the member's death. You must renew this card within 30 days after the member's death in order to continue to have access to these privileges. (For more on getting this card, see page 3.)

Your CACO will make arrangements for you to receive a new card and will accompany you to the nearest Real-Time Automated Personnel Identification System (RAPIDS) site or other military installation authorized to issue ID cards. You should take your old ID card along with a copy of the DD Form 1300 to the issuing office. You may use your old card for identification until a card is obtained.

Educational Benefits and Assistance

Military and veteran dependents are eligible for numerous benefits, including federal and state veterans programs and scholarships. While some assistance is provided only for persons needing financial assistance, some aid is furnished regardless of need. This is particularly true of state benefits. More complete information can be found in Chapter 5.

Survivors and Dependents' Education Assistance Program

Dependents' Educational Assistance (DEA) provides education and training opportunities to eligible spouses and children of deceased or permanently disabled servicemembers. The program offers up to 45 months of education benefits, which may be used for degree and certificate programs, apprenticeships, and on-the-job training. If you are a spouse, you may take a correspondence course. Remedial, deficiency, and refresher courses are also approved under certain circumstances. For more details on this benefit, see page 195.

Eligible dependents between the ages of 18 and 26 (31 in special cases) can use the Survivors and Dependents Education Assistance (DEA) program to get up to $915 a month for 45 months of full-time study. Surviving spouses are eligible for this benefit for up to 10 years from either the original date the VA declared them eligible, or the veteran's date of death.

Take Advantage
For a database of available military scholarships, see www.military.com /scholarships.

Retiree Survivor Benefit Plan

The Survivor Benefit Plan (SBP) is essentially a life insurance (annuity) plan to protect a military retiree's surviving family members in the case of *early* passing, a spouse's outliving the benefits, and inflation.

Relations of a retired servicemember eligible to be insured under the Survivor Benefit Plan include spouses, former spouses, and children and dependent grandchildren. In rare cases, relations such as a business partner or parent can be covered.

As with most other insurance, you are required to pay a monthly premium. SBP premiums and benefits depend on the amount that you elect as the base of your coverage. Your base amount can be your full monthly gross retired pay, or just a portion—as little as $300. Full coverage means your full gross retired pay is your base amount. When retired pay gets a cost-of-living adjustment—adjustments for inflation, known as 'COLA'—so does the base amount, and as a result, so do premiums and benefits.

Take Advantage
Your decision on Survivor Benefit Plan election is critical. If you need help, speak to a financial counselor, or transition program manager, and your spouse before making your final decision.

How SBP Benefits Work

Upon the death of a military retiree, the finance center is notified, and an SBP application form is mailed to the surviving spouse. If all goes smoothly in the application process, the annuity will begin to flow continually about 45 to 60 days after the death of the retired member.

Surviving children are paid the annuity in equal shares until they reach age 18, or 22 if full-time students. An incapacitated child will receive the annuity for life without any reductions for Social Security, provided the child never marries. As each child reaches the age when entitlements no longer exist, the annuity is divided equally between the remaining eligible children.

SBP premiums are tax deductible; however, you cannot enter them as a deductible item on your Form 1040. You will receive an IRS Form 1099-R from DFAS that will show your net taxable pay after deducting the SBP cost.

Enrolling in SBP

Take Advantage

If you want to know exactly how much your premium will cost and how much you will benefit, visit www.military.com/sbp.

Shortly after you submit your request to retire from the military, you will receive an SBP enrollment form. This will be your *only* opportunity to participate in the SBP. If you choose to decline to participate you will not be given a second chance. *The exception to the rule: If you have no dependents when you retire, but later you marry, you may apply within one year to participate.* Should you elect not to participate in SBP or elect not to participate at the maximum level, your spouse has to agree with your decision.

Every retiring servicemember is automatically enrolled in SBP for full coverage *unless* the spouse consents in writing to reduced coverage or no coverage.

Terminating enrollment. Once you have elected to participate, you cannot discontinue participation until after the second anniversary of your retirement. You will not be reimbursed for your premium.

Coverage you choose may be "spouse only," "spouse and children," or "children only." If you do not have a spouse or child, you may be able to choose insurable interest (business partners or parents) coverage, and alter this coverage as your situation changes.

SBP Premiums

Spouse-only coverage. Monthly SBP premiums for spouse coverage are the lesser of the two following options:

- 6.5 percent of your chosen base amount (the amount you wish your spouse to receive each month in SBP pay).

Military Matters

In cases where DIC is involved (DIC reduces the spouse's SBP annuity dollar for dollar), if the DIC amount exceeds the SBP annuity, the surviving spouse is entitled to a refund of all SBP payments. If SBP exceeds the DIC amount, the surviving spouse will receive the difference between the SBP annuity and DIC, plus a refund of SBP payments for that portion of the SBP annuity not received.

- 2.5 percent of the first $616 of your elected base amount (also known as the "threshold amount"), plus 10 percent of the remaining base amount.

The threshold amount increases at the same time and by the same percentage as future active-duty basic pay. In 2005, this amount was $616.

If you joined the military on or after March 1, 1990, and you are retiring for length of service (that is, not due to disability), or at age 60 as a reservist or guard member (nonregular service), your SBP costs will be calculated only as 6.5 percent of your chosen base amount.

Spouse and child coverage. Adding children to your coverage incurs additional costs based on the age of your youngest child, and the ages of both spouses.

Insurable interest. The cost for an insurable interest election is considerably more expensive than for a child. It amounts to 10 percent of the gross retired pay plus an additional 5 percent—up to 40 percent total—for each full five years the beneficiary is younger than the retiree. However, you can discontinue insurable interest at any time.

Child-only coverage. The cost for children alone is based on the age of the retiree and the age of the youngest child. For example, a 40-year-old retiree with a youngest child of 10 would have a monthly cost factor of .0033, or $3.30 per every $1,000 in the base amount.

Take Advantage

Retirees who opted out of the SBP have another opportunity to elect coverage during a special enrollment period that ends on September 30, 2006. See www.military.com/sbp for details.

Survivor Benefits Plan for Active-Duty Deaths

Since the terrorist attacks of September 11, SBP has been made available to all active-duty servicemembers including reserve and guard members called to active duty regardless of years of service. In the event of an active-duty death, the servicemember is treated as if he or she died in a 100 percent disabled status. The retired pay is calculated as 75 percent of the servicemember's final base pay (or "high three" base pay if applicable). The SBP annuity for the servicemember's surviving spouse is 55 percent of that retired pay.

The spouse's SBP annuity continues for his or her entire life unless the spouse remarries prior to age 55. If a spouse dies or remarries prior to age 55, the benefit will pass to eligible children. If SBP terminates due to marriage prior to age 55, and that marriage ends either in death or divorce, the spouse may reapply for the benefit.

Take Advantage

After October 1, 2008, SBP participants who reach 70 years of age and have made 360 payments (30 years), will no longer have to pay premiums for continued SBP coverage and will be placed in "Paid-up SBP" status.

Reserve Component Survivor Benefit Plan

If you are in the Reserve or Guard, this plan is intended to ensure that surviving spouses receive a portion (55 percent maximum) of your monthly retirement for life, adjusted for annual cost of living raises. The election of the Reserve

Component Survivor Benefit Plan (RCSBP) has no effect on other retirement benefits and entitlements.

Eligible Beneficiaries. RCSBP annuities (the amounts paid to survivors each month) can be elected for the following beneficiaries:

- Spouse—An annuity would be paid to the eligible spouse for life, unless the spouse remarries prior to age 55.

- Spouse and Children—The spouse would be the primary beneficiary and the children, contingent beneficiaries (includes former spouses and children).

- Children Only—Children would receive an annuity until age 18, or age 22 if continuing education on a full-time basis.

- Incapacitated Children—Incapacitated children would receive an annuity as long as they remain unmarried and incapacitation exists.

- Former Spouse—An annuity would be paid to the former spouse.

- Insurable Interest Person—This would include a person who depends on your income for support, i.e., parent, dependent or nondependent child, relative, etc.

Electing RCSBP. If you are in the Reserve or Guard, you qualify for RCSBP when you are notified that you are eligible for retired pay at age 60. From that date of notification, you have 90 days to enroll. You have three options for enrollment:

Option A:

You elect not to participate in RCSBP, but you still have the option to enroll in RCSBP when you:

- Marry (election must be made within one year after the marriage).

- Reach age 60 and receive retired pay.

Option B:

You elect coverage, but survivors are not entitled to a monthly annuity until the date you would have reached age 60. This is known as the deferred annuity.

Option C:

You elect coverage requiring that annuity payments to survivors begin immediately upon your death. This is known as the immediate annuity.

For options B and C, your annuity is determined by a base amount that you specify when you enroll. You can elect from $300 up to an amount equal to full monthly retirement pay for your base amount. For example, if you receive full

Take Advantage

To calculate your potential RCSBP coverage and premium costs, go to www.military.com/RCSBP.

retirement pay of $2,000 per month, you may elect between $300 and $2,000 as the base amount, or some other amount less than $2,000. You can only select your base amount once. Premiums are higher for higher base amounts—you should consider this when deciding on your base amount.

To enroll in this plan, fill out DD Form 2656-5 (available at www.military .com/forms), and mail it to the address for your particular service branch, as specified on the form. If you wish to opt out of the plan, you have only one opportunity to do so: between your second and third anniversary of receiving retired pay. (For most, this is between ages 62 and 63.) Once disenrolled, you cannot return to the plan. To disenroll, fill out a "Survivor Benefit Plan Termination Request" (DD form 2656-2, available at www.military.com/forms) and mail it to the Defense Finance and Accounting Service (DFAS) in Cleveland (see page 70 for address).

Take Advantage

If you get divorced, you must send a copy of the divorce decree to DFAS. In the event of a spouse's death, send along a copy of the death certificate. In both cases, your SBP premium will be suspended. If your divorce decree requires that you continue SBP for your former spouse, premiums will not be suspended.

SBP Coverage for Former Spouses

The SBP allows selection of coverage for former spouses. Costs and benefits under this option are identical to those for spouse coverage.

When former spouse coverage is elected, the current spouse must be informed. Only one SBP election may be made. If there is more than one former spouse, the member must specify which one will be covered.

When electing the former spouse option, a member must give the finance center a written statement signed by both the member and the former spouse. It must state if the SBP election is court ordered or part of a voluntary divorce agreement.

Part Five

The
Education
Advantage

Military service offers you a spectrum of great benefits—and the crown jewel of these might just be education benefits. With the recent addition of the new Post 9/11 GI Bill and other related benefit improvements many servicemembers and veterans are now eligible for more than $50,000 in education benefits. Tremendous options to help you finance your education, plus programs and services suited for your military lifestyle, are also at your fingertips. You are in prime position to fulfill your education and career goals—whether through college or a graduate degree, vocational training, certification, or just a few classes.

Too few servicemembers and veterans, however, take full advantage of these opportunities. The Department of Veterans Affairs estimates that 50 percent of the servicemembers who are eligible for GI Bill benefits never use them. In this chapter, we'll help you take advantage of these benefits—so that you can fulfill your goals of earning a degree, getting an edge in the job market, advancing in the military, and more.

Your education benefits break down into two major categories: money for school and education assistance programs. The Department of Veterans Affairs

The Education Advantage at a Glance

estimates that between 30 and 40 percent of eligible veterans and servicemembers never attempt to use their GI Bill benefits. Education assistance programs help servicemembers accelerate their path to completing their degrees by offering college credit for military training and experience, distance-learning programs, and credit-by-exam testing programs.

Money for School: Paying for Your Education

Servicemembers and veterans are eligible for financial aid and educational programs designed to save you time and money, and help you get ahead with your education. Many sources are available to help you, including:

- VA education benefit programs: The New Post 9/11 GI Bill, Montgomery GI Bill, Selective Reserve GI Bill, Reserve Education Assistance Program (REAP), Vocational Rehabilitation and Education (VR&E) and Veterans Education Assistance Program (VEAP).

- Military tuition assistance programs.

Use It or Lose it

The three most common excuses for not pursuing a college degree are: "It takes too long"; "It costs too much"; and "It's too difficult on a hectic work schedule."
But did you know that:

- You may have more than $82,000 in educational funding just waiting to be used.
- Using your GI Bill benefits, tuition assistance, and scholarships, you could get your degree with no out-of-pocket costs.
- In some cases, GI Bill benefits and tuition assistance can be used simultaneously, providing over $16,500 in annual educational benefits.
- Distance learning, on-base coursework, and online courses have been designed to fit your busy schedule and far-flung assignments.
- If you don't take advantage of your benefits, you could lose them.

Take Advantage

If you are a veteran or currently in the Guard or Reserve, the VA Apprenticeship and On-the-Job Training (OJT) Program offers you an alternative way to use your VA (GI Bill) education and training benefits. To learn more, see page 305.

Take Advantage

You can get an extra $150 a month in GI Bill education benefits if you elect to contribute an additional $600 before you leave the service. See the "GI Bill Buy-Up" section on page 195 for details.

- Federal student loans and grants.

- Military scholarships.

In addition to these resources, each military service offers special financial assistance programs, which are covered in the second part of this chapter (see page 205).

The New Post 9/11 GI Bill

On August 1, 2009 many post 9/11 veterans and servicemembers will become eligible for a new comprehensive package of education benefits. This new Post 9/11 GI Bill goes well beyond helping to pay for tuition; many veterans who served after Sept. 11, 2001, will get full tuition and fees, a new monthly housing stipend, and a $1,000 a year stipend for books and supplies. The new bill also gives Reserve and Guard members who have been activated for more than 90 days since 9/11 access to the same GI Bill benefits.

This new GI Bill is set to go into affect on August 1, 2009. However, as with any new legislation, it could take some time for the Department of Veterans Affairs (VA) to begin paying benefits. Benefits will not be paid for any training or education programs completed before July 31, 2009.

There are still many details to be determined and many current details are subject to change before this new benefit goes into effect. Be sure to check for the latest news on this benefit at www.military.com/new-GI-Bill.

New Post 9/11 GI Bill Eligibility

If you have served a total of at least 90 consecutive days on active duty in the Armed Forces since Sept. 11, 2001, you're eligible. However, the amount of benefits you receive under this program are determined by the actual amount of accumulated post 9/11 service you have.

To be eligible for the full benefit, you must have three years of active duty service after 9/11 or have been discharged due to a service-connected disability. If you are an officer who graduated from a service academy or received ROTC scholarships, you also qualify for the new GI Bill benefits. However, your ROTC/Service Academy associated obligated active-duty service time does not count toward the three years necessary to qualify for the full benefits.

Note: You didn't have to opt-in for the Montgomery GI Bill to be eligible for this program.

New GI Bill Payment Rates

The Post 9/11 GI Bill will provide up to 100 percent of your tuition. In addition, the program provides a monthly housing stipend a stipend of up to $1,000 a year for books and supplies. If you attend less than full-time will receive a portion of the payment based on the number of units of study.

The amount of tuition and stipends paid under the Post 9/11 GI Bill will vary depending on your state of enrollment, number of units taken, and amount of post Sept. 11, 2001 active-duty service. Here is a quick reference showing the percentage of total combined benefit eligibility based on the following periods of post 9/11 service:

- 100% - 36 or more total months.
- 100% - 30 or more consecutive days with Disability related Discharge.
- 90% - 30 total months.
- 80% - 24 total months.
- 70% - 18 total months.
- 60% - 12 total months.
- 50% - 6 total months.
- 40% - 90 or more days.

Tuition Rates

Under the new GI Bill you will be provided tuition up to the highest established charges for full-time undergraduate students charged by the public institution of higher education in the State in which you are enrolled.

One of the added features of this tuition payment plan is that the tuition will be paid directly to the school, relieving you of the responsibility. This is similar to the process used for military tuition assistance.

Monthly Housing Stipend

If you are enrolled in a traditional college program as full time student, you will be paid a monthly housing stipend equal to the monthly Basic Allowance for Housing (BAH) for an E-5 with dependents. However, if you attend distance learning programs such as correspondence courses and online you will not qualify for this stipend.

Book and Supply Stipend

You will receive a lump sum payment the first month of each quarter, semester, or term to help cover the cost of books, supplies, equipment, and other educational fees for that academic term. The payment amount will be equal to portion of the annual $1,000 cap for that academic year, depending on how the academic year is divided – quarter or semester terms.

Benefits Expiration Date

Unlike the Montgomery GI Bill, the new Post 9/11 GI Bill will allow you to use this benefit for up to 15 years after your last discharge or separation from active duty.

Benefit Transferability

The Department of Defense (DoD) is authorized to allow individuals who, on or after August 1, 2009, have served at least 6 years in the Armed Forces and **who agree to serve at least another 4 years** in the Armed Forces to transfer unused entitlement to their dependents (spouse, children). The Department of Defense may, by regulation, impose additional eligibility requirements and limit the number of months transferable to not less than 18 months.

Post 9/11 Affects on Existing GI Bill Benefits

If you are eligible for the Montgomery GI Bill and meet the criteria for Post 9/11 GI Bill eligibility, you will have the option to transfer your remaining MGIB benefits to the new program. However it is important to note that this choice is irrevocable.

For many veterans this will be a good option. However, due to the tuition limits set by this new GI Bill, many veterans who are pursuing post-graduate degrees may find the MGIB better suits their needs. This is also true for those students pursuing an online degree, as this new benefit will not pay the housing stipend to students enrolled in distance learning programs.

The Montgomery GI Bill

The Montgomery GI Bill (MGIB) is the VA education program for active-duty servicemembers and veterans. The program can provide up to $47,500 in tax free financial assistance for tuition, books, fees, and living expenses for those seeking a college degree or certification (including undergraduate and graduate degrees). This benefit is normally paid directly to the student on a monthly basis.

Since August of 1985, all active-duty enlistees are automatically enrolled in the Montgomery GI Bill, unless they choose to "opt out," which must be done in the first three days of active-duty service (usually during Military Basic Training).

In addition to helping fund your studies at traditional colleges, the GI Bill can be used to pay for independent study programs if they lead to a certificate that reflects educational attainment equivalent to that offered by an institution of higher learning. It can also be used for required continuing education units, professional certification, and graduate school. Finally, your GI Bill benefits can be used for licensing, certification, apprenticeship, and on-the-job training (OJT) programs.

MGIB Eligibility

To qualify for the GI Bill, you must meet all of the following requirements:

- Completion of high school or an equivalency certificate.

- Service for at least two years on active duty.

- For veterans, an honorable discharge.

In addition to the universal requirements listed above, you must meet eligibility requirements for one of the following four categories.

Category I

- Entered active duty for the first time after June 30, 1985.

- Contributed $100 each month from your military pay to the GI Bill, during the first 12 months of your service.

- Served continuously for three years, *or* two years if that is what you first enlisted for, *or* two years if you entered Selected Reserve within a year after leaving active duty and served for four years (the "2 by 4" program).

Category II

- Entered active duty before January 1, 1977.

- Served at least one day between October 19, 1984, and June 30, 1985, and stayed on active duty through June 30, 1988 (or June 30, 1987, if you entered Selected Reserve within one year after leaving active duty and served four years).

- Had entitlement left from the Vietnam Era GI Bill on December 31, 1989.

Category III

- Not eligible for GI Bill under Category I or II.

- On active duty on September 30, 1990, *and* separated involuntarily after

Take Advantage

There are many disreputable schools—sometimes referred to as "diploma mills"—out there. Be sure that the school you are considering is regionally or nationally accredited. For a database of accredited schools, see www.military.com /schools.

Take Advantage

You can use your GI Bill benefits for reimbursement of the cost of VA-approved licensing and certification tests. Visit www .military.com/ licensing-and-certification to learn more.

Take Advantage
The Reserve GI Bill is worth more than $10,000, and you pay nothing to get it! It requires a six-year commitment to serve in the Reserve or Guard.

February 2, 1991, or involuntarily separated on *or* after November 30, 1993, *or* voluntarily separated under either the Voluntary Separation Incentive or Special Separation Benefit program.

- Before separation, contibuted $1,200 of military pay for the program.

Category IV

- On active duty on October 9, 1996, *and* you had money remaining in a Veterans Education Assistance Program account on that date *and* you elected the GI Bill by October 9, 1997.

- Entered full-time National Guard duty under Title 32, U.S.C., between July 1, 1985, and November 28, 1989, *and* you elected the GI Bill during the period of October 9, 1996, through July 8, 1997.

The Montgomery and the New Post 9/11 GI Bills

The following table highlights the differences between the two bills.

	Montgomery GI Bill Chapter 30	Post 9/11 GI Bill Proposed - Chapter 33
Payment Rate for Full-Time Student	A monthly $1321 payment paid directly to the student.	A lump sum paid directly to the school each term for tuition.
Duration of Program	36 Month entitlement.	36 Month entitlement.
Additional college related expense payments	No additional payments for living expenses.	Monthly housing stipend – for on campus students only. Books and Fees: Up to $1,000 a year
Eligibility Requirements	Those who entered service after June 30, 1985.	90 days or more of active-duty service since Sept. 11, 2001.
VEAP-era Eligibility	No - Except those who elected to convert in the past.	Yes – those who meet the eligibility criteria above.
Benefit Expiration	10 Years after separation or discharge.	15 years from your last period of active duty of at least 90 consecutive days.
Enrollment fee	Yes - $1,200	None

GI Bill Giants

From poet Lawrence Ferlinghetti to chef Julia Child to Presidents George H. W. Bush and Gerald Ford, from congressional leaders Robert Dole and G.V. "Sonny" Montgomery to Supreme Court Justice William Rehnquist, former GI Bill students have succeeded in a wide range of fields. They've received the Nobel Prize in nearly every science-related category, including Milton Friedman in economics and Jack Kilby in physics.

- Had military pay reduced by $100 a month for 12 months or made a $1,200 lump-sum contribution.

Officers who are commissioned through a Service Academy or ROTC students who received more than $3,400 in any academic year are not eligible for the GI Bill.

Multiple VA Education Benefit Eligibility

You may be eligible for more than one VA education benefit. For example, you may be a veteran who has GI Bill benefits based on active-duty service, but you decide to join the Reserve and thus become eligible for the Reserve GI Bill (see page 192). Or you may qualify for vocational rehabilitation for service-connected disabilities of 10 or 20 percent with a waiver from a vocational rehabilitation counselor (see page 305). Not surprisingly, you cannot receive payment for more than one benefit at a given time—you must select which benefit to receive.

In situations such as these, you should discuss your education plans with a VA Education Service Representative, who can help you get maximum use of your benefits.

Contact

To verify the school or degree program is VA approved or to talk to a VA counselor directly, call VA at 888-GIBILL-1 (888-442-4551).

Monthly GI Bill Benefits

This table shows how much VA pays each month while you are going to school.

If you are on active duty or a veteran and go to school:	Each month you'll get:
Full-time (usually 12 or more credits)	$1,321.00
Three-quarters time (usually 9–12 credits)	$990.75
Half-time (usually 4–9 credits)	$660.50
Quarter-time or less (usually 3 or fewer credits)	$330.25

Take Advantage

Having your school registrar's office submit both VA Form 1990 and VA Form 1999 to the VA regional office will help speed the process.

No matter how many VA education assistance programs you are eligible for, you cannot use benefits for more than 48 months. For example, if you use 36 months of active duty-veteran GI Bill benefits and then qualify for the Reserve GI Bill, you can use only 12 months of Reserve GI Bill benefits.

The Reserve Education Assistance Program (REAP)

REAP is a relatively new GI Bill benefit that makes certain Reservists and Guardsmen, who were activated for at least 90 days after September 11, 2001, eligible for increased benefits. Each military service, the Department of Defense (DOD), and the Department of Homeland Security (DHS) will determine eligibility. A Guard or Reserve member who has served on active duty on or after September 11, 2001, under Title 10 U.S. Code for a contingency operation and who serves at least 90 consecutive days is eligible. National Guard members are also eligible if their active duty is under Section 502(f), Title 32 U.S.C., and they serve for 90 consecutive days for a national emergency supported by federal funds. Individuals are eligible as soon as they reach the 90-day point whether or not they are currently on active duty. The DoD identifies contingency operations that qualify for these.

Take Advantage

Eligible members of the National Guard and Reserve are now able to use the MGIB-SR after they separate from military service for the number of months they were activated plus four more months. They may also add multiple periods of activation to further increase this extension, or portability.

Disabled members who are injured or have an illness or disease incurred or aggravated in the line of duty, and are released from active duty before completing 90 consecutive days, are also eligible.

Applying for REAP Benefits

You can apply by filling out VA Form 22-1990, Application for Education Benefits. You can also apply online through the VA VONAPP website at www .vabenefits.vba.va.gov/vonapp.

REAP Benefit Payment Rates

The full-time rate in the table below accounts for full-time institutional training on or after October 1, 2004. If your training took place before October 1, 2004, your monthly rate will be the percentage of the Active-Duty GI Bill in effect at the time of your training.

Time Reserve Member Serves on Active Duty	Full-Time Student Rate (2007 Rates)
90 days, but less than one year	$528.40
One year, but less than two years	$792.60
Two years or more	$1,056.80

Monthly Reserve GI Bill Benefits

The following table shows how much the VA pays each month while you go to school.

If you are in the Reserve or National Guard and go to school:	Each month you will get (2007 rates):
Full-time (usually 12 or more credits)	$329.00
Three-quarters time (usually 9–12 credits)	$246.00
Half-time (usually 4–9 credits)	$163.00
Quarter-time or less (usually 3 or fewer credits)	$82.25

Montgomery GI Bill for Selective Reserve (MGIB-SR)

Through the MGIB-SR, you can get up to 36 months of benefits worth more than $10,000 (tax-free) to help pay for college tuition, books, fees, and vocational training or certification expenses. You qualify for the Reserve GI Bill if all of the following is true:

- After June 30, 1985, you sign a six-year obligation to serve in the Reserve or National Guard.

- You have completed your initial active duty for training.

- You have a high school diploma or equivalency certificate before completing initial active duty for training.

- You remain in good standing while serving in an active Reserve or National Guard unit.

GI Bill—Active Duty Option

Certain Guard and Reserve servicemembers may now be able to qualify for MGIB Chapter 30 Active Duty Benefits. Unlike other reserve MGIB programs this benefit can be used after separating from the service.

In order to qualify you must meet the following criteria:

- Had not been on active-duty service prior to 7/1/85.

- Were activated under Title 10 U.S. Code since 7/1/85.

- Served a minimum of 24 months of continuous active duty.

- Complete DD Form 2366 Election to Participate in the MGIB.

- Contribute $1,200 to enroll in the program.

- Maintained honorable service during your active-duty period.

Take Advantage

The Army has announced a pilot program that will enable eligible enlisted soldiers to transfer part of their GI Bill benefit to a spouse or dependent as part of their selective reenlistment package. Contact your Army retention career counselor for information.

Take Advantage

A new policy may allow transitioning members of the Guard and Reserve to use their GI Bill after leaving the service. Visit www.military.com/education to learn more.

Take AdvantageA

Anew policy may allow transitioning members of the Guard and Reserve to use their GI Bill after leaving the service. Visit www.military.com/education to learn more.

The Veterans Education Assistance Program

The Veterans Education Assistance Program (VEAP) is an educational benefit that was offered instead of the GI Bill from 1977 to 1985. The program matches servicemembers' contributions for education on a $2 for $1 basis. Like the GI Bill, this benefit may still be used for degree and certificate programs, flight training, apprenticeship/on-the-job training, and correspondence courses.

VEAP Eligibility

You qualify for VEAP if:

- You entered service for the first time between January 1, 1977, and June 30, 1985.

- You opened a contribution account before April 1, 1987.

- You voluntarily contributed from $25 to $2,700 to the program.

- You completed your first period of service.

- You were discharged or released from service under conditions other than dishonorable.

How to Get Your GI Bill Benefits

Follow these steps to receive your GI Bill benefits for all three GI Bill programs (active-duty, veterans, Reserve/Guard, and VEAP):

1. Verify the school or degree program is VA-approved by calling the GI Bill phone line.

2. Complete "Application for VA Education Benefits" (VA Form 22-1990), available at www.military.com/forms, and submit it to the school's VA-certifying official (usually the registrar) for verification.

3. The school official will complete VA Form 1999 and submit both VA Form 22-1990 and VA Form 1999 to the appropriate VA regional office.

    If you haven't selected a school yet, simply complete VA Form 22-1990 and submit your application to your VA regional office. You will receive a letter from VA verifying your eligibility within six to eight weeks.

    You only have to submit your VA Form 22-1990 once. While you are attending school, however, you must report to VA each month through the Web Automated Verification of Enrollment (WAVE). In addition, the school must submit a VA Form 22-1999 for you each new academic semester or quarter. Many schools can do this electronically through the VA-Once program. If you are taking correspondence courses you may be required to complete and submit a VA Form 22-1999c for each course, to ensure you continue to receive your benefits.

GI Bill programs expire 10 years after your date of last discharge. This means that any active-duty service (90 days or more) during that 10-year period will reset your 10-year limit. In other words, if you separate from service but reenlist later, your "GI Bill clock" will reset to when you leave the service again.

Additional Montgomery GI Bill Benefits

Two changes based on the Veterans Benefits Improvement Act of 2000 directly affect servicemembers who are currently on active duty: top-up and buy-up.

GI Bill Top-Up

Top-up allows active-duty servicemembers to use their GI Bill to supplement the military tuition assistance program. Top-up will cover the difference between the total cost of a college course and the amount of tuition assistance (TA) paid by the military.

Top-up eligibility. If you are currently on active duty and have completed a minimum of two years' service, and you meet the eligibility requirements for military tuition assistance and the new GI Bill, you qualify for top-up. Follow these simple steps to apply:

1. Complete your service branch's tuition assistance request form.

2. Complete an application for VA education benefits, VA Form 22-1990, which you can find at www.military.com/forms. Indicate "top-up" on the VA application in item 1A under the GI Bill–Active Duty block.

3. Send your TA approval form, along with VA Form 22-1990, to the VA Regional Processing Office that handles your claim. The address is given on the form.

GI Bill Buy-Up

Buy-up allows active-duty personnel to make an additional contribution of up to $600 to increase their total Montgomery GI Bill contribution to $1,800. This buy-up can increase your total GI Bill benefits by as much as $5,400. You get an additional $25 a month in GI Bill benefits for each additional $100 you contribute to your GI Bill account. For example, if you contribute the full $600, your monthly GI Bill benefit will increase by $150. If you contribute $300, your monthly GI Bill benefit will increase by $75.

Take Advantage

Tuition assistance today is at an all-time high—don't take these levels for granted. You never know when they might begin to drop. And remember, tuition assistance is not a loan: you have earned it and don't need to repay it.

Take Advantage

You qualify for Federal Financial Student Aid such as Pell Grants and the Stafford Loan Program even if you are still on active duty.

Take Advantage

To search for DANTES schools, see www.military.com /Education/schools.

Buy-up eligibility. If you enlisted after August 1985, you qualify for making additional contributions. To apply, simply contact your personnel support center to make arrangements to contribute any amount up to $600. You will fill out DD Form 2366, available at www.military.com/forms, and submit it with the help of your personnel office.

Survivors and Dependents Educational Assistance Program

Dependents Educational Assistance provides education and training opportunities to eligible dependents of certain veterans. The program offers up to 45 months of education benefits that can be used for degree and certificate programs, apprenticeships, and on-the-job training. If you are a spouse, you may take a correspondence course. Remedial, deficiency, and refresher courses may also be approved under certain circumstances.

Dependents Educational Assistance Eligibility

Eligibility requirements have been expanded to cover a spouse or child of a person who:

Contact

Find DANTES online at www.dantes .doded.mil.

• VA determines has a service-connected permanent and total disability; and

• at the time of VA's determination is a member of the Armed Forces who is hospitalized or receiving outpatient medical care, services, or treatment; and

• is likely to be discharged or released from service for this service-connected disability.

If you are a son or daughter of a servicemember and wish to receive these benefits, you must be between the ages of 18 and 26. In certain instances, you may begin before age 18 and continue after age 26. Marriage is not a bar to this benefit.

If you are in the Armed Forces, you may not receive this benefit while on active duty. To pursue training after military service, your discharge must not be under dishonorable conditions. VA can extend your period of eligibility by a length of time equal to your time on active duty plus four months. With some exceptions, the extension generally cannot go beyond your 31st birthday.

If you are a spouse, benefits end 10 years from the date the VA finds you eligible, or from the veteran's date of death.

Applying for Dependents Educational Assistance Benefits

You should make sure that your selected program is approved for VA training. If you are not clear on this point, the VA will inform you and the school or company about the requirements.

To apply for DEA benefits, obtain and complete "Application for Survivors and Dependents Educational Assistance" (VA Form 22-5490), available at www.military.com/forms. Then send it to the VA regional office with jurisdiction over the state where you will train. If you are a son or daughter of a servicemember and under legal age, a parent or guardian must sign the application.

If you have started training, take your application to your school or employer. Ask the staff to complete VA Form 22-1999, Enrollment Certification, and send both forms to the VA.

Military Tuition Assistance

The Armed Forces Military Tuition Assistance (TA) program is a benefit provided to eligible members of the Air Force, Army, Coast Guard, Marine Corps, and Navy. Each service will pay up to 100 percent of its members' tuition expenses up to a specified amount. Each branch of the Armed Forces determines how to administer its tuition assistance program—some also offer benefits to their Reserve and National Guard components. Maximum benefits can be as much as $4,500 per year, depending on the branch of service.

Remember, tuition assistance is not a loan; it is money you have earned and do *not* have to repay unless you fail or drop the course. The TA application process differs greatly between services. Visit www.military.com/education to learn more. After registering for classes, TA is paid directly to the school.

Take Advantage

Servicemembers, veterans, and their family members can use the Scholarship Finder at www.military.com/scholarships to find grants and scholarships. Any organization can list its military scholarship on the site.

Take Advantage

You should always attempt to use any available service and state-funded tuition assistance programs before dipping into GI Bill benefits.

Military Matters

Tuition assistance (TA) is usually paid directly to the institution by the individual military service. Active-duty members may elect to use the GI Bill top-up in addition to TA to cover high-cost courses. Tuition assistance is not a loan; it should be seen as money you have earned, just like your base pay. Unlike the GI Bill, tuition assistance is reset each fiscal year, so if you don't use the allotment this year, you can consider it lost. This is why most Education Services Officers recommend that active-duty servicemembers use their TA before dipping into their GI Bill. See the chart on page 201 for further information on deciding which benefit to use.

Active Duty Military Tuition Assistance Benefits

Service	Amount Covered	Covered Fees	Who Is Eligible	Form
Air Force	100% tuition and fees not to exceed: $250 per semester credit hour $166 per quarter credit hour $4,500 per fiscal year	tuition, lab enrollment, and special fees	Active duty, Reserve	New Online Process
Army	100% tuition and fees not to exceed: $250 per semester credit hour $166 per quarter credit hour $4,500 per fiscal year	tuition, lab, and fees	Active duty, Reserve, and National Guard	New Online Process
Coast Guard	100% tuition and fees not to exceed: $250 per semester credit hour $166 per quarter credit hour $4,500 per fiscal year	tuition, lab enrollment, and special fees	Active duty, Reserve, civilian employee	CG-4147
Marine Corps	100% tuition and fees not to exceed: $250 per semester credit hour $166 per quarter credit hour $4,500 per fiscal year	tuition, lab enrollment, and special fees	Active duty	NETPDC 1560/03
Navy	100% tuition and fees not to exceed: $250 per semester credit hour $166 per quarter credit hour 16 semester hour limit per fiscal year	tuition, lab enrollment, and special fees	Active duty, Reserve	NETPDC 1560/03

Federal Financial Student Aid

The federal government offers several low-interest loans and grants that can supplement military or veteran education benefits, if necessary. Federal financial aid is paid directly to the school for disbursement; once the school has taken its share, the remaining loan or grant balance belongs to you.

Whether you are active duty, Reserve, Guard, veteran, retiree, on the GI Bill, or not, you should take advantage of these programs. Your only limitation is that you cannot use military tuition assistance and federal student aid programs at the same time.

Remember: Grants are loans you don't need to repay!

Applying for Federal Student Aid

You can apply for federal student aid programs by filling out the Free Applications for Federal Student Aid (FAFSA) form online (www.fafsa.ed.gov).

After you have submitted your FAFSA form, your school will notify you of the total amounts in loans and grants you are qualified to receive. When you get this notification from the school, simply select the loans and grants you want, and the school will complete the process within two to four weeks.

State Education Benefits

Many states offer education benefits to veterans, active-duty, reserve, and guard servicemembers and their family members. Depending on your home of record, you may be eligible for tuition assistance, reduced fees, scholarships, grants, and tuition waivers. For example, in some states military spouses can enjoy lower in-state tuition rates. To see what your state offers, check out an updated benefits table at www.military.com/education/statebenefits.

Military Scholarships

Military scholarships are designated for servicemembers, veterans, and their family members to help cover the cost of tuition, fees, books, living expenses, and more.

As a member of the military community, you may be eligible for thousands of scholarships, grants, and awards worth millions of dollars. Many of these scholarships go unclaimed each year, often because people don't know they exist or how to access them. Browse more than 1,000 military-specific scholar-

Take Advantage

The Graduate Record Exam (GRE) can be used to earn up to 18 upper-level and 18 lower-level college credits toward an undergraduate degree.

ships at www.military.com/scholarships. Information about benefits for military spouses can also be found at www.military.com/spouse.

Choosing the Best Financial Aid Plan

If you are on active duty, you have several options for how to pay for school. Making the right choice can be critical for two reasons:

- To avoid out-of-pocket expenses.

- To receive the largest amount of benefits when you leave the service. For example, if you use some of your GI Bill benefits during active duty, you will have fewer benefits left over when you are a veteran.

The flow chart on page 201 can assist you as you decide which education option best suits your current and long-term goals.

Education Assistance Programs

Education assistance programs provide access to "nontraditional" education resources such as free credit-by-exam tests, distance learning, and college credit for military experience and training. It all adds up to your gaining course credits and degrees faster than you ordinarily would, as well as saving time and money—an advantage that comes in particularly handy if you're on active duty or have accumulated educational experience in your military career.

DANTES (Defense Activity for Non-Traditional Education Support) is a DoD organization created to help servicemembers pursue their educational goals and earn the degrees or certification they deserve while continuing to serve their country.

DANTES maintains three online catalogs that list distance learning courses and programs:

- DANTES Independent Study Catalog: lists more than 6,200 high school, undergraduate and graduate level, and examination preparation courses from regionally accredited institutions. This catalog is intended for students who need specific courses to meet degree requirements.

Choosing the Right Education Benefit

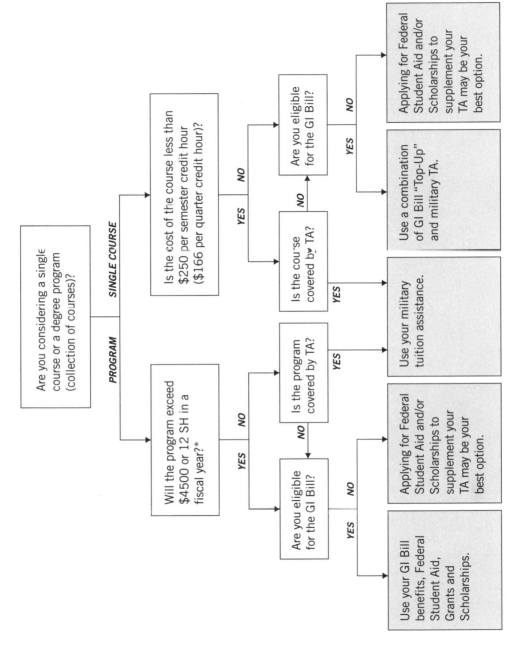

Are you considering a single course or a degree program (collection of courses)?

PROGRAM

Will the program exceed $4500 or 12 SH in a fiscal year?*

YES — Is the program covered by TA?

NO — Are you eligible for the GI Bill?

Is the program covered by TA? **YES** — Use your military tuition assistance.

Are you eligible for the GI Bill? **YES** — Use your GI Bill benefits, Federal Student Aid, Grants and Scholarships.

NO — Applying for Federal Student Aid and/or Scholarships to supplement your TA may be your best option.

SINGLE COURSE

Is the cost of the course less than $250 per semester credit hour ($166 per quarter credit hour)?

YES — Is the course covered by TA?

NO — Are you eligible for the GI Bill?

Is the course covered by TA? **YES** — Use your military tuition assistance.

NO — Use a combination of GI Bill "Top-Up" and military TA.

Are you eligible for the GI Bill? **YES** — Use a combination of GI Bill "Top-Up" and military TA.

NO — Applying for Federal Student Aid and/or Scholarships to supplement your TA may be your best option.

* Note: The 12 semester-hour requirement is for Navy servicemembers only.

SH=Semester Hour, TA=Tuition Assistance

Comparison of Active-Duty Education Benefit Options

Education Benefit	Highlights	Things to Consider
Montgomery GI Bill	• Pays up to $1,321 per month for a full-time student • Not subject to command approval • Money is direct-deposited to your own bank account • Costs are taken from your 36-month GI Bill benefits	• You must be eligible • Cannot be used in conjunction with TA • You are responsible for paying the school since GI Bill benefits are sent to you
GI Bill Top-Up	• Pays the balance remaining after TA • Relatively simple process • Noncompetitive	• Charged against your 36 months of GI Bill benefits • You must be GI Bill eligible • Must be used with TA
Military Tuition Assistance (TA)	• No cost • Simple process • Covers up to 100% tuition and fees • Noncompetitive	Limited to: • $250 per credit hour • $4,500 annually • 16 semester hours (U.S. Navy restriction only) • Subject to command and service approval
Federal Student Aid (FSA)	• Offers low-interest loans • Offers grants (no need to repay) • One application process for all FSA • Needs-based • Noncompetitive	• FSA loans must be repaid • Money goes to school for dispersal • Complex application process
Scholarships and Grants	• Usually no cost • Process varies • Can be worth thousands • Many go unclaimed • Can be used to pay for books and fees in conjunction with TA • Thousands are designed for military, veterans, and dependents	• Process can be time consuming • Based on competition and/or student needs • Wide range in value • May require submitting an essay • Application fees may be required

- DANTES External Degree Catalog: lists academic programs available from regionally accredited colleges and universities that have little or no residency requirements for degree completion. This catalog also has a Teacher Certification Section describing institutions with their Teacher Certification programs available through distance learning.

- DANTES Catalog of Nationally Accredited Distance Learning Programs: lists courses and degree programs from institutions accredited by the various national accrediting bodies. The course and degree subjects range from "Appliance Repair" to "Zionism and Judaism in Israel."

Distance Learning

Increasingly, members of the military community are taking advantage of innovations in coursework delivery—allowing them to complete their degrees from almost anywhere in the world. Distance learning can come in many forms, including videotapes, correspondence courses, on-base courses, and, of course, online. Such user-friendly programs are designed to fit your schedule, lifestyle, and goals. In short, they provide a flexible way to take college or graduate courses or certificate progams while at home, at work, or even on duty, as well as to earn everything from an associate's degree to a doctorate. Thousands of accredited universities and colleges offer distance-learning courses.

Online Opportunities

Online education, in particular, has become a popular option. It doesn't matter where you are stationed or what hours you keep—you can study wherever and whenever you want, and earn the same degree that you would earn on a campus. Online courses generally follow the same format as traditional courses, with a professor, textbooks, assignments, and exams. In addition, they use a combination of message boards, email, chat rooms, CD-ROMs, and textbooks. Online courses can be completely self-paced, or instructor-led; some actually have virtual classrooms, where you can share ideas, ask questions, and learn with other students.

If you're deciding on an online program of study, remember to ask yourself these six important questions:

1. *How is the course presented?* Course content is more easily understood if it's presented in a dynamic, engaging manner. Choose a program that utilizes many different methods to convey information.

2. *How do I interact with the instructor and other students?* Find a program that facilitates, and even requires, student interaction—this is an important aspect of an online program.

Take Advantage

Unless you know for sure that you need to take a particular course, wait until the school gets *all* your transcripts before you sign up for classes. Otherwise you may end up taking courses you don't need.

3. *How will I be evaluated?* Will you actually work to earn your degree? Will you be evaluated properly? Are degrees given away like handouts? Beware of the dreaded "diploma mill."

4. *What kind of library and research materials are available?* Make sure the school has good materials, and that they are accessible from anywhere.

5. *Is the school regionally or nationally accredited?* Degrees from unaccredited schools aren't as valuable as ones from accredited institutions. In fact, the former can be almost valueless to certain employers.

6. *Am I committed and disciplined enough to complete the program?*

Credit-by-Exam

The DANTES Credit-by-Examination Program provides several examination programs through which an individual may:

- Earn a high school credential.

- Satisfy undergraduate- and graduate-level college admission requirements.

- Earn college credit.

- Gain professional certification.

Most tests are offered at DANTES Test Centers on a funded basis for eligible military personnel and increasingly, several of these testing programs are also available at National Test Centers (colleges and universities and commercial test centers). Depending on the testing program, space-available testing may be available for civilian examinees at DANTES Test Centers.

College Level Examination Program (CLEP), DANTES Subject Standardized Test (DSST), and Excelsior College Exam (ECE) examinations are recommended for college credit by the American Council on Education and recognized by most regionally and nationally accredited institutions as a way for students to "test out" of a given course. These exams are worth college credits ranging from 3 to 12 semester hours each.

Military veterans may take these exams at National Test Center locations on a reimbursement basis.

College Credit for Military Experience

Thanks to the efforts of the American Council on Education (ACE), your military training, experience, and specialty can translate into college credits. This can save you time and money as you pursue a degree.

Each individual school determines the number of credits they will accept, and how to apply them toward your degree. Certain schools may choose not to grant any credit for military experience. *This is why it's critical to shop around for the most military-friendly school available.*

The first step to claiming the credits you have earned is to request a transcript from your military service. Each service branch has its own system for recording your military education and experience credits. Your service should provide you with unofficial personal copies of your transcript, and send schools official copies of your transcript at no charge.

Getting Your Transcript

The Army uses the Army/American Council on Education Registry Transcript System (AARTS), which automatically captures your academic credits from military training and standardized tests. The Navy and Marine Corps use the SMART system and the Community College of the Air Force (CCAF) handles transcripts for the Air Force.

The Coast Guard Institute (CGI) requires servicemembers to submit documentation of all training (except correspondence-course records), along with an enrollment form, to receive a transcript. Unlike the other branches, you will be unable to enroll with the Coast Guard transcript system after you leave the service, so it is important to enroll while in the service.

Under most circumstances, veterans are eligible to use their former service branch's transcript program. However, if you are not eligible for the AARTS, SMART, CCAF, or CGI systems, you will need to fill out DD Form 295 (www.military.com/forms), and provide your DD Form 214 (for instructions on how to get your DD Form 214, see page 312) to receive credit for your experience.

Education Advantages by Branch of Service

The Air Force, Army, Coast Guard, Marine Corps, and Navy, along with their affiliated aid organizations, offer you and your dependents college programs, loans, and scholarships. You can use these benefits in addition to your GI Bill and tuition assistance. They are listed below by service.

Take Advantage

If you want to use your GI Bill benefits towards flight training, you must have a private pilot certificate before you begin training. One big exception: You can receive GI Bill benefits for flight training courses that are part of approved standard college degree programs or for a recreational pilot certification or private pilot certification course, provided that the course is part of the standard college degree program.

Contact

U.S. Coast Guard Institute
5900 S.W. 64th St.
Oklahoma City, OK
73169-6990
405-954-0072

SOCCOAST
www.soc.aascu
.org/soccoast

Coast Guard Institute
www.uscg.mil
/hq/cgi.

Take Advantage

GoArmyEd

The Army recently launched GoArmyEd, which is the 24/7 virtual gateway to request tuition assistance (TA) online for classroom, distance learning, and eArmyU online college courses.

Air Force Education

Active Duty Educational Opportunities

Air Force Education Services programs offer cost-effective educational opportunities, from basic skills through graduate-level degrees, and feature tuition assistance, testing, and counseling services.

The Community College of the Air Force (CCAF) is the only degree-granting institution of higher learning in the world dedicated exclusively to educating enlisted personnel. Located at Maxwell Air Force Base in Montgomery, Alabama, CCAF offers career-oriented airmen and NCOs a job-related, two-year associate's degree in Applied Science. The world's largest community college, CCAF is regionally accredited by the Southern Association of Colleges and Schools/Commission on Colleges.

The Air Force Institute of Technology (AFIT), based at Wright-Patterson Air Force Base in Ohio, provides graduate education opportunities at its two resident graduate schools and supervises students enrolled in its civilian institutions program. The Graduate School of Engineering provides advanced education and research focused on aerospace technology, while the Graduate School of Logistics and Acquisition Management teaches officers the expertise to manage complex weapon systems through their life cycles. The AFIT Civilian Institution Program places students in more than 400 civilian universities, research centers, hospitals, and industrial organizations throughout the United States and in several other countries.

Servicemembers Opportunity Colleges (SOC) are a network of more than 1,800 colleges and universities across the nation dedicated to helping servicemembers and their families get college degrees. Basically, you can transfer credits you earn at one SOC school to another SOC school. You can also take courses at an SOC school in your off-duty hours at or near military installations in the United States and overseas.

More Help with Tuition

Air Force Student Loan Repayment Program. If you are a college student or graduate who qualifies for this program, the Air Force will pay, upon enlistment, up to $10,000 of your student loans acquired from a college-level education. This benefit is only available during initial enlistment. Be sure to speak to your local Air Force recruiter for further information.

General George S. Brown Spouse Tuition Assistance Program. If you are the spouse of an active duty airman or officer stationed overseas, and you will be attending high school or college programs, then you are eligible for the

Degrees Defined

Associate's degrees:		
(2 year degree)	Associate of Arts (A.A.)	Usually 60 semester-hour units (L.L.), which typically requires a foreign language
	Associate of Science (A.S.)	Usually 60 semester-hour units (L.L.), which generally requires less arts and more sciences, and has no foreign language requirement
	Associate in Applied Science (A.A.S.)	Usually 60 semester-hour units (L.L.), which are mostly professional in nature, such as electronics technician, machinery technician, etc.
Bachelor's degrees:		
(4 year degree)	Bachelor of Arts (B.A.)	Usually 120 semester-hour units (L.L. and U.L.), predominantly arts and sciences with a foreign language requirement. Includes degrees in mathematics, literature, theology, etc.
	Bachelor of Science (B.S.)	Usually 120 semester-hour units (L.L. and U.L.). Less arts than sciences with no foreign language requirement, such as degrees in business, aeronautics, communications, etc.
Master's degrees:		
	Master of Arts (M.A.)	Graduate-level studies in arts and sciences, such as history, biology, mathematics, etc. Thesis project required in most cases.
	Master of Science (M.S.)	Graduate-level studies in professional areas such as accounting, marketing, etc. Thesis required in most cases.
	Master of Business Administration (MBA)	Graduate-level studies in business-related areas such as human resource management, organization development, e-commerce, etc.

College 101

Lower Level (L.L.)	Associate's level courses	Courses that range from basic to intermediate level, such as English 101, Introductory Algebra 1a, etc.
Upper Level (U.L.)	Bachelor's level courses	Courses that range from intermediate to advanced levels, such as Abnormal Psychology 401, Calculus, Organizational Behavior, etc.
Credit hours	Semester hours (SH)	Most schools run under the semester system. This is how the school grants credit for course completion. A normal course is usually worth 3 credit hours.
	Quarter hours (QH)	Some schools run under the quarter system. This has no effect on the quality of the courses, or the cost, but is simply a different means of measuring credits and organizing the school year. To convert your credits if you plan to transfer from a quarter system to a semester system school, you generally divide your quarter credits by 1.5.
Fees	Tuition and lab fees are the costs associated directly with the course you are taking. Other fees such as administrative, transcript, and evaluation fees are general to college enrollment and are not usually covered by military tuition assistance programs.	
Financial aid	Financial aid refers to any form of grant or loan that is paid directly to the college. This includes Stafford Loans, Perkins Loans, Pell Grants, and military tuition assistance. However, the GI Bill funds are not considered financial aid (because they are paid to you, not the school).	
Fiscal year	A federal fiscal year (FY) runs from the first of October to the 30th of September.	
Registrar's office	The college administration office that normally handles your GI Bill paperwork.	
Distance learning	Any form of education that does not require classroom attendance, such as online, videotapes, correspondence, etc.	
Degree program	The list of courses or modules required to earn a specific degree.	
Residency requirement	The number of credits a student must earn directly from the school (not by transfer) to earn a degree from that school. Example: A college may require you to take a minimum of 30 credits to earn a diploma.	

Air Force Education Contacts

Community College of the Air Force
www.au.af.mil/au/ccaf
Air Force Institute of Technology
www.afit.edu

Air Force Aid Society
www.afas.org

The Servicemembers Opportunity Colleges
www.soc.aascu.org

Spouse Tuition Assistance Program (STAP). STAP provides assistance at a rate of 50 percent of course tuition with a maximum of $1,500 per academic year.

General Henry H. Arnold Education Grant Program. This program provides $1,500 grants to selected sons and daughters of active-duty Air Force servicemembers. Administered by ACT Recognition Program Services, this grant program remains competitive because of its need-based selection criteria. It is uniquely tailored to recognize the proper weighing of family income and education cost factors. ACT, located in Iowa City, Iowa, is an independent not-for-profit organization with more than 40 years' experience in providing support services to scholarship sponsors.

For more information on all these grants and how to apply, visit your Air Force Aid Society (AFAS) Section. AFAS Sections are located at all Air Force Bases worldwide, usually in the Family Support Center.

Educational Opportunities for Guard and Reserve Members

Air National Guard. The Air National Guard (ANG) provides access to all DANTES credit-by-examination programs, Community College of the Air Force associate's degree programs, federal tuition assistance for ANG members for distance-learning courses, and state education benefits for all members.

The ANG currently offers 100 percent tuition assistance for up to $250 per semester hour, or $166 per quarter hour, not to exceed $1,000 annually per servicemember. DANTES manages payment of this program. Contact your Education Service Office on base for information on how to apply for this and other programs.

Air Force Tuition Assistance (Activated Guard and Reserve). In 2004, the tuition assistance for active duty and activated Reserve/Guard was 100 percent tuition and fees up to $250 per semester credit hour or $166 per quarter credit hour, not to exceed $4,500 per fiscal year.

Take Advantage

For tips, practice entrance tests, basic training advice, updated enlistment bonuses and everything else you need to know about joining the military, visit www.military.com/joining.

Take Advantage

For ASVAB study tips, examples of how your score affects your military career options, and practice tests, visit www.military.com/ASVAB.

Take Advantage

For resources, tips, and career news, and for in-depth information on advancement in your branch of service, including the latest promotion alerts, visit the Professional Development Center at www.military.com/militarycareers.

Air Force Reserve. The Air Force Reserve has information on DANTES credit-by-examination, Air Force Institute for Advanced Distributed Learning courses, and Professional Military Education programs that can lead to civilian education credits or an associate's degree in Applied Science from the Community College of the Air Force.

The Air Force Reserve also provides information on other career development and continuing education courses, including the Air Command and Staff College Seminar Program and Non-Commissioned Officer (NCO) Academy Seminar Programs.

For undergraduate degree programs, the Air Force Reserve offers the same amount of tuition assistance as listed earlier for Air National Guard members. For graduate degree programs, the amounts are 75 percent tuition assistance up to $187.50 per semester hour, or $125 per quarter hour, not to exceed $3,500 annually. DANTES manages payment of the U.S. Air Force Reserves tuition assistance program. Contact your ESO for information on how to apply for tuition assistance and the other programs noted earlier.

Army Education

Take Advantage

GoArmyEd is the Army's 24/7 virtual gateway to request Tuition Assistance for classroom, distance learning, and eArmyU online courses. Go to www.earmyu.com to learn more.

Active Duty Educational Opportunities

The **Army Continuing Education System** (ACES) promotes lifelong learning opportunities. This service helps you link up to Army educational opportunities, learning centers, details on money for college, and more.

Army Knowledge Online. The Army Knowledge Online Learning Portal is a burgeoning database for the Army, with guides and information to help soldiers pursue their educational and career goals.

EArmyU. In 2001, the U.S. Army launched this education initiative, giving eligible enlisted soldiers the opportunity to work toward a college degree or certificate anytime, anywhere. EArmyU uses virtual learning systems and provides the following services:

- Distance learning through the eArmyU site.

- A selection of transferable certificate and degree programs.

- 100 percent tuition assistance for tuition, fees, and books up to the established semester hour cap and tuition ceiling.

- Global accessibility—24 hours a day, seven days a week.

- Academic mentoring and credit for prior training and education.

Army Education Contacts

Education Division (AHRC-PDE)
Army Human Resources Command
200 Stovall St., Suite 3N07
Alexandria, VA 22332-0472
703-325-9800

Army Continuing Education System
www.armyeducation.army.mil

Army Knowledge Online
www.army.mil/ako

eArmyU
www.earmyu.com

SOCAD
www.soc.aascu.org/socad

Army Emergency Relief
200 Stovall St.
Alexandria, VA 22332
703-428-0000
866-878-6378
DSN 328-0000

Army National Guard Virtual Armory
www.virtualarmory.com

Army College Fund
www.goarmy.com

- Virtual doorway to support services and interactive learning resources.

- Personal laptop, email account, and account with an Internet Service Provider (ISP) for certain enlisted participants.

Students can select from 146 certificate or degree programs from a home institution, while taking courses across 29 regionally accredited, eArmyU-participating colleges and universities, including Grambling University, St. Leo University, and University of Alabama.

SOCAD is the Servicemembers Opportunity Colleges degree program for the Army. SOCAD consists of colleges that offer associate's and bachelor's degree programs on or accessible to Army installations worldwide. Each college in the network accepts credits from all the others.

SOCAD guarantees that you and your adult family members can continue toward completion of your degree even though the Army may transfer you to several locations. Other degrees available by distance learning require no classroom residency.

More Help with Tuition

Army Emergency Relief Spouse Education Assistance Program. If you are assigned to Europe, Korea, or Japan (including Okinawa), Army Emergency Relief offers your spouse a grant to assist with the costs associated with pursuing his or her education, up to a maximum of $350 per term.

Army Student Loan Repayment Program. The Army will pay, upon enlistment, up to $65,000 of your student loans for a college-level education if you are a college student or graduate who qualifies. This benefit is only available during initial enlistment. Be sure to ask your local Army recruiter for further information.

The Army College Fund. Also known as a GI Bill "kicker," this financial resource is available to those who sign up for the GI Bill. If you're a high school graduate, score a 50 or better on the military's entrance exam, called the Armed Services Vocational Aptitude Battery (ASVAB), and qualify for certain Army jobs or specialties, you can get more than $72,900 in addition to your GI Bill funding for your education upon enlistment. For more on ASVAB, see page 223.

Educational Opportunities for Guard and Reserve Members

Army National Guard. The Army National Guard (ARNG) supports education programs that focus on degree or certification completion, primarily undergraduate degrees for all enlisted soldiers, warrant officers, and officers. A master's degree may be supported if sufficient funding is available. Members of the Army National Guard may qualify for federal tuition assistance (see below).

The Army National Guard "Virtual Armory" Education Support Center (ESC) provides guidance and individual plans for you to complete your degree while maximizing your military experience, already earned college credit, and other nontraditional credit. Degree-planning specialists will turn your military credit as well as any college credit you may already have into a degree plan that can be completed around your schedule.

Federal Tuition Assistance. The maximum amount the Army National Guard will pay for tuition assistance is:

- 75 percent tuition up to $200 per semester credit hour, or $133 per quarter credit hour.

- Fees up to $500.

- A maximum of $4,000 per fiscal year.

Army Continuing Education Tuition Assistance (Activated Guard and Reserve). Tuition assistance for active duty and activated Reserve/Guard covers 100 percent tuition and fees up to $250 per semester credit hour, or $166 per quarter credit hour, not to exceed $4,500 per fiscal year.

Army Reserve. The Army Reserve offers opportunities for selected Reserve soldiers to pursue their education on a voluntary basis. Voluntary education differs from military education and training, which is required for Military Occupational Specialty (MOS) or Army Occupation Code (AOC). By enhancing promotional opportunities, voluntary education plays a vital role in a Reservist's career. If you are interested in participating, voluntary education must be completed on personal time, with financial assistance provided by the Army Reserve.

The Army Reserve currently offers 100 percent tuition assistance up to $250 per semester hour, or $166 per quarter hour, not to exceed $4,500 annually per servicemember. DANTES manages payment of the Army Reserve tuition assistance program. Contact your Reserve Support Center Educational Services Specialist for information on how to apply for tuition assistance and the other programs mentioned earlier.

Coast Guard Education

Coast Guard Educational Opportunities

Coast Guard Institute. The Coast Guard Institute oversees correspondence test proctoring, tuition assistance, education transcripts, degree planning, and DANTES test management for Coast Guard servicemembers, civilian employees, and immediate family members.

SOCCOAST is the Servicemembers Opportunity Colleges (SOC) degree program for the Coast Guard. SOCCOAST consists of colleges that offer associate's and bachelor's degree programs on or accessible to Navy and Marine installations worldwide. Each college in the network accepts credits from all the others.

SOCCOAST guarantees that you and your adult family members can continue toward completion of your degrees even though the Coast Guard may transfer you to various locations. Degrees that require no classroom residency are also available via distance learning.

Advanced Computer and Electronics Training (ACET). The ACET program provides up to 24 months of full-time college education toward a degree in a technology or engineering discipline. If you are an active duty Coast Guard member and an E-6 to E-8 in the Electronics Technician, Information Systems Technician, Electricians Mate, Machinists Technician and Avionics, or Electrical Technician ratings, you qualify for the program. To apply, you must have a minimum of six years of service. Contact your local Career Development Advisor to assist you in preparing an application package.

More Help with Tuition

The Coast Guard Foundation Grant. If you are an active-duty enlisted member, the Coast Guard Foundation offers you an annual education grant. Equaling up to $250 per year, you can use this grant for any education-related expense. It is given on a competitive merit basis, so be sure to follow all directions to the letter.

Coast Guard Mutual Assistance offers a Supplemental Education Grant (SEG) of up to $160 per year. You can use this grant for any family member's education expenses with the exception of actual tuition. For example, you can use the grant to pay for study guides for ASVAB, CLEP, SAT, and other study guides. CGMA also offers several education-related loans.

Additional Education Assistance. The Coast Guard offers dependent spouses and federal Coast Guard employees the opportunity to take CLEP, DANTES, and other tests at no cost.

Contact your local Education Service Office or Command Mutual Assistance representative for further information on the programs mentioned here.

Educational Opportunities for Reserve Coast Guard Members

Coast Guard Reserve (USCGR). Coast Guard Reserve units have integrated with active duty sites, so in the spirit of "Team Coast Guard," USCG reservists have access to all educational programs available to active-duty members.

The Coast Guard offers Selective Reservists 100 percent tuition assistance for up to $250 per semester hour, or $166.67 per quarter hour, not to exceed $4,500 annually per servicemember. Contact your Coast Guard ESO for information on how to apply for tuition assistance and other programs.

Marine Corps Education

Educational Opportunities for Active-Duty Marines

The Marine Corps Lifelong Learning Programs support the Lifelong Learning Offices on Marine Corps bases and installations. They act as a central agency assisting Marines with the following programs: the Marine Deployed Education Programs, United Services Military Apprenticeship Program (USMAP), Marine Corps Satellite Education Network (MCSEN), Military Academic Skills Program (MASP), Military Installation Voluntary Education Review (MIVER), and Sailor/Marine American Council on Education Registry Transcript (SMART). Check with the local Education Service Office on your installation for further information on these programs.

SOCMAR is the Servicemembers Opportunity Colleges (SOC) degree program for the Marines. SOCMAR consists of colleges that offer associate's and bachelor's degree programs on or accessible to Marine and Navy installations worldwide. Each college in the network accepts credits from all the others.

SOCMAR guarantees that you and your adult family members can continue toward completion of your degrees even though the Marine Corps may transfer you to various locations. Degrees that require no classroom residency are also available via distance learning.

The Navy College Program for Afloat College Education (NCPACE) gives Marine Corps and Navy servicemembers the opportunity to continue their education while on sea-duty assignments. Both undergraduate and graduate courses are available through NCPACE.

More Help with Tuition

The Navy-Marine Corps Relief Society (NMCRS) Admiral Mike Boorda Seaman-to-Admiral Educational Assistance Program offers grants and interest-free loans of up to $2,000 a year to eligible active-duty servicemembers accepted to the following programs:

- Enlisted Commissioning Program.

- Marine Enlisted Commissioning Education Program.

- Medical Enlisted Commissioning Program.

This program is also open to midshipmen who have been released from active duty for immediate assignment to the Naval Reserve Officer Training Corps (NROTC) program. Application is made through the Commanding Officer of the NROTC unit, or by contacting NMCRS Headquarters.

Marine Corps Education Contacts

Marine Corps Lifelong Learning
www.usmc-mccs.org/education

The Navy College At Sea Program (NCPACE)
www.navycollege.navy.mil/ncp/pace.html

SOCMAR
www.soc.aascu.org/socmar

Navy-Marine Corps Relief Society
4015 Wilson Blvd., 10th Floor
Arlington, VA 22203-1977
703-696-4904
DSN 426-4904

Spouse Tuition Aid Program (STAP). The Navy and Marine Corps Relief Society (NMCRS) offers financial aid to your spouse if you are an active-duty Marine stationed in an overseas location. Your spouse may be a full- or part-time student studying toward a vocational certificate or an undergraduate or graduate degree.

The undergraduate-level maximum grant is $300 per semester and $1,500 per year. The graduate level maximum is $350 per semester and $1,750 per year.

Vice Admiral E. P. Travers Scholarship and Loan Program. To apply for this program, you must be the spouse of an active-duty member, or the dependent child of an active or retired member of the Marine Corps or Navy. To qualify, you must be a full-time undergraduate student at an accredited college or university. Other details are as follows:

- 1,000 grants are awarded each academic year at $2,000 each.

- Applicants are also evaluated for an interest-free student loan of up to $3,000.

- The loan repayment begins within 30 days after award and must be repaid by allotment within 24 months. (For more on allotments, see page 62.)

To request an application form and information about deadlines, contact your local Navy-Marine Corps Relief Society office, or contact NMCRS headquarters. Late applications will not be considered for the scholarship; however, they will be evaluated for a loan.

Navy Education

Take Advantage

Senior Enlisted Navy personnel (E-7 through E-9) are eligible for the Advanced Education Voucher program, which can pay up to $20,000 a year for baccalaureate and master's degree completion in designated areas of study.

Educational Opportunities for Active Duty

Navy College Program. The Navy College Program (NCP) helps sailors earn college degrees by providing them academic credit for Navy training, work experience, and off-duty education. The NCP also enables sailors to obtain a college degree while on active duty. While the NCP is primarily geared toward enlisted sailors, officers have access to some NCP components.

The Navy College at Sea Program (NCPACE). Part of the Navy College Program, NCPACE allows Navy and Marine Corps servicemembers to pursue education while on sea-duty assignments. Both undergraduate and graduate courses are available through NCPACE.

Navy Knowledge Online (NKO). The Navy Knowledge Online Learning Portal involves a systematic process for acquiring, creating, integrating, sharing, and using information, insights, and experiences to achieve organizational goals, and to help sailors and marines pursue their educational and career goals.

The Seaman to Admiral (also known as STA-21) is a commissioning program in which active-duty sailors receive a scholarship to attend a top-notch university. Through this program, sailors move on to careers as Naval officers. For more on this program, see page 238 in the Career chapter.

SOCNAV is the Servicemembers Opportunity Colleges (SOC) degree program for the Navy. SOCNAV consists of colleges that offer associate's and bachelor's degree programs on or accessible to Navy installations worldwide. Each college in the network accepts credits from all the others.

SOCNAV guarantees that you and your adult family members can continue toward completion of your degree even though the Navy may transfer you to various locations. There are also degrees available by distance learning that require no classroom residency.

More Help with Tuition

The **NMCRS Admiral Mike Boorda Seaman-to-Admiral Educational Assistance Program** offers grants and interest-free loans of up to $2,000 a year to eligible active-duty servicemembers accepted to the following programs:

- Enlisted Commissioning Program.

- Marine Enlisted Commissioning Education Program.

- Medical Enlisted Commissioning Program.

This program is also open to midshipmen who have been released from active duty for immediate assignment to the NROTC Program. Application is made through the Commanding Officer of the NROTC unit, or by contacting NMCRS Headquarters.

Navy Education Contacts

Commanding Officer
Naval Education and Training Professional
Development and Technology Center
Navy College Center, Code N27
6490 Saufley Field Road
Pensacola, FL 32509-5204
877-253-7122
DSN 922-1828

The Navy College at Sea Program (NCPACE)
www.navycollege.navy.mil/ncp/pace.html

The Navy Knowledge Online Learning Portal
www.nko.navy.mil

SOCNAV
www.soc.aascu.org/socnav

Vice Admiral E. P. Travers Scholarship and Loan Program. To apply for this program, you must be the spouse of an active duty member, or the dependent child of an active or retired member of the Navy or Marine Corps. To qualify, you must be a full-time undergraduate student at an accredited college or university. Contact your local NMCRS office for application details. Other details are as follows:

- 1,000 grants are awarded each academic year at $2,000 each.

- Applicants are also evaluated for an interest-free student loan of up to $3,000.

- The loan repayment begins within 30 days after the loan is granted and must be repaid by allotment within 24 months.

The Navy College Fund. Also known as a GI Bill "kicker," this financial resource is available to those who sign up for the GI Bill. If you're a high school graduate, score 50 or better on the ASVAB in recruiting, and qualify for certain Navy jobs or apprenticeships, you can get, upon enlistment, more than $15,000 in addition to your GI Bill funding for your education.

Student Loan Repayment Program (LRP). If you are a college student or graduate who qualifies for the Loan Repayment Program (LRP), the Navy will pay, upon enlistment, up to $65,000 of your student loans for a college-level education.

Navy College Assistance/Student Headstart (CASH). If you are a motivated high school or college student who qualifies for the Nuclear Field, Missile Technician Rating, or Submarine Electronics Computer Field, you can apply for the Navy CASH program. The program will allow you to receive full Navy pay and benefits while attending college for up to 12 months if you are accepted.

Spouse Tuition Aid Program. The Navy-Marine Corps Relief Society of-

Military Matters

The USS *Tennessee* Scholarship Fund provides financial assistance education grants for the dependent children of active-duty and retired Navy personnel who are serving or have served aboard the USS *Tennessee*. *Tennessee* scholarship application forms are available from any Navy–Marine Corps Relief Society office or at www.nmcrs.org/spec-prgm.html. For more on this and other military scholarships, see www.military.com/scholarship.

Education by Service Branch

Programs	Air Force	Army	Coast Guard	Marine Corps	Navy
GI Bill "Kicker"	Buy-up	Buy-up	Buy-up	Buy-up	Buy-up
Student Loan Repayment	Yes, up to $10,000	Yes, up to $65,000	N/A	N/A	Yes, up to $65,000
Loans, Grants, and Scholarships	Air Force Aid Society, et al.	Army Emergency Relief, et al.	Coast Guard Mutual Assistance/ Coast Guard Foundation et al.	Navy-Marine Corps Relief Society, et al.	Navy-Marine Corps Relief Society, et al.

fers financial aid to your spouse if you are on active duty and stationed in an overseas location. Your spouse may be a full- or part-time student studying toward a vocational certificate, or an undergraduate or graduate degree. The undergraduate-level maximum grant is $300 per semester and $1,500 per year. The graduate-level maximum is $350 per semester and $1,750 per year.

Military Professional Studies and Post Graduate Programs

The Department of Defense operates several graduate schools for military officers seeking to earn their post graduate degrees. These include the following schools:

- Air Force Institute of Technology.
- The Judge Advocate General's School of the Army.
- National Defense Intelligence College.
- Naval Post Graduate School.
- School of Advanced Air and Space Studies.
- Uniformed Services University of Health Sciences.

In addition each of the military services have senior enlisted academies, staff colleges, and war colleges. These give servicemembers the opportunity to work toward continuing their education and/or earning advanced degrees in leadership, management and other specialties.

Part Six

The
Career
Advantage

A career in the military offers many opportunities, from the time you begin military service through your upward progression in rank. In this chapter, we review benefits and programs that are directly related to your military career cycle, including enlistment and reenlistment bonuses, advice and inside tips on getting promoted, commissioning programs that could help you become an officer, and benefits related to deployment and relocation. To prepare for your transition or retirement and to make the most of your military experience in a civilian career, see the Transition chapter.

The Benefits of Service

Your military advantage actually begins the moment you enter military service. Before you sign on the dotted line, ask your recruiter about benefits such as the GI Bill, college funds, college loan repayment and deferment, and cash bonuses, all of which are detailed in other chapters of this book.

Enlistment Bonuses

In addition to the training you receive in your occupation or career field, one of

The Career Advantage at a Glance

the first, very tangible benefits you may get when you join the military is an enlistment bonus. The amount depends on your particular service, specialty, and length of service. To qualify for an enlistment bonus, you usually have to fulfill certain academic requirements (i.e., you have completed high school or a certain number of G.E.D. credits) and score well on the Armed Services Vocational Aptitude Battery exam, a generalized test that prospective enlisted recruits must take.

Enlistment bonuses are constantly changing depending on service needs—ask your recruiter about current bonuses if you are considering joining the service.

Take Advantage

For tips, practice entrance tests, basic training advice, updated enlistment bonuses and everything else you need to know about joining the military, visit www.military.com/joining.

Pay Grades

Servicemembers are paid according to their rank and time in service. There are three separate rank systems, and within these rank structures there are numerous pay levels, or pay grades:

Take Advantage

For ASVAB study tips, examples of how your score affects your military career options, and practice tests, visit www.military.com/ASVAB.

• Officers—10 ranks (pay grades) ranging from O-1 to O-10.

• Warrant Officers—5 ranks (pay grades) ranging from W-1 to W-5 (Air Force does not have Warrant Officers.).

• Enlisted—9 ranks (pay grades) ranging from E-1 to E-9.

Advanced Enlistment Rank

Recruiters can offer you the chance to enter the service at a higher pay grade, called an Advanced Enlistment Rank. Of course, an advanced rank means more basic pay, and a head start on reaching higher pay grades. If you qualify, you may enter at Enlisted Pay Grade E–2 or E–3 instead of the usual E-1. To qualify, you generally must score high on the Armed Services Vocational Aptitude Battery (ASVAB) test and meet other criteria, such as having college credit or a special skill. Be sure to ask your recruiter about advanced rank.

You may also have the opportunity to enter service as an officer, depending on your qualifications (if you are a physician, lawyer, or engineer, for example), or if you are eligible to enter an officer training program. For more details on these opportunities, look at programs for specific service branches in the "Professional Development in the Military" section later in this chapter, on page 224.

For more on both enlisted and officer pay, see the Pay chapter, page 46.

Your Everyday Rewards

For every day that you serve, the military rewards you by providing housing, meals, vacation, and more, in addition to your basic pay. Some of the major rewards you receive for serving your country include:

- 30 days' paid vacation or leave.
- Health care (TRICARE).
- Meals, or a cash allowance for meals.
- Housing or an allowance for housing.
- Life insurance.
- Travel.
- Veterans benefits.
- Military discounts.
- Commisary and exchange shopping privileges.
- Training and leadership development.
- Education (Tuition Assistance and Discounts).

Professional Development in the Military

Military service provides opportunities to move up through the ranks, and gain more responsibility, new skills, more pay and benefits. The following section gives you a basic understanding of how military advancement systems work for active-duty personnel, and how you can make them work for you. Although the systems for the Reserve and Guard have some similarities, you can find specific information on reserve and guard promotions and advancements at www.military.com/militarycareers.

Each branch of the Armed Forces has its own process for promoting (also known as "advancing") servicemembers. All promotion systems have the same aim: to select officers and enlisted personnel who have demonstrated that they possess the right qualifications, integrity, and ability to successfully perform the duties expected of the next higher pay grade. Generally, promotions are

Military Matters

How quickly you are advanced or promoted in the military sometimes depends on whether the next highest rank is "undermanned" or not. For example, if you're an E-4 and many E-5 slots are available, you'll have a greater chance of quick advancement to E-5. Of course, your own performance is the other major factor.

made as vacancies occur so that the strength of the military is maintained within each pay grade.

Officer promotions are determined by selection boards, which are composed of senior officers. The Secretary of Defense (or Secretary of Homeland Security for the Coast Guard) convenes the boards every year to select officers for ranks higher than O-2. Selection boards are expected to be impartial and confidential; they submit their findings and recommendations but not the reasons for their decisions. Most officer promotions also require confirmation by the United States Senate.

The officer promotion process is controlled by laws, regulations, and administrative procedures that take the following conditions into account:

- Authorized strength—the number of officers in a particular category specified for a grade or combination of grades.

- Promotion flow point—the number of years of commissioned service at which most officers would be promoted to the next higher grade.

- Promotion percentage—the number of officers in the promotion level to be selected.

Evaluations: Learn How to SCORE

No matter your rank, you are always being evaluated by your chain of command. This evaluation process begins the day you check in, and can make or break your career and promotion opportunities.

The evaluation system focuses on performance. It all boils down to how well you do your job. To make sure you get the best evaluation possible, follow this simple five-step system, which we call SCORE.

Step 1. Start by reading your service's promotion regulations. Understanding how the process works is key to making it work for you. Pay particular attention to appropriate evaluation forms for your rank.

Step 2. Communicate. Talk with your evaluator (most likely your supervisor) about your performance report. Go over the form line by line to determine expectations. Ask your evaluator for advice on how to improve your evaluation report and get the highest score possible.

Step 3. Take every **Opportunity** you can to demonstrate the level of performance suggested by your evaluator. Be sure to take the initiative and show that you're committed to performing at the highest level.

Step 4. Record your personal performance by keeping a performance journal. Note the times and situations when you demonstrated skills, initiative, leadership, and performance.

Step 5. Evaluate yourself. Complete your own evaluation report, including documentation and support information. After all, this is your career, and you are the only one who knows exactly what you have accomplished during the evaluation period.

Your evaluator has a rough job: He or she has to monitor you and your team's performance throughout the entire evaluation period. It is nearly impossible for an evaluator to remember every detail about your performance; in fact, evaluators tend to remember negative situations more often than the positive ones. By following the SCORE system, you make your evaluator's job easier and help support your overall evaluation.

The Perception of Performance

What's the real difference between the top performers and those in the middle of the pack? Are performance evaluations grounded in objective criteria or subjective factors? To this second question, there is almost certainly truth to both possibilities, but how our superiors view us is often the single greatest factor in career advancement. The good news is that each of us has the opportunity to affect this perception to great professional advantage.

In an informal poll, senior military and corporate executives most frequently cited the following five descriptions as belonging to excellent performers. Use this list to help you consider how your boss may view you:

1. **Sets and exceeds expectations.** Can you get the job done? Does your boss count on you to take guidance, ask appropriate questions, shape the objective, and execute the plan? In many cases, setting and exceeding your boss's expectations are even more important than the final outcome. Surprisingly, most senior leaders claim to have only a few "go-to" people that they can consistently rely upon to get the job done. You should be one of these people.

2. **Communicates solidly.** Are you a good presenter, speaker, and writer? The ability to make thoughtful and persuasive arguments, handle expectations, and coordinate assets and resources is a prerequisite for success. Great com-

municators can also operate up and down the chain of command. Good communication, perhaps more than any other single factor, can have a favorable impact on perceptions.

3. Leads effectively. The ability to build, manage, and motivate a great team is probably the most common characteristic of a successful leader. The best leaders identify and nurture the individual talents of team members—utilizing their advantages and compensating for weaknesses.

4. Takes the initiative. Do you approach your job with enthusiasm and a commitment to the organization and team? Do you have a dogged determination to drive toward a favorable conclusion? Taking the initiative is the surest way to signal your desire for advancement and inspire confidence in your ability to assume additional responsibility. Managers want people on their team who eagerly take on challenges and exhibit the kind of energy that spurs others to follow. Having to wage a regular battle to motivate a team member gets old quickly—and rarely leads to high marks for anyone.

5. Demonstrates honesty. Can you be trusted to do the right thing?

Each of us brings to the workplace different levels of each of these five traits. Leaders who offered perspectives for this book said that their best people had a balanced portfolio of skills. Although extraordinary performance in one or more areas is great, top performers usually meet a minimum threshold in each. Generally speaking, superior communication skills, exceeding expectations, and enthusiasm are the three most important indicators of success. The other two can be viewed as subsets of the big three. If you can get the job done, communicate effectively, and do it with energy and enthusiasm, you are destined for great things—managers will rely on you, peers will like you, and subordinates will learn from you.

The ability to view yourself and your performance through the eyes of your superior is a critical part of your career development. In your career, perception *is* reality—and the impression you make should be actively and thoughtfully managed.

Air Force Promotion System

The Air Force has separate promotion systems for enlisted airmen and commissioned officers. In general, both Air Force promotion systems are based on a combination of performance evaluations, experience, and oftentimes selection boards. However, the Airman Promotion System differs by incorporating the Weighted Airman Promotion System (WAPS), which uses points to rate servicemembers' standing for promotion.

Take Advantage

Organize all of your military paperwork. Your files should include folders for pay stubs, promotion papers, medical records, etc. Doing this will save you endless hours of sifting through paperwork before evaluation time. Also, keep copies of everything—this will help you when you build your portfolio.

Take Advantage

Be on time, be motivated, and be known. Make sure you remain a presence in your group. If someone with a higher rank asks for volunteers, make sure that person knows you're available to help. Little things like these will score big when it is time to submit your promotion packet.

The Weighted Airman Promotion System (WAPS)

If you are eligible for promotion based on your time in service, time in grade, skill level, and commander's recommendation, then the WAPS points system will apply to you. If you are among those with the most WAPS points in your Air Force Specialty Code, you will be promoted.

A portion of your WAPS promotion points come from the Promotion Fitness Examination and the Specialty Knowledge Tests, which you are required to take.

The **Promotion Fitness Examination** (PFE) is a 100-question test that covers general Air Force supervisory subjects such as:

- Air Force doctrine.

- Organization.

- Military customs and courtesies.

- Standard of appearance and conduct.

- Enlisted history.

- Non-Commissioned Officer (NCO) leadership.

- The enlisted servicemembers evaluation system.

- NCO management functions.

- Enforcing standards.

- Personnel issues and programs.

- Full Spectrum Threat Response (FSTR).

- Security.

- Communications.

Contact

Visit www.military.com /usafpromotions to learn more about the Air Force promotion system.

You can earn a maximum of 100 PFE points for this test.

Senior Non-Commissioned Officer (SNCO) candidates are required to take the USAF Supervisory Examination (USAFSE). This exam covers topics similar to those on the PFE but at a higher level.

The **Specialty Knowledge Test** (SKT) is a 100-question test concerning your particular job in the Air Force. Most SKT questions are drawn from the Career Development Course that you will have to study to be awarded a five-skill level. The maximum number of SKT points you can earn is 100.

Air Force Commissioning Programs

The Air Force offers several ways to earn a commission and join the Officer Corps. Some programs are accelerated—you get on a faster track to a promotion as well as enhanced pay and benefits. The following are descriptions of each of the Air Force Enlisted to Officer Commissioning Programs.

Air Force Reserve Officer Training Corps (ROTC) units are located at selected colleges and universities throughout the United States. Upon graduation and successful completion of required courses and training, a cadet is appointed a Second Lieutenant in the United States Air Force Reserve.

The Airman Education and Commissioning Program (AECP) offers active-duty enlisted personnel the opportunity to earn a commission while completing a bachelor's degree. You must attend Air Force ROTC (AFROTC) courses, which will be the source of your commissioning.

If you are selected for AECP, you remain on active duty and are assigned to an AFROTC detachment, where your job is to go to school as a full-time college student.

In addition to receiving full pay and benefits, AECP cadets are provided with a tuition/fees scholarship of up to $15,000 per year and an annual textbook allowance of $510. Students may not pay the difference to attend higher-cost schools.

You can participate in this program for one to three years, depending on your major, prior academic preparation, and age limitations. During the program, you attend school year-round, including summer terms. (If no classes are available during the summer, you will attend field training and ROTC classes.) Note, however, that AECP is not an avenue for undergraduate flight training.

The U.S. Air Force Academy awards appointments to young people from all walks of life. Whether they have come directly from high school or from within the enlisted ranks of the Air Force, all have proven their ability to measure up to the physical demands and high standards the academy has established.

Officer Training School (OTS) is located at Maxwell Air Force Base, Alabama, and provides a 12-week basic officer training course that commissions 1,000 officers annually. The program is designed for college graduates pursuing a commission in the Air Force.

Contact

For more information on Air Force ROTC, visit www.afoats.af.mil.

Contact

For more information on the Airman Education and Commissioning Program, see www.afrotc.com /scholarships /enlschol/aecp.

Contact

For more information on how to enter the Air Force Academy, see www.usafa.af.mil.

The basic eligibility requirements for the program are:

- A four-year baccalaureate degree.

- U.S. citizenship.

- 18 to 34 years of age.

- Officer caliber.

- Good moral character and integrity.

- Good health and physical condition.

- Ability to depart within 270 days.

- A passing score on the Air Force Officer Qualification Test.

If you are considering applying for OTS and are not on active duty, you should contact your local Air Force OTS recruiter. If you are considering OTS and are currently on active duty, contact the education office or Military Personnel Flight (MPF) on your base.

Contact

For more information on the Air Force Officer Training School, see www.ots.afoats.af.mil or the Air Force Recruiting Home page at www.airforce.com.

Army Promotion System

The Army's enlisted promotion-system requirements and processes differ for each pay grade. For example, promotions to Sergeant (E-6) and ranks above it are based on command recommendations and evaluation by a promotion board.

The promotion board rates your personal appearance, self-confidence, bearing, communication skills, knowledge of world affairs, awareness of military programs, knowledge of basic soldiering, and attitude. The board may award a candidate up to 150 promotion points. Depending on your current pay grade, the points will determine whether you will be promoted.

Army enlisted promotions for grades E-7 and above are handled by the Centralized Selection Board, which consists of officers and NCOs, with a general officer serving as the board president. The boards are divided into nine to 11 separate panels, which in turn review and score your records.

Contact

Visit www.military.com /armypromotions to learn more about the Army promotion system.

The board members vote independently, scoring your records on a scale of 1 minus to 6 plus. A score of 3 or higher indicates that you are fully qualified, whereas a score of 2 or lower means that you will be retained in your current grade or referred to the Qualitative Management Program (QMP).

All of your records are rank-ordered based on the score given by the board members. The Army then takes all selectees, without regard to Military Occupational Specialty (MOS), and assigns them a promotion sequence number, according to seniority. Monthly announcements include the sequence numbers of those who are promoted.

Army Enlisted to Officer Commissioning Programs

The U.S. Army offers enlisted soldiers several ways to earn a commission and join the Officer Corps. Army Enlisted to Officer Programs include:

U.S. Military Academy/West Point. Each year, about 200 active-duty soldiers are offered admission to the U.S. Military Academy, or the Preparatory School, at Fort Monmouth, New Jersey. Although some soldiers are offered direct admission to West Point, most attend the Prep School first. All applications are made directly to West Point, and if you are not directly admitted to West Point, you will be automatically considered for admission to the Prep School.

Admission to West Point is highly competitive, but if you meet the basic eligibility requirements, have achieved competitive SAT or ACT scores, and have earned better than average grades in high school, you are especially encouraged to apply. Those accepted are generally top performers—academically, in sports, and in extracurricular activities.

Officer Candidate School (OCS) is a 14-week program that consists of Basic, Intermediate, and Senior Officer Candidate Phases. To successfully complete OCS, you have to:

- Pass three standard Army physical fitness tests.

- Run more than 60 miles in formation.

- Foot-march more than 50 miles.

- Complete a three-, four-, and five-mile run.

- Complete the Combat Water Survival Test and confidence and conditioning obstacle courses.

- Pass a land-navigation written test and successfully complete a day and night land-navigation course.

> **Contact**
>
> Learn more about the U.S. Military Academy at www.usma.edu.

> **Contact**
>
> For details on how to enroll in Army OCS, visit the Army OCS site at www.armyocs.com.

Military Matters

The U.S. Army Human Resources Command, formerly known as PERSCOM, is the portal for Active and Reserve enlisted and officer information, including promotions and selections: see www.hrc.army.mil. Army National Guard news and announcements are located at www.arng.army.mil.

Contact

Career resources
for those who wish
to become warrant
officers are
available at
www.usawocc.
army.mil.

- Receive academic instruction in 10 areas, pass nine academic tests, and successfully complete training on 67 precommissioning common-core tasks (must score 70 percent or higher on all academic tests).

- Serve in numerous evaluated leadership positions in both a garrison and field environment, attaining a successful rating.

- Meet the Army's standards of conduct and discipline.

Reserve Officer Training Corps (ROTC) units are located at selected colleges and universities throughout the United States. Upon graduation and successful completion of required courses and training, a cadet is commissioned as Second Lieutenant in the United States Army or Army Reserve.

The Army conducts two ROTC selection boards per year, the Early Board in November and the National Board in February. Selected applicants for the ROTC Scholarship Program are chosen through a highly competitive national selection process, and receive full tuition, as well as funding for books, fees, and a living allowance.

The Army Warrant Officer Appointment Process. Army warrant officers are leaders who specialize in a specific technical area throughout an entire career. The Army Warrant Officer Corps constitutes less than three percent of the total Army. Although their group is small in size, the level of responsibility for warrant officers is immense, and only the very best are selected for the role.

Contact

For more
information on
Army ROTC, visit
www.armyrotc.
com.

Coast Guard Promotion System

Take Advantage

Army Green to Gold
The Army ROTC Green
to Gold Scholarship
Program provides
selected enlisted
soldiers on active
duty an opportunity
to complete their
baccalaureate
degree and obtain
a commission through
participating in ROTC.
Visit www.goarmy.com
to download forms
and application
instructions.

Like the other four branches of the Armed Forces, the Coast Guard enlisted promotion system differs depending on your pay grade. You are advanced to grades E-5 through E-9 based on a servicewide competition to test your knowledge of your rating and Enlisted Performance Military Education (E-PME). E-PME is part of the advancement process for enlisted members.

E-PME is a holistic system that consists of professional development, knowledge, and tools to help you develop into a high performer. This area of education is separate from your particular specialty or expertise; e.g., electrician or mechanic. The E-PME is geared more toward leadership and management development and less toward technical aspects of your world of work.

The E-PME has three parts:

- An E-PME Study Guide to prepare for the Service Wide Examination.

- The Knowledge and Performance Requirements.

- An Advancement Qualification Exam (or AQE).

E-PME topics include leadership, management, administration, Coast Guard history, heritage of enlisted Coast Guard service, organizational structure and management, personal development, training, education, and wellness.

Candidates are rank-ordered based on their final multiple score (FMS), which is derived from seven factors:

- SWE Exam Score.
- Performance Factor.
- Time In Service (TIS).
- Time In Grade in Present Rating (TIR).
- Medals & Awards.
- Sea Duty.
- Surf Duty.

Coast Guard Direct Commissions

For people with special training and skills, the Coast Guard has opportunities to become Coast Guard officers through direct commissions in the following specialties:

- Aviator.
- Engineer.
- Environmental manager.
- Intelligence expert.
- Lawyer.

With a direct commission, you will have the privilege of being a Coast Guard officer from the outset (no boot camp!). Direct Commission Officers (DCOs) are required to complete a three- to five-week course, depending on past military experience. For completely new personnel, the five-week course includes an indoctrination period during which you will be expected to meet strict standards of conduct, uniform appearance, and military bearing.

As a DCO, you will receive an active-duty contract for a period of three years, after which you may apply for extensions. Based on their experience, education, and qualifications, selected applicants will be commissioned as either a Lieutenant (junior grade) or Ensign in the Coast Guard Reserve. If you elect to remain in the Coast Guard after your original three-year contract, you can integrate into the regular Coast Guard after selection for lieutenant.

Coast Guard Commissioning Programs

The U.S. Coast Guard offers enlisted Coast Guard servicemembers several ways to earn a commission and join the Officer Corps, which means better pay

---

Contact

Visit www.military.com /uscgadvancements to learn more about the Coast Guard advancement system.

Take Advantage

Fred's Place, the largest Coast Guard community on the Internet, posts the latest official Coast Guard promotion news, for both active-duty and reserve members. Visit www.fredsplace.org/ announce.

Take Advantage

To improve your servicewide competition score, form or join study groups, review past correspondence course quizzes, and request assignments that will increase your rate knowledge.

Contact

For updated direct commission listings, or for how to apply, see www.gocoastguard .com /dc/dcindex.htm.

and better benefits. The following are descriptions of each of the Coast Guard's Enlisted to Officer Programs:

The U.S. Coast Guard Academy, located in New London, Connecticut, is unique among the service academies because it is the oldest lifesaving service in the world. As with the other service academies, competition for admission is fierce. An average of 290 students enter the Academy each year out of approximately 6,000 applicants.

Officer Candidate School (OCS) is a rigorous 17-week course that prepares candidates to serve as officers in the United States Coast Guard. In addition to indoctrinating students into a military lifestyle, OCS covers a wide range of highly technical information necessary for performing the duties of a Coast Guard officer. When you graduate from the program, you will receive a commission in the Coast Guard at the rank of Ensign and will be required to serve a minimum of three years of active duty. You may be assigned to a ship, flight school, or an operations-ashore billet. First assignments are based on the needs of the Coast Guard, although your personal desires and performance are considered.

Contact

For details on enrolling in the U.S. Coast Guard Academy, see www.cga.edu.

The **Pre-Commissioning Program for Enlisted Personnel** (PPEP) is an opportunity for top-performing enlisted personnel to complete their bachelor's degree, attend Officer Candidate School (OCS), and receive a Coast Guard commission. The Coast Guard will pay all fees for tuition, books, and lab use in addition to regular pay and allowances.

The Coast Guard's College Student Pre-Commissioning Initiative (CSPI) is a scholarship program for students entering their junior year of college. This program provides students with leadership, management, law-enforcement, navigation, and marine science skills and training. The program's benefits include:

- Full payment of school tuition for two years.

- Payment of fees and for textbooks.

- Monthly salary of up to $2,000.

- Life insurance.

- Free dental and medical health care.

- 30 days' paid vacation per year.

- Monthly housing and food allowances.

- Leadership training.

    To be eligible for the program, you must:

- Be between the ages of 21 and 26 when you graduate from college.

Contact

For information on Officer Candidate School, see www.gocoastguard .com/dc /DCPrograms /ocs.htm.

- Be a sophomore or junior (with at least 60 college credits completed toward your degree).

- Be enrolled at a four-year program at an approved institution with a minimum 25 percent minority population.

- Meet all physical requirements for a Coast Guard commission.

- Maintain a GPA of 2.5 or higher.

- Attain a qualifying score of 1100 on the SAT; 23 on the ACT; or 109 on the GT portion of the ASVAB.

- Be a U.S. citizen.

The Chief Warrant Officer Option. While administrative and technical specialty expertise is required in many assignments, chief warrant officers must also be capable of performing in a wide variety of assignments that require strong leadership skills. Enlisted and officer experience provide these officers with a unique perspective on how to meet the Coast Guard's roles and missions.

Marine Corps Promotion System

Like for the other branches of the U.S. Armed Forces, the Marine Corps enlisted promotion system differs depending on your pay grade. For example, promotions to corporal and sergeant (E-4 and E-5) are based on basic eligibility, command recommendation, and a composite score, while a promotion to lance corporal (E-3) depends on whether the candidate has successfully completed nine months' time-in-service and eight months' time-in-grade (i.e., E-2).

For Marine Corps enlisted promotions, composite scores are determined on a quarterly basis, when the Marine Corps announces how many Marines in each MOS will be promoted. In the process to see who gets promoted, composite score points are awarded from each of the following areas:

- General Military Performance score.

- Average of duty proficiency marks.

- Average of conduct marks.

- Time-in-service points.

- Time-in-grade points.

- College credits/voluntary education bonus point.s

Contact

For details on the Pre-Commissioning Program for Enlisted Personnel, see www.gocoastguard .com/dc /dcprograms /ppep.htm.

Contact

To apply to the CSPI program, contact a Coast Guard recruiter at 877-NOW-USCG (877-669-8724), ext. 205, or visit www.gocoastguard .com.

Contact

For details on the Chief Warrant Officer Appointment Process, or for how to apply to become a Chief Warrant Officer, see www.military.com/ militarycareers.

Contact

Official Marine Corps updates on promotions for both active-duty and reserve members are available at www.usmc.mil /maradmins.

- Special assignments points.

- Command Recruiting Program bonus points.

For promotions to Staff NCO (E-6 and above), candidates must be evaluated by a centralized promotion board, in addition to meeting the basic requirements and command recommendations.

Marine Enlisted Marks System

Your duty performance and conduct are rated on a scale of 0 to 5, 0 being "unsatisfactory" and 5 being "outstanding." Average Duty Performance and Average Conduct Marks together can equal up to 1,000 points of the composite score system used in the corporal and sergeant promotion systems.

The Marine Officer and NCO Performance Evaluations System

The Marine Corps Performance Evaluation System (PES) provides for the periodic reporting, recording, and analysis of the performance and professional character of Marines in the grades of sergeant through major general.

The system recognizes the inherently high quality of the individual Marine and accounts for the outstanding nature of the "average" Marine. Listed under the five main areas of evaluation are 14 attributes in the form of Performance Anchored Rating Scales (PARS).

Marine Corps Commissioning Programs

The U.S. Marine Corps offers enlisted Marines several ways to earn a commission and join the Officer Corps. The following are descriptions of each of the Marine Corps Enlisted to Officer Programs:

U.S. Naval Academy (USNA). Enlisted active-duty Marines as well as Marines serving in the Active Reserve (AR) program can apply for nomination and appointment to the United States Naval Academy (see page 239). This is a highly selective program. Naval Academy midshipmen can choose to pursue the "Marine option," which leads to a commission in the U.S. Marine Corps. All other graduates receive a commission in the U.S. Navy.

The **Marine Corps Enlisted Commissioning Education Program** (MECEP) provides outstanding enlisted Marines the opportunity to become Marine Corps Officers. Marines successfully completing the program receive a baccalaureate degree and a commission as a ssecond lieutenant in the United States Marine Corps Reserve.

Contact

To learn more about the Marine Corps promotion system, visit www.military.com/ usmcpromotions.

The **Enlisted Commissioning Program** (ECP) allows qualified enlisted Marines in the Regular Marine Corps and the Marine Corps Active Reserve program to apply for assignment to Officer Candidates School (OCS) and for subsequent appointment to unrestricted commissioned officer grade in the U.S. Marine Corps Reserve.

The **Meritorious Commissioning Program** (MCP) allows commanding officers to nominate qualified enlisted Marines in the Regular Marine Corps and the Marine Corps Active Reserve program who have demonstrated exceptional leadership potential for assignment to Officer Candidates School (OCS) and subsequent commissioning in the Marine Corps Reserve.

The **Reserve Enlisted Commissioning Program** (RECP) allows qualified enlisted Marines in the Selected Marine Corps Reserve (SMCR) program to apply for assignment to Officer Candidates School (OCS) and subsequent appointment to unrestricted commissioned officer grade in the U.S. Marine Corps Reserve.

Broadened Opportunity for Officer Selection and Training (BOOST) provides an educational enhancement opportunity if you are seeking a college education and also want to be commissioned. BOOST is a demanding 10-month academic-improvement course providing remedial high school and college preparatory level instruction, and is open to all enlisted active-duty Marines as well as Marines in the Active Reserve program who meet the basic eligibility and academic requirements. BOOST graduates compete for entry into the U.S. Naval Academy, the Enlisted Commissioning Education Program (MECEP), and the Naval Reserve Officer Training Corps (NROTC) scholarship program.

The **Navy Reserve Officer Training Corps** (NROTC) educates and trains qualified young men and women for careers as commissioned officers in the United States Marine Corps. NROTC midshipmen seeking a commission in the Marine Corps can select the "Marine option" program at their NROTC unit.

Marine option NROTC units are located at selected colleges and universities throughout the United States. Upon graduation and successful completion of required courses and training, you will be appointed Second Lieutenant in the United States Marine Corps Reserve. While attending a university on scholarship, active-duty Marines who are selected to receive NROTC scholarships are released to the Inactive Ready Reserve (IRR) and do not receive pay and allowances.

Selected applicants for the NROTC scholarship program are awarded scholarships and receive full tuition, along with funding for books, fees, and other benefits.

The Enlisted to Warrant Officer Program allows qualified enlisted Marines who are technical experts in their fields to apply for appointment to become warrant officers in the MOS in which they are considered qualified to serve.

There are five categories of warrant officers: Regular Active Duty, Active Reserve, Selected Marine Corps Reserve, Marine Gunner, and Career Recruiter.

Contact

For more on the Marine Corps commissioning programs, see www.military.com /militarycareers.

Contact

For information on the NROTC, see www.nrotc. navy.mil.

Contact

For more information on the Marine Corps Enlisted to Warrant Officer Program, see www.military.com/militarycareers.

Navy Promotion System

The Navy has two basic systems for promotion. Enlisted promotions are referred to as "advancements," while in the officer system, they are referred to as "promotions."

The **Navy Enlisted Advancement System** (NEAS) determines advancements through a Navy-wide examination. After each exam cycle, Final Multiple Scores (FMS) and quotas are used to select personnel for enlisted advancement. The FMS system is based on a member's knowledge, performance, and experience and considers the "whole person" in determining who will be advanced to fill quotas (or vacancies) within each rating. FMSs and quotas for each rating and pay grade are used to calculate a cutoff score. If your FMS is at or above the cutoff score, you will be advanced.

The components of your FMS differ depending on your pay grade. For E-4 through E-6, the FMS includes points for your Navy-wide exam score, performance evaluations, awards, time in service, and pass-not-advanced factors.

The Navy E-7 (Chief Petty Officer) promotion process is similar to the process for E-4 through E-6, but it also includes a Chief Petty Officer Selection Board. Advancements to E-8 and E-9 are made solely based on the candidate's meeting basic eligibility requirements and the Senior Chief and Master Chief Selection Boards.

Navy Commissioning Programs

The U.S. Navy offers enlisted sailors several ways to earn a commission and join the Officer Corps. The following are descriptions of the Navy Enlisted to Officer Programs:

The **Seaman to Admiral Program** (STA-21) is a commissioning program in which sailors keep their active-duty benefits, pay, and privileges while they attend college on scholarship to obtain their degree and their commission as Naval Officers.

The **Chief Warrant Officer Appointment Process** advances members who have performed exceptionally in the enlisted ranks in various technical specialties. Chief Warrant Officer Programs are open to chief petty officers with at least 12 but no more than 24 years of Naval service, and appointments are made to the permanent grade of chief warrant officer.

The **Limited Duty Officer Appointment Process** provides technically skilled servicemembers to perform duties requiring the authority, responsibility, and managerial skills of commissioned officers. Duties are limited to broad enlisted occupational fields.

Contact

For information on the U.S. Naval Academy, see www.usna.edu.

Enlisted active-duty and active reserve sailors can apply for nomination and appointment to the **United States Naval Academy** (USNA). The Naval Academy Preparatory School (NAPS) gets many of its students from USNA applicants who, in the opinion of the USNA Admissions Board, could profit from an additional year of academic preparation. Sailors who wish to be considered for admission to NAPS must state their willingness on their USNA application.

The **Navy Reserve Officer Training Corps** (NROTC) educates and trains qualified young men and women for careers as commissioned officers. NROTC units are located at selected colleges and universities throughout the United States. Upon graduation and successful completion of required courses and training, a midshipman is appointed officer in the Navy Reserve. Active-duty sailors who are selected as NROTC scholarship recipients are released to the Inactive Ready Reserve (IRR) while attending school and do not receive pay and allowances.

Navy Officer Candidate School (OCS) is one of five officer training schools located at Naval Station Newport in Rhode Island. The twelve week OCS course is designed to give candidates a working knowledge of the Navy (afloat and ashore) to prepare them to assume the responsibilities of a Naval Officer

Contact

Visit www.npc.navy.mil /Reference Library/Messages to learn about the Navy scores for each pay grade and official promotion announcements and news for Navy activeduty and Navy Reserve members.

Deployment and Mobilization

If you're in the military, you know that deployment—the assignment of military personnel to temporary, unaccompanied tours of duty—is always a possibility. In plainer language, deployment refers to the sending of soldiers, sailors, airmen, Marines, and Coast Guardsmen to training, special assignments, or combat. If you are in the Reserve or National Guard, you could also be mobilized for active duty in times of war or national need. Guard members may be mobilized for individual state emergencies as well.

Deployment and mobilization can be tough, especially if you have a family, but being prepared when it's time to ship out can help make a hard situation easier. This section covers the basics of deployment preparation. You need to be prepared.

Contact

For details on the Seaman to Admiral program, see www.sta-21.navy .mil.

Military Matters

The Pentagon recently approved a new wartime policy that allows servicemembers to carry up to 120 days of leave in one year. To qualify, you must be continuously deployed for at least 120 days on a contingency or contingency-support mission. Check with your commanding officer, who will determine if you are eligible and what procedures you will need to follow.

Contact

For details and guidelines on the Chief Warrant Officer Process and Limited Duty Officer Appointment Process, see www.persnet.navy. mil/pers211.

The Deployment Process

Deployment is defined by the Department of Defense (DoD) as a troop movement for 30 continuous days or more to a land-based location outside the United States, either for peacekeeping or during a conflict. Deployment generally has five phases:

1. **Pre-deployment Activities**—These activities take place at your installation, prior to your leaving for the port of embarkation, and include any necessary training for when you reach your destination, as well as briefings for you and your family on your benefits and entitlements. This phase can last for a few months, or even a few days, depending on the situation.

2. **Movement to Port of Embarkation**—When your unit receives orders to deploy, you will be sent to your port of embarkation, the location in the United States from which you will be deployed.

3. **Strategic Lift**—Your unit will be transported by air or sea to your point of debarkation, which will be in the theater of operations to which you have been assigned. If you are assigned to duty on a vessel, your unit will proceed directly to your destination.

4. **Reception at Point of Debarkation**—Your unit will arrive at the point of debarkation, and its onward assignment, travel, and support logistics will be coordinated.

5. **Onward Movement**—Your unit will be organized (or reconfigured, if necessary) and move on to the staging area (the location where you will be stationed) to await tactical assignment.

Pre-Deployment Tips for the Servicemember

Below are some suggestions to help you prepare for deployment.

Service Record—Check your service record to make sure your contact information is correct. In the case of an emergency, an incorrect phone number can delay a response.

Vehicle Storage—If you own a car or truck, make storage arrangements if necessary. If your registration will expire while you are deployed, you should renew your registration prior to deployment. You should also check with your insurance company to see if it offers reduced rates to deployed servicemembers.

Bills—You are responsible for your bills while you are deployed, including expenses such as rent, mortgage payments, car payments, credit cards, etc. Before deploying, be sure to make arrangements for these payments to be taken care of.

Take Advantage

Before deployment, confirm the information in your Military Pay Account to avoid pay issues later (see page 64).

Direct Deposit—You will receive your pay through direct deposit while you are deployed. For more information on direct deposit, check with your bank or credit union.

Income Tax—If you will be deployed when your income taxes are due, decide in advance how the taxes will be filed and who will do it. You may also want to file for an extension. For more details, see the tax section on page 12.

Power of Attorney—A power of attorney is a legal designation you can grant another person so that the other person can sign documents in your name. While you are deployed, it may be necessary for your spouse, family member, or friend to act on your behalf. Before you execute a power of attorney, be sure you know exactly what you want this person to do in your place. You can limit the duration of the power of attorney to the period of time you expect to be deployed.

Life Insurance—Before deploying, you should verify whom you have designated as a beneficiary on your life insurance, and make changes as necessary. An eligible beneficiary can be any person or legal entity designated by you. For more information on life insurance and SGLI, see page 28.

Make a Will—A will is a legal expression or declaration of your wishes concerning the disposition of your property after death. It is always easier for survivors to take care of things if you have prepared a legally executed will. If you die without leaving a will, your property is distributed according to state law, which might not be the same way you would have wanted it. For assistance in preparing, updating, or changing your will, you should contact the legal office at your installation (see page 160).

Family Readiness for Deployment

Before you deploy, make sure that you and your family have prepared for the difficulties that may arise during deployment. A full section on family deployment issues and support programs can be found on page 339, but you should also keep the following points in mind before deployment:

- Prepare a sheet of important phone numbers, addresses, and financial records, which should include everything from utility bills to veterinarians. Don't wait until deployment to do it.

- Designate a "backup." Things don't always go as planned, so call on a trusted person to handle all your affairs, then select another person in case that person falls through.

Take Advantage

If you are deployed with a ship or squadron for 90 days or more, and you are single, you may be eligible to store household goods at government expense. Check with your base transportation office for more details.

Contact

The Department of Defense has guard and reserve deployment support information, guides, and related links at www.defenselink.mil/ra.

- Get a power of attorney. This will be a big help for those handling your financial affairs while you are away. Unfortunately, in this day and age, getting a "general power of attorney" can be risky, unless you completely trust the person handling your affairs. A safer choice might be a "specific power of attorney," which allows only certain portions of your finances to be controlled by the individual you choose.

- Check in with the ombudsman at your installation for information on support services (see page 339 for more details).

- Use military family-support services. You're not alone—there are many official and unofficial sources of aid and assistance. Contact your base family services office for assistance. More details are in the Family chapter.

- Make sure your family's military ID cards are up to date (see page 3).

- Get your legal and financial affairs in order. Develop a family care plan, and make sure you're up to date on your insurance payments, will, pay, and finances.

- Update your medical benefits. Keep up with the paperwork, and Defense Enrollment Eligibility Reporting System (DEERS) enrollment, and make sure you have all necessary immunizations and vaccinations.

- Don't neglect the home front. Make arrangements for your family's security and safety. Work together in preparing checklists for what to do in case of emergencies at home.

- Be ready for the worst. It's not pleasant to think about, but be sure your family will be taken care of should you be severely injured or worse. You and your family should be familiar with survivor benefits and the beneficiary information should be up to date (see page 172).

Mobilization

When possible, members of Reserve and National Guard units are provided with as much time as possible between the date they are alerted and the date they are required to report for active duty. Some units may be alerted but will not actually begin active duty for several weeks. Under mobilization conditions, however, an emergency situation may require extremely short activation notice—as short as a few days. Fortunately, there are protections and benefits in place to ease this significant burden.

Reserve and guard members have special financial and legal protections that go along with being activated or mobilized. These rights can provide support for everything from keeping your regular civilian job while you're away to getting a stay on court judgments. The key benefits you should be familiar with are the Servicemembers Civil Relief Act (SCRA) and the Uniformed Services Employment and Reemployment Rights Act (USERRA), both of which are explained in detail in the Benefits chapter (see 139).

Mobilization Levels

Generally, the type and degree of a given emergency determines the level of mobilization. Selective Mobilization takes place in response to natural disasters or civilian disturbances that do not threaten U.S. national security. Examples of a domestic emergency that might require a selective mobilization would include a natural disaster, such as an earthquake, or a national crisis, such as a postal strike.

The National Guard can be mobilized by either their home state or the federal government. Mobilization or activation under federal law (Title 10) brings the same benefits that activated reservists get, depending on the length of time for which you are activated. Activation under state law rarely increases your benefits.

Phases of Mobilization

Preparation. Under normal peacetime conditions, the National Guard and Reserve plan, train, and prepare for mobilization. Under some circumstances, a unit may be mobilized and sent to another military command to receive specialized training prior to assuming their mission.

Alert. A unit receives notice of orders to active duty. The unit prepares for a transition to Active Component status.

Mobilization at home station. The unit assembles at home station and begins active duty.

Movement to mobilization stations. The unit departs from its home station and travels to the mobilization site—either in the United States or overseas.

Operation Readiness Improvement. The unit makes final preparation before actual deployment at the mobilization site.

Deployment Support for the Family

All Services Deployment Guide: www.military.com/deployment

Air Force
Air Force Crossroads
www.afcrossroads.com

Air Force Family Programs
http://public.afsv.net/FMP/

Army
Army Community and Family Support Center
www.armymwr.com

Army Family Team Building
www.armyfamilyteambuilding.org

Coast Guard
Coast Guard Ombudsman
www.uscg.mil/mlcpac/iscseattle/pw/ombudsman.htm

Coast Guard Work-Life
http://www.uscg.mil/hq/g-w/g-wk/wkw/index.htm

Marine Corps
Marine Corps Community Services
www.usmc-mccs.org

National Guard
Army National Guard Family Readiness Program
www.arng.army.mil/soldier_resources

National Guard Family Readiness Program
http://www.arng.army.mil/familyresources.aspx

Navy
Fleet and Family Support Link
www.ffsp.org

LIFELines
www.lifelines.navy.mil

Navy Morale, Welfare, and Recreation Headquarters
www.mwr.navy.mil

Navy Family Ombudsman Program
www.ffsp.org

Spouse Support and Relocation
www.surfacespouses.navy.mil

Reserves
Army Reserve Family Programs:
http://www.arfp.org/skins/ARFP/home.aspx?AllowSSL=true

Navy Reserve Ombudsman Online
www.ffsp.org

Air Force Reserve Family Programs
http://www.afrc.af.mil/library/family.asp

Coast Guard Reserve Family Programs
http://www.uscg.mil/hq/g-w/g-wk/wkw/index.htm

Post-Deployment and Demobilization

With the ongoing War on Terror, active-duty, reserve, and guard members are being deployed worldwide in great numbers. Your military training has prepared you for these combat situations, but what about when you return home? Below, you'll learn about the services available to aid you in your demobilization or return to civilian life.

Post-Deployment and Demobilization Programs and Benefits

You will undoubtedly face some challenges upon returning from deployment: you may be in the National Guard or Reserve, and need to get back to the job you held before you were deployed. Or you may be transitioning out of the military. Or perhaps you have a health problem that needs addressing. In this section, the major benefits and services available for returning servicemembers are described. If you are transitioning out of the military, you should also read the Transition chapter for more on transition services and benefits.

Post-Deployment and Demobilization Financial Protection

The Servicemembers Civil Relief Act (SCRA) is your protection against certain financial difficulties that may have occurred while you were away on service. For a full rundown of SCRA protections, see page 150.

Post-Deployment and Demobilization Employment Protection

The Uniformed Services Employment and Reemployment Rights Act (USERRA) protects your job if you are a reservist or guard member, so that you can resume working when you return from deployment. For more details on the protections USERRA offers, see page 155. The National Committee for Employer Support of the Guard and Reserve (ESGR) can also provide assistance

Take Advantage

Don't forget that you may be eligible for a Combat Zone Tax Exclusion on your basic pay or any reenlistment bonuses—even the Redux retirement bonus—you may receive while deployed to certain regions of the world. See page 14 for details.

Take Advantage

Operation Child Care is a service that offers free child care to the families of returning Reserve and National Guard members. If you are returning home (or if your spouse will be returning home) from Operation Iraqi Freedom or Operation Enduring Freedom for two weeks of R&R leave, you are eligible to receive a minimum of four hours of free child care. For more details, see www.childcareaware.org/en/operationchildcare.

Take Advantage

Help for PTSD

The Department of Veterans Affairs offers free counseling sessions and other resources to help deal with PTSD. For more information on PTSD or VA assistance, go to the National Center for Post-Traumatic Stress Disorder website.

and mediation services for those encountering difficulties in regaining their old jobs. For a description of ESGR's services, see page 158.

Post-Deployment Health Benefits

If you are returning from deployment, several programs are in place to provide you with transitional or continued health care. For details on these benefits, see the Health chapter. The benefits include:

- VA health care for combat veterans (see page 111).

- Transitional health care coverage (see page 112).

- TRICARE Reserve Select (see page 113).

Service Aid Organizations

Among the resources available to assist you when you return from deployment are military service aid organizations. Each service branch has its own aid society or mutual assistance organization that can provide you with grants, loans, financial advice, and scholarships. Check out the Service Aid Organizations section on page 281, for more information.

Contact

For more information on post-traumatic stress disorder services, visit www.military.com /PTSD.

Post-Traumatic Stress Disorder

Post-traumatic stress disorder (PTSD), a psychiatric disorder that can follow life-threatening events such as military combat, natural disasters, terrorist incidents, serious accidents, or violent personal assaults, affects more service-members than you may think. According to the National Center of Post-Traumatic Stress Disorder, about 30 percent of the men and women who have spent time in war zones experience PTSD. People who suffer from PTSD often relive the traumatic experience through nightmares and flashbacks, have difficulty sleeping, and feel detached or estranged. These symptoms can be severe enough and last long enough to significantly impair the person's daily life.

PTSD frequently occurs along with related disorders such as depression, substance abuse, memory problems, and other mental and physical health problems. The disorder can limit a person's ability to function in his or her social or family life and career, with consequences including occupational instability, marital problems and divorce, family discord, and difficulties in parenting.

Take Advantage

TurboTAP is an easy to use, interactive web portal that provides life-long support to separating military servicemembers and their families. For more information, visit www.TurboTAP.org.

Post-Deployment Blues

The post-deployment blues can sneak up on you without warning. They can begin innocently enough—a sudden loss of temper, an extra drink at the bar—but the situation can snowball into a long-lasting depression, or it may be related to post-traumatic stress disorder (PTSD). Be on the lookout for these warning signs when you return from deployment:

- Disillusionment or displacement: You have doubts about whether you are making a difference in the world, or if life is worth living. You feel disconnected from life and the people around you and have difficulty fitting in.

- Low functioning: You no longer have enthusiasm for work, communicating with others, being with your family, or even an interest in your personal hygiene.

- Unusual behavior: Possibilities range from overindulging (in food, drink, etc.), becoming more irritable or depressed, performing poorly on the job, or retreating into a "shell."

- Rage: You are more likely to lash out or even fight with friends and family in situations where ordinarily you would not lose your cool.

If you are experiencing these symptoms, communication is the key. Talk it out with friends or family. Your on base community services can offer help or point you in the right direction. Your chaplain can also provide advice, no matter what your religious beliefs are. For more on these services, see the Family chapter or contact Military OneSource for 24 hours a day, seven days a week assistance at 800-342-9647.

VA offers inpatient and outpatient services for those suffering from PTSD, including counseling, therapy, education, and a variety of treatments.

All About Relocation

In the military, you can count on moving to new locations every few years, either to an installation somewhere in the United States or overseas. There are definite advantages to relocation—you gain a full range of experiences in different communities and even cultures—but it's also easy to get overwhelmed by the actual logistics of a move. The following section contains the crucial information you need about how to make moving as economical and smooth as possible.

Permanent Change of Station Orders

Take Advantage

For guides and tips on on-base and off-base housing, see www.military.com/relocation.

Permanent Change of Station (PCS) orders are issued when you move to a new duty station at a different base or in a different area. This can be either a local or an overseas move that involves shipment of household goods from the current duty station to the new permanent duty station.

If you have been given PCS orders, you have two options: a government move, or a Personally Procured Move (PPM). The advantage of a government move is that you do not have to pay for your moving expenses, or worry about organizing everything—the government will plan it all with you. Another major advantage is that if you are moving within the continental United States (CONUS), you have certain protections in case your belongings are damaged in the move (more details on page 252).

Take Advantage

Navy personnel can use a pilot program called SmartWeb-Move, which allows you to set up moves of household goods on the Internet. For more details, visit www.smartwebmove.navsup.navy.mil.

In a PPM, you volunteer to move yourself, taking care of all your planning, expenses, and the actual move, and you are entitled to 95 percent of what it would cost the government to pay a government-contracted Transportation Service Provider (TSP) to move you. Most members can receive up to 60 percent of this amount in advance to help cover the expenses of their move.

Which option should you choose for your move? It will depend on your situation. If you can plan well in advance and handle the challenge of taking care of your own move, moving on your own might cost less than a government-contracted move. So when the government pays you your PPM allowance, you may actually end up making money. However, if you are short on time, or don't have the resources or expertise to handle your own moving arrangements, having a government-sponsored move may be your easiest, safest option.

For more on PPMs, see page 254.

Relocation Categories

Take Advantage

If you have renters or homeowners insurance, your household goods may be covered during your relocation—check with your insurance company.

Your move will fall under one of these categories:

Continental United States (CONUS). Moves within the continental United States make up the majority of relocations, and they are conducted either by government-hired moving contractors, or as a Personally Procured Move (PPM).

Home of Record or Combination of Orders Move. This move involves shipment of household goods from a location other than where you currently live, or another area in the continental United States (CONUS) or overseas. It is the most complex move because of the paperwork involved. For example, if you are stationed overseas (OCONUS) and choose to place property in storage near your last CONUS duty station, you are entitled to ship that property to your next unit when you depart your OCONUS assignment.

Local Move. This is a door-to-door move within your local area, with no storage involved—these moves are usually into and out of government quarters.

Overseas Move. Such moves include relocation to Alaska and Hawaii, as well as to other overseas locations. Approval of family member entry is required for some locations. If you receive orders to relocate overseas (Overseas Duty Orders), you qualify for:

- Unaccompanied baggage shipment (see page 261 for weight limits).

- Long-term storage for household goods for the length of the tour.

- Shipment of household goods and unaccompanied baggage to a designated location in CONUS.

- Shipment of a privately owned vehicle to your new location, if permitted in the specific area (see page 260).

Temporary Duty (TDY). This refers to a temporary reassignment to a location other than your Permanent Duty Station. You return to your Permanent Duty Station upon completion of the temporary duty. The length of TDY can

Take Advantage

Prior to moving be sure you have the following three critical documents:

- Household Goods Descriptive Inventory

- DDForm619

- Government Bill of Lading

Military Matters

You—not your transportation officer or the mover—are responsible for staying within the weight allowance for your mover. If the weight of items packed, shipped, or stored exceeds your weight allowance, you must pay all charges connected with the excess weight, so estimating the weight of your household goods is very important. An easy and fairly dependable method for making this estimate is to count on about 1,000 pounds per room (not including storage rooms or bathrooms) and then add the estimated weight of large appliances and items in the garage, storage rooms, basement, etc. See the weight limit tables on page 261 to determine your weight allowance.

Take Advantage
Be sure to check out www.military.com/discounts to find coupons and get military discounts on relocation services.

vary, depending on the situation, and is not defined. You may qualify for a per diem from the government to handle lodging and other personal expenses. (See the Pay chapter for details.)

Separation. When you separate or retire from service, you are eligible for moving and storage services, whether you are headed to your home of record or to a new location. (See the Transition chapter, page 274.)

Know Your Relocation Benefits

One of the biggest relocation challenges is managing the cost of your move. Below are the military's 10 core relocation-reimbursement programs. Make an appointment with the relocation manager in your family center (see page 252) for help estimating what each program will provide you.

The **Advance Basic Allowance for Housing** (BAH) is an advance on monthly pay that helps you pay for off-base rental housing. It is generally limited to three months' BAH pay. To request an advance, fill out and submit Form DA 4187. To learn more about standard BAH, see page 47.

Advance Basic Pay is basically an interest-free loan for when you make a Permanent Change of Station move. The collateral is your military salary, and you may draw up to three months' basic pay in advance, interest free. Normally, you pay back basic pay advances over a period of 12 months, starting a month after the allowance is drawn. A 24-month payback period is allowed under certain conditions. Your base pay and finance office can provide details. For more on standard basic pay, see page 47.

The **Advance Overseas Housing Allowance** (OHA) is an advance that covers the difference between the cost of nonbase rental housing and the Base Housing Allowance (BAH). Except in unusual cases, advances are limited to 12 months' OHA. For more on regular OHA, see page 50.

Dislocation Allowance (DLA). For more details on this benefit, see page 50.

Family Separation Allowance for Housing (FSH) compensates you for additional expenses incurred when dependents need to find quarters other than with you. It is not payable to a member assigned to any duty station under permissive, humanitarian, or mutual exchange of station orders, or to a member who elects an unaccompanied tour in the continental U.S.

Payment is in a monthly amount equal to BAH without dependents (in the 50 states and District of Columbia) or OHA without dependents (at any OCONUS location where BAH is not payable).

The Family Separation Allowance for Housing is only payable if:

Contact
The Official Military Table of Distances is accessible at www.dtod.sddc.army.mil/default.aspx.

- No government quarters are available at the permanent duty station (PDS).

- Dependents don't reside at or near the PDS.

- Dependents are prevented from residing with the member.

Monetary Allowance in Lieu of Transportation (MALT). MALT is the amount paid when you and/or your family drives to your new duty station. It is based on the Official Military Table of Distances. This allowance is available for both stateside and overseas bases.
MALT Rates:

One Authorized Traveler (AT)—$.15 per mile
Two Authorized Travelers—$.17
Three Authorized Travelers—$.19
Four or more Authorized Travelers—$.20

Move-in Housing Allowance (MIHA). This allowance, only for overseas locations, reimburses you for costs associated with living in privately owned or privately leased quarters overseas. It addresses three specific needs: one-time rent-related expenses, modification of homes for security protection, and the initial cost of making a home habitable. Rates will change depending on currency values and your location. Claim MIHA by submitting Form DD 2556. See your base relocation manager for details.

Per diem allowance. See page 49 for more details.

Temporary Lodging Allowance (TLA). See page 51 for more details.

Temporary Lodging Expense (TLE). The TLE partly reimburses you and your family for the cost of meals and lodging incurred when temporary housing is needed. This allowance is figured according to a formula that factors in the member's pay grade, number of family members, cost of actual quarters, availability of cooking facilities, and the local per diem rate. The maximum TLE rate is $110 per day. Ask your family center relocation manager for help in figuring your TLE.

Relocation Basics and Tips

Moving doesn't involve physical relocation alone; it's like starting a new life. There will be many questions to answer, many necessities to take care of—everything from storage and packing to learning about your new community to finding schools for your children. Taking the following steps should cover all the necessary bases.

Set up a meeting with your base transportation office. Depending on your service branch, the government office to handle your relocation will vary as follows:

Contact

Find information on relocation offices at your specific installation at www.military.com/ installations. Contacting experts at your current and future duty stations may be helpful.

Take Advantage

If you are moving, you can ship essential items such as pots, pans, clothing, dishes, etc., as "unaccompanied baggage." Having these items sent ahead will help you set up house at your new address as soon as possible.

Take Advantage

A one-stop resource for all of your moving needs is available at www.military.com/relocation.

- Department of Defense: Joint Personal Property Shipping Office.

- Air Force: Personal Property/Transportation Office.

- Army: Installation Transportation Office.

- Coast Guard: Household Goods Shipping Office.

- Marine Corps and Navy: Personal Property Shipping Office.

Remember, it is mandatory to make an appointment with your transportation office as early as possible. At your meeting, you will find out about all the moving options available to you—including a PPM—as well as required forms and preliminary arrangements for your move. If you are moving to a new installation, you should also contact the relocation office at your new location, which can supply sponsor and support services.

Make an appointment with your finance office at your current installation. Making a move will be a drain on your bank account—the finance office can give you the lowdown on your options, as well as relocation benefits and pays that you are eligible for.

If you're living in government quarters, notify the housing office of your projected move date. Make sure you also know all the regulations about cleaning your home before you move out. For tips on preparing your house for inspection, contact your local housing office.

Damage/Loss Protection and Claims

The Department of Defense is now offering Full Replacement Value (FRV) Protection for damage or loss claims. FRV is an important new benefit for the servicemembers, DoD Civilian Employees and DoD Families, which is available at no additional cost.

Take Advantage

Don't ship small, extremely valuable items such as stock or bond notes, jewelry, coins or coin collections, and items of great sentimental value such as photo albums. Carry them with you, as well as your purchase receipts, health records and appraisals.

For personal property lost, damaged or destroyed while in the care of the Transportation Service Provider (TSP), the member can recover the greater of $5,000 per shipment or $4.00 times the weight of the shipment (in pounds) up to a maximum of $50,000 as compensation for loss.

FRV coverage is in effect for personal property shipments occurring on or after the following dates:

- 1 October 2007 for International shipments (to / from OCONUS)
- 1 November 2007 for Domestic shipments (within CONUS)
- 1 March 2008 for Non-Temporary Storage (NTS) shipments and Local Move / Direct Procurement Method (DPM) shipments

There is no additional cost for FRV coverage, but the servicemember must file the claim directly with the TSP within nine months of delivery by using the DD Form 1844 to receive FRV. The TSP will settle the claim by repairing or paying to repair damaged items. The TSP will pay FRV cost on items that need replacing or have been lost or destroyed. When the claim is filed directly with the TSP, the TSP will be responsible for obtaining all repair and replacement costs.

An important difference between depreciated value coverage and FRV is that with FRV, the member files his or her claim with the TSP rather than with the Military Claims Office (MCO). As before, the member records loss or damage on DD Form 1840 (for damage or loss discovered at delivery) or the DD Form 1840R (for damage or loss discovered after delivery) and submits these forms to the TSP within 75 days of delivery. The member must contact the TSP within 9 months of delivery to file a claim. If the TSP does not respond to the claim, the member may then turn the claim over to the MCO.

The Military Surface Deployment and Distribution Command (SDDC) has published a detailed set of guidelines that governs FRV coverage on its website. DoD Customers can find the website at http://www.sddc.army.mil/ click Full Replacement Value Protection. Also, more FRV information can be found on the various Military Claims Offices web pages.

Personally Procured Moves (PPM)

The Personally Procured Move (PPM) program—formerly known as the DITY move—offers a monetary incentive for you to pack, crate, and transport your own household goods.. If you're eligible to move personal property at government expense, you're eligible to use the PPM program. This includes PCS and TDY moves, as well as separating, retiring, and moving to or from government quarters under orders.

If you make a PPM and your total move costs are *less* than the PPM allowance provided by the government, you keep the difference. In other words, if you go about your move in an economical manner, you will have money left for yourself—a nice reward for the time you have personally invested to take care of your move.

The program is voluntary and may be used in whole or in part. You may, for example, ship some household goods on a government bill of lading and the balance, up to the maximum weight allowance, under the PPM program.

Under the PPM program, you may use your own vehicle or a borrowed or rental vehicle. You are entitled to travel allowances, per diem, and payment for mileage through the government; for more on per diem, see page 49. You also

What to Expect from Your Mover

Your moving company is required to:

- Unpack and unwrap all cartons, boxes, and crates.

- Place each item or carton in the room you indicate.

- Place unpacked articles in cabinets and cupboards or on kitchen shelves when convenient, safe, and your desired location. Have placement planned out before the carrier arrives. Movers are required to place each item only once.

- Assemble all furniture and equipment disassembled by the movers at the place of origin.

- Remove packing and blocking materials from appliances. The mover is not required to connect appliances to electric, gas, or water outlets.

- Remove all packing material during the unpacking.

receive $25,000 in insurance coverage. An advance monetary allowance, not to exceed 60 percent of the estimated government cost of your move, can be paid under certain circumstances. Ask your transportation office representative for more details on these benefits.

Four Types of Personally Procured Moves

Rental equipment. You rent a truck or trailer, and receive an advance operating allowance based on authorized mileage and estimated weight of shipment. You are responsible for packing, loading, driving, unloading, and unpacking the shipment. Although you pay up front for storage at your destination, you will receive reimbursement.

"You Load, They Drive." You pack and load a commercial moving van or truck, the commercial moving company drives to the destination, and you unload and unpack the commercial vehicle. The commercial firm must provide you with state/federal regulation numbers. You must request that the company provide you with weight tickets.

Privately Owned Vehicle. For this option, you may use your own or a borrowed vehicle for the move. If you are borrowing the vehicle, you must have

Tips for Moving Claims

The following action items will help ensure your claims are accepted.

Before your move:
- Take photos or videos of valuable and unique items. Carry them with you during the move rather than shipping them with your boxes.

- Have your valuables appraised before the move. If you can get a specific dollar value for your items, you should get a better replacement value if they are lost or damaged.

- Prepare inventory lists, especially for items in large numbers, i.e. CDs or kitchenware. If you are having movers pack these items, have them sign inventories that confirm each package's contents. Also write the exact contents of each box on the outside.

- Write down serial numbers and model numbers for your electronics on the boxes in which they are packed, and keep your own list.

- Take inventory lists, receipts for valuable items, and your photographs with you, along with your other important records.

- Check with your insurance company regarding coverage. Some policies cover only lost items, not damages. If you need extra insurance, take care of it before the move.

During your move:
- Supervise movers as they pack and load your goods, checking off items on your inventory lists.

After you arrive at your new duty station:
- Check your inventory lists again when your belongings are unloaded at your destination. On your DD Form 1840, make a note of any missing or damaged items. Don't sign anything until the truck is completely unloaded.

- If you find missing or damaged items after the movers leave, note the items on DD Form 1840R and submit the completed form to your local claims office less than 70 days after your goods were delivered.

- Contact the claims office at your new duty station if any of your property has been lost or damaged, or if you have questions.

- Do not throw away any damaged items until the damage has been inspected by all authorized parties, or you have been instructed to do so by the claims office. You must allow inspection of the property by both the government and the carrier at either's request.

Source: Dept. of Defense

Military Matters

If you have an inconvenience claim, file it directly with the mover. An inconvenience claim covers any expenses you have to shoulder because the carrier failed to pick up or deliver household goods on schedule. The base transportation office can help you with these claims, as well as any appeals you may need to file.

Take Advantage

Visit Military Homefront's "Plan My Move" website to access a powerful new set of tools to help you and your family make your next move a smooth one. Visit http://www.militaryhomefront.dod.mil/ to access the Plan My Move website.

written permission from the vehicle owner to conduct the move. Current vehicle registration is also required. The vehicle must be a van or a car with a trailer, not one designed for passenger transport.

The Move in Connection with a Government-Arranged Mobile Home Shipment. Household goods that can be authorized for shipment at government expense but must be removed from a mobile home to satisfy safety requirements can be moved under the PPM program. This includes heavy appliances and furniture, air conditioners, awnings, etc.

Making a PPM

Decide on your type of move. Choose one of the four types of PPMs (see page 256) that best fits your needs.

Apply for the PPM by scheduling an appointment with your Personal Property Transportation Office (PPTO). The office will cover the program in detail, and provide you with the forms and instructions you need.

You must be authorized before you proceed with your PPM. If you are making a partial PPM (only shipping a certain amount of household goods), make sure you work out all the details with your PPTO representative. Note that you will not receive full government payment for your PPM until after your move.

Get receipts for all moving expenses. All costs associated with your move are nontaxable, and they will be deducted from the allowance you receive from the move to determine your actual financial profit. Although only your profit will be taxed, be sure to keep track of all costs to maximize what money you do make. Authorized expenses include:

• Rental vehicles/trailers.

• Packing materials.

- Moving equipment (including hand trucks and dollies).

- Gas and oil expenses.

- Highway tolls, weight tickets, and any other transportation expense directly related to the move.

Confirm your insurance coverage. Make sure you are up to date on paying your car and accident insurance. If you are using a trailer, check your auto insurance policy to make sure you are covered. State laws regarding liability for accidents during a PPM vary, so if you are involved in an accident while performing a PPM, contact the legal office at the military installation nearest the accident site as soon as possible.

If you opted to have an advance operating allowance (up-front cash to help defray the costs of moving), pick up the allowance from your local dispersing office.

When your vehicle (whether you own it or are renting) is ready, calculate the total weight of what you are moving. You will need to weigh your vehicle both fully loaded and unloaded. This is extremely important, as your PPM payment will be based on this weight ticket. You can usually find certified scales at a local moving or trucking company office. To calculate the weight of your shipment, follow this formula:

Personally Procured Move Paperwork

Forms you may need to fill out or provide for a do-it-yourself move include:

- "Application for PPM and Counseling Checklist" (DD Form 2278), available at www.military.com/forms.

- "Advance of Funds Application and Account" (Standard Form 1038; for advanced operating allowance), at www.psc.gov/forms/SF/SF-1038.pdf.

- Certified empty weight ticket for each shipment, with name, your Social Security number, and signature of weight master.

- Certified loaded weight ticket for each shipment, with name, your Social Security number, and signature of weight master.

- "Travel Voucher or Subvoucher" (Original DD Form 1351-2). Ask your PTO representative if you have specific questions about this form, which is available online at www.military.com/forms.

- Copy of registration for your boat(s) and/or trailer(s) if applicable.

Source: Dept. of Defense

Take Advantage

Before you move, make sure you know what weigh stations are located at your destination—some locations don't have them in the immediate area.

LW (Loaded Weight) = Your vehicle with a full tank of gas plus all of your property loaded with no driver or passengers inside

EW (Empty Weight) = Your vehicle with a full tank of gas with no driver, passengers, or property loaded inside

LW – EW = Net Weight of Property

You must have weight tickets from both your origin and destination points to prove you moved the entire weight to the destination.

Each weight ticket should have the following information:

- Name, grade, Social Security number.
- Name and location of scales.
- Vehicle/trailer identification.
- Date of weighing.
- Weight master's signature.
- Legible written weight amounts.

Make your move, and submit your settlement. Once you have completed your actual move, you have 45 days to submit a claim for full payment of your PPM allowance. This should include the following items, all of which are available from your Personal Property Installation Office.

- Empty and loaded weight tickets (two copies of each).
- DD Form 2278.
- PPM certification (attach all receipts for moving expenses).
- PPM expense sheet.
- Change of station orders.
- Advance operating allowance paperwork (if you are renting a truck or trailer).
- Vehicle/trailer rental contract (if you are renting a truck or trailer).

Temporary or Short-Term Storage

Whether you use a Transportation Service Provider (TSP) or perform a PPM, you are entitled to 90 days of temporary storage of your household goods if they are being moved at government expense on Permanent Change of Station (PCS) orders. You can request an extension of this storage period by filling out

DD Form-1857, available at www.military.com/forms. Storage may be used at your point of origin, en route, or at your final destination.

Try to avoid using temporary storage by planning for a realistic date when your goods can be moved into your new home. This will save your property from additional handling and possible damage.

Firearms are considered part of your household goods, but you may be restricted from transporting them based on national, state, and local laws. Check with your transportation counselor to see if such a provision might affect your move.

Nontemporary or Long-Term Storage

Long-term storage is usually authorized in specific cases—check with your base transportation office to see if you qualify. Take great care in separating items to be shipped and stored because once in storage, they may be difficult to retrieve.

Privately Owned Vehicle Storage

In some instances, the government does not allow shipment of a privately-owned vehicle (POV) to the member's new duty station. If you are ordered to a foreign overseas Permanent Duty Station to which a POV is not permitted to be transported, or sent TDY on a contingency operation for more than 30 days, you are authorized storage of a POV. The POV must be stored in a government-procured storage facility or another commercial storage facility not to exceed the government's storage cost limit. If the service does not transport the POV to and from the storage facility, the member is reimbursed for delivery and pickup of the POV at the storage facilities in the same manner as he or she would be reimbursed for travel to ports for shipment or pickup of a POV.

Shipping a vehicle overseas. If you need to ship your vehicle overseas, you can ship through Surface Deployment and Distribution Command (SDDC) and its Global Privately Owned Vehicle (POV) System, which handles more than 75,000 vehicles through 35 full-service processing sites worldwide every year. You are limited to shipping one vehicle that doesn't exceed a volume of 20 measurement tons. One measurement ton equals 40 cubic feet; a typical compact car is nine measurement tons; a full-size car, 15. When shipping a vehicle at government expense, you will pay for each measurement ton over the limit. Some large pickup trucks and sport utility vehicles (SUVs) may exceed the limit, for instance.

If you use the POV system, remember to remove personal items, such as CD players, and other small electronic devices, before you drop off your car for shipment. Other items that must be removed before shipping include house-

Contact

Directions and maps to the processing centers, and more detailed information on shipping a vehicle, can be found at the POV site: www.whereismypov.com. The phone number for overseas centers is 800-TRANSCAR (800-872-6722).

hold supplies, camping equipment, and flammable and hazardous substances such as waxes, oils, paints, solvents, and polishes. Propane tanks must be purged and certified before the vehicle is turned in. You *can* leave items you will need when you pick up your vehicle, including jacks, tire irons, tire chains, fire extinguishers, nonflammable tire inflators, first aid kits, jumper cables, warning triangles, trouble lights, and tools valued at less than $200. A spare tire, two snow tires, portable cribs, children's car seats, and luggage racks may also be left in the vehicle.

Separation and Storage

If you are separating from the service, you have 180 days from your effective date of discharge to have your personal property moved at government expense. If you are searching for a new home during this period, you can request local storage of your items. If you are living in government quarters and separating or retiring, you may move locally out of the quarters and still retain shipping rights within the authorized time limit.

If you are a veteran separating from the service on a Voluntary Separation with Incentive (VSI) or a Special Separation Bonus (SSB), or you are separating on the Transition Management Program (TAMP) or separating involuntarily, you have the same entitlements as retirees.

Retirement and Storage

If you are retiring from military service, you are entitled to store your household goods at your last duty station while you look for a new home. This privilege is for one year after your date of retirement.

You can request an extension on this time limit due to medical, training, educational, or other valid reasons. When requesting an extension for shipment rights, you should contact your base moving office in person or by mail. You will need:

- Your retirement orders (with accounting data).

- Your service record (DD Form 214).

- Documentation (i.e., from your school verifying commencement, or a letter from your doctor showing your hospitalization or treatment).

- A letter requesting the extension.

Take Advantage

If you are separated from the military and in school, you can apply for a waiver to have your household goods stored for an extended amount of time.

Weight Limits

Weight is indicated in pounds.

Grade	PCS without Dependents	PCS with Dependents	Temporary Duty Allowance
0-10	18,000	18,000	2,000
0-9	18,000	18,000	1,500
0-8	18,000	18,000	1,000
0-7	18,000	18,000	1,000
0-6	18,000	18,000	800
0-5	16,000	17,500	800
0-4/W-4	14,000	17,000	800
0-3/W-3	13,000	14,500	600
0-2/W-2	12,500	13,500	600
0-1/W-1	10,000	12,000	600
E-9	13,000	15,000	600
E-8	12,000	14,000	500
E-7	11,000	13,000	400
E-6	8,000	11,000	400
E-5	7,000	9,000	400
E-4	7,000	8,000	400
E-3	5,000	8,000	400
E-2	5,000	8,000	400
E-1	5,000	8,000	400

Source: Dept. of Defense

Transporting Pets

Military regulations allow for a maximum of two pets (dogs and cats only) per family to travel with their owners on Air Mobility Command (AMC) flights. To travel with pets, you must be able to travel within a 14-day window of time. The weight limit for each pet is 99 pounds (including carrier). The cost is $85 per pet up to 70 pounds, paid at the owner's expense. Pets between 71 and 99 pounds cost $170 per pet. There are no travel entitlements for pet transportation or preparing pets for travel.

Take Advantage

You must be flexible when you transport your pets—you may find that they will be prohibited from certain flights due to extreme conditions on board (i.e., too hot or too cold).

Depending on the season, transporting pets may be problematic due to lack of space on flights. If no pet space is available on AMC Flights, you and your family will be booked on the lowest-cost commercial air carrier, with a courtesy reservation for the pet traveling as baggage in the cargo hold of the aircraft. Servicemembers should personally confirm all pet travel arrangements in the event of last minute airline decrees, which could change pet shipment plans. You are responsible for all pet shipment requirements, such as documentation, immunization, and pet entry requirements for foreign countries.

Most commercial carriers now require pets to have a health certificate from a veterinarian. Some countries and states (Hawaii, for instance) ban certain types of pets or require a quarantine period. Pets may also require inspection by the customs service in the country from which they are departing. Veterinary clinics and animal rights groups can provide more information and help set up a transportation plan for pets. Required documents usually include a veterinary health certificate (DD Form 2209), which must be issued within 10 days of your departure, and a rabies vaccination certificate (DD Form 2208), both available at www.military.com/forms. This must be issued at least 30 days prior to your departure but cannot be more than one year old.

Check on the type and size of kennel needed for overseas shipment of pets. You must provide a hard-shell U.S.-approved International Air Transport Association (IATA) kennel. The cage must be large enough for the animal to be able to stand up, turn around, and lie down with normal movements.

Take Advantage

During moves, attach an ID tag to your pet's collar.

Take Advantage

If you're traveling within the United States, check on pet-friendly hotels on your route at www.petswelcome.com.

Moving Checklist:
Three Months Before the Move

- Make an appointment for a counseling session at your base transportation office.

- Decide whether you want to make a PPM or have the government handle everything for you.

- Start saving for nonreimbursable moving expenses.

- Discuss the moving process with your children to help them overcome their fear of relocation.

- Start planning for special moving needs if you have an infant.

- If you live in a private residence, notify your landlord that you will be moving, but do not give him or her an exact date right now.

- Begin making shipping arrangements for your vehicle(s), if necessary. If you are presently using your base transportation office, schedule a counseling session.

- Start to keep track of tax-deductible moving expenses (i.e., the cost of pre-move house hunting).

- Make an inventory of possessions and valuable items (take photographs or videos). Get appraisals for antiques or collections.

- Start organizing personal records such as birth certificates, insurance papers, and warranties.

- Make a list of whom to notify concerning your move and forwarding address.

- Let clubs and organizations that you belong to know you are leaving. Transfer your membership if possible.

- Take care of necessary medical, optical, and dental appointments. Obtain your records or find out how to forward them later.

- Have a power of attorney or letter of authorization drawn up to prepare for unforeseen circumstances.

- Sort through closets and drawers to decide which clothes and other items to give away or sell.

- Make sure all stickers from previous moves have been removed from furniture.

- Do not make any more mail-order purchases.

Moving Checklist: Two Months Before

- Start using up canned foods, spray paints, and other consumables.

- Have an "inventory session" in which you decide what you need to take with you and what you can get rid of.

- Begin sorting out and disposing of items you don't need. You can sell them through local classifieds, go to an online marketplace such as eBay, or donate them.

- If you are buying a home at your new location, you should choose one as soon as possible, and then arrange financing and set tentative closing dates. For more on the home-buying process, see www.military.com/homebuying.

- If your spouse has a job, he or she should give required notice of termination and get a referral letter. Your spouse should also update his or her résumé for finding a job at your new location. For more help, see the Spouse Career Center at www.military.com/spouse.

- If you require child care at your new location, start looking into options. (See page 333.)

- If you have school-age children, check school schedules and enrollment requirements at your new location.

- If you plan to take a vacation on the way to your new address, make all your reservations as soon as possible.

- If you have a car or truck, be sure that all maintenance and repairs are taken care of now. Be sure you still have your proof of insurance for the car.

- Contact your insurance company about protection for automobiles, home and household storage, and high-value items.

- If you are using your base transportation office, let the staff know if you plan to ship your vehicle, and provide the estimated shipping weight.

- If you have pets, have them checked by a local vet, and be sure that all vaccinations and inoculations are up to date. Get a copy of your pet's medical records.

- Close out any local charge accounts.

- If necessary, open up an account and a safe deposit box at a bank at your new location.

- If you need help organizing your finances, visit your military base finance center.

- Check expiration dates on major credit cards you plan to use during travel.

- Contact the Department of Motor Vehicles at your new location for information on a new driver's license and registration.

Moving Checklist: One Month Before

- Schedule pickup and delivery dates with your mover, and arrange for storage if needed.

- Verify your move-in schedule with real estate agents and landlords, or your destination housing office, and arrange for temporary housing or lodgings if needed.

- Obtain change-of-address cards from the post office. If your new address is not yet known, you can still address cards now to save time later.

- If you haven't found a new residence yet, obtain a post office box or forwarding address for your mail until you have a permanent address.

- If you haven't done so already, visit your military financial center or private advisor for counseling. Check with your transportation center on base to see if you are entitled to advanced pay or other benefits.

- Get rid of any unwanted items around your house (furniture, clothes, etc). You can sell them through the classifieds, hold a garage sale, or donate them to charity. Keep any receipts from your donations for tax purposes.

- Arrange to pick up your children's school records or learn the proper procedures for having them sent to their new school.

- Arrange for letters of transfer from your local religious groups and clubs, including Boy Scouts and other national organizations.

- If you or someone in your family is employed, arrange with your employer to forward tax-withholding forms.

- Spouses and children with part-time jobs should give notice.

- Make arrangements for transporting your pets.

- Ensure that all health, life, fire, and auto insurance are up to date by informing these companies of your new address.

- Return library books and borrowed items.

- Ensure that your vehicle(s) are in good running condition and that all required maintenance has been completed.

- Record serial numbers of electronic and other important equipment.

- Fill out an IRS change of address form (available from www.irs.gov).

- Have appliances serviced for moving.

- Switch utility services to your new address. Inform electric, disposal, water, newspaper, magazine subscription, telephone, and cable companies of your move, and cancel any local services (i.e., pool, diaper, fuel delivery). If you have placed any deposits, get your refunds.

Moving Checklist:
Three Weeks Before the Move

- Contact your military pay office to recertify Basic Allowance for Quarters (BAQ) and have them sign-off on your PCS.

- Reconfirm your packing, pickup, and delivery dates with your mover.

- If you have a military ID card, check the expiration date and update it if necessary.

- Notify your credit card companies of your new or temporary address.

- Transfer bank accounts and your safe deposit box.

- If possible, settle all your outstanding bills.

- Cancel all local deliveries and services, such as newspapers and diaper service.

- Retrieve all items you have loaned out.

- Retrieve any developed film, dry cleaning, or other items.

- Send out a change-of-address card to the post office, your friends, and relatives.

- Plan menus from what you have remaining in the freezer and cabinets.

- If you are using the Personal Property Shipping Office (PPSO), reconfirm moving dates.

- Have drapes and carpets cleaned; *do not* leave them in plastic wrappers.

- Clean up your current living space or quarters.

- Renew and pick up any necessary prescriptions. Obtain prescription slips in case you need refills on the road. Pack medicine in leakproof, spillproof containers.

- If you are making use of military weight allowances, separate your professional books, papers, and equipment. These items will be weighed and listed separately on your shipping inventory. Make sure the packers know these are your professional items—their weight will not be counted into your weight allowance.

Moving Checklist:
One Week Before the Move

- Close out your safety deposit box, if you have one.

- Buy a bunch of plastic zip bags. These will come in handy when packing large sets of small items, like silverware, or for components of furniture that need to be broken down (i.e., screws, bolts).

- Make copies of any important documents before mailing or hand-carrying them to your new address.

- Remove wall accessories such as drapery rods, small appliances, and food and utensil racks.

- Pull out all items from beneath stairways, attics, and any other area that does not allow full standing room.

- Drain garden hoses.

- Drain oil and gas from lawn mowers and other gas-operated tools. Disconnect spark plugs.

- Dispose of flammables such as fireworks, cleaning fluids, matches, acids, chemistry sets, aerosol cans, ammunition, oil, paint, and thinners.

- Refillable gas tanks must be purged and sealed by a local propane gas dealer. Discard nonrefillable tanks. Some movers and the military do not permit shipment of any propane tanks.

- Disassemble outdoor play equipment and structures such as utility sheds.

- Disassemble electronic components such as stereos and VCRs. Place original packing boxes (if they are in good condition and you want the movers to use them) by the equipment. If you decide to pack the item in the original carton yourself, leave the boxes open so that items can be inventoried.

- If you have a computer, "park" hard disk drive units, then disconnect computer systems.

- Give a close friend or relative your travel route and schedule so that you may be reached if needed.

- Set aside cleaning materials to be used after packing and loading.

Moving Checklist: A Few Days Before the Move

- Separate items that will *not* be packed, including suitcases. If you are making more than one shipment, separate items for each shipment into groups.

- Ship as "unaccompanied baggage" items that you'll use immediately, such as linens, dishes, etc.

- Keep a household inventory list on hand to carry with your personal luggage.

- Make a complete inventory of all the boxes you will have moved to your new location— you will need to check this later, after you move in.

- Attach colored stickers to your boxes to correspond with the rooms in your new home where you want your boxes to go. If you are using movers, prepare a color-coded map of your new house so that they'll know exactly where to take your belongings.

- Make sure that cash, jewelry, important documents, your checkbook, and other valuable items are secure and placed with the suitcases and other items you are hand-carrying. Do not ship jewelry.

- If you are renting a truck or other vehicle for your move, check it over to make sure everything is running properly.

- Make sure the condition of belongings is accurately noted. If you have marked anything "scratched," "dented," or "soiled," also note the location of the particular problem.

- If you are leasing phones from the phone company, return them.

- Confirm child care and pet arrangements, if necessary.

- Clean and dry your refrigerator and freezer. Allow them to dry one or two days with doors propped open. Note: Families with children or pets present should block the doors from closing accidentally. To avoid a musty odor, you can place several charcoal briquettes in a stocking or sock in both the freezer and refrigerator compartments.

- Discard partly-used cans and containers of substances that might leak.

- Carefully tape and place in individual waterproof bags any jars of liquid you plan to take with you.

- Remove outside TV and radio antennas, if applicable.

- Remove air conditioners from windows, if applicable.

- Remove pictures and mirrors from walls.

- Disconnect gas and electrical appliances. Moving companies are *not* required to perform the disconnects or to reconnect at the destination address. Call your power company if you have questions.

- Remove all light bulbs from lamps.

Moving Day

- Get up early and be ready for movers to arrive. *Do not* have dirty dishes in the kitchen, or dirty clothes in hampers or lying around the house. Take all trash out of the residence.

- Have coffee, cold drinks, and snacks for yourself (and packers if you wish). This is going to be a very long day.

- Be sure that you or someone assisting in your move is at home at all times—military and most regular moves are conducted during normal business hours.

- Make sure cash, jewelry, important documents, checkbooks, and other valuable items are secure. (Put them in the trunk of your car along with your suitcases and whatever else you take with you.) *Do not ship jewelry.*

- Get pets under control before movers arrive. If necessary, ask a neighbor to keep them for you if you haven't made boarding arrangements.

- Double-check closets, drawers, shelves, the attic, and the garage to be sure you have packed everything.

- Have a marker handy to make extra notes on boxes.

- If you are hand-carrying any boxes with you, be sure to mark "DO NOT MOVE" on them clearly.

- Carry a box of "basics" you'll need on move-in day (i.e., tools, paper products, pens, markers, housecleaning supplies, emergency kits, etc.).

- Verify that the mover's inventory is detailed, complete, and accurate. Do not accept any "miscellaneous" labels or entries (especially on high value items).

- Watch loading and unloading, and examine all items carefully before signing a receipt.

- Make sure the condition of your belongings is accurately noted.

- If the military is taking care of your move, obtain a copy of the GBL, the DD-619 (if CONUS), and the Household Goods Inventory from the packers before they leave. Ensure the inventory reflects the true condition of the property, and be certain everything is listed on the inventory. Review it carefully and keep a copy with other important records you are hand-carrying.

- Check the entire house *before* releasing the packers to make sure that nothing is left behind which needs to be moved. *The packers are not required to return to the residence after they have been released.*

- Leave all the old keys that the new tenant or owner will need with your realtor or a neighbor.

- Consider carrying traveler's checks for quick, available funds. You should have enough to cover the cost of moving services and expenses until you are settled in.

- Hand-carry financial, medical, and dental records.

When You Arrive

- You will be given the telephone number of the transportation office at your new duty station. You should contact the office as soon as possible, and provide them with a phone number where you or a family member may be reached.

- If you are listing Household Goods Office as a destination, contact the staff to arrange for delivery of personal property.

- Arrange for phone, gas, and electricity to be connected.

- Check the pilot lights on the stove, water heater, incinerator, and furnace.

- If you are moving to a new state, register your car and get a new driver's license as soon as possible.

- Register your children in school.

- Connect with medical services in your new location, such as doctors, dentists, etc.

- Before the moving van arrives, clean the hard-to-reach places in your new residence.

- When the movers arrive, check their inventory against the one you made prior to departure—they should match.

- Know in advance where to place each piece of furniture. The mover is required to place each piece only once.

- If you're moving into government quarters, do a thorough inspection, noting and photographing any damage—this will save you time and trouble when you move out.

Part Seven

The
Transition
Advantage

Whether you serve three years or 30, transitioning out of the military is a sure thing. Fortunately, the skills and values you have learned in the military are sought after in the civilian world. You have also earned valuable benefits that will serve you throughout your career and life.

As you are planning your transition, you should focus on two areas: making sure that you're receiving all of the benefits you're entitled to and advancing your career. This chapter will prepare you for these goals and help ensure a smooth transition.

Prepare to Transition Out of the Military

Servicemembers transitioning out of the military fall into two major groups: veterans (servicemembers who are separating from military service) and retirees. Both veterans and retirees can take advantage of the programs in this section; retirees should also consult "Military Retirement" on page 277.

The Transition Advantage at a Glance

Transition Assistance Programs

A variety of workshops and seminars are available through your Transition Assistance Office to help you and your spouse become more competitive in the job market. Topics include enhancing job search skills, goal setting, and preparation of standard and optional forms for federal civil service employment, resumes, and interviewing techniques. One of the most popular job-hunting workshops is sponsored by the Department of Labor. Their 2½-day Transition Assistance Employment Workshop is one component of the overall Transition Assistance Program (TAP). You can sign up for this important workshop through your Transition/ACAP Office, or through your Command Career Counselor. Some local installations may combine this workshop with other specialty workshops.

During your first visit to the Transition Assistance Office or with your Command Career Counselor, you should ask to be scheduled to attend the next available workshop (your spouse should attend if space is available). You should plan to attend employment workshops at least 180 days prior to separation. TAP addresses such useful subjects as the following:

- Employment and training opportunities.
- Labor market information.
- Civilian workplace requirements.
- Resume, application, and standard forms preparation.
- Job analysis, job search, and interviewing techniques.
- Assistance programs offered by federal, state, local, military, and veterans' groups.
- Procedures for obtaining verification of job skills and experience.
- Obtaining loans and assistance for starting a small business.
- Analysis of the area where you wish to relocate, including local employment opportunities, the local labor market, and the cost of living (housing, child care, education, medical and dental care, etc.).

At the TAP workshops, you will receive a participant manual. Among other valuable information, this manual contains points of contact around the nation for many of the services you will need after your separation.

Note: Not all installations offer the Department of Labor TAP Employment Workshop. If the workshops are not available at your installation or base, the Transition Counselor will refer you to other sources where similar information is available.

Take Advantage

The Department of Labor has found that on average, service-members participating in the Transition Assistance Program find their first post-military job three weeks sooner than those who do not participate in TAP.

Contact

For more on Transition Assistance and related programs, visit www.dol.gov/vets/programs/tap/main.htm.

Take Advantage

TurboTAP.org is an official DoD website that provides information for transitioning service-members. Also supported by the Departments of Labor and Veterans Affairs, TurboTAP.org is intended to supplement the services offered by Transition Assistance Offices and other groups. Visit www.turboTAP.org to learn more.

Transition Services and Benefits

If You Are	Years of Service	Transition Counseling	Veterans Benefits	Household Goods Storage	Relocation Costs Covered (based on destination)
Voluntarily separating	0–19	Yes	Yes	6 months	Home of record[1]
Involuntarily separating under other than adverse conditions	0–8	Yes	Yes	6 months	Home of record[1]
	8–19	Yes	Yes	1 year	Home of selection[1]
Retiring	15 or more	Yes	Yes	Up to 1 year	Home of selection[1]
Separating due to medical condition (Less than 30% disability rating)	0–19	Yes	Yes	1 year	Home of selection[1]
Retiring due to medical condition	0 or more	Yes	Yes	1 year	Home of selection[1]

Note 1: "Home of Record" is defined as the residence used prior to entering the military; this may be changed at the time of re-enlistment. "Home of Selection" is the declared relocation destination that is at the discretion of the servicemember.

Note 2: 60 days for less than 6 years of service and 120 days for more than 6 years of service.

Note 3: 20 days for relocation in continental US (CONUS) and 30 Days for overseas relocation.

Commisary and Exchange Privilege Benefits	Medical and Dental	Separation or Retired Pay	Continued Health Insurance	Disability Separation Pay	Leave for Transition and House Hunting
No	No	No	18 months	No	No
No	60 days	No	18 months	No	Yes[3]
No	120 days	Yes	18 months	No	Yes[3]
Yes	Yes	Yes	Yes	No	Yes[3]
No	60 to 120 days[2]	No	18 months	Yes	Yes[3]
Yes	Yes	Yes	Yes	No	Yes[3]

Transition Tips

Keep the following pointers in mind as you work with your transition planner:

- Take the lead. Let your transition planner know your needs, and work on the best ways to accommodate them.

- Don't leave questions unanswered. Find out everything you need to know about transition, and how it's done.
- Engage in dialogue with your transition planners. Accept feedback. They're here to help you.

Take Advantage

The key to a smooth transition is to prepare well before you separate. Start early. Build networks that will help you make connections in the civilian world (see page 290). Use your education benefits discussed in Chapter 5 to get a degree or certification that will provide you with additional credentials.

Take Advantage

Transitioning military personnel are required to receive pre-separation counseling no less than 90 days prior to leaving active duty. To get a head start, you can set up a pre-separation counseling appointment for as soon as 180 days prior to separation. Retirees can get started as early as one year prior to retirement.

Pre-Separation Counseling

By law, all transitioning military personnel are required to receive pre-separation counseling in order to learn about benefits and rights as well as available services. You should schedule this counseling with your local personnel office or on-base transition program manager at least six months before separation. During this process you will receive help in completing the Pre-Separation Counseling Checklist (DD Form 2648). The checklist helps you identify your needs and develop a personal plan to meet those needs. It covers the following topics:

- Effects of a career change.

- Employment assistance.

- Relocation assistance.

- Education and training.

- Health and life insurance.

- Finances.

- Reserve / guard affiliation.

- Disabled veterans benefits.

- Individual transition plan.

The Pre-Separation Counseling Checklist is considered so important that you will not be allowed to leave your installation until you have completed it. You'll be given a copy when you complete your counseling—don't lose it.

Individual Transition Plan

A carefully thought out Individual Transition Plan (ITP) is your game plan for a successful transition to civilian life—it is not an official form, but something you create by yourself, for yourself. Your Transition Assistance Office will give you a head start with your Pre-Separation Counseling Checklist (DD Form 2648), which can serve as an outline for your ITP. On this checklist, you indicate the benefits and services for which you want counseling. You then are referred to subject experts. Your Transition Assistance Office will furnish additional information; you can also visit www.military.com/ITP to see a sample plan.

Prepare for Military Retirement

Preparing for military retirement is essentially the same process as separating. The pre-separation time line on page 278 applies, along with the TAP workshops and other pre-separation planning measures. However, there are some extra benefits and additional steps to be taken, forms to fill out, and decisions to be made. Understandably, military retirees have many questions about pay, taxes, the Survivor Benefit Plan, health care, and more. You can find detailed information on these issues in other chapters. (See page 280 for an index.)

Retirees are encouraged to attend a TAP workshop as early as one year prior to retirement. If members are unable to attend a TAP seminar while on active duty, they may attend one within six months after retirement. Travel to and from seminars is at the retiree's expense.

It's important to attend retirement transition seminars offered by your command. The decisions you make at the time of retirement will affect the amount of your retirement benefits. Each of the armed services will provide you with an estimated calculation of your future retired pay, survivor benefits cost and annuity options, and other pay-related matters. Armed with this ballpark figure of your complete retirement package, you will be able to carefully consider all your options.

Transition Assistance Tips

You are entitled to major benefits once you're out of the military. Most related programs are described in other chapters, including Money, Health, Education, and Benefits. (See page 281 for an index of benefits.) In addition, the Department of Veterans Affairs has an active role in the Transition Assistance Program and Disabled Transition Assistance Program, providing benefit information to separating servicemembers and their families.

Take Advantage

For a sample Individual Transition Plan, see www.military.com/ITP.

Take Advantage

It's crucial to make sure all the information on your "Discharge from Active Duty" (DD Form 214) is accurate—your awards, your completed school and training, your time under way or deployed, your rank, specialty, and so forth. The individuals preparing the DD Form 214 for you can make or authorize corrections quickly.

Take Advantage

Many states have individual programs for veteran benefits, home loans, education, business assistance, homeless veterans, and veteran-assisted living homes. Visit www.military.com /stateVA to see what your state has to offer.

Pre-Separation Time Line

The following is a suggested time line for pre-separation planning. It's possible that, because of operations tempo, deployment, and command pressures, your actual planning may follow a different schedule—just remember that it's better to finish these tasks sooner than later. Taking care of the items below will help ensure access to benefits and support even after you've departed service.

Six Months Prior to Separation (or Earlier)

- Schedule your pre-separation counseling appointment with your local personnel office or transition program manager on base.
- Attend a Transition Assistance Program workshop, or if you qualify, the Disabled Transition Assistance Program workshop.
- Develop your Individual Transition Plan (see www.military.com/ITP). Seek assistance from your Transition Office or Command Career Counselor if needed.
- Review the Pre-separation Counseling Checklist (DD form 2648) located at www.military.com/forms. You can also contact your installation's Transition Office, Command Career Counselor's Office, or the Transition Counselor's Office for a copy.
- Assess your career skills and interests. To determine how they relate to today's job market, take a vocational interest inventory.
- Kick your job search into gear. Create a career plan. Start checking online resources for posting résumés and conducting job searches.
- Review and make copies of your personnel records, medical records, and family records.
- Discuss with your family possible career options and where to live next.

- If you are considering self-employment/small business ownership, the Transition Assistance Program offers U.S. Small Business Administration (SBA) sessions on business assistance programs and financing resources. See page 301 for more on Small Business Administration.
- If applicable, arrange for your discharge review.

Five Months Prior to Separation

- Contact friends or family who may help you find a job. Start networking. See page 290 for more on networking opportunities.
- Begin attending job fairs.
- Develop a fallback plan in case your first career plan falls through.
- Research specific job possibilities, job markets, and the economic conditions in the geographic areas where you want to live.
- Establish a financial plan to make ends meet during your transition to civilian life.
- If you are considering self-employment, begin researching economic data and business resources in the new community where you will live.

Four Months Prior to Separation

- Continue to network.

- Fill out your Verification of Military Experience and Training form (DD Form 2586), available at www.military.com/forms, and get a copy of your transcript.
- Complete the first draft of your résumé, and get feedback from your transition office.
- If you are considering government employment, check with the relevant civilian personnel office to determine what documents you will need to apply. Explore special federal programs and hiring opportunities for veterans.
- Visit the Relocation Assistance Program Office to learn about relocation options, entitlements, and assistance. See page 248 for more on relocation.
- If you live in government housing, arrange for a preinspection and obtain termination information.
- See the Education chapter for details on your veterans education benefits.
- If you decide to go back to school, consider taking an academic entry exam, college admission test, or challenge exam, free to servicemembers on active duty.
- Schedule your separation physical examination.
- Contact appropriate offices at your installation to discuss extended medical care (if you are eligible) or conversion health insurance. If you have specific questions about veterans medical care, contact VA or make an appointment with your local VA counselor.

Three Months Prior to Separation

- Continue to network.
- Send out résumés.
- Continue job searches for you and your spouse using resources such as www.military.com/careers, Transition Bulletin Board, Department of Defense Job Search, the Federal Job Opportunities Listing, and other available employment data banks.
- Assemble a civilian wardrobe for interviewing.
- Once you know where you will live next, arrange for transportation counseling. Learn about your options for shipment and storage of household goods. See page 250 for details.
- Schedule a final dental examination.
- If you would like to prepare a will, or if you have legal questions or problems, seek free legal advice through your service. See Legal Assistance on page 159 for more details.

Two Months Prior to Separation

- Plan a visit to the area where you plan to move.
- Continue to send out your résumé.
- Continue to network.
- Choose your transitional health care option. You can use military medical facilities or, if eligible, sign up for TRICARE. Decide whether to sign up for the optional Continued Health Care Benefit Program medical coverage. See the Health chapter on page 85.

- Be sure you are up-to-date on VA benefits, and other programs such as disability compensation for which you may qualify.

One Month Prior to Separation

- Continue to network.
- Review your Certificate of Release or Discharge from Active Duty (DD Form 214), and make any necessary revisions.
- Decide what to do with any unused leave.
- Review and copy your medical and dental records. Get a certified true copy of each.
- Make sure all DEERS information is up to date. See page 90.

- Set up your Thrift Savings Plan rollover if you want to switch to an IRA. See page 38.
- Contact a Veterans Service Office for assistance in completing your Veterans Affairs Disability Application (VA Form 21-526). Check with your local Transition Office or VA representative.
- Make sure your life insurance plan is up to date. For more on life insurance plans, see page 28.

Three Transition Tips

VA disability compensation. Contact a Veterans Service Officer (VSO) while you are still on active duty and before you take your separation or retirement physical. This way you may be able to arrange to have your physical and VA compensation evaluation performed at the same time. This could shorten your VA compensation rating process by nearly a year. For more on disability compensation, see page 80; for more on VSOs, see page 282.

Major Benefits Retirees May Qualify For

- Retired Pay (page 67).
- Combat Related Special Compensation (page 73).
- TRICARE for Life and Retiree Dental Program (page 116).
- Survivor Benefit Plan (page 172).
- Commissary and Exchange Privileges (page 5).
- Space A Travel and Military Lodging Privileges (page 141).
- Concurrent Retirement and Disability Pay (CRDP).

Retirees also qualify for veterans benefits—see the "Transition Assistance" section on page 277.

Major Veterans Benefits You May Qualify For

- GI Bill (page 188).
- VA home loans (page 20).
- VA pension (page 80).
- Disability compensation (page 81).

- Veteran health benefits (page 121).
- Burial benefits (page 165).
- Insurance (page 32).
- Relocation (page 247).

Leave. Unless you already have a job lined up, avoid "selling back" your leave. (More details on leave are on page 52.) Terminal leave can give you up to three months (sometimes more) of job hunting time and allow you to continue drawing benefits.

VA health care enrollment. Enroll with the VA health care system even if you don't currently need it. Enrollment is free and ensures that if the need arises, you will already have coverage in place. It also helps VA demonstrate a need for more funding.

Service Aid Organizations

In addition to state and federal programs, each service branch has an aid society or mutual assistance organization that can provide you with grants, loans, and scholarships to ease your transition into the civilian world. These programs can help with housing, debt, and education. To find out exactly what programs you may qualify for, check your service branch aid society's website.

Military Matters

Many veterans are unaware of a particular resource that can help them get the vital benefits they deserve: the Veterans Service Office (VSO). Although often located at VA regional offices and VA hospitals and clinics, VSO offices are not operated by VA employees. Instead, they are run by one of many military groups, including the Veterans of Foreign Wars (VFW), Disabled American Veterans (DAV), and American Veterans (AMVETS). Counselors are referred to either as Veterans Service Officers (VSOs) or District Service Officers (DSOs). These counselors are often dedicated veterans who are committed to assisting you with the process of getting enrolled in VA, filing claims, and pursuing your hard-earned benefits and compensation. To find a VSO near you, visit http://www1.va.gov/vso/index.cfm

Contact

Air Force Aid Society
www.afas.org

Army Emergency Relief
www.aerhq.org

Coast Guard Mutual Assistance
www.cgmahq.org

Navy-Marine Corps Relief Society
www.nmcrs.org.

Veteran Service Organizations

Literally hundreds of organizations have been created by veterans to assist other veterans and their families. The following are some of the better-known groups dedicated to the mission of serving those who have served our nation:

Air Force Association
www.afa.org
American Foreign Service Association (AFSA)
www.afsa.org
The American Legion
www.legion.org
American Veterans (AMVETS)
www.amvets.org
Association of the U.S. Army
www.ausa.org
Disabled American Veterans (DAV)
www.dav.org
Fleet Reserve Association (FRA)
www.fra.org
Iraq and Afghanistan Veterans of America
www.IAVA.org

Military Officers Association of America (MOAA)
www.moaa.org
Non-Commissioned Officers Association (NCOA)
www.ncoausa.org
Student Veterans of America
http://www.studentveterans.org
The Veterans Affairs VSO Directory
www1.va.gov/vso/index.cfm?template=view
Veterans of Foreign Wars (VFW)
www.vfw.org
Vietnam Veterans of America (VVA)
www.vva.org
For a complete list of veteran and aid organizations, visit www.military.com/community.

A Successful Transition to a Civilian Career

Take Advantage

Translate your military skills to civilians' terms and find jobs related to your military specialty: Military.com offers a skills translator at www.military.com /skillstranslator.

Job hunting is often a major issue for the soon-to-be civilian, whether separating or retiring from military service. The skill sets that you have learned in the military are very much in demand in the civilian world. Employers value the skills, leadership, and experience that the military offers. You may also have special qualifications, such as security clearance, that provide you with an edge in highly competitive fields. You also have access to a tremendous network of veterans willing to help you.

The first step to finding your ideal job is to clearly define your objectives—otherwise known as career or life planning. A key to having a satisfying transition is to effectively evaluate your strengths and weaknesses, and position yourself for success. Career counselors say that one of the most common problems people encounter in job seeking is that they fail to consider how well suited they are for a particular position or field.

Assess Your Goals and Priorities

The first step in your job search should be assessing your career goals. Exploring your goals will enable you to conduct a more focused search for positions and career fields that match your interests and qualifications.

As you consider your goals and evaluate different career fields, you should answer key questions such as:

- What are your specific goals for your career? For example, do you want to simply earn a living, or acquire new skills in a particular field?

- Are there certain types of work that you enjoy—for instance, do you like writing or prefer working with numbers?

- What type of environment do you prefer? For instance, do you want to travel?

- Do you prefer working independently or working closely with others?

- What are your preferences for salary, geographic region, and so forth?

You can use many resources to help you understand your goals and priorities, such as personality assessment tests. A list of books is on page 291.

Job Search: A Portfolio Strategy

Finding that first civilian job after separation can be stressful and frustrating. Fear of the unknown can lead you to seek a safe option—such as turning over your job search to an employment agency, or taking the first job

Where the Jobs Are

The Southeast United States continues to outpace the rest of the nation when it comes to new jobs. In fact, more than half of the top 10 cities for job creation are in the South and South East, according to the Milken Institute. The top 10 are:

- Fayetteville, Arkansas
- Las Vegas, Nevada
- Fort Myers, Florida
- West Palm Beach, Florida
- San Diego, California
- San Luis Obispo, California
- Laredo, Texas
- Brownsville, Texas
- McAllen, Texas
- Monmouth, New Jersey

Source: Dept. of Labor

Today's Top Jobs

The following table reflects 10 of the fastest growing professions/career fields and associated salaries for 2008–2016

FASTEST GROWING JOBS	MEDIAN ANNUAL INCOME
Database Administrator	$64,670
Computer Software Engineer	$79,780
Veterinary Technician	$28,920
Personal Financial Adviso	$66,120
Health Care Professionals (Nurses/Aides)	$57,280
Veterinarian	$71,990
Financial Analyst	$66,590
Gaming Surveillance Officer	$27,430
Forensic Science Technician	$50,310
Mental Health Counselor	$39,450

Source: Dept of Labor

you are offered. Neither is necessarily a bad solution, but don't let transition anxiety limit your ability to find a job you love. The best job seekers don't use any single method to find a job; they come up with a portfolio of strategies to increase opportunities.

Military Staffing Firms and Junior Military Officer Recruiters

Companies like Orion, Lucas, and Cameron-Brooks provide specialized services to help transitioning personnel, especially junior military officers or enlisted technicians. Many provide "high-touch" career services like assessment, résumé writing, and interviewing skills, which lead to a job placement with one of their client companies. In some cases, these firms host job fairs as a way to connect employers and candidates.

The biggest advantage of military staffing firms is that you get personalized assistance and direct connections to employers actively seeking to hire military personnel. Some recruiting firms, however, represent a limited set of employers and career fields—be sure to ask to see a client list when you contact each firm. In addition, a few of them may insist that you stop actively looking while they represent you, which potentially limits your options. All in all, however, they provide a great service and have helped countless transitioning personnel find jobs. For more details on these services, see www.military.com/staffing.

Online Job Boards

Be sure to spend time browsing the hundreds of thousands of job postings out there. This will give you a feel for available openings, and a sense of careers that might fit your skills. Many of these sites have automated search agents that automatically scan postings and alert you for potential matches. The best boards, such as Monster and HotJobs, also have content on dressing for success, negotiating a salary, and assessing your interests. Don't just use one job board—use a few national and specialized career sites. Job boards offer you choice, but generally do not provide personalized career services. For more on job boards, see page 298.

Your Network

Not surprisingly, this is often the best way to develop a set of career options. You will almost certainly know someone who is in an interesting career field, or works for an employer you find appealing. It pays to start networking early. Employers often view their internal employee referral programs as one of their most consistently productive sources of great employees—so they are looking for you, too. For more on networking, see page 290.

Direct Applications

Almost every employer website lists career opportunities under the "About Us" section of their site. Pay special attention to government positions, as they are required by law to give preference to veterans in the hiring process. For more on "Veterans Preference," see page 286.

Associations

Most military associations and service academies offer career services. Often, they host career fairs and provide help with resume writing, networking, etc. Like military staffing firms, they tend to bring together a smaller, but highly

Contact

Military Staffing Firms:

Cameron-Brooks
www.cameron-brooks.com

Leaders Professional Recruiting
www.leadersinc.com

Lucas Group
www.lucasgroup.com/military

Orion International
www.orioninternational.com

The Compass Group
www.thecompassgroup.cc

USA Placements
www.usaplacements.com

Military Recruiting Institute
www.jrofficer.com/jmoServices.htm.

Bradley-Morris, Inc.
www.bradley-morris.com.

Contact

Heidrick &
Struggles
www.heidrick.com

Korn-Ferry
www.kornferry
.com

Spencer Stuart
www.spencesrstuart
.com.

focused network of employers who are actively seeking to hire veterans. (For more on associations that can help, see page 298.)

Executive Recruiters

Executive recruiters like Korn-Ferry, Heidrick & Struggles, and Spencer Stuart focus on helping companies recruit senior executives. Corporations have come to value military leadership as they fill executive positions. Generally, executive recruiters are not interested in mid-level managers—so, unless you are quite senior, they are probably not a viable option.

Your Educational Options

Using your education benefits to get additional training, certification or a degree is a great option. To check out all the education options available to you, see the Education chapter.

An early start to your portfolio-driven job search will result in greater choice, increased confidence, and a better outcome, so when you set off on your civilian career, you won't need to look back.

Government Employment

As a veteran, you have the edge on the competition when it comes to getting a job with the federal government. Veterans often find that their skill sets are highly sought after by government agencies, especially the DoD and Department of Homeland Security (DHS). Military bases encourage you to apply for employment positions, especially if you have years of technical and support skills.

Veterans Preference

The Veterans Preference system was created to ensure you are in a competitive position for government employment, and to acknowledge a larger obligation owed to disabled veterans. In line with this belief, federal, state, and municipal government agencies have a "veterans preference" hiring law. This policy doesn't guarantee you any job—it means that because of your veteran status you could be selected over an equally qualified non-veteran.

Once you qualify for the basic requirements of a given job, the employer uses the following guidelines to choose among candidates:

First of all, the employer selects those who are among the best qualified and interviews them; veterans preference is not a factor in deciding who is qualified. After interviews are conducted, a finalist pool is determined. The position is then awarded to the most qualified candidate. If there is a veteran in that pool and his or her related qualifications are substantially equal to a "best-qualified" applicant, the position must be offered to the veteran.

Veterans Preference Points, Eligibility, and Civil Service Exams

Veterans preference points are used when civil service examinations are part of the hiring process. These exams are conducted by the Office of Personnel Management and related agencies for most service jobs including Veterans Recruitment Appointments, and when agencies make temporary, term, and overseas limited appointments. Preference in hiring applies both to permanent and temporary positions.

To receive preference, you must have separated from active duty with an honorable or general discharge. (Reserve and guard members on active duty also qualify, although active duty for training purposes does not qualify.) You must also be eligible under one of the following preference categories:

1. Five points are added to your examination score or rating if you served in one of the following:

   * Between December 7, 1941, and July 1, 1955.

   * For more than 180 consecutive days at any point between January 31, 1955 and October 15, 1976.

   * During the Gulf War, from August 2, 1990 through January 2, 1992.

   * In a campaign or expedition for which a campaign medal has been authorized, including El Salvador, Grenada, Haiti, Lebanon, Panama, Somalia, Southwest Asia, Bosnia, and the Persian Gulf.

2. Ten points are added to the examination score or rating of:

   * Veterans who served at any time and who have a disability connected to their military service or are receiving compensation, disability retirement benefits, or pension from the military or Department of Veterans Affairs.

   * Veterans who received a Purple Heart.

   * Unmarried spouses of certain deceased veterans and spouses of veterans unable to work because of a service-connected disability.

Take Advantage

Expanded Veterans Preference Eligibility
Those who have served for more than 180 consecutive days, any part of which occurred during the period beginning September 11, 2001, and ending on the date yet to be prescribed by Presidential proclamation or by law as the last day of Operation Iraqi Freedom.

Take Advantage

Veteran Career Network
Join the world's largest Veteran Career Network and get connected with over 200,000 veterans. Find veterans working in companies, government agencies, career fields, industries, or locations that interest you: www. military.com/mentor

- Mothers of veterans who died in service or who are permanently and totally disabled.

Military retirees with a pay grade of 0-4 or higher are not eligible for preference in appointment unless they are disabled veterans. This does not apply to those who will not begin drawing military retired pay until age 60.

Using your veterans preference points is relatively simple. When applying for federal jobs, you claim preference on the application or your résumé. Complete the "Application for 10-Point Veteran Preference," Standard Form 15, and submit the requested documentation. You can download the form at www.opm.gov/forms/pdf_fill/SF15.pdf. When you apply for government jobs online, indicate your veteran status.

Employment with a Foreign Government

If you are a military retiree and contemplating employment with a foreign government, you must obtain approval from the Secretary of your service as well as the Secretary of State, or be subject to having your retirement pay withheld. For more information, contact your specific service branch:

Air Force
  HQ AFMPC/DPMARR3
  550 C St. West, Suite 11
  Randolph AFB TX 78150-4713
  210-565-2508

Army
  U.S. Army Reserve Personnel Command
  Attn: ARPC-SFR-SCI
  1 Reserve Way
  St. Louis, MO 63132-5200
  800-452-0201

Coast Guard
  Commanding Officer (RAS)
  Coast Guard PSC
  444 SE Quincy
  Topeka, KS 66683-3591
  800-772-8724

Marine Corps
  HQMC (MMSR-6)
  3280 Russell Rd.
  Quantico, VA 22134-5103
  800-336-4629

Navy
  The Office of the Judge Advocate General
  200 Stovall St.
  Alexandria, VA 22332-2100
  703-325-8122

The Security Clearance Advantage

One of the most valuable qualifications that a transitioning servicemember can bring to the table is active security clearance. Today, thousands of employers including defense contractors and government agencies are in a desperate hunt for cleared individuals. Qualified job seekers will find they have a tremendous advantage over noncleared candidates. Unfortunately, many people let their security clearances lapse. An active clearance is a commodity that must be maintained and managed.

Contact

For additional information about your security clearance, check out the Military.com Security Clearance Career Center at www.military.com/clearance.

Security Backlog

There has never been a greater demand for employees to work on classified programs than now. This strong demand has put a significant strain on the Defense Security Service (DSS), the government agency responsible for conducting background checks for the Department of Defense and other agencies. A recent report on the DSS indicated it had a backlog of more than 500,000 applicants.

Employers value people with active security clearance since it can take between six months and two years for a person to receive a clearance. In addition, the clearance process often is very expensive.

A government security clearance requires a reinvestigation every 15 years for a "confidential" clearance, every 10 years for "secret," and every five years for "top secret." When a clearance becomes inactivate (because the individual switches jobs or leaves the military), it can be fairly easy to reinstate within the first 24 months, as long as that period falls within the reinvestigation window. After that, the task becomes significantly more difficult. In other words, if your clearance is going to lapse, you should consider some options to reactivate it within the first two years.

The easiest way for you to maintain your clearance is to take a "cleared" position with a company or government agency. The job board of the U.S. government, www.USAJobs.com, run by the Office of Personnel Management, lists more than 2,000 positions requiring some type of clearance.

Another approach for keeping your clearance active is service in the National Guard or Reserve (see page 307). Finally, you can turn to specialty staffing companies that assist defense contractors and government agencies to fill temporary and full-time positions with cleared individuals.

Here are three ways your clearance helps you in your career:

Take Advantage

Like many other federal agencies, the Department of Homeland Security is still growing. It is a great career fit for many veterans.

- You have increased marketability with employers that require cleared employees.

- Even if your security clearance has lapsed, employers are more willing to hire people with prior clearance. The firm will often sponsor you after you have been hired.

- Depending on how long it has been since you last had clearance, the investigation process can take much less time than for people who never had clearance.

Networking Works

Many people use their personal or professional networks to find employment. Using your network to get ahead is no longer optional. With a rapidly changing business environment, each of us needs to take time to build, nurture, and use our networks. In this endeavor, military people are luckier than most—they have millions of fellow servicemembers and veterans waiting to help. And thanks to the Internet, staying connected and in touch has never been easier.

"Networked" people get more than just annual holiday cards. They likely are the first to know about job openings, to know whom to call to get something done, and to hear the latest news on a variety of topics. They are the ones who get requested "by name" from detailers when on active duty, and often continue to have career options as they network after separation. They are able to walk into commands and companies and establish personal relationships quickly and with ease. Frankly, they have a leg up on almost everyone else. Sure, networking involves some hype—but a well-built network can make all the difference.

Good networking is not a one-time activity; it is about staying in touch, providing value to your contacts, and giving back. The sincerity of your relationships matter—no one wants to hear from you only when you need something. The best networkers do not see networking as a shortcut to a job—they thrive on connecting with people, helping others, and staying in touch throughout their lives.

Take Advantage

Military.com/mentor can connect you with one of the largest networks in existence: the military community. Through Military Mentor Network, you can tap millions of servicemembers, veterans, and retirees who want to help you in your career.

Almost any career counselor will tell you that the best route to a better job is through somebody you already know, or through somebody to whom you can be introduced. Counselors recommend that you build your contact base beyond your current acquaintances by asking each one to introduce you, or refer you, to additional people in your field of interest.

As you make connections, keep in mind the four components of building a good network:

- Size (How many people are you in contact with?)

- Visibility (Can you find the right person to help you?)

Jobhunter's Reading List

Some excellent books to support your career exploration and job search include:

The 10-Day MBA: A Step-by-Step Guide to Mastering the Skills Taught in Top Business Schools by Steven Silbiger (Quill, 1999)

The Book of U.S. Government Jobs: Where They Are, What's Available & How to Get One (9th Edition) (Book of U. S. Government Jobs) by Dennis V. Damp (Bookhaven Press, 2005)

Does Your Resume Wear Combat Boots? : How to Turn Your Military Experience into a Good Civilian Job Offer by William Fitzpatrick (Prima Lifestyles, 1993)

From Air Force Blue to Corporate Gray (Impact Publications, 1996)

From Army Green to Corporate Gray (Impact Publications, 1997)

From Navy Blue to Corporate Gray all by Carl Savino (Impact Publications, 1994)

I Don't Know What I Want, but I Know It's Not This: A Step-By-Step Guide to Finding Gratifying Work by Julie Jansen (Penguin, 2003)

Monster Careers: How to Land the Job of Your Life by Jeffrey Taylor, Douglas Hardy (Penguin, 2004)

Occupational Outlook Handbook: 2004-2005 by U.S. Department of Labor (Jist Publishing, 2004)

PCS to Corporate America: From Military Tactics to Corporate Interviewing Strategy by Roger Cameron (Odenwald Press, 2000)

Ten Steps to a Federal Job: Navigating the Federal Job System, Writing Federal Resumes, KSAs and Cover Letters with a Mission by Kathryn Kraemer Troutman (Jist Publishing, 2002)

Weddle's Guide to Employment Web Sites by Peter Weddle (Weddle's, 2004)

What Color Is Your Parachute? 2005: A Practical Manual for Job-Hunters and Career-Changers by Richard Nelson Bolles, Mark Emery Bolles (Ten Speed Press, 2004)

- Access (Do you have an easy way of contacting that person?)

- Relationship (Does the person care enough to help you?)

Recently, "social networking" services have emerged on the Internet, such as Monster.com, Spoke.com, ZeroDegrees.com, and LinkedIn.com. Most of these services allow you to share in the network of your friends and their friends. You could use one of these services, for example, and learn that your former shipmate knows the vice president for marketing at Lockheed and request an introduction. These services extend the success of online dating into the world of business networking. Though they are valuable services for connecting, they are not substitutes for good relationship building.

Networking is not an end in itself; it should be an enjoyable, interesting, and useful part of professional and personal development.

Contact

Find a list of job fairs at www.nationalcareerfairs.com /military/

Job Fairs and Hiring Events

Job fairs and career events provide valuable opportunities to meet with employers who are actively hiring. These events vary widely in format, employer attendance, and focus. Some, for example, specialize in connecting job seekers with security clearances to employers requiring those credentials. Others are specific to a given location or industry. Some provide opportunities to schedule on-site interviews in addition to informal discussions or the chance to submit resumes and cover letters.

Events are hosted by a range of organizations, from Transition Assistance offices to associations such as the Military Officers Association of America and the Non-Commissioned Officers Association as well as state employment agencies, local municipalities, professional associations, or companies like Military.com.

Doing some homework ahead of time pays off, helping you select events as well as allowing you to identify and research employers of interest. These events can provide valuable opportunities for you to learn about organizations and make a solid first impression.

Job Fair Tips

- Before you go to the event, research the companies that will be attending—you'll want to target those that you are most interested in, so you can make the most of your time there.
- When you go to the event, dress as you would for an official job interview. Since you will be at the fair with many other prospective employees, you need to make a good first impression.
- Be ready to hand out multiple copies of your résumé to employers. If you are interested in occupations in different fields, bring several types of résumés with you that are tailored for those fields. (For more on creating your résumé, see page 293.)
- When you arrive at the event, get the lay of the land—take note of where the companies you are interested in are located, and work out a schedule for yourself so you get a chance to talk with all of them. Get business cards of contacts and follow up.
- At the job fair, be alert and prepared—you should be ready to answer any questions, and be at the top of your game in presenting yourself.

A Winning Résumé and Cover Letter

A good résumé and cover letter are crucial for getting your foot in the door in any job search, but particularly so for those leaving the military. During your service, you've been bombarded with all sorts of jargon to describe your occupation, skills, and achievements—now it's time to translate that jargon into language that civilian employers can understand.

Your résumé and cover letter should be customized for the particular job you are seeking. It's important that you research the employers you apply to and position yourself as someone who can hit the ground running and deliver. Because we've been coded to "go anywhere and do anything," many military résumés try and communicate that the applicant can do almost anything. Although the sentiment is good, employers will almost always choose someone whose skills, qualities, and experience most closely match the open position. Your résumé must therefore "match the hatch" and address the employer's needs. The steps below will help you create a résumé and cover letter that will showcase your practical skills, education, and demonstrated successes. Get your foot—along with the rest of you—through the door.

Step 1. Target Your Career Field

Although your experience in the military gives you a wide variety of skills, for the sake of writing a winning résumé, you need to focus on only one career at a time. It's best to create different résumés for different jobs; for instance, you may be interested in a human resources job and personnel management too. Tailor your résumé for the specific position you're interested in so that it emphasizes your strengths in that particular field.

Step 2. Create a Portfolio

Throughout your military service, you have been evaluated, awarded, certified, cited, and acknowledged for your outstanding abilities. A portfolio is simply a collection of these past evaluations, awards, letters of recommendation, military and college transcripts, course certificates, college theses, and successful projects. Your portfolio has two purposes—as a great resource for filling in your résumé, and as documentation of your experience to carry to interviews.

Take Advantage

For résumé samples, visit www.monster.com and www.military.com /resume.

Step 3. Choose the Right Format and the Right Words

In general, there are two types of résumé formats: functional and chronological. You can use one or a combination of both.

The type of format you use depends largely on your career field. For example, a résumé for a management position is usually arranged in a chronological format. For skill-intensive jobs, the functional résumé format works best.

You should use dynamic verbs no matter what format you choose. Each of your verbs should be active and your nouns energetic. Simply reducing the number of syllables can add zip.

Step 4. Use a Template

A foolproof way to ensure you get your résumé format and flow correct is to use a proven winning résumé as a model. You will notice that some résumé examples include a statement of objectives and some do not. Opinions are mixed on this question, so it is strictly up to you whether or not to include an objective statement. If you decide not to use one, make sure your cover letter includes your career goals.

Here are two examples of how to effectively state your objective:

> "Seeking a position in contract administration utilizing six years of increasing responsibility, education, and on-the-job knowledge of purchasing, proposal preparation, and contract administration."

> "Seeking a challenging position as a technical recruiter, offering skills in interviewing, occupational assessment, and as an employee supervisor liaison."

Step 5. Show Off Your Record

Take Advantage

Many employers use phone interviews to weed out applicants. If you are telephoned, be enthusiastic and confident, remain calm, and smile— these traits are communicated even over the phone.

Your evaluations, awards, and citations contain a wealth of documented results. Use your portfolio to create a list of accomplishments. Employers need to see results of your performance that they can relate to the open job position. Military Performance Evaluations and Fitness Reports usually describe your duties and the number of people you were responsible for, and they typically contain bulleted, performance-related results. Past performance is the best indicator of future success, so quantify your accomplishments with numbers and percentages. Explain how often you did your tasks, the percentage of increased productivity, the cost savings, the number of people you supervised or trained, or the dollar value of equipment you were responsible for. For example:

- Supervised 14-member staf.f

- Produced 150 percent over quota for eight consecutive months.

- Saved unit $250,000.

- Administered travel budget of $15 million.

- Reduced inventory loss by 20 percent.

- Developed training program for a 600-person organization.

Your previous evaluations should have this type of results-oriented information. One caution: Never exaggerate on your résumé—it could come back to haunt you later.

As you are developing your résumé, it is crucial that you avoid using military acronyms, slang, jargon, or obscure terms. Most civilian employers do not understand military terminology, and the last thing you want is for a potential employer to be confused, or concerned about your ability to communicate clearly in a civilian setting. Spell out acronyms, and explain them when necessary. Translate the specialized military training and professional and technical courses you have taken into civilian terminology. Use a line or two to describe or list some of the topics studied in the course that may be pertinent to the job you are applying for, and include dates and locations. For example, write "Leadership and Management" as a course title. Then add the course content, including course objectives (e.g. decision-making, communications, using resources, giving directions, providing counseling, etc.).

Step 6. Proofread, Proofread, and Proofread

There is nothing that will earn your résumé a quicker trip to the wastebasket than misspelled words and improper punctuation. The following three tips can help you avoid having your résumé dumped in the "round-file express":

1. After you have completed your résumé, let it cool. Take a break and return later to give it at least one more look.

2. Read it backwards. Start with the last sentence and read each sentence for clarity and meaning from the end to the beginning of the page.

3. Have someone else proofread it. Another set of eyes may catch errors you missed.

The Perfect Cover Letter

In a cover letter or cover e-mail you introduce yourself, summarize the most important parts of your résumé and communicate how you could effectively fill the open position. A good cover letter will:

- Catch the employer's attention.

- Highlight key points in your résumé.

- Persuade the employer of your benefit or value.

- Convince the employer to call you for an interview.

In your cover letter, your tone should be formal, polite, and honest, but assertive. Employers don't want to take time to read much, so make your cover letter one page with three parts. The first paragraph identifies the position you are interested in, and how you learned about it. The second part (one or two paragraphs) should highlight your value to the employer, backed up by factual evidence. Match your skills, training, and experience with those qualities required for the position. Avoid simply repeating the contents of your résumé in the letter. In the third paragraph, you refer the reader to your résumé, indicate how and when you can be contacted, and ask for an interview. Limit each paragraph to four sentences or fewer.

Interviews: Do Your Homework

Doing your homework on the employer can save you time and help you feel confident during the interview process. Most organizations have websites where you can research the company—there is usually a link labeled "About Us." If you've done your homework you should be able to answer these questions before you go in for the interview:

- What are the company's goals, mission, and culture?

- Who is interviewing you and what is their role within the company?

- What job are you applying for and how do you meet all the criteria?

The Interview Drill

The following seven steps will help you prepare for your interview and present yourself in the best light.

1. Appearance counts. When you look good, you feel good. Make sure you are groomed and neat.

2. Your clothes and accessories should be conservative and neutral. Your clothes are your packaging and should not take attention away from the product—you.

3. Nonverbal communication is just as important verbal communication. Avoid slouching, and sit up straight.

4. Eye contact and smiles indicate a confident and upbeat attitude. This is a good opportunity to demonstrate your social and interpersonal skills as well as your excitement about the opportunity for which you're interviewing.

5. The handshake sends a strong tactile message. Whether your hands are hot and sweaty or cold and clammy, you can try some tricks to control the temperature. To cool your hands, try running cold water on the insides of your wrists. Use hot water if your hands are cool. If you have particularly sweaty hands, try using a deodorant gel (antiperspirant) as a lotion.

6. Your voice and the volume of your speech convey a strong impression. Whether the interview's over the phone or face-to-face, you should speak with enthusiasm and energy. Use a firm voice to demonstrate your confidence.

7. Your vocabulary reveals your communication skills and ability to interact with people, especially those you haven't met before. The words you choose will say something about you, as well as your knowledge.

Take Advantage

Create a one-minute verbal resume that quickly highlights your experience and skills. Then practice delivering it aloud until you're comfortable. This will give you the confidence to answer the "Tell me something about yourself..." interview question.

The Follow-Up Strategy

Your work is not over when you finish the interview. A good follow-up could give you the edge you need to get the job offer, and the contacts you make can become part of your network in the future even if you don't get the job. Consider the points below as you follow up your job interview:

• Ask when the employer expects to make the hiring decision.

• Get the correct titles and names of all the people who interviewed you.

• Write thank-you notes or letters (within two days) to each person who interviewed you.

• Remind the employer why you are the one they should hire in your thank-you letter.

• Be sure to proofread your thank-you letters.

Sample Interview Questions

1. Describe your strengths and weaknesses.
2. Describe your best accomplishment in your previous job.
3. How do you handle working under deadlines or with multiple tasks?
4. How do you handle working with a tough manager?
5. Do you think there is such a thing as "working too hard"? How do you know when you're working too hard?
6. What are the ways in which you manage stress?
7. If you are hired, what would be your personal goals for the first 30 days on the job? 60? 90?
8. Where do you see yourself in five to 10 years?

- Remind your references that they may be hearing from your prospective employer.

- Follow up with a telephone call to the employer within a week to 10 days. Use the phone call as an opportunity to resell your strengths.

- Be patient. The hiring process often takes longer than the employer expects.

- Use other job offers as leverage in your follow-up—to get the offer you really want.

Employment Resources for Veterans and Retirees

Many organizations, resources, and websites can aid you in your career transition, ranging from services that help you start your own business to VA organizations that support veterans with disabilities.

Major Job Search Websites

The Internet has transformed how we all look for jobs. Instead of pounding the pavement, you can hit your keyboard to find a variety of career opportunities.

Army Credentialing Opportunities On-Line (COOL)

The Army Credentialing Opportunities On-Line (COOL) program enables you to find civilian credentials related to your military occupational specialty. Then it helps you understand what it takes to obtain those credentials and check on available programs that will help pay credentialing fees.

Career Center for the Military Severely Injured

This site is a collaboration between military organizations, government agencies, private organizations, and employers who have rallied to support those seriously injured during service to America. The Career Center for the Severely Injured builds on efforts by the Military Severely Injured Joint Support Operations Center to ensure that servicemembers with severe injuries have easy access to all available resources to assist with their recovery and rehabilitation.

Employment Websites and Programs

Army Credentialing Opportunities Online
www.cool.army.mil

Career Center for the Severely Injured
www.military.com/support

CareerOneStop Portal
www.careeronestop.org

Department of Labor's FirstGov for Workers
http://dev-workers.xpandcorp.com

Helmets to Hardhats
www.helmetstohardhats.com

Military and Veteran Career Center
www.military.com/careers

Monster.com
www.monster.com

Office of Personnel Management
www.opm.gov/veterans/html/vetguide.htm

Spouse-to-Teachers
www.spousestoteachers.com

Troops-to-Teachers
www.dantes.doded.mil/Dantes_web/troopsto
teachers/index.asp

USAJobs
www.usajobs.opm.gov

Spouse Career Center
www.military.com/spouse

CareerOneStop Portal

The CareerOneStop Portal is a single point-of-entry to the Department of Labor tools that can help you find a job: America's Job Bank, America's Career InfoNet, and America's Service Locator. Content is organized both by customer (jobseekers, employers, students, and workforce professionals) and by topic. The portal is also a gateway to access state and local resources.

Federal Employment Opportunities

You may want to join the large number of veterans who are continuing to serve America as civilian employees of the federal government. Opportunities for federal employment exist across the United States and in many foreign locations. The Office of Personnel Management (OPM) has developed a guide to federal employment. In addition, the Department of Labor's FirstGov for Workers website offers links to major federal job centers as well as specific agencies.

Applying for a federal job can be a challenge, and certainly the federal job search process is unique, but the OPM has developed a site that provides useful information on federal job opportunities and the application process, along with application forms. Don't forget that your local Transition Assistance Office can help you find local federal jobs.

HireVetsFirst

The National Hire Veterans Committee, under the President's guidance, has designed a website to help employers find qualified veterans, and to help veterans make the best use of a national network of employment resources. The site allows employers to contact veterans, and provides tips and a one-stop career center for veterans.

Contact

The National Hire Veterans Committee's website is located at www.hirevetsfirst .gov or you can call 877-US2-JOBS (877-872-5627).

Local Veterans Employment Programs (LVERs)

LVERs conduct active outreach programs with employers, community and veterans organizations, unions, and local counseling and social services agencies to ensure that veterans know about and receive the services for which they are eligible. They can work with you to find placement in federally-funded employment and training programs, and assist you in developing job interviewing and resume writing skills. They can also help you conduct a productive job search, and access job listings through electronic databases.

Military Spouse Career Center

Commissioned by the Department of Defense Office of Military Community and Family Policy, the Military Spouse Center connects military spouses with education options, scholarships, training programs, career planning tips, and more than 500,000 employment opportunities. For more details on the Military Spouse Career Center, see page 329.

see page 329.

Operation Transition and Transition Bulletin Board

Operation Transition provides the Transition Bulletin Board, an automated system that contains a listing of job want ads and other useful information to separating and retiring military and federal civilian personnel and their spouses. On average, more than 10,000 want ads representing more than 30,000 jobs can be viewed on the bulletin board every day. For more information, visit the Operation Transition website.

Troops-to-Teachers

The Department of Education's Troops-to-Teachers program provides referral assistance and placement services to military personnel interested in beginning a second career in public education as a teacher. The DANTES Troops-to-Teachers office helps applicants identify teacher certification requirements, programs leading to certification, and employment opportunities.

U.S. Small Business Administration

Veterans have achieved self-employment at a higher rate than any other group of identifiable Americans over the past 25 years, according to recent Small Business Administration research. And a joint population survey by the U.S. Bureau of the Census and the Bureau of Labor Statistics indicates that of the 11.6 million individuals with some self-employment earnings in 1999, 1.6 million, or 13.9 percent, were veterans. With the programs and benefits available to veterans today, running your own business is not only viable, but an attractive option.

If you're thinking of starting your own business, the U.S. Small Business Administration (SBA) and other ancillary organizations, such as the Veterans Administration Center for Veterans Enterprise, can help you succeed with your business.

The SBA Office of Veterans Business Development provides guidance,

Take Advantage

With more than 500,000 jobs available, the Military.com Veteran Job Search is the largest online veteran job search resource: www.military.com /careers.

Contact

SBA Office of Veterans Business Development
www.sba.gov/vets

Telephone:
202-205-6773

Programs for reservists and National Guard members:
www.sba.gov/ reservists

SBA local offices directory:
www.sba.gov/local resources/index.ht ml

Contact

For more on Veterans Business Outreach Centers and their services, visit www.sba.gov /VETS/vbop.html.

Contact

Visit the Center for Veterans Enterprise at www.vetbiz.gov.

Contact

The Small Business Administration's Pro-Net database is located at www.ccr.gov.

Take Advantage

The Service Corps of Retired Executives (SCORE) is a non-profit association which offers free and confidential advice to help you build your small business – from idea to start-up to success. For additional information about SCORE visit www.score.org.

tools, and ombudsman services if you are interested in starting or growing a small business. The office's programs include Veterans Business Outreach (VBO) Centers that provide services to veterans, service-disabled veterans, and Reserve and Guard members. Here you will find outreach, business training, counseling, mentoring, e-counseling, nationwide services coordination, and directed referrals for owning or starting a small business. If you are a self-employed member of the Reserve and Guard, you can receive help when you are activated and then reestablish or restart your small business following deactivation. The SBA Office of Disaster Assistance provides what is known as Military Reservists Economic Injury Disaster Loans for small businesses affected by the activation of an essential employee or owner.

It is estimated that 5 million veteran-owned businesses could benefit from the services provided by VBO Centers. If 51 percent of the ownership and control of an enterprise is maintained by a veteran, you can claim to have a veteran-owned business.

Any veteran or service-disabled veteran owning a small business who is interested in federal procurement opportunities must be registered in the Central Contractor Registration (CCR). This database is also known as SBA's Pro-Net database, which has merged with the CCR. Federal contracting officials and federal prime contractors utilize this database to locate veteran and service-disabled veteran-owned businesses.

USAJobs

USAJobs is the federal government's official jobs site. In addition to a job board, the site features skills assessment tools, a database to which you can add your résumé, forms for veterans preference and federal employment, and tutorials and tips.

Veteran Career Center

A one-stop resource for job postings, transition advice, and military-friendly employers is Military.com's Veteran Career Center. In addition to a job board with over 500,000 openings nationwide, you'll find career tips, résumé and salary tools, a military-to-civilian skills translator, a list of military-friendly employers, guides to finding employment, and more.

Military Matters

RESUMIX is a computer software program that allows you to use an online application to create a résumé specifically to apply for federal jobs. It's used by both military and civilian organizations. You can print the résumé or save it to the system to retrieve and edit for future use. For some federal jobs, you may be able to submit your résumé electronically. Find more information on the USAJobs website.

Contact

The following websites contain information on the Veterans Employment Training Service:

VETS home page
www.dol.gov/vets

e-VET Advisor
www.dol.gov/elaws
/vets/evets/evets.
asp

DOL Transition
Assistance
Program
www.dol.gov/vets
/programs/tap
/main.htm.

Veterans Employment Training Service (VETS)

The Veterans Employment Training Service (VETS) helps active-duty, guard, and reserve servicemembers find civilian employment after separation from the military. VETS also helps enforce veterans' preference regulations, which give veterans an advantage in getting government jobs. (For more on veterans' preference, see page 286). Other major services include disabled veterans outreach programs, employment and training services, a homeless veterans reintegration project, and a federal contractor program.

Veteran Franchise Program

A special program called VetFran was created by a community of franchising companies wishing to honor those who have served our country. With the co-operation of the Department of Veterans Affairs and the U.S. Small Business Administration, and with outreach initiatives to other military and veteran organizations, the program continues to expand. More than 130 participating member companies have agreed to help qualified veterans acquire franchise businesses by providing financial incentives not available to other investors.

Contact

For information on the Veteran Franchise Program, visit
www.franchise.org
/memservice
/vetfran.asp.

Vocational Rehabilitation and Employment Services

If you are a veteran with a disability that affects your employment prospects, Vocational Rehabilitation and Employment (VR&E) Services can assist you. The program helps you achieve the following goals:

• Identifying all viable employment options.

• Identifying an appropriate career goal.

• Exploring labor market and wage information.

Take Advantage

VetSuccess.gov is a Department of Veterans Affairs website that provides information about vocational counseling available to active duty service members and veterans who have recently separated from active duty. Visit www.vetsuccess.org to learn more

- Investigating training requirements.

- Identifying physical demands.

- Developing an individualized vocational plan to achieve your career goal.

Customized for your situation, a vocational plan is a detailed outline of services that will be provided for you. The following types of plans are available:

Individualized Employment Assistance Plan (IEAP). Outlines steps that will be taken to assist you in obtaining employment; such assistance may be offered for up to 18 months.

Individualized Extended Evaluation Plan (IEEP). Used to help determine if you are able to obtain and maintain employment; typically does not exceed 12 months.

Individualized Written Rehabilitation Plan (IWRP). Outlines the training or education you should complete, leading toward a job goal; cannot exceed 48 months.

Individualized Independent Living Plan (IILP). Outlines the steps needed to assist you in becoming more independent in daily living within the family and community; such services usually do not exceed 24 months.

Once a plan is developed, you will continue to work with a case manager who will assist you toward your goal of gainful employment or independent living. Specialized employment services will also be provided by a case manager, employment specialist, and/or Disabled Veterans Outreach Placement coordinator. Specialized services include job placement assistance and follow-up support, job-seeking skills training, and employer education.

Applying for VR&E services. To apply for vocational rehabilitation, fill out and submit VA Form 28-1900 to your local VA office. You will then be scheduled for an evaluation with a counselor. To qualify for VR&E services and assistance under this program, the answers to all three of the following questions must be yes.

1. Do you meet one of these basic entitlement requirements to qualify?

Vocational Rehabilitation and Employment

- Main Page www.vba.va.gov/bln/vre/index.htm
- Employment Counseling www.vba.va.gov/bln/vre/vec.htm
- Vocational Education www.vba.va.gov/bln/vre/vec.htm
- GI Bill OJT Program www.military.com/OJT
- Online Self Help www.vba.va.gov/bln/vre/self_serv.htm

- You are a veteran or servicemember awaiting a disability discharge, have a 20 percent disability rating or higher, and are judged by the counselor to have an employment handicap.

- You are a veteran, have a 10 percent disability rating or higher, and are judged by the counselor to have a serious employment handicap. (Those rated at 20 percent or higher may also qualify for independent living services and assistance.)

An "employment handicap" means that you have difficulty in getting or holding a job that is suitable for your interests and abilities, and is compatible with your disabilities. Your difficulty in getting and keeping a job must result in substantial part from your service-connected disability. A "serious employment handicap" means that this difficulty greatly limits your ability to get or hold a suitable job.

2. If you could meet the requirements in question 1, is it reasonable to expect you to be able to reach an employment or independent living goal?

3. Are you within the time limit for receiving this benefit? (Generally this is 12 years from the date VA notified you that you had at least a 10 percent service-connected disability.)

If it is determined that you don't qualify for VR&E services, the counselor can assist you in finding other options, goals, and programs that should help, so it is in your best interest to apply for VR&E services even if you are unsure you qualify.

On-the-Job Training Program

If you are a veteran or currently in the Guard or Reserve, the On-the-Job Training (OJT) program offers you an alternative way to use your VA (GI Bill) education and training benefits. While you are being trained for a new job, you can receive monthly training benefits in addition to your regular salary—that means you can receive up to $913 a month ($262.65 for Reserve) tax-free, on top of your regular salary, or up to $14,000 in cash benefits over two years, for training in an on-the-job or apprenticeship training program.

To qualify, you must meet the following criteria:

- You must be supervised at least 50 percent of the time in your job.

- Job training must lead to an entry-level position. (Management training programs do not qualify.)

- You must be a full-time paid employee, not on commission.

Contact

Unemployment Compensation for Ex-Servicemembers Program: www.workforce-security.doleta .gov/unemploy /ucx.asp.

- Your training must be documented and reported.

- You cannot be already qualified for the job through previous experience.

- You must be recently hired (within one to two years).

- The job must require that you be trained for at least six months.

- The employer may be private, or else local or state government.

Eligibility

You may be eligible if you are otherwise eligible for the GI Bill under either the Active Duty (Veteran) or Reserve GI Bill programs and:

- You are no longer on active duty.

- You were recently hired or promoted.

- It's been less than 10 years since you left the service.

- You are currently a member of the Guard or Reserve (Reserve GI Bill).

In some cases the VA will even pay retroactively for OJT that occurred during the past 12 months.

Note that you may not receive GI Bill OJT benefits at the same time you are receiving GI Bill education benefits.

To apply for the OJT program, contact your nearest VA office or local State Approving Agency (SAA), who will help you get started on the process and answer any questions you may have.

Unemployment Compensation

If you are separating from active duty, you may qualify for unemployment compensation if you are unable to find a new job. The Unemployment Compensation for Ex-Servicemembers (UCX) program provides benefits for eligible ex-military personnel. You may be entitled to benefits based on your service, but you must have been separated under honorable conditions. There is no payroll deduction from your wages for unemployment insurance protection. Benefits are paid for by the various branches of the military.

Contact

You can locate local state employment offices in the Department of Labor directory: www.dol.gov/dol/ location.htm.

Receiving separation pay may also influence your receipt of unemployment compensation. (Retirees will almost certainly receive a lesser amount, or no amount, since the weekly amount of retirement pay would usually be offset against the amount of unemployment compensation.)

Your state employment office handles unemployment compensation. Benefits vary from state to state, so only the staff at the office where you apply will be able to tell you the amount and duration of your entitlement. To receive unemployment compensation, you must apply to the state employment office. Bring your Certificate of Release or Discharge from Active Duty (DD Form 214), your Social Security card, and your civilian and military job history or résumé.

See page 310 for instructions on how to get a DD Form 214 if you don't have one or have lost it.

Continue to Serve: The Guard and Reserve

When you're getting ready to leave the military, it makes sense to consider your options in the Reserve or Guard. It's worth exploring for the pay, educational and advancement opportunities alone. For example, while you cannot collect VA disability and be on active duty at the same time, you can collect VA disability and serve in the Guard or Reserve as long as you can meet the retention criteria for that job.

Reserve/Guard Prior Service Enlistment Bonus

If you were formerly enlisted in any armed force, choose to enlist in the Reserve or National Guard for three or six years, and perform a critical military skill, you may be eligible for a prior enlistment bonus. A bonus may only be paid if you meet each of the following requirements:

- You have completed a military service obligation, but have less than 14 years of total military service, and received an honorable discharge at the conclusion of that military service obligation.

- You were not released, or are not being released, from active service for the purpose of enlistment in a reserve component.

- You are projected to occupy, or currently occupy, a position as a member of the Selected Reserve in a specialty in which you:

  —while a member on active duty, successfully served and attained a level of qualification commensurate with your grade and years of service; or

Take Advantage

Prior to reenlisting or extending your enlistment, make sure you talk with your career counselor or recruiter to explore what bonus options are available.

Reserve/Guard Affiliation Bonus Eligibility

To be eligible to receive a bonus, you must:

- Be eligible for reenlistment or for an extension of active-duty service.
- Have completed satisfactorily any term of enlistment or period of obligated active-duty service.
- Hold and be qualified in a military specialty designated for such purposes.
- Have a grade for which there is a vacancy in the reserve component in which you are to become a member.
- Enter into a written agreement to serve as a member of the Selected Reserve, Ready Reserve, or National Guard of an armed force for the period of obligated service you have remaining or, if you are on active duty, will have remaining at the time of your discharge or release from active duty.
- Meet all the other requirements for becoming a member of the Selected Reserve, Ready Reserve, or National Guard.

—have otherwise completed training or retraining in the specialty skill and attained a level of qualification commensurate with your grade and years of service.

- You have not previously been paid a bonus for enlistment, reenlistment, or extension of enlistment in a reserve component.

Reenlistment bonuses usually do not exceed $15,000, in the case of a person who enlists for a period of six years; $7,500, in the case of a person who, having never received a bonus of this type, enlists for a period of three years; and $6,000, in the case of a person who, having received a bonus for a previous three-year enlistment, reenlists or extends his or her enlistment for an additional period of three years.

Each branch of the military has authority to vary the amounts and eligibility criteria of enlistment bonuses based on the specific needs of the service—for updates, see www.military.com/bonus.

Records and Awards

Your military records and the awards should not only be a great source of pride, but also an important part of your portfolio as you apply for civilian jobs. Your records are also the key to unlocking many of your military benefits. That's why proper documentation of your military career, achievements, and awards is critical. Read on to learn how to get your complete service record, the awards you've earned, and what to do in case you need corrections or replacements.

Verification of Military Experience and Training

Your military service gives you valuable training and experience that can improve your chance of getting a good job or achieving your educational goals—but sometimes it can be difficult to remember all the details. The military makes life a little easier with the Verification of Military Experience and Training (DD Form 2586), which is generated from your electronic records. This form lists your military job experience and training history, recommended college credit information, and civilian equivalent job titles. This document is not a résumé but is designed to help you apply for jobs.

If you discover an error or omission in your Verification of Military Experience and Training (VMET) document, you should read thoroughly the "Frequently Asked Questions" on the VMET website. Errors in the VMET may be correctable, but you must contact your parent service. It is not a simple process to make changes to an individual DD Form 2586, so be patient; the changes must pass through official channels, and the process can sometimes take months. To request corrections, follow the procedures identified for your specific military service in the chart on page 314.

Correcting Military Records

The secretary of a military service can change any military record when necessary to correct an error or remove an injustice, including a review of a discharge issued by courts martial.

A veteran, survivor, or legal representative generally must file a request with a board for correction within three years after discovery of an alleged error or injustice. The board may excuse failure to file within that time, however, if it finds that justice warrants such an exception. It is an applicant's responsi-

How to Correct Your Verification of Military Experience and Training Document

First, check Frequently Asked Questions at www.dmdc.osd.mil/vmet.

Air Force: Active and separated or retired members can email VMET@afpc.randolf.af.mil.

Air Force Reserve should contact their Reserve Military Personnel Flight (MPF).

Air National Guard should call DSN 327-5908.

Army: Active, Reserve, and National Guard personnel should contact your local personnel records manager. Submit additional questions to the Army VMET online help desk at vmet@resourceconsultants.com.

Marine Corps: All active-duty and Reserve Marines should contact your local administrative office or the Mobility and Mobilization Support Branch at DSN 278-9523 or fax 703-784-9825.

Navy: Seek assistance via e-mail at p662c12a@persnet.navy.mil or call 901-874-4384.

Take Advantage

Prior to transition, review your military records. If you can, have another military person review them with you, and write down all questions you have. Ensure your personnel administrative specialist corrects any and all deficiencies. Once discharged or retired, you will face a long process to correct your military records.

bility to show why the filing of the application was delayed and why the board should consider it despite the delay.

To justify any correction, you must show the board that the alleged entry or omission in the records was in error or unjust. Applications should include all available evidence, such as signed statements of witnesses or a brief of arguments supporting the requested correction.

Discharge Review

Each of the military services maintains a discharge review board with authority to change, correct, or modify discharges or dismissals that are not issued by a general court martial. The board cannot review medical discharges. The veteran or surviving spouse, next of kin, or legal representative may apply for a review of discharge by writing to the military department concerned, using DD Form 293. If more than 15 years have passed since discharge, apply to the Board for the Correction of Military Records using DD Form 149.

If you were discharged because of more than 180 days of unauthorized absence, you are ineligible for VA benefits unless VA decides there were compelling circumstances for the absences. Boards for the correction of military records may consider such cases. To apply, use DD Form 149.

Veterans with disabilities incurred or aggravated during active military service may qualify for medical or related benefits regardless of separation and characterization of service. Veterans separated under other than honorable conditions may ask that their discharge be reviewed for possible recharacterization within 15 years after the date of separation.

Getting or Replacing Military Personnel Records

The National Personnel Records Center (NPRC) in St. Louis is the repository of millions of military personnel, health, and medical records of discharged and deceased veterans of all services during the 20th century. The NPRC can make your complete service record available to you or your next of kin. Limited information, such as dates of service, awards, and training, is available to anyone. Such information excludes anything that would invade your privacy, such as medical records, Social Security number, and present address.

If you wish to replace your military record, or obtain a copy, fill out Standard Form 180 and mail or fax it directly to the NPRC (address listed on page 312). Be sure to have as much of your service information available as possible when you fill out Form 180. This will make it easier for the NPRC to find your records. Be sure this information is available for your next of kin as well—many servicemembers do not follow up with their lost or misplaced military records until it is too late.

The NPRC Military Records Facility currently has a backlog of 180,000 requests, and receives approximately 5,000 requests per day. The average turnaround time on all requests is currently about 12 weeks, so don't be surprised if your records request takes some time.

If you are requesting the records of a relative, note your relationship to the former servicemember (brother, uncle, etc.). There is no charge for this service to former servicemembers or their next of kin. For others, a nominal fee is charged for research and reproduction costs. You may submit more than one request per envelope or fax, but submit a separate request for each individual whose records are being requested. The National Personnel Records Center will respond by mail.

Military personnel records can also be requested online. The system will allow you to create a customized order form to request information from military personnel records. You may use this system if you are a military veteran or the next of kin of a deceased, former member of the military.

Alternative Sources of Military Service Data

If you are a veteran and do not have a copy of your military record, and National Personnel Record Center files are not available, you may be able to get essential information about your military service from a number of other sources:

- The Department of Veterans Affairs maintains records on veterans if the veteran or a beneficiary filed a claim before July 1973. For more details, see www.aac.va.gov/vault/default.html.

Contact

Write the discharge review board at the following addresses:

Air Force Military Personnel Center Attn: DPMDOA1 Randolph AFB, TX 78150-6001

Army Discharge Review Board (ADRB) Attn: SFMR-RBB 1901 S. Bell St. Arlington, VA 22202-4508

www.arba.army. pentagon.mil /index.htm

Coast Guard Attn: GPE1 Washington, D.C. 20593

Navy Discharge Review Board (Navy and USMC) 801 N. Randolph St., Suite 905 Arlington, VA 22203.

Take Advantage

Online Process for Records Requests
The new eVetRecs system allows military veterans or their next of kin to create a customized order form to request copies of military personnel records. Visit www.archives .gov/veterans/ evetrecs/ to learn more.

Military Records and Awards Application Forms

Verification of Military Experience and Training, DD Form 2586

Department of Defense Form 293 (DD-293)

Application for Correction of Military Record, DD Form 149

Request Pertaining to Military Records, Standard Form 180

Certification of Military Service, NA Form 13038

Report of Separation from Active Duty, DD Form 214

All forms are available at www.military.com/forms.

Contact

Mail or fax requests for military records to:

National Personnel Records Center Military Personnel Records 9700 Page Ave. St. Louis, MO 63132-5100 www.archives.gov /facilities/mo /st_louis.html fax: 314-801-9195

Access records online at www.archives.gov /veterans/research /online.html.

- Organizational records such as unit morning reports, payrolls, and military orders are on file at the NPRC or other National Archives and Records Administration facilities.

- Records of the State Adjutants General, and other state veterans services offices, can provide a great deal of information. For a directory of state veterans offices, see page 357.

By using alternative sources, the NPRC often can reconstruct a veteran's beginning and ending dates of active service, the character of service, rank, time lost during active duty, and periods of hospitalization. The NPRC can then issue a Certification of Military Service (NA Form 13038), considered the equivalent of a Report of Separation from Active Duty (DD Form 214), to use in establishing eligibility for veterans benefits.

Military Matters

On July 12, 1973, a disastrous fire at the National Personnel Records Center destroyed between 16 and 18 million official military personnel files. If you are a veteran and believe your records may have been lost in the fire, send photocopies of any documents you possess—especially separation documents—to the NPRC. The NPRC will add those documents to the computerized index and file them permanently.

Necessary Information for File Reconstruction

The key to reconstructing military data is to give the NPRC enough specific information so that the staff can properly search the various sources. The following information is normally required:

- Full name used during military service.

- Branch of service.

- Approximate dates of service.

- Service number or Social Security number.

- Place of entry into service.

- Last unit of assignment.

- Place of discharge.

Replacing Awards, Medals, and Decorations

Medals and decorations earned in the military are usually among servicemembers' and veterans' most prized possessions, as well as symbols of pride in service and country. You or your family can request the issuance or replacement of military service medals, decorations, and awards. These requests should be directed to the specific branch of the military in which you or your military family member served. However, for Air Force (including Army Air Corps) and Army veterans, the National Personnel Records Center verifies the awards to which a veteran is entitled, and forwards requests and verification to appropriate service departments for issuance. (For an overview of military awards and decorations, see Appendix, page 359.)

The paperwork involved in requesting medal replacement is relatively simple. Use the Request For Military Records, Standard Form 180 (www.military.com/forms). The request must contain the veteran's signature, or the signature of the next of kin if the veteran is deceased. If available, include a copy of the discharge or separation document, WDAGO Form 53-55 or DD Form 214. There is no charge for medal or award replacements. The length of time it will take to receive a response or your actual medals and awards varies depending upon the branch of service sending the medals. See the "Medal Replacement" section on page 318 for information on where to send your request.

Take Advantage

Army veterans and their families can track and receive medals and decorations online at www.veteranmedals .army.mil. Award criteria and background for the different service medals can also be found on the site.

Military Service Records

Most veteran's records are stored at the National Archives and Records Administration's National Personnel Records Center, Military Personnel Records (NPRC-MPR). This includes records of veterans who are completely discharged (with no remaining reserve commitment), or who are retired or have died. Starting in 1995, the service departments gradually began retaining their personnel records in electronic format and all but the Coast Guard have stopped transferring them to NPRC-MPR. NPRC-MPR does not have records of members who are still in the active or inactive reserves or in the National Guard. The locations of most personnel records are listed by service branch.

Older military personnel records (generally prior to WWI, depending on the service branch) are on file at the National Archives and Records Administration, Old Military and Civil Records Branch (NWCTB), Washington, DC 20408.

New Online System for Requesting Military Records

Veterans and Next of kin can now request a copy of military records through the National Archives website. Called eVetRecs, the new system can be used to create a customized order form to request information from your, or your relative's, military personnel records.

Take Advantage

Find old friends by searching over 20 million records at: www.military.com /BuddyFinder.

You may use this system if you are:

- A military veteran, or

- Next of kin of a deceased, former member of the military.

- The next of kin can be any of the following: surviving spouse that has not re-married, father, mother, son, daughter, sister, or brother.

Note: If you are not the veteran or next of kin, you must complete the Standard Form 180 (SF 180).

Initiating a Request for Military Personnel Records:

1. Go to the National Records Archives website at www.archives.gov/veterans /evetrecs/index.html.

2. Click on the "Request Military Records" button to start. This will launch a separate window.

3. Enter the required information in the system to create your customized re-

quest form. There are four steps that you need to navigate. The system will guide you through the steps and tell you exactly which step you are on.

4. **Print, sign** and **date** the signature verification area of your customized form. If you don't have a printer, have a pen and paper handy and the system will guide you through the process. The Privacy Act of 1974 requires that all requests for records and information be submitted in writing. **Each request must be signed and dated by the veteran or next of kin.**

5. Mail or fax your signature verification form to the National Records Archives, to process your request. **You must do this within the first 20 days of entering your request, or your request,** will be removed from our system.

Military Health Records

Military health records used to be archived at NPRC-MPR with the personnel record portion when a member was released, discharged, or retired from active duty. That practice has been discontinued. Starting in 1992, most service branches now forward health records to the Department of Veterans Affairs (VA).

The Department of Veterans Affairs (VA), Records Management Center, St. Louis, MO, now maintains or manages the active duty health records when on loan within the VA. Call the VA toll free number at 1-800-827-1000 to identify the current location of specific health records and to find out how to obtain releasable documents or information.

Requesting Awards and Decorations

The new eVetRecs system can also be used to request Army and Air Force awards and decorations. However requests for Navy, Marine Corps, or Coast Guard awards and decorations must be submitted by mail to:

> Bureau of Naval Personnel
> Retired Records Section
> Room 5409
> Attn: PERS-313E
> 9700 Page Avenue
> Saint Louis, MO 63132-5100

Tarnished Medals

Prior to the Civil War, veterans of military service did not receive medals for valor. The display of medals on a uniform was considered a European tradition usually reserved for royalty. In other words, medals were considered marks of status rather than tokens of honorable duty or behavior. During the Civil War, Congress first authorized a Medal of Honor to "promote the efficiency of the Navy." More than 2,000 men (and one woman) received a medal—some under dubious circumstances. Ultimately, in an attempt to protect the dignity of the award, a review board of five retired generals scrutinized all 2,625 Medals of Honor awarded to members of the U.S. Army prior to 1917. Eventually, 910 Medals of Honor were revoked as not having been properly earned. In the years since, a military review board has created a Pyramid of Honor, a hierarchy of military awards with the Medal of Honor at the peak.

Special Awards, Special Benefits

There have been a few more than 3,400 recipients of the Medal of Honor in this country's entire history, as befitting one of the most prestigious and respected military awards for heroism under fire. Each person whose name is placed on the Medal of Honor Roll is entitled to receive a special pension, a supplemental uniform allowance, special identification cards and commissary and exchange privileges, automatic admission for the recipient's children to the United States military academies, and a 10 percent increase in retired pay.

Medal Replacement

Service Branch	Where to Write for Medals	Where to Write in Case of a Problem or an Appeal
Army	National Personnel Records Center Medals Section (NRPMA-M) 9700 Page Ave. St. Louis, MO 63132-5100	Commander PERSCOM Attn: TAPC-PDO-PA 200 Stovall St. Alexandria, VA 22332-0471
Air Force	National Personnel Records Center Air Force Reference Branch (NRPMF) 9700 Page Ave. St. Louis, MO 63132-5100	Headquarters Air Force Personnel Center AFPC/DPPPR 550 C St. West, Suite 12 Randolph AFB, TX 78150-4714
Navy	Bureau of Naval Personnel Liaison Office Room 5409 9700 Page Ave. St. Louis, MO 63132-5100	Chief of Naval Operations (OPNAV 09B33) Awards and Special Projects Washington, D.C. 20350-2000
Marine Corps	Bureau of Naval Personnel Liaison Office Room 5409 9700 Page Ave. St. Louis, MO 63132-5100	Commandant Headquarters United States Marine Corps Awards Branch (MMM) Washington, D.C. 20380-0001
Coast Guard	Bureau of Naval Personnel Liaison Office Room 5409 9700 Page Ave. St. Louis, MO 63132-5100	Commandant U.S. Coast Guard Medals and Awards Branch (PMP-4) Washington, DC 20593-0001

Locating Another Servicemember or Veteran

On a regular basis, servicemembers and veterans search for old buddies, sometimes to verify their periods of service as well as injuries and illnesses, and sometimes just to reconnect with a friend. In recognizing the importance of servicemembers, contributions, the five branches of the military each have procedures for contacting active or past servicemembers that make hiring a private investigator unnecessary. The locator service is free to immediate family members and federal and state government officials. Other family members, civilian friends,

Finding a Military Friend

Air Force

The Air Force Worldwide Locator can find active-duty personnel, as well as retirees, reservists, and guardsmen. Parents, spouses, and government officials may call 210-565-2478. Letters requesting locator service should be mailed to:
HQ AFPC/MSMIDL
550 C St. West, Suite 50
Randolph AFB, TX 78150-4752
210-565-2660 (Monday through Friday 7:30 a.m. to 4:30 p.m., Central Time)

The Air Force will not help in locating separatees or Army Air Corps retirees. To seek help in locating these persons, you may write to the National Personnel Records Center below or contact one of the various veterans service organizations.

National Personnel Records Center
9700 Page Ave.
Saint Louis, MO 63132-1500

Army

The Army will help you locate individuals on active duty only. Mail your request to:
Commander
U.S. Army Enlisted Records & Evaluation Center
ATTN: Locator
8899 East 56th Street
Fort Benjamin Harrison, IN 46249-5301
1-866-771-6357

businesses, and any others must pay a nonrefundable fee of $3.50 in the form of a check or money order made payable to the U.S. Treasury. Before you use the locator, check with your service on what is required. You will need to provide information such as full name, assigned unit, retired or nonretiree, and last known address. The more information you have available, the easier it will be to locate someone.

A locator notice can also be posted on www.military.com/BuddyFinder, or in Veteran Service Organization (VSO) magazines and other veteran-affiliated publications. (See page 282 for more information on VSOs.)

Coast Guard

The Coast Guard will help you locate individuals on active duty only. Call or E-mail your request to:
Call: (202) 493-1697
e-mail: ARL-PF-CGPCCGlocator@uscg.mil

Marine Corps

The Marine Corps can provide the duty station for active-duty personnel and Reservists. For retired individuals, city and state can be provided, but not an address. Requests can be (800) 336-4649 Option #0, and are free of charge to immediate family members and government officials calling on official business. Service will also be free for any individual, business, or organization, if the Marine locator decides the information would benefit the individual. Send written locator requests to:

Headquarters U.S. Marine Corps
Manpower and Reserve Affairs (MMSR-6)
3280 Russell Road
Quantico, VA 22134-5103

Navy

To locate a retiree or separatee of the U.S. Navy, write to:
Navy Worldwide Locator
Bureau of Naval Personnel
Pers-312
5720 Integrity Dr.
Millington, TN 38055-3120
901-874-3388 (Recording 24 hours per day; live assistance available from 7:00 a.m. to 4:30 p.m, Central Time)
Limited service is available by writing to the address above. Letters will be forwarded, if possible, to the retiree.

You can also search an extensive online database of servicemembers and veterans at www.military.com/buddyfinder.

Part Eight

The Family Advantage

J ust as servicemembers make tremendous sacrifices for their country, so do the military families who support the servicemembers behind the scenes. The typical military family faces many challenges: frequent relocations, long deployments, interrupted careers, financial obstacles, and the real consequences of war. There are many benefits and support systems offered to help military families with these challenges, and you'll learn about them in this chapter. These include career resources, quality child care and school programs, and service organizations.

Military Families on the Move

There's no denying that the modern military is a mobile force, and this mobility

The Family Advantage at a Glance

Relocation Support 323
- Family Support Resources
- Helping Your Children
- Family Housing

Relocating Spouses 326
- Spouse Preference Programs
- Portable Careers
- Employment Resources
- Education and Scholarships

The Military Child 333
- Child Development Centers
- Family Child Care
- School-Age Care
- Resource and Referral Programs

Deployment Support 337
- Family Care Plan
- Deployment Checklist

Family Support Resources 339
- Family Liaison/Ombudsman Programs
- Chaplains
- Tragedy Assistance Program for Survivors
- Armed Services YMCA
- National Military Family Association
- Red Cross
- United Service Organization (USO)

places perhaps the biggest strain on the military family. With reassignments come relocation, the need to adjust your family to a new community, and a host of financial and practical questions. While many of the issues and programs associated with the actual move are addressed in the Career chapter, page 247, the following section relates directly to family members.

Official Military Family Support Resources

Military Spouse Career Center
www.military.com/spouse

Air Force Crossroads
www.afcrossroads.com/spouse/main.cfm

Army Community Services
www.myarmylifetoo.com/skins/malt/home
.aspx?mode=user

Navy Lifelines Family Line
http://www.lifelines.usmc.mil/Familyline/index.htm

Marine Corps Community Services
www.usmc-mccs.org

Military OneSource
www.militaryonesource.com

MilSpouse.org
www.milspouse.org

Military Child Care Initiative
http://www.naccrra.org/MilitaryPrograms/

Military Homefront – Plan My Move
http://apps.mhf.dod.mil/pmm

Military Student.Org
http://www.militarystudent.dod.mil/

Military Spouse Network -
http://www.military.com/military-spouse
-network

According to a survey by the Air Force Institute of Technology, the typical military family relocates around six to seven times during the course of a servicemember's 20-year career, or an average of once every three years. It goes without saying that the decision to move often means leaving family, friends, and maybe even a career behind. But while the servicemember is quickly submerged into the new duty assignment (which could include joining a new command during a deployment overseas), the spouse and family may have to handle the issues of arranging a move, finding a home, getting the kids in new schools and activities, making new friends, finding a new job, and so forth.

In order to help you plan your move and settled into a new community, stop by your installation's family center. This center will have many special programs and services to help you find the resources you need. It also offers opportunities to attend activities where you can become acquainted with other spouses on both ends of a move. Through them you will undoubtedly pick up tips for making the most of a mobile military lifestyle.

Take Advantage

Certain allowances and payment advances your family can use when you relocate are detailed in "Know Your Relocation Benefits" on page 250.

Take Advantage
Military spouses often feel isolated. Spouse-BUZZ, a virtual Spouse Support Group, is a place where you can instantly connect with thousands of other milspouses. The site celebrates and embraces the tie that binds us all - military service. Get connected at www.spousebuzz.com

Another important on-base resource is your command's spouse club. Through this club, spouses come into contact with other spouses who have been through the same situations, helping you get a head start on learning about your new community.

Home is about people as much as anything, and relationships with friends, neighbors, teachers, and coworkers. Much of it can be attributed to the challenge of making new relationships. So, be patient but be active, and use the formal and informal services available to you.

Family Housing

Active-duty servicemembers with families are eligible to apply for on-base housing. The type and size of housing is normally based on the number of family members and their ages. Due to limited availability, newly arriving families are often placed on a waiting list until housing becomes available. In this case servicemembers are given either temporary housing or a monthly Basic Allowance for Housing (BAH) to offset the cost of finding housing in the local civilian housing market (page 47).

Family Support Centers

Family Support Centers are available on all installations to address family questions and needs. To find the support center closest to you, visit www.military.com/installations. Family Support Centers can help with the following programs:

- Exceptional Family Member (EFM) program and training for parents of special needs children.

- Elder care.

- Women, Infants, and Children (WIC) program, within the United States and overseas, through the DoD.

- Adoption reimbursement.

- Family advocates who work to prevent child and spouse abuse.

- New Parent Support Program for first-time parents.

- Healthy Parenting and Healthy Families initiatives.

- Family Literacy Foundation and reading programs for military parents and children.

- Child care.

- Youth and recreation programs.

Helping Your Children During Relocation

A critical part of relocation is helping your children make the move. The home you are leaving may be the only home your child has ever known. There's a sense of familiarity, not only with the home, but everything around it. If you can understand what your children's concerns and needs are, you can help avoid distress. Here are some ideas to get started:

- Get information on the schools, child care, and sports and recreational activities available in your new area.

- If you can, visit local schools with your child and meet some of the teachers. You can find reports on off-base schools at www.military.com/relocation.

- Try to get your children involved in the moving process. Have them pack some of their own special belongings and mark their name on the outside of the box. Also, ask them to help you pack a couple of special boxes marked "First Night." These will include items that you will need the first night in your new home (sheets, a few cooking and eating utensils, can opener, TV remote control, videos or DVDs, games or playing cards, flashlight and batteries, clock, small lamp, and electrical cord, etc.).

- Contact the local Chamber of Commerce for maps and pamphlets on your new area. Sit down with your family and visualize what the new town will be like.

- Throw a going-away party with your children's friends, and take pictures to make a scrapbook for them to look back on. Give them a stationery set, an address book, and prestamped cards, so that they can stay in touch with friends.

- Visit the Military Student website to learn about the many things you can do to help your school-age child transition successfully into a new school and new local activities. This site also has resources for children who have a deployed parent or a parent who has suffered a traumatic injury during military operations.

If your child is having serious adjustment problems related to relocation, you can also contact Military OneSource to speak to a trained consultant who can refer you to local support resources.

Contact

To contact the military spouse club on your base, go to www.military.com/installations. You can also contact the National Military Family Association, at www.nmfa.org.

Helping Your Children:

The following resources offer a range of services to relocating families.

Military.com: www.military.com/relocation
Military teens on the Move: http://www.defenselink.mil/mtom/
Military Student: http://www.militarystudent.dod.mil/
Military OneSource: 800-342-9647

Career, Education, and Training Resources for Spouses

One of the biggest considerations a military family has is the career prospects for the servicemember's spouse. If you are a military spouse, the dangers of unemployment (or a job with a lower salary) can have a direct impact on your family's economic and psychological quality of life, which in turn can affect the overall quality of the military force.

The military has several programs in place to address these challenges:

- Military Spouse Career Center (page 327).

- Priority Placement Program (Spouse Preference Program) (page 328).

- Spouse and Family Employment Assistance Program (page 330).

Military Matters

Status of Forces Agreements (SoFAs) determine the legal status of members of the Armed Forces stationed abroad. These agreements may have an impact on spouse employment opportunities, depending on where you are stationed. In some cases, military spouses cannot work off-base in the local economy. Check with the Family Support Center or legal office to understand the rules.

- Non-Appropriated Fund (NAF) Job Opportunities (page 334).

  As you use these resources, consider the following questions:

- What are your long-term family, career, and education goals?

- What type of personal needs for fulfillment do you have?

- Do you have any current or unique family responsibilities you need to take care of?

- Do you have any special needs yourself—handicaps, lack of transportation, language skills—that need support?

- Does your servicemember spouse support your career and employment goals?

- Can you take classes or get a degree to help you achieve your goals? (See the Education chapter for benefits you can use.)

  When you present answers to these questions, the staff at each program will be better able to assist you.

The Military Spouse Career Center

The Military Spouse Career Center, developed under contract to the Department of Defense, offers a job search with over 500,000 private sector and gov-

State Benefits for Military Families

In recognition of the contributions of military families, states are placing more emphasis on military family assistance programs, certifications, and benefits. These programs include:

- Family support, including credit counseling, family survivor benefit plans, and support groups.

- Education benefits, including tuition assistance and scholarships for spouses and children.

- Licensing and registration benefits, including extended deadlines for professional licenses.

- Tax and financial benefits, including tax relief and extension of filing deadlines.

- State employees benefits, including health care and life insurance benefits.

- Other support benefits, including reemployment protection and hiring preferences.

To see the benefits available in your state, go to www.military.com/statebenefits.

Contact

Visit the Military Spouse Career Center at www.military.com/spouse.

ernment job openings. Find spouse-friendly employers, scholarships, resume resources, popular career fields, and jobs at military installations. View resources for childcare, relocation, family support, and licensing or certification. In addition, you can participate in discussion forums and sign up for a military spouse newsletter to stay current on benefits updates, educational opportunities, training programs, and career advancement tips.

DoD Priority Placement Program

If you're a spouse looking for a job, and you are a current or former federal employee, one of the first programs you should check is the DoD Priority Placement Program (PPP). Under the PPP, a computerized system matches the skills of relocated employees with vacant DoD positions and helps match you based on your skills. The DoD Data Support Center (DDSC) serves as the operating center for the PPP program. To register, visit your Civilian Personnel Office (CPO) on base, which provides counseling and registers employees for jobs on the basis of their skills. Employees are permitted to register for up to five skills for which they are fully qualified at their current federal grade. They can also register for positions as many as three grades lower than their current grade level.

Take Advantage

A free career networking tool that matches you up with more than 150,000 military personnel veterans and spouses employed in industries nationwide is available at www.military.com/Careers/Network. You can search for mentors by location, career field, or employer.

On a weekly basis, the DDSC issues a computer listing to all DoD activities that reflects the skills and employees available for that location. This is called the stopper list. CPOs will continuously match vacant positions against the stopper list. When a match of occupational series and grade is found, a requisition is telephoned into the DDSC and positions are offered to qualified registrants.

If you are not eligible for PPP, check out the Military Spouse Preference Program, which is described below.

Military Spouse Preference Program

Contact

For more on priority placement, visit the DoD Civilian Personnel Management website located at www.cpms.osd.mil.

An outgrowth of legislation to increase employment opportunities for spouses of active-duty personnel, the Spouse Preference Program is a subset of the Priority Placement Program. If you are a spouse who has relocated to accompany your partner on a Permanent Change of Station (PCS) move to an active-duty location, you may be given priority for Department of Defense jobs if an employment opportunity that matches your skills becomes available.

Eligibility

If you are the spouse of an active-duty member, you can register 30 days prior to the member's reporting date for DoD service positions in the United States and its territories and possessions, provided the servicemember (sponsor) belongs to one of these categories:

- Assigned by a PCS move from overseas to United States, or to a different commuting area within the states, including the U.S. territories and possessions.

- Relocating to a new and permanent duty station after completing basic and advanced individual training.

- Permanently assigned to the same duty station where initial entry training was received.

- Assigned by a PCS to a service school, regardless of the duration of training.

- A former military member who reenlists and is placed in a permanent assignment.

- Reassigned on an unaccompanied tour by a PCS, with orders specifying the sequential assignment.

Contact

Office of Personnel Management: www.opm.gov. USAJobs: www.usajobs .opm.gov.

Registering for the Military Spouse Preference Program

To request use of the Military Spouse Preference Program when applying for a position, you will need the following documents:

- Résumé.

- Copy of SF Form 50 documenting current or previous appointment(s).

- Copy of last performance appraisal if currently working for the federal government.

- DD Form 214, Member 4 copy, if you were previously a military member and have an honorable discharge. (For more on DD Form 214, see page 312.)

- SF Form 15, if you are a veteran claiming 10-point preference and you have a letter from the Department of Veterans Affairs dated within the last year showing your percentage of disabilit

- Transcripts (may be necessary if education is relevant to qualifications for the position. (For more on veteran's preference, see page 286.)

- Licenses/certifications (if applicable).

- PCS orders documenting your spouse's assignment.

Many standard forms are available to download from www.military.com/forms.

Local military service human resources offices serve as the registration points for the Military Spouse Preference (MSP) Program. Information regarding spouse preference is also available at military installation family centers.

To register for the Military Spouse Preference, contact the Office of Personnel Management or a DoD Delegated Examining Office. If you are moving overseas, you will be considered for employment under the local duty station, and you may file 30 days ahead of anticipated arrival.

If you are traveling to overseas areas, you cannot receive preference until you actually arrive. You remain eligible for preference throughout your spouse's military tour—accepting or declining a temporary position expected to last less than one year does not end your spouse preference. However, preference ends if your job is extended for a total period of one year or longer, or if you are offered and decline such an extension.

Spouses employed under temporary appointments of less than one year (either part-time or full-time) continue to receive spouse preference when referred for permanent or temporary employment of one year or longer.

Spouse and Family Member Employment Assistance Program

All the military services have special spouse employment assistance programs. The Family Member Employment Assistance Program (FMEAP) provides employment assistance; resource libraries; use of computers for completing federal employment applications, résumés, and accompanying letters; as well as workshops on the local job search, job information fairs, and federal employment. FMEAP also maintains a listing of current openings in the U.S. Government Appropriated and Non-Appropriated Fund (NAF), nongovernment on- and off-base employment opportunities, as well as publications and computer programs listing worldwide vacancies as a clearinghouse for job information.

Your local Employment Assistance Manager (EAM) can provide worldwide employment assistance, review résumés and federal employment applications, and conduct counseling with clients during individual appointments.

Get more information about your service branch's FMEAP program by contacting your local Family Support Center.

Non-Appropriated Fund (NAF) Job Opportunities

You may find the job opportunity you're looking for on an installation near where the servicemember in your family is stationed. These jobs are provided for by non-appropriated funds (NAF), which are directed towards programs that support the well-being of military families. Examples of NAF jobs include positions at base clubs, recreational centers, craft shops, lodging facilities, day care and youth programs, and food service. To see what jobs are available at your installation, contact your MWR center directly or go to military.com/spouse for job search by installation.

Portable Careers

As a military spouse, you might consider a portable career—a career that goes with you no matter where you go. Portable careers, including home-based business ventures, give you flexibility and don't tie you down to one physical

Spouse Employment Resources

AAFES
odin.aafes.com/employment/default.asp

Adecco Career Accelerator
usworkflowpro.olecenter.com/careercenter/Default.aspx

Air Force Civilian Employment
www.afpc.randolph.af.mil/library/airforcecivilianemployment.asp

Army Civilian Personnel Online (CPOL)
acpol.army.mil/employment

Coast Guard Jobs Site
www.uscg.mil/hq/cgpc/cpm/jobs/vacancy.htm

DeCA
www.commissaries.com/inside_deca/HR/index.cfm

Military Spouse Career Center
www.military.com/spouse

Navy-Marine Corps Civilian Human Resources Department
www.donhr.navy.mil

USA Jobs
www.usajobs.opm.gov

Contact

Spouses to Teachers phone number: 800-342-9647 Toll Free

location. With the availability of the Internet, you can carry on your virtual career from virtually anywhere, including overseas locations. More and more, career fields and employers are allowing employees to telecommute from many locations.

Examples of portable careers include writing, editing, customer support, translating, transcription, and research. If you have self-discipline and are comfortable working alone and using technology, a portable career may be right up your alley. Remember that if you are starting your own portable business, you should check the local laws; if you want to start a business from government quarters, check in with your base housing and legal office for permission.

For more advice on portable careers and home-based businesses, plus a job board, see the Military Spouse Career Center website.

Spouses to Teachers

Built on the Troops-to-Teachers initiative, the Spouses-to-Teachers program helps spouses enter the teaching ranks. You are eligible for this program if you are a spouse of an active-duty member or a member of the Reserve or Guard on active duty. If you qualify, the program provides information, counseling, and guidance regarding teacher certification requirements, and assists you with the certification process and employment searches. Some funding is also provided to reimburse the cost of tests required for state teacher licensure/certification.

Take Advantage

Technology has made it easier than ever for you to get your education online, through distance-learning classes and programs. This option gives you more flexibility in planning and taking classes. To connect with distance-learning courses and programs, use www.military.com /schools.

Education Opportunities and Benefits

As a military spouse or family member, you face the challenge of gaining an education while being on the move, but you also have educational opportunities and benefits not available to civilians. The education benefits offered by the military to military spouses and families, including scholarship programs, tuition assistance, and service-specific programs, are detailed in the Education chapter, page 185. You should also check your particular state's education benefits. School and care programs for children are covered later in this chapter, on page 333.

Spouse Career Advancement Accounts

The Department of Defense Career Advancement Accounts program provides assistance to military spouses seeking to gain the skills and credentials necessary to begin or advance their career. The Career Advancement Account (CAA) program covers up to $3,000 a year for training and education, enabling participants to earn a degree or credential in in-demand, portable fields in almost any community across the country. CAA may be renewed for one additional year, for a total two-year account amount of up to $6,000 per spouse. This program is currently being piloted at a limited number of military installations. Visit http://military.com/spouse to learn more about this pilot program.

More information on education benefits for military spouse and family members can be found in Part 5 of this book.

The Military Child

It can be a challenge for any parent to locate affordable, quality child care and education. Certainly child care is among the top concerns of military families. If you're looking for the right care program or school, be sure to check with the services and resources that follow to help you find the right situation.

Child Care Programs

Over the years, the Department of Defense (DoD) has responded to the need to provide military families with quality, affordable child care. Depending on where you are stationed, finding child care can be somewhat challenging. DoD has created programs to help meet those challenges and to improve the quality of life for military families.

DoD currently oversees 800 Child Development Centers (CDCs) located on military installations worldwide. These centers offer a safe child care environment and meet professional standards for early childhood education. Child care is typically available through these centers for children ages six weeks to twelve years. The centers are generally open Monday through Friday between the hours of 6:00 AM and 6:30 PM. Commanders may decide to extend hours to meet the work and deployment needs and schedules of their installation population.

DoD also oversees the Family Child Care (FCC) programs. These programs provide in-home care by installation-certified providers. FCC helps bridge gaps

Contact

Find child development center phone numbers, listed by state or country, on the Military Home Front site at www.military homefront.dod .mil.

in child care when the CDC does not entirely meet the child care needs of the family. Family Service Centers, youth centers, referral offices, and the CDC have lists of approved homes and providers.

An additional component of military child care is the School Age Care (SAC) program. SAC meets the needs of children ages six to twelve years and provides before and after school care as well as summer and holiday programs. Additional support for families with children over the age of twelve can be found through the youth and teen programs often sponsored by youth services and community centers.

Family Child Care

If you have a child between two weeks and 12 years old, you can also choose in-home child care, also known as family child care (FCC) or child development home care. In this system, providers care for a small group of children in their own homes, which may be on or off the installation. A caregiver may tend to no more than six children under the age of eight, including a maximum of two children under age two.

In addition to operating typical workday hours, these homes may provide before- and after-school hours, extended hours, weekend and vacation hours, summer care, and care during events and briefings. Also, many in-home providers can care for children who are under the weather. In-home providers must meet the DoD's certification requirements, including training, background checks, and inspections. Standards for in-home care are similar to those for child development centers (i.e., for learning materials and activities). All FCC providers are encouraged to achieve accreditation as determined by the National Association of Family Child Care (NAFCC).

School-Age Care

School-age care (SAC) programs are offered for children between six to 12 years old before and after school, during holidays, and on summer vacations. The SAC programs complement, rather than duplicate, activities during the school day. This type of care is currently expanding, with new initiatives being implemented at the Service level to more fully meet the need. At present, about 43,250 (25 percent) of the total number of military child care spaces are accommodated by school-age care. Not all SAC is provided in CDCs—much of it is provided in youth centers or other facilities. Contact your local CDC to see what options are available in your community.

Local YMCA and Boys and Girls Club programs, as well as some elementary and middle schools, offer after-school care programs that include arts and crafts, music, sports, recreational and homework help activities at your child's school. Military OneSource can help you find more information on local community programs such as these.

Resource and Referral Services

Resource and referral services (R&Rs) on your installation can guide you through the process of finding child care. Your local R&R can give you the names of child care providers and information about waiting lists and costs. If you are in a country where it's common for care providers to come to your home, the R&R can help you find someone to do this. If you are in a country where language barriers make it difficult to find care off the installation, the R&R can help you find solutions. When you are on a waiting list but need child care immediately, the R&R can also help you find alternative care. To access R&R services on your base, check in with your CDC.

Schools for Military Children

A civilian agency of the U.S. Department of Defense, the Department of Defense Education Activity (DoDEA) runs schools to serve the children of servicemembers. All schools within DoDEA are fully accredited by U.S. accreditation agencies. The DoDEA instructional program provides a comprehensive pre-kindergarten through 12th grade curriculum that is competitive with that of most school systems

Take Advantage

The Armed Services YMCA also offers child care services, often located on installations. For more on its programs, see page 341.

Take Advantage

For more on family child care options, visit www.military.com /spouse.

Military Matters

A recent child care relief initiative aimed to help reduce the cost of child care for families of those serving in the Global War on Terror, Operation Military Child Care is aimed specifically at those who are not located near an installation. National Guard, Reserve, and active-duty military families with servicemembers serving in the Global War on Terror can receive financial assistance, as well as help locating quality child care in their communities.

Contact

National Association of Family Child Care (NAFCC): www.nafcc.org.

Take Advantage

The Military OneSource program offers referrals to child care in the civilian community, and coaching on how to look for quality care outside the installation. For more information, call Military OneSource at 800-342-9647.

in the United States. DoDEA maintains a high school graduation rate of approximately 97 percent, significantly higher than the U.S. public school rate.

DoDEA monitors student progress through the use of standardized tests. Such tests include the Terra Nova Achievement Test, a norm-referenced test for students in grades three through 11. DoDEA fourth and eighth grade students also take the National Assessment of Educational Progress (NAEP), known as "the nation's report card."

No tuition is charged to military students, although some schools will take civilian children for varying amounts of payment.

DoDEA operates 222 public schools in 15 districts located in 13 foreign countries, seven states, Guam, and Puerto Rico. All schools within DoDEA are fully accredited by U.S. accreditation agencies. Approximately 8,785 teachers serve DoDEA's 102,600 students.

Contact

Families eligible for Operation Military Child Care can call the Child Care Aware hotline at 800-424-2246 or go to www.childcareaware.org for help in applying for subsidies and location assistance.

Family Support During Deployment

Deployment can be a difficult experience for both the servicemember and the family. Having a loved one mobilized or deployed means shifting roles and changing responsibilities while maintaining a stable family life. Being aware of the programs and issues that can affect your family prior to deployment or mobilization can ease the transition. Family readiness ensures that your family is taken care of during drills, annual training, mobilization, and deployment.

Making a Plan for Family Care

A personal plan is important for all families in planning for potential emergencies, and is especially critical for single parents and dual military parents. Whether you expect to be deployed or not, you should develop a plan; in fact, many military units will require you to develop a formal Family Care Plan.

In preparing your plan, be sure to do the following:

- Assign a guardian for your family in a special power of attorney, and make sure the guardian understands his or her responsibilities.

- Obtain ID and commissary cards, register in DEERS (page 90), and check to make sure no ID cards have expired.

- Sign up for life insurance (page 28), and update all beneficiary information.

- Arrange for housing, food, transportation, and emergency needs.

- Inform your spouse or any caretakers about your financial matters.

- Discuss your plans with your older children.

Contact

To learn more about military school locations and enrollment, visit the DoDEA website at www.dodea.edu.

Predeployment Family Checklist

A predeployment checklist for the family can supplement your family care plan. The following list can be a useful tool even if you don't anticipate being deployed.

Budgeting tasks. Managing the family budget while a spouse is away can be challenging, but it can be done. Prior to deployment, discuss your banking and credit card situation with your spouse. Sit down and calculate your family's monthly expenses, including:

- Utility bills.

- Long-distance bills.

- Rent or mortgage.

- Monthly living expense.

- Credit payments.

- Insurance and taxes.

- Savings.

(See the Money chapter on page 1 for more on household budget planning.)

Vehicles. Make certain you have the name of a trusted mechanic or automotive garage where you or a friend has taken a car for service. Repair costs can mount rapidly if you simply select a repair shop out of the phone book.

Be sure to keep a record (on the refrigerator is a good place) of the correct type of battery, tires, oil, etc., for the car.

Finally, keep track of when automotive registration, insurance payments, emissions inspections, or oil changes are due.

Home/apartment maintenance. Know what to do or whom to call if something in your home breaks down. Untested plumbing, roofing, or repair contractors can be very costly.

Take Advantage

The Red Cross publishes a guide for military families at www.redcross.org /pubs/afpubs /welcome.pdf. Titled "Welcome Home: A Guide to a Healthy Family Reunion," it deals with family reunion and post-deployment concerns.

Contact

For more specific information, and help in developing your Family Care Plan, visit www.military.com/deployment.

Give your home a security check inside and out. This should include testing (or installing) smoke alarms, and checking door and window locks as well as outdoor lights or motion detectors (if you have them).

If your family expects to move during your deployment, discuss the process for moving your household goods.

Review your homeowners' or renters' insurance policies.

Military Family Support Organizations

Many military and nonmilitary organizations offer support to military families, especially in times of deployment and postdeployment. These services range from financial aid to emotional support and legal services. In addition to organizations described in earlier chapters, the resources described in the following pages can be useful.

You can also find assistance and services at your current or next installation. For a base directory that includes important phone numbers and contact information, visit www.military.com/installations.

Take Advantage

Many organizations offer ways for military families to keep in touch with deployed servicemembers, whether through email, phone cards, or video connections. The Support the Troops page is located at www.military.com/benefits/resources/support-our-troops

Family Liaison or Ombudsman Program

The Family Liaison Officer, or Ombudsman, is a communication link between servicemembers' commanding officers and family members. Ombudsmen are mainly information and referral specialists or military spouses who help family members in the command gain the assistance they need. This is especially relevant for deploying units. Keep in mind that ombudsmen are not counselors or social workers, but they can help connect you with the help and services you need.

The Army Family Liaison Officer serves as the Ombudsman for all Army soldiers, civilians, and families of active and retired army, guard and reserve members. The Marine Corps's version of the program is the Key Volunteer Program, while the Navy has the Command Ombudsman program. The Air Force does not have a program.

Unit Liaison or Family Readiness Officer

Some commands have a small unit of administrative personnel assist with ongoing family support needs in times of deployment. One of their roles is to facilitate communications between the command and its families. Check with your servicemember's command to see if there is a designated Family Readiness Officer (regardless of whether a rear-detachment unit has been left behind). This person will have resources for your family during deployments and mobilizations, and can address questions about command-related issues.

Chaplains

For more than 200 years, military chaplains and their religious support staff have accompanied U.S. forces wherever they have served, supporting military members and their families.

Chaplains are ordained by individual religions or denominations before they join the military but are trained to serve all denominations. Once commissioned as officers in the Air Force, Army, or Navy (Navy chaplains serve with the Marine Corps and Coast Guard), they provide religious worship services, rites, sacraments, and ministrations to military members and their families worldwide. Their stated mission is to "Nurture the living, care for the sick or wounded, minister to prisoners or prisoners of war, and honor the dead."

Chaplains also assist military personnel and family members in dealing with personal concerns such as faith issues, stress, anxiety, redeployment or reunion issues, moral and ethical values, marriage counseling, and social concerns. You can find chaplains through your base chapel, senior enlisted advisor, or Family Support Center.

For many servicemembers and families, chaplains are the first people they can turn to for help outside their chain of command. In this role, chaplains help to resolve problems by making appropriate referrals to command channels or social service agencies. They also assist military personnel in requesting emergency leave, compassionate reassignments, and hardship discharges.

In addition, VA has a Chaplain Corps available to provide services to veterans and their families.

Tragedy Assistance Program for Survivors

If your family has suffered the loss of a servicemember, the Tragedy Assistance Program for Survivors (TAPS) is foremost among organizations that can help.

Take Advantage

Spouses and children of deployed active-duty, reserve, and guard personnel can receive up to six free counseling sessions with nonmilitary professionals by contacting Military OneSource at 800-342-9647. You can also join other Spouse Discussion Forums on the Military Spouse Network: www.military.com/military-spouse-network

Contact

Army Family Liaison Office www.armyfamilies online.org/skins/W BLO/home.aspx

Navy Ombudsman www.navyombuds man.org/

Key Volunteer Program www.usmc-mccs .org/kvn/index.cfm

Coast Guard Ombudsman Program www.uscg.mil /mlcpac/iscseattle /pw/ombudsman .htm.

Military Matters

Military Exchanges (see page 5) offer gift certificates and prepaid phone cards to deployed service personnel, families, and friends. They can also arrange for phone service that supports deployed troops and coordinate "free phone calls home" programs. In addition, in some installations and in theaters of operation they have cyber-cafes for use by troops and families so they can have email access. Contact your local exchange to see what they can provide for you.

Take Advantage

Don't hesitate to use chaplains as a resource, even if you don't consider yourself to be religious or you are not of the same faith as your local chaplain. Chaplains are trained to provide assistance to servicemembers and families of all faiths.

Contact

For a full directory of VA chaplains, visit www1.va.gov /chaplain /page.cfm?pg=14.

See also Navy/Marine Corps Chaplain-CARE located at www.chaplain care.navy.mil.

The services this nonprofit organization offers to bereaved families include a crisis hotline, support networks, counseling referrals, and assistance with surviving family benefits. For more on TAPs, see page 273. For more on benefits related to death of a servicemember, see page 172.

The Armed Services YMCA

The Armed Services YMCA (ASYMCA) is a national affiliate of the nonprofit YMCA, and it works with the Department of Defense. With headquarters in Alexandria, Virginia, the ASYMCA more than 20 branches around the country provide support to military families. At the local level, ASYMCA has programs for after-school youth care, daily child care, along with single-soldiers' centers, hospital assistance, transportation, adult classes, aerobics, English as a Second Language classes, and so on. ASYMCA also coordinates with military installations to work with regular YMCAs. Some ASYMCA branches are located on military installations, but the majority are not.

Services ASYMCA provide include:

- Crisis counseling.

- Respite care.

- In-Home parenting education.

- Emergency food supplies.

- Young family support.

- Family abuse shelter.

The Four Chaplains

During World War II some 8,000 Army chaplains dedicated their lives and service to the fighting men of "the Greatest Generation," according to homeofheroes.com. Though these chaplains earned 2,453 high military awards for their valor, none received the Medal of Honor. Four of the 77 who gave their lives in service, however, received one of the most unusual and distinct medals in history. Ordered by special congressional action, this medal was meant to carry the same weight and prestige as the Medal of Honor. It is known simply as the Four Chaplains Medal, and calls to memory four men of God—one Jewish, one Catholic, and two Protestant.

- Child abuse prevention.
- Parenting workshops.
- Spouse support groups.
- Tuition assistance.
- Financial management classes.
- Child literacy program.
- Before- and after-school tutoring.

Contact

Call TAPS at 800-959-TAPS (800-959-8277).

Take Advantage

A complete directory of volunteer organizations that offer gifts and services to deployed troops and their families can be found at www.military.com/supportthetroops.

National Military Family Association

The National Military Family Association (NMFA) was first organized by a group of wives and widows seeking financial security for survivors of uniformed service personnel and retirees. Thanks in large part to efforts of this organization, the Survivor Benefit Plan (see the Benefits chapter, page 172) came into being.

The NMFA has members from all ranks of the uniformed services worldwide, and their families. Its programs educate the public, the military community, and Congress on the rights and benefits of military families. Its accomplishments include work in major areas such as medical and dental benefits, dependent education, retiree and survivor benefits, and relocation and spousal employment.

Contact

To find further information on the Armed Services YMCA, visit www.asymca.org.

Contact

More information about the NMFA and its services is available at www.nmfa.org, or call 703-931-6632.

Red Cross Emergency Services

The American Red Cross has programs specifically designed to aid service-members and families, including financial assistance for emergency travel or urgent needs (food, temporary lodging, medical needs), confidential counseling, guidance, and referrals to social services, and assistance with veterans benefits and claims.

Family members of servicemembers can use the Red Cross emergency communication system to notify military personnel at any duty station of an emergency or other important event. Servicemembers stationed in the United States and their immediate family members can call the Red Cross Armed Forces Emergency Service Centers for help seven days a week, 24 hours a day, 365 days a year. The toll-free telephone number is available through base or installation operators and from local on-base Red Cross offices.

Contact

To find your local Red Cross office, go to www.redcross.org/where/where.html and enter your ZIP code.

Red Cross services are available through your local Red Cross chapters, which are listed in local telephone books and on the American Red Cross website. To reach the Red Cross overseas, personnel stationed on military installations should call base or installation operators or the on-base Red Cross office. At overseas deployment sites, contact the American Red Cross deployed staff.

When calling the Red Cross to send an emergency message to a family member, please have ready the following information, which will speed the process of sending your message:

- Servicemember's full name.

- Rank/rating.

- Branch of service.

- Social Security number.

- Military address and phone number.

Contact

In cases of emergency, call the National Contact Center toll-free at 800-FED-INFO (800-333-4636), Monday through Friday, from 8 a.m. to 8 p.m., Eastern time. Provide as much identifying information as possible about the person you wish to locate, such as full name, rank, last duty assignment, last known military address, service number, and Social Security number.

The USO

If you've been in a major airport and heard an announcement about a certain lounge over the loudspeakers, or you've seen famous entertainers perform for the troops, you know something about the USO. Since 1941, the USO has been synonymous with a "home away from home" for the U.S. military. A nonprofit organization not directly affiliated with the U.S. government, the mission of the USO is to boost morale and provide welfare and recreational services to uniformed military personnel and their families.

The USO serves as a backbone for overseas deployment centers. Carrying on the tradition started by Bob Hope, the USO produces some 60 entertainment tours each year, both stateside and overseas, reaching tens of thousands of servicemembers. USO Canteens offer high-tech services such as free Internet access so that service personnel can keep in contact with friends and family. The USO also sponsors social events for servicemembers stationed in remote areas. Other USO-led campaigns include distribution of prepaid phone cards, DVDs, and video games, servicemember and family services in airports, and helping access email.

Take Advantage

The National Next-of-Kin Registry is a free emergency contact system that can help citizens find missing loved ones in the event of serious accidents or catastrophic national emergencies. Registry users include families and individuals who input personal information about themselves, their children, other relatives, and friends. For more information, visit www.nokr.org.

Contact

The USO website is www.uso.org.

Acknowledgments

This is the book I wanted to read nearly 20 years ago when I joined the United States Navy. Thanks to the marvelous support I've received over the years, it's now a reality.

This book would not have been possible without the contributions of many colleagues and friends. I would like to thank them for their assistance and for supporting those who have answered the call to serve. This book was written by them.

On the Military.com team, I would like first and foremost to thank Terry Howell and Ho Lin for their central role in preparing the manuscript for the original edition. I would also like to thank Ward Carroll, Tom Aiello, Barb Chiles, Pete DeLauzon, Anne Dwane, David Grayson, Vince Patton, and Alina Pavlovich. Thanks to my former Monster.com colleagues Brad Baker, Paul Camara, and Marc Stoever for their unwavering support for this project and the military community.

Many friends at the VA, DoD, and other agencies contributed ideas, gave feedback and tips, and shared their store of wisdom. At the DoD, I would like to express my gratitude to Leslye Arsht, Jane Burke, Aggie Byers, Gary Woods, and David Mitchell at the Office of Military Community and Family Policy. I'd also like to thank Katherine Chamberlain, Randy Eltringham, and Gene Gomulka. I would like to thank the following colleagues at the VA: Phil Budahn, Roscoe Butler, Regis Cooney, Dan Cooper, Bill Elmore, Tom Harvey, Raymond P. Kempisty, Dorilyn Martz, Janet Moorman, Tom Pamperin, and Stephen Stafford. At the Defense Finance and Accounting Service (DFAS), I would like to acknowledge Deatta Minter, Tom Roberts, Roger Still, and Sean Wuethrich.

We at Military.com are fortunate to work with many talented contributors and advisors, who also contributed to the book: John Brunelli; Steve Etheridge; Tom Hall; Dr. Jeff Cropsey; Master Gunnery Sergeant Jim O'Keefe, USMC; Carol Osborn; Michael McHugh; Anthony Principi; Lou Reda; Jack Tilley; Michael Volkin; and Marshall Williams.

I would also like to thank Bob Bailey; Al Bemis; Eric Benson; Bonnie Carroll; William Chatfield; Max Cleland; Geoff Culver; John Fales; Nick Glakas; Dawn Hemming-Rich; Jim Holley; Steve Keith; Thomas McAtee; Bo Maske; David McIntyre; Tom McKnight; General Norman Schwarzkopf, USA (ret.); Kim Myers; Robert Palmer; Chris Paul; Jeff Phillips; Ned Powell; Fred Rainbow; Michael Selleck; Keith Weaver; Walter Weintz; Kevin Wensing; Owen West; Captain Ben Girtman, USNR (ret); Linda Rothleder; and Tom Wilkerson. I also owe a debt of gratitude to my editor at Simon & Schuster, Jack Sallay, and to Robin Dellabough at Lark Productions. Robin graced the original edition of this project not only with her expertise but also with enthusiasm, patience, and good humor. Finally, I would like to thank our 10 million members. Fundamentally, it was their insight, know-how, and passion that made this book possible

Appendices

Active Duty Pay Charts

Based on the proposed January 2009 - 3.9 percent pay increase.

Commissioned Officers

Pay Grade	Years of Service																	
	<2	2	3	4	6	8	10	12	14	16	18	20	22	24	26	30	34	38
O-10												$14,689	$14,760	$15,067	$15,602	$16,382	$17,201	$18,061
O-9												$12,847	$13,032	$13,299	$13,766	$14,454	$15,177	$15,936
O-8	$9,090	$9,387	$9,585	$9,641	$9,887	$10,299	$10,395	$10,786	$10,898	$11,235	$11,722	$12,172	$12,472	$12,472	$12,472	$12,784	$13,104	$13,104
O-7	$7,553	$7,904	$8,066	$8,196	$8,429	$8,660	$8,927	$9,193	$9,460	$10,299	$11,007	$11,007	$11,007	$11,007	$11,063	$11,284	$11,284	$11,284
O-6	$5,598	$6,150	$6,554	$6,554	$6,579	$6,861	$6,898	$6,898	$7,290	$7,983	$8,390	$8,796	$9,028	$9,262	$9,717	$9,911	$9,911	$9,911
O-5	$4,667	$5,257	$5,622	$5,690	$5,917	$6,053	$6,352	$6,571	$6,854	$7,287	$7,493	$7,697	$7,929	$7,929	$7,929	$7,929	$7,929	$7,929
O-4	$4,027	$4,661	$4,972	$5,042	$5,330	$5,640	$6,025	$6,326	$6,534	$6,654	$6,723	$6,723	$6,723	$6,723	$6,723	$6,723	$6,723	$6,723
O-3	$3,540	$4,013	$4,332	$4,723	$4,949	$5,197	$5,358	$5,622	$5,760	$5,760	$5,760	$5,760	$5,760	$5,760	$5,760	$5,760	$5,760	$5,760
O-2	$3,059	$3,484	$4,013	$4,148	$4,233	$4,233	$4,233	$4,233	$4,233	$4,233	$4,233	$4,233	$4,233	$4,233	$4,233	$4,233	$4,233	$4,233
O-1	$2,655	$2,764	$3,340	$3,340	$3,340	$3,340	$3,340	$3,340	$3,340	$3,340	$3,340	$3,340	$3,340	$3,340	$3,340	$3,340	$3,340	$3,340

Commissioned Officers with more than 4 years Active Service as an Enlisted or Warrant Officer

Pay Grade	<2	2	3	4	6	8	10	12	14	16	18	20	22	24	26	30	34	38
O-3E				$4,723	$4,949	$5,197	$5,358	$5,622	$5,845	$5,973	$6,147	$6,147	$6,147	$6,147	$6,147	$6,147	$6,147	$6,147
O-2E				$4,148	$4,233	$4,368	$4,596	$4,772	$4,902	$4,902	$4,902	$4,902	$4,902	$4,902	$4,902	$4,902	$4,902	$4,902
O-1E				$3,340	$3,568	$3,699	$3,834	$3,967	$4,148	$4,148	$4,148	$4,148	$4,148	$4,148	$4,148	$4,148	$4,148	$4,148

Warrant Officers

Pay Grade	<2	2	3	4	6	8	10	12	14	16	18	20	22	24	26	30	34	38
W-5												$6,505	$6,835	$7,081	$7,354	$7,721	$8,108	$8,513
W-4	$3,658	$3,936	$4,049	$4,160	$4,351	$4,541	$4,732	$5,021	$5,274	$5,515	$5,711	$5,903	$6,186	$6,417	$6,682	$6,815	$6,815	$6,815
W-3	$3,341	$3,480	$3,623	$3,670	$3,820	$4,114	$4,421	$4,565	$4,732	$4,904	$5,213	$5,422	$5,547	$5,680	$5,861	$5,861	$5,861	$5,861
W-2	$2,956	$3,236	$3,322	$3,382	$3,573	$3,871	$4,019	$4,164	$4,342	$4,481	$4,607	$4,757	$4,856	$4,935	$4,935	$4,935	$4,935	$4,935
W-1	$2,595	$2,874	$2,950	$3,108	$3,296	$3,573	$3,702	$3,882	$4,060	$4,200	$4,328	$4,484	$4,484	$4,484	$4,484	$4,484	$4,484	$4,484

Enlisted Servicemembers

Pay Grade	<2	2	3	4	6	8	10	12	14	16	18	20	22	24	26	30	34	38
E-9							$4,421	$4,521	$4,647	$4,796	$4,945	$5,185	$5,388	$5,602	$5,928	$6,225	$6,536	$6,863
E-8						$3,619	$3,779	$3,878	$3,997	$4,125	$4,357	$4,475	$4,675	$4,786	$5,060	$5,161	$5,161	$5,161
E-7	$2,515	$2,745	$2,850	$2,990	$3,099	$3,285	$3,390	$3,577	$3,733	$3,839	$3,951	$3,995	$4,142	$4,221	$4,521	$4,521	$4,521	$4,521
E-6	$2,176	$2,394	$2,500	$2,602	$2,709	$2,951	$3,045	$3,226	$3,282	$3,323	$3,370	$3,370	$3,370	$3,370	$3,370	$3,370	$3,370	$3,370
E-5	$1,994	$2,127	$2,230	$2,335	$2,499	$2,671	$2,811	$2,828	$2,828	$2,828	$2,828	$2,828	$2,828	$2,828	$2,828	$2,828	$2,828	$2,828
E-4	$1,827	$1,921	$2,025	$2,128	$2,218	$2,218	$2,218	$2,218	$2,218	$2,218	$2,218	$2,218	$2,218	$2,218	$2,218	$2,218	$2,218	$2,218
E-3	$1,650	$1,754	$1,860	$1,860	$1,860	$1,860	$1,860	$1,860	$1,860	$1,860	$1,860	$1,860	$1,860	$1,860	$1,860	$1,860	$1,860	$1,860
E-2	$1,569	$1,569	$1,569	$1,569	$1,569	$1,569	$1,569	$1,569	$1,569	$1,569	$1,569	$1,569	$1,569	$1,569	$1,569			
E-1	$1,400	$1,400	$1,400	$1,400	$1,400	$1,400	$1,400	$1,400	$1,400	$1,400	$1,400	$1,400	$1,400	$1,400	$1,400			
E-1 with less than 4 months of service				$1,294														

Guard and Reserve Monthly (4 Drills) Pay Charts

Based on the proposed January 2009 - 3.9 percent pay increase.

Commissioned Officers

Pay Grade	<2	2	3	4	6	8	10	12	14	16	18	20	22	24	26	30	34	38
O-7	$1,007	$1,054	$1,076	$1,093	$1,124	$1,155	$1,190	$1,226	$1,261	$1,373	$1,468	$1,468	$1,468	$1,468	$1,475	$1,505	$1,505	$1,505
O-6	$746	$820	$874	$874	$877	$915	$920	$920	$972	$1,064	$1,119	$1,173	$1,204	$1,235	$1,296	$1,321	$1,321	$1,321
O-5	$622	$701	$750	$759	$789	$807	$847	$876	$914	$972	$999	$1,026	$1,057	$1,057	$1,057	$1,057	$1,057	$1,057
O-4	$537	$622	$663	$672	$711	$752	$803	$843	$871	$887	$896	$896	$896	$896	$896	$896	$896	$896
O-3	$472	$535	$578	$630	$660	$693	$714	$750	$768	$768	$768	$768	$768	$768	$768	$768	$768	$768
O-2	$408	$465	$535	$553	$564	$564	$564	$564	$564	$564	$564	$564	$564	$564	$564	$564	$564	$564
O-1	$354	$368	$445	$445	$445	$445	$445	$445	$445	$445	$445	$445	$445	$445	$445	$445	$445	$445

Commissioned Officers with more than 4 years Active Service as an Enlisted member or Warrant Officer

Pay Grade	<2	2	3	4	6	8	10	12	14	16	18	20	22	24	26	30	34	38
O-3E			$630	$660	$693	$714	$750	$779	$796	$820	$820	$820	$820	$820	$820	$820	$820	
O-2E			$553	$564	$582	$613	$636	$654	$654	$654	$654	$654	$654	$654	$654	$654	$654	
O-1E			$445	$476	$493	$511	$529	$553	$553	$553	$553	$553	$553	$553	$553	$553	$553	

Warrant Officers

Pay Grade	<2	2	3	4	6	8	10	12	14	16	18	20	22	24	26	30	34	38
W-5											$867	$911	$944	$980	$1,030	$1,081	$1,135	
W-4	$488	$525	$540	$555	$580	$605	$631	$669	$703	$735	$762	$787	$825	$856	$891	$909	$909	$909
W-3	$445	$464	$483	$489	$509	$549	$589	$609	$631	$654	$695	$723	$740	$757	$781	$781	$781	$781
W-2	$394	$431	$443	$451	$476	$516	$536	$555	$579	$597	$614	$634	$648	$658	$658	$658	$658	$658
W-1	$346	$383	$393	$414	$439	$476	$494	$518	$541	$560	$577	$598	$598	$598	$598	$598	$598	$598

Enlisted Servicemembers

Pay Grade	<2	2	3	4	6	8	10	12	14	16	18	20	22	24	26	30	34	38
E-9							$603	$620	$639	$659	$691	$718	$747	$790	$830	$871	$915	
E-8						$504	$517	$533	$550	$581	$597	$623	$638	$675	$688	$688	$688	
E-7	$335	$366	$380	$399	$413	$438	$452	$477	$498	$512	$527	$533	$552	$563	$603	$603	$603	$603
E-6	$290	$319	$333	$347	$361	$393	$406	$430	$438	$443	$449	$449	$449	$449	$449	$443	$449	$449
E-5	$266	$284	$297	$311	$333	$356	$375	$377	$377	$377	$377	$377	$377	$377	$377	$377	$377	$377
E-4	$244	$256	$270	$284	$296	$296	$296	$296	$296	$296	$296	$296	$296	$296	$296	$296	$296	$296
E-3	$220	$234	$248	$248	$248	$248	$248	$248	$248	$248	$248	$248	$248	$248	$248	$248	$248	$248
E-2	$209	$209	$209	$209	$209	$209	$209	$209	$209	$209	$209	$209	$209	$209	$209	$209	$209	$209
E-1	$187	$187	$187	$187	$187	$187	$187	$187	$187	$187	$187	$187	$187	$187	$187	$187	$187	
E-1 with less than 4 months of service	$173																	

Military Service Requirements for VA Loan Eligibility

Wartime—Service during:

WWII	September 16, 1940 to July 25, 1947
Korean	June 27, 1950 to January 31, 1955
Vietnam	August 5, 1964 to May 7, 1975

You must have at least **90 days** on active duty and been discharged under other than dishonorable conditions. If you served less than 90 days, you may be eligible if discharged for a service-connected disability.

Peacetime—Service during periods:

> July 26, 1947 to June 26, 1950
> February 1, 1955 to August 4, 1964
> May 8, 1975 to September 7, 1980 (enlisted)
> to October 16, 1981 (officer)

You must have served at least **181 days** of continuous active duty and been discharged under other than dishonorable conditions. If you served less than 181 days, you may be eligible if discharged for a service-connected disability.

Service after September 7, 1980 (enlisted) or October 16, 1981 (officer)

If you were separated from service that began after these dates, you must have:

- completed 24 months of continuous active duty or the full period (at least 181 days) for which you were ordered or called to active duty, and been discharged under conditions other than dishonorable

- completed at least 181 days of active duty and been discharged under the specific authority of 10 USC 1173 (hardship) or 10 USC 1171 (early out), or have been determined to have a compensable service-connected disability

- been discharged with less than 181 days of service for a service-connected disability. Individuals may also be eligible if they were released from active duty due to an involuntary reduction in force size, certain medical conditions, or, in some instances, for the convenience of the government.

Gulf War-Service during the period beginning August 2, 1990 to a date yet to be determined

If you served on active duty during the Gulf War, you must have:

- completed 24 months of continuous active duty or the full period (at least 90 days) for which you were called or ordered to active duty, and been discharged under conditions other than dishonorable

OR

- completed at least 90 days of active duty and been discharged under the specific authority of 10 USC 1173 (hardship) or 10 USC 1173 (early out), or have been determined to have a compensable service-connected disability

OR

- been discharged with less than 90 days of service for a service-connected disability. Individuals may also be eligible if they were released from active duty due to an involuntary reduction in force size, certain medical conditions, or, in some instances, for the convenience of the government.

Active Duty Service Personnel

If you are now on regular active duty (not active duty for training), you are eligible after having served 181 days (or 90 days during the Gulf War) unless discharged or separated from a previous qualifying period of active duty service.

Selected Reserves or National Guard

If you are not otherwise eligible and you have completed a total of six years in the Selected Reserves or National Guard (member of an active unit, attended required weekend drills and two-week active duty for training) and you:

- were discharged honorably.

- were placed on the retired list.

- were transferred to the Standby Reserve or an element of the Ready Reserve other than the Selected Reserve after service characterized as honorable; or

- continue to serve in the Selected Reserves.

Individuals who completed less than six years may be eligible if discharged for a service-connected disability. Eligibility for Selected Reserves expires September 30, 2009.

You may also be determined eligible if you:

- are an unremarried spouse of a veteran who died while in service or from a service-connected disability (spouses who are remarried after age 57 retain their eligibility).

- are a spouse of a servicemember missing in action or a prisoner or war.

Eligibility may also be established for:

- certain United States citizens who served in the armed forces of a government allied with the United States in WWII.

- individuals with service as members in certain organizations, such as Public Health Service officers, cadets at the United States Military, Air Force, or Coast Guard academy, midshipmen at the United States Naval Academy, officers of National Oceanic and Atmospheric Administration, merchant seaman with WWII service, and others.

Retirement Systems Summary

Retirement System	Basis	Multiplier	Cost of Living Allowance	Bonus
Final Pay	Last month's basic pay	2.5% for each year of service	Consumer Price Index	No
High 36	Average of highest 36 months basic pay	2.5% for each year of service	Consumer Price Index	No
CSB REDUX	Average of highest 36 months basic pay	3.5% for each year of service beyond 20	Consumer Price Index minus 1%	Yes

Choosing Retirement Options

Let's look at three servicemembers who all retire at the same pay grade with exactly 20 years of service, and who made three different choices at the 15-year point of their careers. The CSB is $30,000 before taxes.

Servicemember one, Jones, decides to take the High 36 option; numbers two and three, Smith and Cruz, choose the CSB/REDUX option. Smith spends his $21,000 bonus on a new car, while Cruz invests his $21,000 bonus.

Cruz and Smith paid 28 percent tax on their CSB, but they could have shielded more than $10,000 of their CSB in the Thrift Savings Plan to help protect it from taxes.

Each year during their retirement, all three will receive cost of living adjustments (COLAs) based upon the consumer price index (CPI), which measures inflation. Jones's High-36 COLA is the full CPI (3.5 percent each year for our example), so Jones gets a 3.5 percent raise. Smith and Cruz, however, get a 2.5 percent raise because COLAs under the REDUX system are equal to the CPI minus 1 percent. But Cruz's CSB investment continues to grow (at an annual rate of 8 percent for our example).

The following table demonstrates the different growth in value for the two options.

	Jones	Smith	Cruz
Time of Retirement			
Savings After 5 years at 8%	$0	$0	$28,600
Retirement Percentage	50%	40%	40%
End of First Year of Retirement			
Savings	$0	$0	$30,200
Total Annual Pay	$18,000	$14,400	$14,400
Total Retirement Value	$18,000	$14,400	$44,600
Age 61			
Savings	$0	$0	$98,000
Total Annual Pay	$37,100	$24,200	$24,200
Total Retirement Value	$581,000	$415,600	$513,600
Age 62-REDUX Readjustment Year			
Savings	$0	$0	$103,600
Total Annual Pay	$38,400	$38,400	$38,400
Total Retirement Pay	$620,300	$454,000	$557,600
Age 75			
Savings	$0	$0	$214,600
Total Annual Pay	$60,000	$52,900	$52,900
Total Retirement Value	$1,260,000	$1,049,000	$1,264,000
Total Difference		-$211,000	+$4,000

Military Clothing Allowance
To help pay for your uniform and other clothing costs, you may be given a clothing allowance (if appropriate clothing is not furnished).

2008 Standard Initial Clothing Allowances

Army		Navy (E-1 to E-6)		Air Force		Marine Corps		Coast Guard	
Male	Female	Male	Female	Male	Female	Male	Female	Male	Female
1330.70	1,622.36	1,203.64	1,432.15	1,292.89	1,499.21	1,596.43	1,879.05	1142.36	1,244.28

2008 Cash Clothing Replacement Allowances

Type	Army		Navy		Air Force		Marine Corps		Coast Guard	
	Male	Female	Male	Femae	Male	Female	Male	Female	Male	Femae
Basic	370.80	432.00	464.40	475.20	316.80	349.20	360.00	385.20	337.78	346.47
Standard	529.20	619.20	662.40	680.40	453.60	496.80	514.80	550.80	478.26	494.97
Special	0	0	871.20	939.60	0	0	0	0	0	0

2008 Military Clothing Maintenance Allowance

Type of Duty	Male		Female	
	Basic	Standard	Basic	Standard
Active (monthly)	27.89	39.85	28.87	39.85
Reserve (per drill)	3.35	4.79	3.45	4.93

The CRSC Benefit

The following table shows how much compensation you may get each month based on your VA disability rating. *Note: These results do not reflect the annual COLA.*

Combat related VA Disability Rating	Monthly CRSC
100%	$2,193
90%	$1,317
80%	$1,171
70%	$1,008
60%	$801
50%	$633

The CRDP Benefit

Air Force Assoc.
Universal Benefits Corp.
P.O. Box 17480
Baltimore, MD 21289-9012
866-769-3263
www.afa.org

Air Force Sergeants Assoc.
AFSA Group Insurance Plans
1776 West Lakes Pkwy.
West Des Moines, IA 50398
800-882-5541
www.afsahq.org

The American Legion
American Legion Insurance
Plans
1776 West Lakes Pkwy.
West Des Moines, IA 50398
800-542-5547
www.legion.org

**American Assoc. of
Uniformed Services**
Neat Management Group
P.O. Box 3686
Austin, TX 78764
800-222-0207

American Military Assoc.
Fort Snelling Station
P.O. Box 76
Minneapolis, MN 55440
800-562-4076

**American Military Retirees
Assoc.**
Group Plan Administrator
P.O. Box 2510
Rockville, MD 20847
800-638-2610, ext. 257

American Military Society
USI Administrators
P.O. Box 96987
Washington, D.C. 20090-6987
800-808-4514 or 301-925-1420

AMVETS
4647 Forbes Blvd.
Lanham, MD 20706-4380
301-459-9161
www.amvets.org

**Armed Forces Benefit
Assoc.**
5 Star Life Insurance Co.
909 N. Washington St.
Alexandria, VA 22314
800-403-7745 or 703-549-4455

**Armed Services Mutual
Benefit Assoc.**
Group Plan Administrator
P.O. Box 2510
Rockville, MD 20847
800-638-2610

**Army Aviation Assoc. of
America**
USI Administrators
P.O. Box 96987
Washington, D.C. 20090-6987
800-808-4514 or 301-925-1420
www.quad-a.org

**Assoc. of Military Surgeons
of the U.S.**
AMUS Group Insurance
P.O. Box 2510
Rockville, MD 20852
800-638-2610 or 301-816-0045
www.amsus.org

Assoc. of U.S. Army
AUSA Insurance Plans
1776 West Lakes Pkwy.
West Des Moines, IA 50398
800-882-5707
www.ausa.org

Credit Unions
Group Plan Administrator
P.O. Box 2510
Rockville, MD 20847
800-638-2610 or
301-816-0045

First Coast Fleet Inc.
FCFI Group Insurance
3996 Confederate Point Rd
Jacksonville, FL 32210
800-566-0420 or 904-778-1565
www.waop.net/page2.html

Fleet Reserve Assoc.
FRA Insurance Plans
1776 West Lakes Pkwy.
West Des Moines, IA 50398
800-424-1120
www.fra.org

**Government Employee
Benefits Assoc.**
P.O. Box 241324
Montgomery, AL 36124-1324
800-240-2020 or 334-272-4313

**Harris Methodist Health
Insurance Co.**
Texas Military Healthcare
P.O. Box 90100
Arlington, TX 76004-9882
800-373-9779

Marine Corps Assoc.
MCA Group Benefit Program
P.O. Box 21357
Santa Barbara, CA 93121-9911
800-368-5682
www.mcainsurance.org

Marine Corps League
USI Administrators
P.O. Box 96987
Washington, D.C. 20090-6987
800-808-4514 or 301-925-1420
www.mcleague.org

Military Benefit Assoc.
14605 Avion Pkwy.
P.O. Box 221110
Chantilly, VA 20153-1110
800-336-0100 or 703-968-6200
www.militarybenefit.org

**Military Insurance
Specialist Inc.**
208 Gunn Road
Montgomery, AL 36117
800-852-9162
www.tricare.osd.mil

**The Military Officers
Association of America**
P.O. Box 9126
Des Moines, IA 50306
800-247-2192
www.troa.org

**Military Order of the
Purple Heart**
USI Administrators
P.O. Box 96987
Washington, D.C. 20090-6987
800-808-4514 or 301-925-1420
www.purpleheart.org

**Military Order of
the World Wars**
USI Administrators
P.O. Box 96987
Washington, D.C. 20090-6987
800-808-4514 or 301-925-1420
www.militaryorder.org

**National Armed
Forces Assoc.**
Neat Management Group
P.O. Box 163010
Austin, TX 78716-3010
800-336-3219 or 512-328-8610
www.neatmgmt.com

**National Assoc. for
Uniformed Services**
USI Administrators
P.O. Box 96987
Washington, D.C. 20090-6987
800-808-4514 or 301-925-1420
www.naus.org

**National Defense
Transportation Assoc.**
USI Administrators
P.O. Box 96987
Washington, D.C. 20090-6987
800-808-4514 or 301-925-1420

National Officers Assoc.
USI Administrators
P.O. Box 96987
Washington, D.C. 20090-6987
800-808-4514 or 301-925-1420

**Naval Enlisted Reserve
Assoc.**
Marsh Affinity Group Services
1776 West Lakes Pkwy.
West Des Moines, IA 50398
800-424-9883
www.nera.org

Naval Reserve Assoc.
Marsh Affinity Group Services
1776 West Lakes Pkwy.
West Des Moines, IA 50398
800-424-9883
www.navy-reserve.org

Navy League
Monumental General
Insurance Group
P.O. Box 17480

Baltimore, MD 210203-7480
800-752-9797 or 800-883-5378
www.navyleague.org

**Noncommissioned Officers
Assoc.**
5 Star Life Insurance Co.
909 N. Washington St.
Alexandria, VA 22314
800-403-7745 or 703-549-4455

**Pentagon Federal
Financial Services**
Group Plan Administrator
P.O. Box 2510
Rockville, MD 20847
800-638-2610 or 301-816-0045
www.pentagonfcu.org

The Reserve Officer Assoc.
ROA Insurance Plans
1776 West Lakes Pkwy.
West Des Moines, IA 50398
800-247-7988
www.roa.org

**Retired Assoc. for the
Uniformed Services**
Group Plan Administrator
P.O. Box 2510
Rockville, MD 20847
800-638-2610 or 301-816-0045

The Retired Enlisted Assoc.
USI Administrators
P.O. Box 96987
Washington, D.C. 20090-6987
800-808-4514 or 301-925-1420

Society of Military Widows
1101 Mercantile Lane
Springdale, MD 20774
800-808-4514
www.naus.org

**Uniformed Services
Benefit Assoc.**
P.O. Box 418258
Kansas City, MO 64141-9528
800-368-7021
www.usba.com

**United Military and
Government Employee
Assoc.**
UM & GA Group Insurance
P.O. Box 2510
Rockville, MD 20852-0510
800-638-2610 or 301-816-0045
www.militarybenefit.org

United Services Assoc.
USA Group Insurance
P.O. Box 2510
Rockville, MD 20852
800-636-2610 or 301-816-0045

**United Services
Automobile Assoc.**
USAA Life Insurance Co.
9800 Fredricksburg Road
San Antonio, TX 78288
800-531-9017 or 800-531-6978

**U.S. Coast Guard
Chief Petty Officers
Assoc./Coast Guard En-
listed Assoc.**
Seabury & Smith Administrator Group Insurance
1255 23 St. NW, Suite 300
Washington, DC 20037
800-424-9883 or 202-457-6820
www.uscgcpoa.org

**U.S. Coast Guard Chief
Warrant & Warrant
Officers Assoc.**
Seabury & Smith Administrator Group Insurance
1255 23rd St., Suite 300
Washington, D.C. 20037
800-424-9883 or 202-457-6820
www.cwoauscg.org

Veterans Affairs Regional Offices

Alabama
345 Perry Hill Rd.
Montgomery, AL 36109
800-827-1000

Alaska
2925 DeBarr Rd.
Anchorage, AK 99508
800-827-1000

Arizona
3225 N. Central Ave.
Phoenix, AZ 85012
800-827-1000

Arkansas
P.O. Box 1280
Little Rock, AR 72115
800-827-1000

California
Federal Bldg.
11000 Wilshire Blvd.
Los Angeles, CA 90024
800-827-1000

1301 Clay Street, Rm. 1300 N.
Oakland, CA 94612
800-827-1000

8810 Rio San Diego Dr.
San Diego, CA 92108
800-827-1000

Colorado
155 Van Gordon St.
Lakewood, CO 80228
800-827-1000

Connecticut
450 Main St.
Hartford, CT 06103
800-827-1000

Delaware
1601 Kirkwood Hwy.
Wilmington, DE 19805
800-827-1000

District of Columbia
1722 I St. N.W.
Washington D.C., D.C. 20421
800-827-1000

Florida
9500 Bay Pines Blvd.
St. Petersburg, FL 33708
800-827-1000

Georgia
1700 Clairmont Rd.
Decatur, GA 30033
800-827-1000

Hawaii
459 Patterson Rd., E-Wing
Honolulu, HI 96819
800-827-1000

Idaho
805 W. Franklin St.
Boise, ID 83702
800-827-1000

Illinois
2122 W. Taylor St.
Chicago, IL 60612
800-827-1000

Indiana
575 N. Pennsylvania St.
Indianapolis, IN 46204
800-827-1000

Iowa
210 Walnut St.
Des Moines, IA 50309
800-827-1000

Kansas
5500 E. Kellogg
Wichita, KS 67211
800 827-1000

Kentucky
545 S. 3rd St.
Louisville, KY 40202

Louisiana
701 Loyola Ave.
New Orleans, LA 70113
800-827-1000

Maine
1 VA Center
Togus, ME 04330
207-623-8411

Massachusetts
J.F.K. Federal Bldg.
Government Center
Boston, MA 02114

Maryland
Federal Bldg.
31 Hopkins Plaza
Baltimore, MD 21201
800-827-1000

Michigan
Patrick V. McNamara Federal
Bldg.
477 Michigan Ave.
Detroit, MI 48226

Minnesota
Fort Snelling
1 Federal Dr.
St. Paul, MN 55111-4050
800-827-1000

Mississippi
1600 E. Woodrow Wilson Ave.
Jackson, MS 39216
601-364-7000

Missouri
Federal Bldg.
400 S. 18th St.
St. Louis, MO 63103
800-827 1000

Montana
William St. off Highway
Fort Harrison, MT 59636
800-827-1000

Nebraska
5631 S. 48th St.
Lincoln, NE 68516
800-827-1000

Nevada
1201 Terminal Way
Reno, NV 89520
800-827-1000

New Hampshire
Norris Cotton
Federal Bldg.
275 Chestnut St.
Manchester, NH 03101
800-827-1000

New Jersey
20 Washington Place
Newark, NJ 07102
800-827-1000

New Mexico
Danis Chavez
Federal Building
500 Gold Ave. S.W.
Albuquerque, NM 87102
800-827-1000

New York
Federal Bldg.
111 W. Huron St.
Buffalo, NY 14202
800-827-1000

245 W. Houston St.
New York, NY 10014
800-827-1000

North Carolina
Federal Bldg.
251 N. Main St.
Winston-Salem, NC 27155
800-827-1000

North Dakota
2101 Elm St.
Fargo, ND 58102
Phone: (701) 451-4600

Ohio
A.J. Celebrezze
Federal Bldg.
1240 E. 9th St.
Cleveland, OH 44199
800-827-1000

Oklahoma
125 S. Main St.
Muskogee, OK 74401
800-827-1000

Oregon
1220 S.W. 3rd Ave.
Portland, OR 97204
800-827-1000

Pennsylvania
5000 Wissahickon Ave.
Philadelphia, PA 19101
800-827-1000

1000 Liberty Ave.
Pittsburgh, PA 15222
800-827-1000

Rhode Island
380 Westminister Mall
Providence, RI 02903
800-827-1000

South Carolina
1801 Assembly Street
Columbia, SC 29201
800-827-1000

South Dakota
2501 W. 22nd St.
Sioux Falls, SD 57117
800-827-1000

Tennessee
110 9th Ave. S.
Nashville, TN 37203
800-827-1000

Texas
6900 Almeda Rd.
Houston, TX 77030
Phone: 1 800 827 1000

1 Veterans Plaza
701 Clay Ave.
Waco, TX 76799

Utah
550 Foothill Dr.
Salt Lake City, UT 84158
Fax: 800-827-1000

Vermont
N. Hartland Rd.
White River Jct, VT 05009
800-827-1000

Virginia
210 Franklin Rd. S.W.
Roanoke, VA 24011
800-827-1000

Washington
Federal Bldg.
915 2nd Ave.
Seattle, WA 98174
800-827-1000

West Virginia
640 Fourth Ave.
Huntington, WV 25701
800-827-1000

Wisconsin
5400 W. National Ave.
Milwaukee, WI 53295
800-827-1000

Wyoming
2360 E. Pershing Blvd.
Cheyenne, WY 82001
800-827-1000

Guam
222 Chalan Santo Papast, Reflection Center, Ste. 102
Agana, GU 96910
(705) 475-7161

Philippines Islands
1131 Roxas Blvd.,
Ermita
0930 Manila, PI 96440
Phone: (011) 632-528-6300

Puerto Rico
150 Carlos Chardon Ave.
Hato Rey, PR 00018
800-827-1000

Military Awards

Medal of Honor
Defense Distinguished Service
   Medal
Silver Star
Bronze Star
Legion of Merit
Purple Heart
Distinguished Service Medal
Defense Superior Service
   Medal
Defense Meritorious Service
   Medal
Meritorious Service Medal
Air Medal
Distinguished Flying Cross
Joint Service Commendation
   Medal
Joint Service Achievement
   Medal
Presidential Unit Citation
POW Medal
National Defense Service
   Medal
Korean Service Medal
Antarctica Service Medal
Armed Forces Expeditionary
   Medal
Joint Meritorious Unit Award
Good Conduct Medal
Army of Occupation Medal
Vietnam Service Medal
Southwest Asia Service Medal
Kosovo Campaign Medal
Armed Forces Service Medal
Humanitarian Service Medal
Military Outstanding
   Volunteer Service Medal
Armed Forces Reserve Medal
Philippine Presidential Unit
   Citation
Republic of Korea
   Presidential Unit
   Citation
Republic of Vietnam
   Gallantry Cross Unit
   Citation
United Nations Service Medal
United Nations Medal
NATO Medal (Yugoslavia)
NATO Medal (Kosovo)
Republic of Vietnam
   Campaign Medal

Kuwait Liberation Medal
   (Kingdom of Saudi
   Arabia)
Kuwait Liberation Medal
   (Kuwait)
Republic of Korea War
   Service Medal

**Awards approved since
September 11, 2001**
Afghanistan Campaign Medal
Iraq Campaign Medal
Global War on Terrorism
   Expeditionary Medal
Global War on Terrorism
   Service Medal
Korean Defense Service
   Medal
Air Force Expeditionary
   Service Ribbon
Air Force Expeditionary
   Service Ribbon with
   Gold Border
Gallant Unit Citation
Meritorious Unit Award

**Military Awards by Service
Branch**

Air Force
Air Force Cross
Airman's Medal
Aerial Achievement Medal
Air Force Commendation
   Medal
Air Force Achievement Medal
Air Force Outstanding Unit
   Award
Air Force Organizational
   Excellence Award
Combat Readiness Medal
Air Force Good Conduct
   Medal
Air Reserve Forces
   Meritorious Service Medal
Outstanding Airman of the
   Year
Air Force Recognition Ribbon
Air Force Overseas Ribbon-
   Short
Air Force Overseas Ribbon-
   Long

Air Force Longevity Service
   Award Ribbon
Air Force Basic Military
   Training Instructor
   Ribbon
Air Force Recruiter Ribbon
Air Force NCO Professional
   Military Education Gradu-
   ate
   Ribbon
Basic Military Training Honor
   Graduate
Small Arms Expert
   Marksmanship Ribbon
Air Force Training Ribbon

Army
Distinguished Service Cross
   Soldier's Medal
Army Commendation Medal
Army Achievement Medal
Army Reserve Components
   Achievement Medal
NCO Professional
   Development Ribbon
Army Service Ribbon
Overseas Service Ribbon
Army Reserve Components
   Overseas Training Ribbon
Inter-American Defense Board
   Medal
Multinational Force and
   Observers Medal
Valorous Unit Award
Meritorious Unit
   Commendation
Army Superior Unit Award
Republic of Vietnam
   Presidential Unit
   Citation
Republic of Vietnam Civil
   Actions Unit Citation

Coast Guard
Navy Cross
Department of Transportation
   Gold Medal
Coast Guard Medal
Gold Lifesaving Medal
Silver Lifesaving Medal
Department of Transportation
   Silver Medal
Coast Guard Commendation
   Medal

Department of Transportation
Bronze Medal
Coast Guard Achievement
Medal
Commandant's Letter of
Commendation
Combat Action Ribbon
Coast Guard Unit
Commendation
Coast Guard Meritorious Unit
Commendation
Coast Guard "E" Ribbon
Coast Guard Bicentennial
Unit Commendation
Coast Guard Reserve Good
Conduct Medal
Naval Reserve Meritorious
Service Medal
Navy Expeditionary Medal
China Service Medal
Navy Occupation Service
Medal
Coast Guard Artic Service
Medal
Coast Guard Special
Operations Service
Coast Guard Sea Service
Coast Guard Restricted Duty
Coast Guard Basic Training
Honor Graduate
Air Force Basic Military
Training Honor Graduate
Ribbon
Coast Guard Recruiting
Service Ribbon
Naval Reserve Medal
Republic of Vietnam
Presidential Unit
Citation
Republic of Vietnam Civil
Actions Unit Citation
Multinational Force and
Observers Medal
Inter-American Defense Board
Medal

Marine Corps
Navy Cross
Navy and Marine Corps Medal
Navy and Marine Corps
Commendation Medal
Navy and Marine Corps
Achievement Medal
Combat Action Ribbon
Navy Unit Commendation
Navy "E" Ribbon
Marine Corps Good Conduct
Medal
Selected Marine Corps
Reserve Medal
Marine Corps Expeditionary
Medal
China Service Medal
Navy Occupation Service
Medal
Sea Service Deployment
Ribbon
Navy Arctic Service Ribbon
Navy and Marine Corps
Overseas Service
Ribbon
Marine Corps Reserve Ribbon
Republic of Vietnam
Presidential Unit
Citation
Republic of Vietnam Civil
Actions Unit Citation
Multinational Force and
Observers Medal
Inter-American Defense Board
Medal

Navy
Navy Cross
Navy and Marine Corps Medal
Navy Commendation Medal
Navy Achievement Medal
Combat Action Ribbon
Navy Unit Commendation
Navy "E" Ribbon
Naval ReDittoserve
Meritorious Service
Medal
Fleet Marine Force Ribbon
Navy Expeditionary Medal
China Service Medal
Navy Occupation Service
Medal
Sea Service Deployment
Ribbon
Navy Arctic Service Ribbon
Naval Reserve Sea Service
Ribbon
Navy And Marine Corps
Overseas Service Ribbon
Navy Recruiting Service
Ribbon
Navy Recruit Training Service
Ribbon
Naval Reserve Medal
Republic of Vietnam
Presidential Unit
Citation
Republic of Vietnam Civil
Actions Unit Citation
Multinational Force and
Observers Medal
Inter-American Defense Board
Medal
Expert Rifleman Medal
Expert Pistol Shot Medal

Index

The Naval Institute Press is the book-publishing arm of the U.S. Naval Institute, a private, nonprofit, membership society for sea service professionals and others who share an interest in naval and maritime affairs. Established in 1873 at the U.S. Naval Academy in Annapolis, Maryland, where its offices remain today, the Naval Institute has members worldwide.

Members of the Naval Institute support the education programs of the society and receive the influential monthly magazine *Proceedings* or the colorful bimonthly magazine *Naval History* and discounts on fine nautical prints and on ship and aircraft photos. They also have access to the transcripts of the Institute's Oral History Program and get discounted admission to any of the Institute-sponsored seminars offered around the country.

The Naval Institute's book-publishing program, begun in 1898 with basic guides to naval practices, has broadened its scope to include books of more general interest. Now the Naval Institute Press publishes about seventy titles each year, ranging from how-to books on boating and navigation to battle histories, biographies, ship and aircraft guides, and novels. Institute members receive significant discounts on the Press's more than eight hundred books in print.

Full-time students are eligible for special half-price membership rates. Life memberships are also available.

For a free catalog describing Naval Institute Press books currently available, and for further information about joining the U.S. Naval Institute, please write to:

Member Services
U.S. Naval Institute
291 Wood Road
Annapolis, MD 21402-5034
Telephone: (800) 233-8764
Fax: (410) 571-1703
Web address: www.usni.org